Global Recession – Causes, Impacts and Remedies

After the Crisis: Rethinking Finance

GLOBAL RECESSION – CAUSES, IMPACTS AND REMEDIES

Additional books in this series can be found on Nova's website under the Series tab.

Additional E-books in this series can be found on Nova's website under the E-books tab.

GLOBAL RECESSION – CAUSES, IMPACTS AND REMEDIES

AFTER THE CRISIS: RETHINKING FINANCE

THOMAS LAGOARDE-SEGOT
EDITOR

Nova Science Publishers, Inc.
New York

Copyright © 2010 by Nova Science Publishers, Inc.

All rights reserved. No part of this book may be reproduced, stored in a retrieval system or transmitted in any form or by any means: electronic, electrostatic, magnetic, tape, mechanical photocopying, recording or otherwise without the written permission of the Publisher.

For permission to use material from this book please contact us:
Telephone 631-231-7269; Fax 631-231-8175
Web Site: http://www.novapublishers.com

NOTICE TO THE READER

The Publisher has taken reasonable care in the preparation of this book, but makes no expressed or implied warranty of any kind and assumes no responsibility for any errors or omissions. No liability is assumed for incidental or consequential damages in connection with or arising out of information contained in this book. The Publisher shall not be liable for any special, consequential, or exemplary damages resulting, in whole or in part, from the readers' use of, or reliance upon, this material. Any parts of this book based on government reports are so indicated and copyright is claimed for those parts to the extent applicable to compilations of such works.

Independent verification should be sought for any data, advice or recommendations contained in this book. In addition, no responsibility is assumed by the publisher for any injury and/or damage to persons or property arising from any methods, products, instructions, ideas or otherwise contained in this publication.

This publication is designed to provide accurate and authoritative information with regard to the subject matter covered herein. It is sold with the clear understanding that the Publisher is not engaged in rendering legal or any other professional services. If legal or any other expert assistance is required, the services of a competent person should be sought. FROM A DECLARATION OF PARTICIPANTS JOINTLY ADOPTED BY A COMMITTEE OF THE AMERICAN BAR ASSOCIATION AND A COMMITTEE OF PUBLISHERS.

Additional color graphics may be available in the e-book version of this book.

LIBRARY OF CONGRESS CATALOGING-IN-PUBLICATION DATA
After the crisis : rethinking finance / editor, Thomas Lagoarde-Segot.
p. cm.
Includes index.
ISBN 978-1-61668-924-7 (hbk.)
1. Finance. 2. International finance. 3. Financial crises--Prevention.
4. Global Financial Crisis, 2008-2009. I. Lagoarde-Segot, Thomas.
HG173.A357 2009
332--dc22
2010022571

Published by Nova Science Publishers, Inc. ✦ New York

CONTENTS

Preface		vii
About the Editor		ix
Contributor Bios		ix
Chapter 1	Capital is Dead: Long Live Ultra Capital? *Jon Cloke*	**1**
Chapter 2	The Individual-Collective Dialectic in Management Sciences: A Re-Reading Based on the Interpellation of Finance from a Marketing Standpoint *Bernard Paranque and Bernard Cova*	**17**
Chapter 3	Ireland and the Crisis *Ciarán mac an Bhaird*	**35**
Chapter 4	The Global Mortgage Crisis Litigation Fallout *William V.Rapp*	**47**
Chapter 5	From Finance to Green Technology Activist States, Geopolitical Finance and Hybrid Neoliberalism *Federico Caprotti*	**81**
Chapter 6	Globalization and Economic Crisis: Does Information Really Matter? *Leonardo Baccini, Soo Yeon Kim and Fabio Pammolli*	**101**
Chapter 7	Towards a New Political Economyof Central Banking *Roy Allen and Kristine Chase*	**125**
Chapter 8	In Search of Relevant Regulatory Policies: A Minskyian Analysis of the CurrentFinancial Crisis *Faruk Ülgen*	**149**
Chapter 9	Mortgage Markets Matter: Why we Need a Better Understandingof the Mortgage Market to Understand the Financial Crisis *Manuel B.Aalbers*	**169**

Chapter 10	Private Equity and the Current Financial Crisis: Risk and Opportunism *David Weitzner and James Darroch*	**185**
Chapter 11	Sub-Prime Crisis: Market Failuresor Human Follies? *Arvind K. Jain*	**209**
Chapter 12	Portfolios, Information and Geometry: *Simplex Orbis Non Sufficit* *Eric Briys, Brice Magdalou and Richard Nock*	**225**
Index		**245**

PREFACE

The 2007-2010 economic crisis has profoundly shaken the foundations of mainstreamfinancial economics. The apparent falsification of core concepts such as risk diversification, informational efficiency and valuation efficiency by an unexpected course of events has revealed the need to redefine the objectives and direction of research today. In a context where global public opinion has begun to doubt the merits of a deregulated economy, a conceptual void has been opened up, thereby rendering more complex the elaboration of appropriate policy responses. As a result, academics are now facing the challenge of revising their working assumptions, renewing their theoretical models and reframing their empirical conclusions.

This book seeks to carve out new paths in economic research by examining the crisis from perspectives which fall outside the conventional theoretical paradigm and which, by virtue of their nonconformity, are in a position to provide a refreshed gaze on former ways of thinking.

Rather than engaging in a one-dimensional critique of orthodox economics, this approach may be viewed as a necessary step towards the productive 'deconstruction' of mainstream academic discourse. It is our hope that through the analysis and questioning of tacit assumptions within this discipline, we might see the emergence of innovative research strategies. This collection of exclusive chapters should shed some light on what lies ahead for theoretical and empirical economic research in the 21st century.

Thomas Lagoarde-Segot

ABOUT THE EDITOR

Thomas Lagoarde-Segot is Associate Professor of Finance and Development at Euromed Management, School of Management Marseille and a research fellow at DEFI, Aix-Marseille Université, France. He holds aPhD from Trinity College Dublin, an Msc in International Economics from Aix-Marseille Université, and a Bsc in Economics from the University of Durham (ERASMUS program). A recipient of the franco-irish Ulysses scholarship, his research has been published in academic journals such as the *Journal of Banking and Finance*, *TheWorld Economy*, and the *Journal of International Financial Markets, Institutions and Money*, among others. He is an associate editor of the *Review of International Business and Finance* and coordinator of the Global Research on Innovative Development Strategies (GRIDS) network at Euromed Management. He has consulting experience with the European Commission on economic transition in the Euro-Mediterranean region, as well as with the private sector on corporate social responsibility.

CONTRIBUTOR BIOS

Manuel B. Aalbers, a human geographer, sociologist and urban planner, is a researcher at the Amsterdam Institute for Metropolitan and International Development Studies (AMIDSt), University of Amsterdam. From January 2007 till August 2008 he was a post-doc researcher at Columbia University, New York. Previously, he was a guest researcher at City University New York, the University of Milan-Bicocca and at the University of Urbino (Italy). He is the associate editor of the Encyclopedia of Urban Studies, the guest editor of a special issue of the International Journal of Urban and Regional Research on mortgage markets, and the book review editor of Rooilijn, a Dutch urban studies/planning journal. His main research interest is in the intersection of housing and finance. He has published on redlining, social and financial exclusion, gentrification, the privatization of social housing, financialization, and the Anglo-American hegemony in academic research and writing. He is the author of a book on housing and community development in New York City and is preparing a manuscript for a book titled Place, Exclusion and Mortgage Markets.

Roy E. Allen is Professor of Economics and Dean, School of Economics and Business Administration, Saint Mary's College of California. His most recent publications are *Financial Crises and Recession in the Global Economy, Third Edition* (forthcoming 2010,

Edward Elgar Publishing), and "New Thinking on the Financial Crisis" (In *Critical Perspectives on International Business*, Vol. 5, 2009). His current interests include globalization, sustainable systems research, and financial market instability.

Leonardo Baccini is a research fellow at IMT Lucca. He completed his PhD in Political Science at Trinity College Dublin, Ireland, in September 2009. He hold an MA in International Relations from University of Bologna and a Laurea in Economics from University of Florence. Before joining IMT, he was a post-doctoral fellow at New York University from September 2008 to June 2009. His main research interests are political economy of international trade, international cooperation, international organizations, development studies, democratic transition, and spatial econometrics.

ÉricBriys, is the co-founder of www.cyberlibris.com and adjunct professor of finance at the CEREGMIA of the University of French West Indies. He has been a professor of Finance at HEC (Paris) for ten years. He has also an investment banking background, having led the Insurance Strategies Groups at Deutsche Bank, Merrill Lynch and Lehman Brothers. He graduated from HEC (Paris) and received his PhD degree in Economics from the University of Geneva.

Federico Caprotti's research is on the processes which influence decision-making at the investor level in the case of renewable energy technologies. His current project is an international, comparative analysis of the emergence of the cleantech sector in the US, China and the UK, with a particular focus on wind energy and aeolian technologies. The project's focus on the links between investors and green technologies has seen Federico involved in research in the world's premier cleantech market centres – Shanghai, San Francisco, NewYork and London – as well as at the sites of major renewables technology deployment, such as California and Inner Mongolia. Federico's research has been funded by the British Academy, the Sino-British Fellowship Trust, the Nuffield Foundation, and the Royal Geographical Society. Federico is currently a lecturer at the Department of Geography, University of Plymouth, and has also worked at University College London (UCL), Oxford University, and Leicester University.

Kristine Chase is Professor of Economics in the School of Economics and Business Administration and Director of the Center for the Regional Economy at Saint Mary's College of California. Her most recent presentation is "Fed Lending Policy: A Return to Its Roots?" She speaks frequently in the San Francisco area on banking and monetary policy. Her publications have addressed Canadian vs. U.S. banking systems, biographies of U.S. Treasury Secretaries, and the role of deposit insurance. Her current interests include the history of central banking and the regulation of financial intermediaries.

JonCloke currently works as a lecturer at Loughborough and a research associate with the Globalization and World Cities network based in the Geography Department there. He completed his PhD as a mature candidate at Loughborough in 2003, having come from a background of working in the homeless sector in the UK and since then has been working in a variety of different research areas including corruption, corporate social responsibility and alternative energy. He has taught at a number of different universities including Durham, Newcastle and Nottingham Trent and combines his research with consultancy work and working with NGOs in the UK; his most recent post previous to arriving at Loughborough was as Project Officer for a European Community and Foreign and Commonwealth-funded project called EnergyCentral, intended to encourage the spread of alternative energy use in Central America and particularly in poor rural communities. His particular interest in the global economic crisis comes from examining the political economy of the discourse on corruption as it relates to the development project, and from examining the wider relational spaces of corruption within the global financial services sector as they relate to 'normal', as opposed to 'aberrant' practices within the global development *dispositif.*

Bernard Cova is Professor of Marketing at Euromed Management, Marseilles and Visiting Professor at Università Bocconi, Milan. A pioneer in the Consumer Tribes field since the early nineties, his internationally-influential research has emphasized what he calls "the Mediterranean approach" of tribal marketing. His work on this topic has been published in the International Journal of Research in Marketing, the European Journal of Marketing, Marketing Theory and the Journal of Business Research. He is also known for his groundbreaking research in B2B marketing, especially in the field of project marketing. The companies he recently worked with are: Alfa-Romeo, EDF, Hachette, Macif, Snai, etc. His latest major publications include books - Consumer Tribes, with Robert V. Kozinets and Avi Shankar, Butterworth-Heinemann, Oxford, 2007, 340 pages; Consuming Experience, with Antonella Caru, Routledge, Oxon, 2007, 204 pages; Il Marketing Non Convenzionale, with Alex Giordano and Mirko Pallera, Il Sole 24 Ore, Milan, 2007, 280 pages – and articles - Cova, B. (2009), "Marketing tribale e altre vie non convenzionali : quali ricadute per la ricerca di mercato?", *Micro and Macro Marketing,* N°3, pp. 437-447; Cova, B. and Salle, R. (2008), "Marketing Solutions in Accordance with the S-D Logic: Co-Creating Value with Customer Network Actors", *Industrial Marketing Management,* Vol. 37, pp. 270-277; Cova, B. and Elliott, R. (2008), "Everything you always wanted to know about interpretive consumer research but were afraid to ask", *Qualitative Market Research, an International Journal,* , Vol. 11, N°2, 2008, pp. 121-129; Cova, B. and Salle, R. (2008), "The Industrial/Consumer Marketing Dichotomy Revisited: A Case for Outdated Justification?", *Journal of Business and Industrial Marketing,* Vol. 23, N°1, pp. 3-11; Carù, A. and Cova, B. (2007), "Nuove opportunità: L'immersione nelle esperienze di consumo", *Economia and Management,* N°6/2007, pp. 65-69.

James L.Darroch is an Associate Professor of Strategic Management and International Business and Director of the Financial Services Program at the Schulich School of Business, York University. He holds an M.B.A. and Ph.D. in Strategic Management and International Business from York University. His research focuses upon strategic management with an emphasis on governance and enterprise risk management especially in financial services firms. Representative of his current research focus are: "The Limits of Strategic Rationality: Ethics, Risk Management, and Governance," Journal of Business Ethics, forthcoming (with David Weitzner), "A Comprehensive Framework For Strategic CSR: Ethical Positioning and Strategic Activities," (with David Weitzner), Best Paper Proceedings Academy of Management Chicago 2009, "Why Moral Failures Precede Financial Crises," Critical Perspectives on International Business (2009) (with David Weitzner), "Entry Barriers and Evolutions of Banking Systems: Lessons from the 1980s Canadian Western Bank Failures," Canadian Public Administration 50:2 (Summer 2007), pp. 141-166. (with Charles McMillan), "Globalization Restricted: The Canadian Financial System and Public Policy," Ivey Business Journal, . (with Charles McMillan) and "From Partners in Nation Building to the Two Solitudes: An Analysis of Canadian Chartered Bank-Federal Government Relations" (with Gerry Kerr) in Tom Wesson, editor Canada and the New World Economic Order.

Arvind K. Jain has been a faculty member at Concordia University in Montreal since 1990. He earned his Ph. D. from The University of Michigan, Ann Arbor. His other degrees are from Indian Institute of Technology, Bombay, Indian Institute of Science, Bangalore, and Carnegie-Mellon University, Pittsburgh. Before joining Concordia, he had taught at Indiana University, McGill University, The University of Michigan and the University of Dar es Salaam. He has held short-term or visiting appointments at Pennsylvania State University, International University of Japan, and University of Otago (New Zealand). He has taught international financial management and other courses in Canada, the United States, Finland, India, Mexico, New Zealand, Poland and other countries around the world at doctoral, MBA and other levels. Besides teaching, he has worked in industry or in public sector in India, the United States, Tanzania and Mexico. His current research interests focuses on the impact of international financial imbalances on the contemporary financial and economic crisis and on the impact of corruption on poverty and economic development. His research papers dealing with corruption, the third world debt crisis, capital flight, international lending decisions of banks, oligopolistic behavior in banking, foreign debt and foreign trade of developing countries, impact of culture on saving behavior, and commodity futures markets have appeared in *Journal of International Business Studies, Journal of Money, Credit and Banking, Economics Letters, Journal of Economic Psychology, Journal of Economic Surveys,* and other academic journals. His papers dealing with political risk, investor behavior, exchange rates, and other topics have appeared in volumes edited by scholars around the world. He has written three books, *Commodity Futures Markets and the Law of One Price* (1981), *International Financial Markets and Institutions* (1994), and *Essentials of International Financial Management* (2009),and has edited two volumes on corruption: *Economics of Corruption* (Kluwer Academics, 1998)and*The Political Economy of Corruption* (Routledge, 2001). Besides teaching and writing, he enjoys travelling and trekking around the world, flying gliders and blowing glass.

Soo Yeon Kim is Assistant Professor of Government and Politics at the University of Maryland. She holds a Ph.D. in Political Science from Yale University, and B.A. in Political Science and Diplomatic Relations from Yonsei University (Seoul, Korea). Her main research area is international political economy, with a focus on trade politics that includes the politics of the GATT/WTO, WTO disputes, and trade agreements. Her forthcoming book, entitled "Power, Institutions, and International Trade: from the GATT to the WTO" (Series in Political Economy, Cornell University Press) examines the origins and development of the GATT/WTO and its consequences for the evolution of the global trading system. She is currently pursuing a project on economic institution-building in post-Cold War Asia that focuses on the role of trade agreements.

Ciarán mac an Bhaird is currently lecturer of Business and Management, and Chair of the undergraduate degree programmes at Fiontar, Dublin City University. He holds a PhD in finance and management from Trinity College Dublin, as well as B. Comm. and L.L.B. degrees from the National University of Ireland, Galway, and an M.Sc. in Finance from University College Dublin. His research interests include capital structure and financial management issues in medium sized enterprises; serial entrepreneurship, particularly opportunity recognition, and regional development. He also examines policies on the provision of support to SMEs. Previously he worked at the European Commission, prior to managing a famine relief project in Wollaita, Southern Ethiopia. His book, "Resourcing

Small and Medium-Sized Enterprises: A Financial Growth Life Cycle Approach", is published by Springer in January 2010.

Brice Magdalou received is PhD degree in Economics from the University of Montpellier I, France, in 2006. He joined the University Antilles-Guyane in 2008, where he is now assistant professor in the Department of Economics. He is currently member of the CEREGMIA research laboratory. His research interests mainly focus on public economics, behavioral and experimental economics, and information.

Richard Nock received the agronomical engineering degree from Agro Montpellier, France (1993); a MSc in Computer Science (1993), the PhD in Computer Science (1998) and an accreditation to lead research in computer science (HDR, 2002), all from the University of Montpellier II, France. He joined the University Antilles-Guyane in 1998, where he is currently full professor of computer science. His research interests include machine learning, data mining, computational complexity, image processing, information geometry. He won the best paper award at the European Conference on Artificial Intelligence in 2006. His research is being funded by the French ANR (Young Researcher, White and Thematic programs).

Fabio Pammolli is Full Professor of Economics and Management, University of Florence (on leave), director of IMT Institute For Advanced Studies, Lucca, Italy, and director of CERM, Rome, Italy. Pammolli's research deals with business firms growth, network evolution, the economic analysis of pharmaceutical, biotechnology and health care industries, the macroeconomics of health, as well as the interplay between institutional/regulatory variables and patterns of industrial dynamics. He has published in journals such as: The Proceedings of the National Academy of Sciences (cover article, dec 27, 2005, vol. 102, n. 52), The Journal of the European Economics Association, The International Journal of Industrial Organization, Management Science, Physical Review E, Physica-A, Revue d'Economie Industrielle, Research Policy, Small Business Economics, Health Affairs, RandD Management, E. Journal of Health Economics, Europhysics Letters, Economics Letters, The European Physical Journal B.

BernardParanque joined Euromed Management in September 2004 as Professor of Finance. He is now Associate Dean for Research and Faculty. He is AG2R/La Mondiale - Prémalliance Chair in "Alternative financing: Investment, Solidarities and Responsibility". His research refers to the "économie des conventions". He is focused on the financial behavior of the non-financial organization and the promotion of specific tools and assessment procedures designed to enhance SMEs' access to financing. He is also interested by the action economic coordination problem. Some of his papers are on line on www.ssrn.com. He has published "Construire l'Euroméditerranée" L'Harmattan, 2008. He is co-author with Bernard Belletante and Nadine Levratto of "Diversité économique et mode de financement des PME" published in 2001 and with Nadine Levartto and Corinne Grenier "L'Euroméditerranée:.de l'espace géographique aux modes de coordinations socio-économiques" published in 2007, both by L'Harmattan. He is also the co-author of "" Structures of Corporate Finance in Germany and France" with Hans Friderichs in" Jahrbücher für Nationalökonomie und Statistik", 2001. He is associate researcher of the CNRS research team UMR 604 IDHE-ENS Cachan « Institutions et Dynamiques Historiques de l'Economie ». He belongs to the Scientific Committee of "Techniques Financières et Développement" and to the Editorial Board of Corporate Governance: an International Review, International Journal of Business and Globalisation, EuroMed Journal of Business, Euro-Mediterranean Economics and Finance Review.

William V. Rapp is the first Henry J. Leir Professor of International Trade and Business at The New Jersey Institute of Technology's School of Management and former Director of the International Relations Program at Yale University. He received his doctorate from Yale in Economics as a National Science Foundation Fellow. His Masters degrees in Economics and Japanese Studies are from Yale and Stanford, the later as a Ford Foundation Fellow. His JD with honors is from Pace. He received his Bachelor degree in Economics is from Amherst College, magna cum laude and Phi Beta Kappa. His teaching and research focuses on international business, strategy, financial institutions, law and economics and using technology to gain competitive advantage. He has had an extensive international career in academia, business and government and joined NJIT after completing a year in Japan as a Fulbright Scholar. His book, Information Technology Strategies, was completed under a Sloan Foundation grant. His current research focuses on issues related to how to create a sustainable advantage in a global environment. Dr. Rapp has been the Chair in Economic Relations with Japan and International Business at the University of Victoria in Canada, a Senior Research Fellow at Columbia University's Center on Japanese Economy and Business and its East Asian Institute, and the Toyota Visiting Professor of International Business at Columbia. He continues as a Senior Research Associate at Columbia. Before entering into fulltime teaching and research, Dr. Rapp was active in business and government as Executive Director for Bank of America's Corporate Finance Group in Tokyo responsible for North Asia and Commercial Counselor at the US Embassy in Tokyo. He has written more than 80 individual and joint publications on various aspects of trade, international business, and corporate strategy plus presented many papers, given congressional testimony and public speeches on these topics. His website is found at http://web.njit.edu/~rappw.

Faruk Ülgen is an Assistant Professor of Economics at the University of Grenoble 2-France since 1994 and the Director of the Department of Economics and Management of the Branch Campus of Valence. He has a PhD degree from the University Paris X – Nanterre. He is specialised in monetary and financial economics (monetary theories, monetary policies, banking and financial systems, regulatory and supervisory schemes of monetary and financial markets), financial and development economics (links between financial markets' development and economic development in emerging countries, links between financial liberalization, institutional infrastructure and macroeconomic stability) and in industrial and organizational economics. He has authored two books on market theories and on the coordination problems in market economies, contributed several chapters to books, and published in academic journals.

David Weitzner is the Associate Director of the Strategic Field Study program at the Schulich School of Business, York University. He teaches strategic management, business ethics and the capstone management simulation course. David completed his MBA and PhD in Strategic Management and Business Ethics at the Schulich School of Business. David maintains an active research program which focuses on the intersection between strategy and ethics, particularly as it relates to the development of organizational virtue. Representative of his current research focus are: "The Limits of Strategic Rationality: Ethics, Risk Management, and Governance," Journal of Business Ethics, forthcoming (with J. Darroch), "A Comprehensive Framework for Strategic CSR: Ethical Positioning and Strategic Activities," (with J. Darroch), Best Paper Proceedings Academy of Management Chicago 2009, "Why Moral Failures Precede Financial Crises," Critical Perspectives on International Business (2009) (with J. Darroch),

"Deconstruction Revisited: Implications of Theory over Methodology". Journal of Management Inquiry (2007), and a recently edited anthology "Corporate Social Responsibility" (with W. Cragg and M. Schwartz) for Ashgate Publishing (2009).

In: After the Crisis: Rethinking Finance
Editor: Thomas Lagoarde-Segot

ISBN 978-1-61668-924-7
© 2010 Nova Science Publishers, Inc.

Chapter 1

CAPITAL IS DEAD: LONG LIVE ULTRA CAPITAL?

Jon Cloke

ABSTRACT

This chapter re-visits the more abstract take on capital expressed by Marx in the Grundrisse, that "capital is not a simple relationship but a process in whose moments it is always capital." It does so with the intention of showing that a series of global events and processes, beginning with the first deployment of derivatives in the 1970s, accelerated by the fall of the socialist bloc in 1989, the development of an off-shore cyber-reality and the widespread de-regulation of financial services, and culminating in the rapid expansion of financial services cyber-space, has brought about the first global crisis caused by a new form of capital that I refer to as ultra-capital. Ultra-capital stands alone through being the creation of none of the traditional mechanisms through which capital has historically been created, as outlined by (inter alia) Castree; class exploitation, social domination, technological innovation and inter-capitalist competition. Ultra-capital stands detached from value as an expression of labour time, social necessity or commodification and cannot be used as a specific measure of wealth, being dependent on artificial cyber-constructs, themselves depending on temporary, shifting and evanescent financial services relational space. The analysis uses the social and qualitative aspects of capital to examine the global crisis as being separate from individual legislative and political events, economic policy and the technocratic aspects of commercial structures and functions, and instead a product of a complex, constantly degrading and coalescing nebula of financial actor-network relationships.

1. INTRODUCTION

The last three decades of the twentieth century bore witness to an explosive growth in the development of new kinds of capital instruments and flows, concurrent with a growing domination by radical ideas of governance under neoliberalism that changed the ways in which they were understood and regulated. These kinds of capital owe their existence, not only to innovations in financial engineering and technological developments, but also to the development of crucial political and socio-cultural networks and relational spaces. Because of the new possibilities inherent in the development of new politico-financial actants, networks, technologies and processes, the global financial crisis from 2007 onwards comprised the first crisis brought about by substantively new, hybrid forms of capital, here termed ultra-capital. This chapter endeavours to set out a preliminary approach to understanding the interrelationships between this collection of flows, processes and events, using the concept of ultra-capital as a key.

At first glance this may seem like hyperbolae; forms of what Marx referred to as 'fictitious capital'[1] are not exactly new. What is new, however, are the levels of technological, IT-enabled complexity of such types of capital, their reliance on social and political relational spaces that have eroded the state/private boundary to the point of non-existence, their durability and their dramatic effects on the 'real' economy. Marx in addition could scarcely have envisaged the connectivity and concealment permitted by developments in financial engineering and finance-related IT over the last three decades of the millennium. These have dramatically increased the depth, speed and complexity of capital types and flows, as well as their connection to layers of offshore cyber-space that conceal ownership and their ability to impact on the productive/goods economy.

Because the global economic crisis is still with us and the after-shocks will be experienced for decades, much current writing on the topic is highly politicized and empirical analysis is in its infancy. The bursting of the US housing market bubble and the concomitant collapse in Mortgage-Backed Securities (MBS), the consequent drying up of liquidity and the virtual disappearance of credit globally has had an all-too-real impact on productivity, enterprise and employment, making analysis by different social science disciplines critical:

> "The conditions of economic circulation, hypermobility, timespace compression, and cultural insignia warrant a completely new conceptualization of space (Jones, 2009: 6)."

By trawling across disciplinary literatures, moreover, it becomes obvious that a substantial quantity of academics and professionals had already been writing about the frailties and dangers of the developing global financial services sector for some time and with remarkable prescience[2]. But in the main such pre-crisis research has tended to concentrate one or at best a few phenomena associated with current global weaknesses, whereas with hindsight a far more complex picture has been emerging.

As to the nature of ultra-capital, financial, technical and political analyses by themselves (or in tandem) are not sufficient – such forms of capital are as much as anything social capital, being dependent on the highly complex relational spaces that have developed in the financial services sector.

In addition, this analysis is not definitional in the sense of giving the term fixity, if not an examination of process intended to discuss ultra-capital characteristics and a preliminary exploration of the concept. It does so in the certainty that the socio-cultural mechanisms, actors, networks and financial relational spaces which led to the evolution of ultra-capital are still firmly in place and that current global proposals for institutional, legal and regulatory changes to the financial services sector will do little to affect the creation and development of new forms of ultra-capital in the future.

---

[1] Capital, Vol. 3, Chapter 29.
[2] A good example of this is Adam Tickell's seminal (2000) article on the dangers of financial derivatives.

Although the analysis of ultra-capital below analyzes the development of financial derivatives as one key to an understanding of ultra-capital, their importance lies not in their development as financial instruments*per se*. Complex derivatives are not ultra-capital by themselves, they are one socio-political, financial manifestation of an ultra-capital process. Their central role is to facilitate an understanding of the legal, socio-political and cultural processes crucial to their existence. There is still controversy over the role (for instance) of the particular mortgage-backed securities and their more complex derivatives that evolved from the sub-prime mortgage lending in the US, but the debate is frequently ideological and an effort to shift blame. For the purposes of a more ontological analysis, the key to understanding derivatives comes from an examination of their role in the crisis, but more importantly how they came to be, what they are of themselves, and the complex, interrelated and rarified nature of the financial services environment necessary to develop and sustain them.

2. CONSIDERING SECURITIES AND DERIVATIVES

2.1. The Development of Derivative

Financial derivatives have come a long way since the deregulation of foreign currency exchanges and the introduction of the first standardised options in 1973, two key events unlocking the path to their development. Whereas derivative is merely a term given to any financial instrument derived from an underlying asset, the complexity in the use of such instruments comes from the assumptions underpinning any future contract (and thus future value) based on that underlying instrument. A rapid increase in that complexity grew not only from developments in financial engineering and regulation, but also the computer-enabled clearance systems and financial IT that developed from the 1980s onwards.

The instrumentation of financial derivatives proceeded rapidly after the 1970s; from the 1980s onwards, the packaging of US mortgage bonds to create collateralised debt obligations (CDOs) was followed by the development of default protection via credit default swaps. Subsequently, the low interest rates of the NICE (Non-Inflatinory Continuous Expansion) era during the 1990s created a substantial flow of investment funds seeking a higher rate of return (BIS, 2008), a phenomenon familiar as Harvey's (2006) capital surplus absorption problem. Whereas the amount outstanding in derivatives contracts by the end of the 1990s was by no means insubstantial, it was at the beginning of the millennium that the explosive growth began (see Figure 1) – the investment flows thus absorbed (with hindsight) constituted Harvey's crisis-creating "ever-increasing quantities of surplus-value" (2006: xxiii).

The rapid growth in numbers and types of derivatives was caused not only by the ease with which a new financial instrument could be developed, but by the way in which their underlying assumptions (and those of the contracts constructed to insure them) were limited only by the ability to find contractor and contractee willing to believe in them. The CEO of Berkshire Hathaway, Warren Buffett (2003: 13) suggested that:

"The range of derivatives contracts is limited only by the imagination of man (or sometimes, so it seems, madmen)."

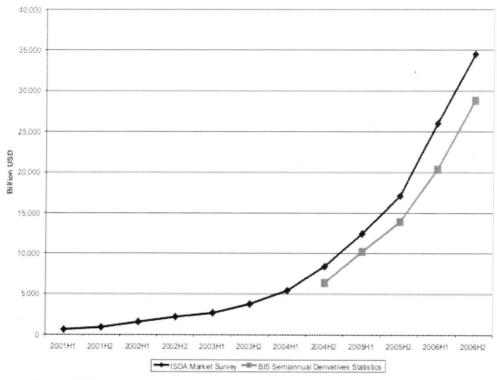

(Source: Gibson, 2007).

Figure 1. Notional amounts of credit derivatives outstanding.

The majority of derivatives traded globally are what is referred to as over-the-counter[3] (OTC) derivatives, which are contracts traded privately and which do not pass through an exchange or market. It is this very private, non-market character and how it is devised that makes even notional value very hard to estimate and regulate. This virtual secrecy and regulatory invisibility is one contributor to their rapid expansion in numbers and at the same time a vital characteristic of ultra-capital. In evading the informational visibility of a market transaction the value remains notional and subject to the malleable relation spaces of internal accounting measures, whilst at the same time helping to evade regulatory control and possible taxation. It is precisely because of this that these new financial instruments are so important to financial services and banking institutions.

2.2. The Subversion of Securitization

Co-constitutive with (and a *sine qua non* of) the evolution of ultra-capital was the process of securitization. Although there is no formal definition, put simply securitization is the

---

[3] According to the Bank for International Settlements Quarterly Review for June 2008, the total outstanding notional amount of OTC derivatives was is $684 trillion.

conversion of illiquid assets into a security (or derivative thereof) through frequently complex financial engineering. It involves:

"the aggregation and pooling of assets with similar characteristics in such a way that investors may purchase interest or securities backed by those assets." (Borod, 1991: 5-7)

Securitization was greatly assisted by the creation of Special Purpose Vehicles (SPVs) and Off-Balance-Sheet Entities (OBSEs) that helped the originator avoid capital adequacy safeguards under the Basel I agreement. In doing so, they also helped evade problems in case of bankruptcy and developed increasingly complex intermediation networks that made ownership and liability for some products almost impossible to determine. Because of the size of the global OTC trade in derivatives this had the added effect of rapidly and substantially increasing the complexity and interconnectedness of the global financial services system (Shin, 2009).

In theory, securitization is monitored by counterparties buying into the product, the accountants charged with verifying a corporation's accounts and by securities rating agencies whose responsibility it is to assess the quality of the finished product before it can be sold. Accompanying the development of derivatives and securitization since the 1970s, however, were a series of rapid infrastructural, legal and commercial changes to regulatory, accounting and credit rating systems alike. The changes meant that these three key sets of actors in the developing global financial services sector, instead of constituting a system of checks and balances, were rapidly co-opted into supporting the dynamic growth of different types of securities and their derivatives. As the International Monetary Fund's (IMF) Global Financial Stability Report for 2009 points out:

"One of the reasons that securitization grew so quickly and became such a large market was the willingness of credit rating agencies to give their highest ratings (AAA or Aaa)."(2009: 81)

This willingness on the part of the large credit ratings agencies (Moody's, Standard and Poor and Fitch) derived at least in part from the changes after the 1970s in the business models which these firms employed. Increasing competition meant that they were effectively trying to sell services to the investment banks whose securities and derivatives they were responsible for rating, advising clients on how to achieve an AAA rating for their products. The competition also allowed clients of the ratings agencies to 'cherry pick' the agencies willing to give them the highest ratings for particular products, something that intensified rapidly during the period leading up to the crisis (Benmelech and Dlugosz, 2009).

A similar process was happening in the global accountancy sector, strengthening that social capital component so vital to the development of ultra-capital. Clients for accountancy firms shopped around more for the best deal towards the end of the century (Boyd, 2004), increasingly looked for accounting firms that would give interpretations as close as possible to those desired by the board, so-called "opinion shopping" (Magill and Previts, 1991:124).Firms were paid to audit banks/financial services firms in order to "properly audit" capital, cash flow and assets of the bank/firm and at the same time to asses the "fair value" for existing and new derivative products, mark-to-market (or 'mark-to-myth' (Buffett, 2003: 13)) pricing. This notional value was therefore arrived at by using selected information provided by the originator of a derivative product and by using models devised by the same originator.

2.3. The Political and Regulatory Components of Ultra-Capital

The picture thus far has been of an evolution of securitization, securities and derivatives that depended on the rapid coalescing of new financial engineering methodologies, global financial services institutions, investment banks, accountancy firms and credit rating agencies, all supposedly components of a counter-party surveillance system to ensure that the system was self-regulating. The market for derivative products, however (as well as its concealment and proofing against regulatory ambitions) could not have proceeded as far or as fast without the assimilation of the last vital components, the political and regulatory sectors.

The increasingly global transition to a neoliberal economic and geopolitical environment, which began in the 1970s and gathered pace throughout the 1980s, substantially reduced regulation of the financial services sector. Chief amongst the impacts were a rapid increase in the freedom of capital to move across borders, the abandonment of Depression-era regulation and substantial increases in the amount of leverage (debt per unit of concrete asset) allowed to investment banks[4]. Financial services institutions were devolved powers to measure their own internal risk and there was a rapid movement towards 'light-touch' and self regulation by stock exchange supervisory bodies; regulations covering forms of financial innovations became outdated and failed to keep pace.

In the UK and the USA in the paramount financial services dyad comprised by the two globally pre-eminent stock markets, London and New York, the power and influence of the finance sector grew rapidly. The de-regulation (Big Bang) of the London Stock Exchange from the mid-1980s was followed in the US by a wave of deregulation initiated through increasingly close links between financial services institutions and regulators. In 1998 (for instance) US President Clinton's Working Group on Financial Markets blocked initiatives to regulate of the market in derivatives and in 1999 the Gramm-Leach-Bliley Act repealed the Glass-Steagall Act of 1933 which had enforced the separation of bank types, thus facilitating the consolidation of commercial and investment banks. The Commodity Futures Modernization Act of 2000 removed federal oversight of derivatives and in April 2004 the New York Stock Exchange Commission (SEC) allowed investment banks to greatly increase their ratios of debt leverage.

At the heart of the increasing intimacy between state and financial services sector lay a pervasive neoclassical theorizing of the globalizing economy in the liberal democracies of the North/West, an intimacy theorized by what was referred to as New Public Management (NPM). This effectively constituted a post-hoc rationalization of a purportedly post-bureaucratic organizational process of de-layering government and empowering both private and public sectors (Theobald, 2002: 437). The practical effects were a substantial increase in the number and complexity of interrelationships between public and private actors involved in the financial services sector. These interrelationships involved *inter alia* the use of special advisors, industry appointments to public posts (so-called 'revolving-door' government) and in the US at least increasing dependence on the massive financial assistance that financial sector lobbyists could bring to bear on political campaigns. Rapid changes in perceptions of the role of the state acted: "as part of a strategy to block criticisms of the new entrepreneurial ethos." (Theobald, 2002: 437-438).

---

[4] The Quiet Coup, Simon Johnson, The Atlantic, Economy section May 2009, available at http://www .theatlantic. com/doc/200905/imf-advice, last accessed 11/01/10.

The Joint US Congressional Economic Committee Report of June 2008 described the consequences of this politico-financial intimacy as the growth of "an alternative financial system evolved to rival the traditional bank-centric system (US Congress, 2008: 1)". The system described in the report is based on the development of new financial institutions, highly leveraged non-depository financial institutions (HLNDFIs) which accompanied the evolution of securitization. The congressional report also analyses what are referred to as misaligned private incentives, securitization models, credit rating problems, regulatory and supervisory factors. Although the congressional committee points out that this system evolved specifically to avoid state and international regulatory authorities, it fails to point out that it did so by effectively absorbing them into the body corporate, so that structurally and in terms of personnel and ideology they were no longer discrete entities. This politico-financial system was also increasingly shaped to avoid the purported disciplines of the market and counter-party surveillance through processes such as securitization of the OTC system and was responsible for the subversion of mark-to-market, accountancy models and standards, the credit rating agencies etc. described above. An interrelated and contiguous set of actor-networks developed that were absorbed in the same relational spaces, designed to produce capital flows that avoided objective mechanisms for assessing value or utility and which became a state/market hybrid whilst maintaining the simulacrum of difference.

3. CONSIDERING CAPITAL AND ULTRA CAPITAL

3.1. The Nature of Ultra-Capital

The preceding analysis gives a generalized basis for suggesting some characteristics of ultra-capital before going on to consider why it should be considered different from forms of 'fictitious' capital or normal financial capital. It is important to stress firstly that these are preliminary outlines of the ultra-capital process rather than an attempt to examine specific instruments and manifestations and, as such, not intended to be exclusive. Some common characteristics of capital derived from the ultra-capital process, therefore, would be that it is:

1. Capital directed towards and derived from the exclusivity of HLNDFIs through the subversion of central banking regulatory mechanisms – as such it is effectively an inverted 'cyber-fix' (see Harvey's 'spatial fix' – 2001, 2006: xviii) whose purpose through velocity of circulation and complex intermediation is to conceal value, ownership and location.
2. Capital created through socio-political systems operating in financial spaces designed to be concealed from objective valuation, regulation and taxation.
3. Capital that has been enabled by the erosion of difference at the state/private regulatory interface into a contiguous politico-financial relational space.
4. Capital that is almost purely social capital, whose book value is the product of intricate, complex and co-constitutive relationships between quantitative analysts, risk assessors, credit-raters, company officials, bank officials and accountants.

3.2. The Different Natures of Capital and Ultra-Capital

The global financial crisis can be visualized in orthodox economic terms as what Harvey (2006: 269) describes as the 'height of distortion' in a cyclical crisis – there is no currency globally whose measure of value is stable, particularly the dollar and the pound. But the ability of the system to seek 'a more solid monetary basis' has been substantially eroded, if not destroyed, by the development of forms of ultra-capital outside the control of central bankers, even of supranational financial institutions such as the IMF. This is not just because the levers of control have been legislated away, but also because the regulation of the financial services sector as a whole has been 'perverted and undermined' (Harvey, 2006: 281) by an ideology, institutions and people, a 'specific faction of capital'. As a direct corollary to this, the development of forms of ultra-capital mean that it is no longer true that: "The central bank is the pivot of the credit system. And the metal reserve, in turn, is the pivot of the bank (Marx, 1894: 572-3)."

In The General Formula for Capital in Volume 1 of Capital, Marx suggests that: "All new capital, to commence with, comes on the stage, that is, on the market, whether of commodities, labour, or money, even in our days, in the shape of money that by a definite process has to be transformed into capital (Marx, 1887)".The analysis of ultra-capital thus far, however, shows how actual instruments of ultra-capital such as complex derivatives are developed through the process of securitization (effectively the creation of false or indeterminate surplus-value), which is only capable of survival in the special cyber-environment created for it through the relational space surrounding HLNDFIs. Securitization itself has evolved into a process where the most sought-after products are those which avoid markets, involve only electronic transfers and for which immediate profits are accountancy creations.

Ultra-capital is capital that in certain critical areas is created by complex social and relational aspects that put it outside, beyond capital. These relational and social components impart to ultra-capital, through intermediation processes, not a value but in effect a spectrum of values. In this respect it follows Castree:

> "For value, though real, is strangely intangible and "phantom-like": it is a real abstraction that is qualitatively homogenous and quantitatively determinate but also imperceptible (2002: 136)."

Ultra-capital certainly qualifies in terms of its intangibility and "phantom-like" qualities, as well as in being a social relation; in the appropriation of surplus value, however, it differs substantially, abstract value being allocated arbitrarily through social/commercial networks designed to avoid marketability.

Furthermore, the concept of surplus-value itself becomes attenuated and malleable with reference to derivatives and other forms of ultra-capital; these are not after all items/commodities which are bought outright, but suppositional capital flows in which rights and options of various kinds are traded. The original 'value' of income streams from that which is securitized is not derived from any objective, market-based appraisal but, as outlined above, the end-product of an extended, mutually-beneficial collaboration between various sets of actors temporarily conjoined in one area of closed and exclusive relational space, politicians, public officials, lobbyists, financial engineers, credit-raters, accountants and so forth. In this respect, that set of processes, actants and relationships leading to politico-financial manifestations of ultra-capital conforms to ideas of phase space as being:

"the active product of reciprocal relationships between economic behaviour, the politics of representation and identity, state power geometries, and the sedimentation of these practices in spacetime" (Jones, 2009: 15).

It is because of this aspect of relational space that ultra-capital blends into theorizing social capital, given that definitions of social capital do not preclude the profit motive. A part of ultra-capital is certainly: "the expectations for action within a collectivity that affect the economic goals and goal-seeking behaviour of its members (Portes and Sensenbrenner, 1993: 1323)." It shares "the ability to facilitate certain actions of individuals who are within the structure (Coleman 1990; Robison, Schmid and Siles 2000: 3) and is critically inclusive of features such as trust, norms and networks (Putnam, 1993), but none of these generalizations describe exactly what it is. The missing component is provided by an analysis of Marx's discussion of the contradictory nature of capital (Capital Vol. 1, Chapter 5) and his assertion that 'surplus-value cannot be created by circulation'; ultra-capital effectively substitutes 'social-value' for surplus-value, thereby apparently solving the contradiction:

"It is therefore impossible for capital to be produced by circulation, and it is equally impossible for it to originate apart from circulation. It must have its origin both in circulation and yet not in circulation."(Marx, 1887)

Examining such a contradiction (to all intents and purposes overcome by the development of ultra-capital) requires an interdisciplinary examination of the global/local links in financial services interrelations between technology, time, space and social life (Graham, 1998). The development of markets in derivatives, the development of technology to sustain incalculable numbers of market transactions every day, the development of sophisticated second-/third-/nth party insurance and hedging instruments, the rapid development of an offshore cyber-reality specifically tasked with anonymity and secrecy, have all contributed to a rapidly expanding environment in which ultra-capital has developed from: "Complex, contingent and subtle blendings of human actors and technical artefacts, to form actor-networks (which are sociotechnical 'hybrids')" (Graham, 1998: 167). Ultra-capital and its manifestations emerge: "between interactions in geographical space and place, and the electronic realms accessible through new technologies. (ibid: 172).

4. THE FUTURE OF ULTRA-CAPITAL

4.1. Financial and Economic Indicators: Where we are Now

At the time of writing, the Bank for International Settlements reports what it terms a slow return to growth within the financial services sector globally (BIS, 2009a). The direct global financial cost of this growth as of September 2009 has been over $3.5 trillion in country/regional bailouts, over $7 trillion in country/regional guarantees and nearly $9.5

trillion in country/regional stimulus packages[5]. The 2009 Global Financial Stability Report of the IMF reports an:

> "unprecedented $1.5 trillion of bank debt due to mature in the euro area, the United Kingdom, and the United States by 2012.... reflecting the higher leverage and the worsening business climate, and overall loan quality is likely to deteriorate further in the next 12 to 18 months (2009: 12)"

What has been achieved thus far by international action on a vast scale through the state component of politico-financial relational space, is a slow unravelling of a tiny part of the skein of intermediation created through ultra-capital. This unravelling however has not in any way changed the set of processes, flows and relational spaces vital to the development of ultra-capital and neither has it affected the vast, complex global mesh of intermediation connectivity in any substantive way.

As the Bank for International Settlements (2009b: 1) reported, for the first half of the year: "notional amounts of all types of OTC contracts rebounded somewhat to stand at $605 trillion at the end of June 2009, 10% above the level six months before." These are now contracts owned and traded by many financial services institutions that are (nominally) majority-owned by states on a global basis, operating in a financial relational space whose activities have been guaranteed by the state component of ultra-capital, within a global financial services sector that is inoperable without supra-national taxpayer support. The same instability that caused the current crisis has been set in aspic within ultra-capital, as various actants hoard substantial quantities of bailout funds, using them to try and avoid 'unnecessary' de-leveraging and loss write-downs.

The development of the crisis since 2007 has also acted to concentrate politico-financial power amongst fewer actants within ultra-capital. In the USA, for instance, the Big Four banks (Citigroup, JPMorgan Chase, Bank of America and Wells Fargo) held 31.8% of all US banking deposits in 2007; by June 2009 (as Figure 2 below shows) this figure had increased to 38.6% (at least two of these entities, Citigroup and Bank of America, would no longer exist without the substantial financial assistance transferred from the US state/corporate hybrid). Neither did concentration in the US banking proceed in isolation. The mergers in the US that rapidly concentrated banking power in a dwindling number of banks throughout the 1990s and into the new millennium also included banks from outside the USA. Deutsche Bank AG linked up with Banker's Trust, Credit Suisse with First Boston and HSBC (Hong Kong and Shanghai Banking Corporation) bought into Wells Fargo and Wachovia Corporation. Outside the US a similar movement towards mergers saw the Banque Nationale de Paris (BNP) acquire Paribas to create what was claimed to be one of the world's largest banks (Chossudovsky, 2003).

This pre-crisis concentration was intensified on a global scale with the onset of the crisis. The Bank of America (for instance) took over the remnants of Merrill Lynch, the Bank of China acquired a 20% stake in liquidity-starved banks such as Rothschild and Barclays Bank acquired what was left of Lehman Brothers.

---

[5] Global Financial Crisis Bailout/Stimulus Tracker, September 12 2009, available at http://www.grailresearch.com/pdf/ContenPodsPdf/Global_Bailout_Tracker.pdf.

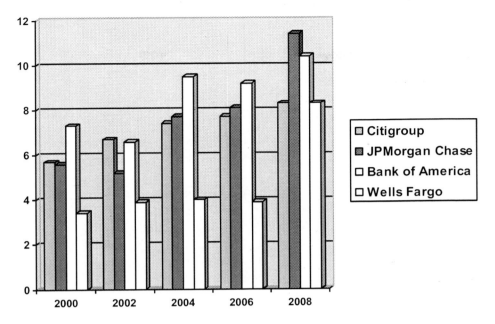

(Sources: Sources: FDIC, NCUA, Federal Reserve Bank of Cleveland).

Figure 2. Share of total bank deposits held by the Big Four US Banks

Banco Santander of Spain, now the largest bank in the Eurozone and in profits the third largest in the world, took advantage of the crisis to absorb banks such as Sovereign Bancorp in the US and the Alliance and Leicester and Bradford and Bingley building societies in the UK. A crisis precipitated by the development of ultra-capital, therefore, has caused severe problems in the productive economy and severely financially damaged the manoeuvring capabilities of nominal nation-state governance; the resultant re-shaping and re-concentration of power within ultra-capital has made a few financial attractors within financial services relational space more powerful by an order of magnitude.

4.2. The Political Capitalscape

In the UK and the USA, epicentres of unravelling securitization processes and de-leveraging financial services networks (as well as evolutionary centres for the spread of ultra-capital), moves to re-regulate the financial services sector are under discussion. The Financial Services Authority in the UK has put forward a series of proposals designed to overhaul some mechanisms of the current crisis (strengthening UK liquidity regulations, reforming the UK mortgage market[6], etc.). In the USA the House of Representatives passed the Wall Street Reform and Consumer Protection Act of 2009 on December 11 2009, whilst in January 2010 US President Obama announced plans to legislate towards significant curbs on

---

[6] See 'FSA finalises far-reaching overhaul of UK liquidity regulation', FSA/PN/132/2009, 05 October 2009; 'FSA sets out major reforms for the mortgage market', FSA/PN/140/2009, 19 October 2009.

bankingactivities and size, in recognition of his claim that: "While the financial system is far stronger today than it was a year one year ago, it is still operating under the exact same rules that led to its near collapse."[7] The weakness of all of these suggested reforms is that they stem from a re-assertion of the false state/market binary that is undermined by the reality of ultra-capital. In the USA, for instance, no meaningful regulatory reform is likely to pass through both the House and Senate, given the overwhelming involvement of representatives and senators alike within ultra-capital. There will be legislation, but it will be symbolic, without effective power.

Ideas for forestalling future crises emanating from supra-national institutions such as the IMF suffer from similar problems. The GFSR talks of the need to broaden the perimeter of regulation to preclude the build-up of 'too big to fail' institutions, encouraging market discipline through greater transparency and disclosure, enforcing adequate capital provisions for banks and improving international regulatory collaboration (2009: xiii). Again, the systemic/spatial ability of ultra-capital to simply side-step clumsy regulatory barriers into the privacy and anonymity of offshore cyber-space precludes any limits on institutional size or strictures on disclosure and transparency. In addition (as discussed above) the financial services institutions that have been 'saved' already constitute overwhelming politico-financial strength; they are powerful attractors in chaotic, dynamic ultra-capital space.

5. CONCLUSION

The current crisis acts both to illuminate the tracery of global ultra-capital and to underline the impossible complexity of regulating it, given the involvement of regulatory, legislative and executive gatekeepers in financial services generally. Heads of state, ministers, senators, representatives, MPs and deputies responsible for drawing up and enacting financial services legislation have a theoretical electoral accountability depending on the breadth and effectiveness of democratic practices. In practice these responsibilities are compromised by a range of party political and personal interests, coloured by ideology.

The increasing penetration of NPM practices throughout the state component of ultra-capital has increasingly compromised the effectiveness of representational democracy. Actants and actors are accustomed to taking up dual functions related to lobbying, special interest pleading and corporate representation that represent concrete conflicts-of-interest. This is what Treanor (2005) refers to in discussing neoliberalism as: "the desire to intensify and expand the market, by increasing the number, frequency, repeatability, and formalisation of transactions" – the drive towards a system in which there is nothing which is not market. Within the neoliberal take, conflicts of interest are de facto attempts to limit the market against its free flow and the functional state must combat that internal contradiction by giving the market precedence.

Further out from various nexuses of state-component power within ultra-capital vast arrays of actors in the financial services sector have arisen to interact and overlap with state-component actors and actants. Accountants, credit agencies, risk analysts, banking corporations, bankers, management consultants, quantitative analysts, financial economists,

---

[7] See 'President Obama Calls for New Restrictions on Size and Scope of Financial Institutions to Rein in Excesses and Protect Taxpayers', Office of the Press Secretary, The White House, January 21, 2010.

mortgage brokers, mortgage packagers and mortgage wholesalers have some form of regulatory and commercial interrelationship with the state component. The urgent quest for innovation and capital expansion has shaped an unceasing, intensifying flow of pressure inwards towards the state component, shaping it around the needs of finance towards a constant 'maximalisation of volume of transactions' (Treanor, ibid.).

Further out still in this relational space in hierarchical terms but contiguous in ultra-capital space are an array of specialist actors and actants providing velocity-enhancing services. These include specialist tax avoidance services linked to the use of anonymous trusts and offshore banking centres, the centres themselves and the anonymous cyber-reality in which they operate. Since the 1970s secrecy and privacy services on offer have become ever more important in increasing both the volume and intensity of transactions within ultra-capital, as well as enabling the exponential growth of complex financial instruments and engineering processes. The also serve as a vital conduit for the manipulation and control of markets and financial contracts.

Feeding these convoluted and co-constitutive spaces have been a growing number of service processes related to housing, property and property development. These spheres of activity are comprised of property developers, real estate agents, property appraisers, constructors, land valuers, estate agents and various sales agents acting as gatekeepers not only to possession of land and property, but also as gatekeepers to mechanisms by which fictitious value, and hence fictitious capital, can be developed from the processes by which land and property are bought and sold. Land valuations, property valuations, mortgage access, mortgage packaging and the insurance relating to these activities, not to mention the complex derivatives arising from them, all have their origins in these spaces of activity.

Last but not least, since the displacement of Keynesian economics in the 1970s a substantial intellectual hinterland has grown in support of ultra-capital, to provide a range not only of theoretical underpinnings but also management and financial engineering techniques. Research and business management institutes and universities have become increasingly locked into systems of corporate funding, down to individual school level. As access to funding became increasingly dependent on the private sector, so intellectual/academic endeavours (in the same manner as those of the accountants and credit rating agencies) became locked into client-shopping activities. Replicating and enhancing a neoclassical orthodoxy represented the path to career advancement and access to research funding; in this respect the educational system linked increasingly into pressure from politico-financial space to teach acceptable economic theory and to develop acceptable models.

As a direct consequence of this historical development of ultra-capital, much of the outpouring of ideas on both causation and prevention (so far as the current crisis is concerned) tends to follow two paths. The first path is a technical/econometric one, which is to say based on analysis of internal structures, incentives and procedures within financial services institutions, markets and economies. The second path is ideological, which is to say derived from either a free market take on market discipline as the ultimate cure-all for what is claimed to be the ills of 'crony capitalism', or it is (for want of a better term) left/progressive in looking to the state, the legal system and international regulation to put limits on a hostile corporate capitalism.

In the analysis outlined in this chapter, the technical approach will fail because it has no means to measure or model the socio-political, cultural components of ultra-capital. Either ideological approach must also fail because on the one hand ultra-capital is the direct product of previous efforts to de-regulate and free markets and is 'really-existing' capitalism, and on the other hand expecting the politico-financial hybrid that is the state to regulate effectively is expecting one component of ultra-capital to control an artificially constructed other which is in fact itself. Ironically, then, in this reading both 'left' and 'right' end up expecting ultra-capital to regulate itself. Ultra-capital will continue to defy such theoretical and technical approaches because it is the purest evocation yet of Harvey's dictum: "Value is a social relation in relational time-space" (Harvey 2006: xx)

REFERENCES

Bank for International Settlements (2008) Financial market developments and their implications for monetary policy, BIS Papers No 39 , BIS Monetary and Economic Department, April 2008.

Bank for International Settlements (2009a) BIS Quarterly Review, December 2009, Statistical Annex, available at http://www.bis.org/publ/qtrpdf/r_qs0912.pdf, last accessed 7/1/10.

Bank for International Settlements (2009b) OTC derivatives market activity in the first half of 2009, Monetary and Economic Department, November 2009, available at http://www.bis. org/publ/otc_hy0911.pdf?noframes=1, last accessed 7/1/10.

Benmelech, E. and Dlugosz, J. (2009) The Credit Rating Crisis, NBER Working Paper No. 15045 (Cambridge, Massachusetts: National Bureau of Economic Research), available at http://ssrn.com/abstract=1415208, last accessed 10/01/10.

Borod, R. (1991) Securitization, Asset Backed and Mortgage Backed Securities, 3rd Edition (New Hampshire: Butterworth Legal Publications): 1-7.

Boyd, C. (2004) The structural origins of conflicts of interest in the accounting profession, Business Ethics Quarterly, Vol. 14 No. 3, pp. 377-98.

Buffett, W. (2003) Berkshire Hathaway Inc. 2002 Annual Report, Berkshire Hathaway Inc., available at http://www.berkshirehathaway.com/2002ar/2002ar.pdf, last accessed 7/1/10.

Castree, N. (2002) False Antitheses? Marxism, Nature and Actor-Networks, Antipode 34 (1): 111 – 146.

Chossudovsky, M. (2003) The Globalization of Poverty and the New World Order (Canada: Centre for Research on Globalization).

Cloke, J. (2009) An economic wonderland: derivative castles built on sand, *Critical Perspectives on International Business* 5(1/2): 107-119.

Coleman, J. (1990) Foundations of Social Theory (Cambridge: Belknap Press/Harvard University Press).

Gibson, M. (2007) Credit Derivatives and Risk Management, Finance and Economics Discussion Series 2007-47, Divisions of Research and Statistics and Monetary Affairs, Federal Reserve Board, Washington, D.C.

Graham, S. (1998) The end of geography or the explosion of place? Conceptualizing space, place and information technology, Progress in Human Geography 22: 165.

Jones, M. (2009) Phase space: geography, relational thinking, and beyond, Progress in Human Geography (2009): 1–20.

Magill, H. and Previts, G. (1991) CPA Professional Responsibilities: An Introduction (South-Western Publishing: Cincinnati, OH).

Marx, K. (1887) Chapter 4: The General Formula for Capital, Part II: The Transformation of Money into Capital, Capital Volume One (Moscow, USSR: Progress Publishers), available at http://www.marxists.org/archive/marx/works/1867-c1/index.htm, accessed 14/1/10.

Marx, K. (1887) Chapter 5: Contradictions in the General Formula of Capital, Part II: The Transformation of Money into Capital, Capital Volume One (Moscow, USSR: Progress Publishers), available at http://www.marxists.org/archive/marx/works/1867-c1/index.htm, accessed 14/1/10.

Marx, K. (1894) Chapter 25: Credit and Fictitious Capital, Part V: Division of Profit into Interest and Profit of Enterprise, Capital Volume 3 (New York: International Publishers), available at http://www.marxists.org/archive/marx/works/1894-c3/index.htm, last accessed 10/01/10.

Marx, K. (1894) Chapter 35: Precious Metal and Rate of Exchange, Part V: Division of Profit into Interest and Profit of Enterprise, Capital Volume 3 (New York: International Publishers), available at http://www.marxists.org/archive/marx/works/1894-c3/index.htm, last accessed 10/01/10.

Pilling, G. (1980) Chapter 3: The Concepts of Capital, Section V: Capital and the productive forces, Marx's Capital, Philosophy and Political Economy (London: Routledge and Keagan Paul), available at http://www.marxists.org/archive/pilling/works/capital/index.htm, last accessed 14/1/10.

Portes, A. and Sensenbrenner, J. (1993) Embeddedness and Immigration: Notes on the Social Determinants of Economic Action, *American Journal of Sociology* 98: 1320-1350.

Putnam, R. (1993) Making Democracy Work, Princeton: Princeton University Press.Is Social Capital Really Capital?

Robison, L., Schmid, A. and Siles, M. (2002) Is Social Capital Really Capital? Review of Social Economy, 2002 60 (1): pages 1-21.

Shin, H. (2009) Securitisation and Financial Stability, *The Economic Journal* 119 (536): 309–32.

Tickell, A. (2000) Dangerous derivatives: controlling and creating risks in international money, Geoforum 31: 87 –99.

Treanor, P. (2005) Neoliberalism: origins, theory, definition, available at http://web, last accessed 14/1/10.

US Congress (2008) The US Housing Bubble and the Global Financial Crisis: Vulnerabilities of the Alternative Financial System, Joint Congressional Economic Committee, June 2008, Washington DC, available at http://www.house.gov/jec/studies/2008/The_US_Housing_Bubble_June_2008_Study.pdf, last accessed 12/1/10.

In: After the Crisis: Rethinking Finance
Editor: Thomas Lagoarde-Segot

ISBN 978-1-61668-925-4
© 2010 Nova Science Publishers, Inc.

Chapter 2

THE INDIVIDUAL-COLLECTIVE DIALECTIC IN MANAGEMENT SCIENCES: A RE-READING BASED ON THE INTERPELLATION OF FINANCE FROM A MARKETING STANDPOINT

Bernard Paranque and Bernard Cova[*]

ABSTRACT

The management sciences are largely based on the figure of an economic agent who seeks to maximise his or her own individual interests, in the same way as the celebrated *homo economicus*. The whole corpus of finance relies on this fundamental hypothesis. However, developments in this field, as well as in the neighbouring field of marketing, in the last decade reflect the effects of collective actors or actors whose motives are more collective than individual. This paper describes those developments and proposes to make new progress in this direction by offering a critical reading of the role and place of financial markets.

1. INTRODUCTION

As the question of the source of value is no longer in vogue (cf. the physiocrats, classical economists, Marx etc, versus neoclassical and Keynesian thoughts), the market - i.e. the institutionalised form of exchange - has taken centre stage. While we may accept this exclusive shift, we should nevertheless examine the actual possibilities of economic action, one of the key vectors of which are the financial markets where wealth is allocated and which affects the ability to live together and corporate strategies. These strategies are in fact the basis and reasons for investment decisions and the allocation of resources.

---

[*] This work benefits from the support of: Chaire AG2R/Prémalliance « Finance Autrement : Investissement, Solidarités, Responsabilités ».

Can it therefore be said that finance displays arrogance, to borrow from the title of the work by Briys and Bourguignat (2009)? Yes, in our opinion, it can, at least if we consider the debate regarding stock options, the performance levels of financial markets and the impact of their activity on the real economy. Yes it can, especially if we refer to the axiom underlying the theoretical hypotheses of finance which quite simply maintains that collective welfare, is achieved if it is ensured share value is maximised (Jensen, 2001, for example).

This ambition (arrogance?) nevertheless comes up against the fundamental axiom that only sees that collective welfare as the sum of individual welfares. This dispenses with to need to ponder the meaning of collective action (see Cefaï, 2007, for a general description). We feel, however, that we should question that axiom. An individual, whether he or she be an ordinary citizen or a trader on the financial markets, exists only as a person, i.e. through a process of socialisation and appropriation of his or her environments - a "practice" as defined by Ricoeur (1997, pages 278 and 298, for example).

We therefore opt for an ontological rather than an epistemological standpoint[1]. This standpoint recognises that the "collective" in which each one of us lives out his or her life is dated and situated and that, in return, every one of us produces conditions of existence which then modify that collective. The history of sciences clearly shows that "knowing and acting" are not a straightforward, long, natural process and there are those who remind us that conviction sometimes carries more weight than demonstration: Galileo (Redondi, 1983; Feyerabend, 1979, 1989) and Kepler (Simon, 1979; Hallyn, 1987).

Recent developments in management sciences thus show the emergence of an interrogation concerning the fundamental hypothesis of the discipline of a *homo economicus* seeking to maximise his or her individual interests, with emphasis on the necessary allowance for collective actors, or actors who motives are more collective than individual. These developments therefore call into question the Anglo-Saxon Protestant inspired foundations of the management sciences (Witkowski, 2005). Here we propose to back up this process of questioning by examining how some management disciplines have dealt with it and by plotting paths for the future.

Finance is, by construction, a matter of anticipation. In its edition of October 26 and 27, 2008, the "Le Monde" French leading newspaper reviewed the year on the stock market as from January 2, 2008, under the headline: "25,000 billion dollars vanish". In fact, what it should have said was that, on top of real losses suffered in some quarters, it was above all a question of a drastic revision of initial expectations - a spectacular revision of forecasts. The performance levels required by current financial management (strengthening of margins and stock prices) lead to managerial decisions which may be contrary to the collective interest (see "Les Echos" of June 23, 2009, page 15, or "Les Echos" of June 17, 2009, which published a survey by Grant Thornton revealing that more than half of heads of companies were reticent about pro-environmental measures).

Financial markets and finance in general are however bestowed with virtues of rationality, objectivity and efficiency the limits of which only become apparent to the general public in times of crisis, illustrating the similarity between the market and public opinion, as we are reminded by Cefaï (2007) referring to Park, comparing the shaping of public opinion with the formation of prices on the securities market. The public is described as a cousin to

---

[1] See Defalvard (1992), Hodgson (2007) and Birnbaum and Leca (1991) for a presentation of the terms of the debate between methodological individualism, holism, dialectics and convention. .

the market (Cefaï, 2007, p. 48). Further on, he states that this clearly displayed, asserted rationality cannot stand up to the test of facts: "the speculative market becomes like a panicking crowd: everyone copies each other through rational anticipation to generate the irrational phenomenon of market implosion" (Cefaï, 2007, p. 50).

What more can be said about finance other than that, as regards its role in allocating resources, we should perhaps consider another possible "driver" as an alternative to the shareholder alone with regard to the needs and practices of consumption? Marketing could then be a key to understanding and supplementary action which could help us identify another model through new consumer and user practices which are increasingly off-market, as illustrated by peer-to-peer networks and Facebook.

So how, then, can we contribute to finding solutions to the issues and needs for the co-ordination of our world without rethinking it? The latest theoretical and practical developments in two of the most important disciplines of management science (finance and marketing) offer an initial embryonic answer and they do so by viewing our societies and our economies from a so-called postmodern perspective.

In this chapter, we will proceed by a number of stages. Firstly, we will recontextualise this dialectic in our current society, highlighting societal changes conducive to a return to the collective and to co-ordination. We will then propose an "oriented" review of theoretical discussions regarding the individual-collective dialectic in management sciences. Next, we will illustrate those discussions by examining financial theory and its limits in relation to that dialectic. We will then describe some theoretical advances in marketing and propose going beyond those updated limits. In a final section, we will propose a revision of finance objectives by integrating the described advances in marketing.

2. POSTMODERNITY AND RETURN TO THE COLLECTIVE

Our questioning is not so very different from that engaged in the 13th century with regard to the relationship between the divine order and concrete man[2]. We have moved on from a world in which man is responsible, on earth, for divine plans to a world in which self-interest serves to control individual passions which may be detrimental to the carrying out of divine plans and then those of the "Prince", all with the aim of avoiding eventual social disorder (Hirschman, 1980)[3]. However, this vision in which particular material interest may lead to the collective welfare was contested as soon as it was asserted, as revealed by Hirschman who quotes Barnave (as above, page 107) and Tocqueville (as above, page 111) echoing the physiocrats for whom *"the public good is the result of the free pursuit by everyone of his own self-interest"* (as above, page 89). We cannot therefore ignore these debates, or even their echoes, as emphasised for example by reflections regarding financial "stakeholders" (Jensen, 2001).

In broad outline, it may be said that, in the opinion of the upholders of postmodern sociology (Bauman, 2007; Lipovetsky, 2006; Maffesoli, 2007), we are experiencing a change

---

[2] Voir Onfray, 2005, for a critical reading, especially pages 214, 232 and 256. Caustic and interesting, on the place of religion in the construction of collective welfare in our thought and imagination.

[3] "It's that passions are fiery and dangerous, whereas looking after one's material interests is an innocent and inoffensive activity." page 56; see also pages 70-71, 89, 116, 119.

of epoch as important as the transition from the Middle Ages to the Renaissance. Thus, the entire modern project that has occupied and guided our western societies since the Renaissance is, in fact, based on the idea of freeing the individual from the straightjacket of blood ties and religious superstitions typifying the Middle Ages to create an individual who is able to freely choose who to be tied to and who to believe. The range of individual freedom was then gradually widened and has now become almost unlimited. Having initially been confined to the fields of economics, politics and knowledge, it has eventually spread to customs and day-to-day life as a whole (Lipovetsky, 1983).

But the continuous quest for social progress, through the process of individual liberation, quietly ran aground during the 1980s and has disappeared from the imagination of westerners who have lost confidence in the myth of growth. This period of millenary transition has seen the disintegration, or collapse, of an ensemble of systems and utopias constituting reference points for the individual: work, politics, the family and religion, etc. This disintegration went hand in hand with the predicted end of ideologies and "grand narratives" (Lyotard, 1979) which comes down to noting that, if we go along with Ricœur (1997), that there is nothing more to be said about power – i.e. the capacity for action (Cecconi, 1978) – or about the way in which it is exerted, despite the fact that this very topic resurfaces in connection with our responsibility with regard to the future of our planet and the rise of fundamentalisms. Through the successive stages of liberation of the individual (free choice of spouse, women's liberation, free time, sexual freedom, etc.), with external constraints falling one after another, the subject of freedom has lost its flame and has ceased to be a positive ideology, i.e. an openness to others. To quote from Bakunin (Munoz, 1965): "My personal freedom, confirmed by the liberty of all, extends to infinity," (page 48), to become a source of anxiety and rootlessness.

A postmodern society, anticipated by sociologists in the 1980s, may therefore be rising from the ruins of the belief in freedom and progress, and it is in that sense that it is postmodern. Against a modern imaginary featuring the uprooting of the individual, we can set a postmodern imagery featuring attempts to develop new roots illustrated by the ecological anti-globalisation movements. "Attempts" only, because there is no question of going back to a premodern world (except for a few movements which may be described as sectarian) which we would be unable to live in because that "return", apart from being reactionary in the primary sense of the word, may be described a nonsense based on the illusion that what constituted the past can also constitute our future. If we accept the postmodern hypothesis, the imaginary of our western societies and, thus, the values around which they are structured are in the process of switching from "progress" to "regress" or, at least, a rebalancing of the values of progress with those of regress, placing the individual in a state of tension between those two imaginaries (Figure 1).

In what way may this state of tension be said to be postmodern rather than the much more "classical" opposition between tradition and modernity? In the opinion of upholders of the postmodern, we are experiencing a unique situation as, for the first time, at the beginning of the 21st century, we truly realised and were able to experience the state of the free individual, which is that of the "free fox in a free chicken coop". If is for this reason that this epoch has been described by some as the age of individualism. This age of individualism has undoubtedly led us to forget that an individual is only apparent as a socialised being or, in other words, a person, i.e. in interaction with others.

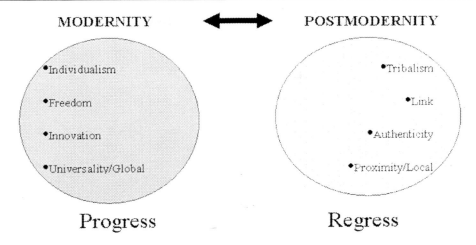

Figure 1. The individual in a state of tension between two imaginaries.

It could even be said, following on from Piaget (1972, 2005), that the individual is only "revealed" and constructed by way of such interactions. That is no doubt why the modern and global future is no longer a dream: it is a reality, and experiencing that reality of the liberated individual is not as exalting as all that, unlike the process of liberation which has exalted a great many generations. "Liberty is a critical form; liberation, on the other hand, is a potentially catastrophic form. The former confronts the subject with his/her own alienation and transcendence. The latter leads to metastases, to chain reactions, to the disconnection of all the elements and finally to the radical expropriation of the subject. Liberation is the effective fulfilment of the metaphor of liberty and, in this sense, it is also its end" (Baudrillard, 1992, p. 151). Something we dream of today is the lost world that we idealise; the attraction of the past and proximity seem to be increasingly gaining ground at the expense of that of a magnificent future on an interconnected planet. A reversing of poles is thus taking place: what is traditional today is modernity and progress. And what is modern, if we can call it, that is tradition and regress: it is what does not exist or no longer exists; it is what can constitute the object of an idealistic quest.

Consequently, while many people see postmodernity as of period of intense social dissolution and frantic individualism, we feel we may be able to detect attempts at social recomposition. The individual who has at last managed to become completely free from archaic or modern social ties triggers a reverse movement seeking social recomposition, on the basis of a free emotional choice. It appears that, today, it is not so much differentiation as dedifferentiation that must guide individual action. Thus, according to a second sociological current led by Michel Maffesoli (1988, 2007), postmodernity is the consecration not of the triumph of individualism but of the beginning of its end, with the emergence of a reverse movement of desperate searching for community social ties. Seen in this perspective, individualism corresponds to only a short period of transition: "late modern", as architects would say, rather than postmodern.

We can thus show that social dynamics, characteristic of our postmodern age, are based on a multiplicity of daily experiences, representations and emotions that are often misunderstood. While such dynamics can generally be explained by the contraction around individualism, it can be linked with the tribalism that is developing in our western societies.

The concept of tribe calls to mind the revival of archaic values - local particularisms, spatial accentuation, religiosity, syncretism and group narcissism - the common denominator of which is the community dimension. It is therefore a question of reintegrating the community, the tribe and the collective, etc, into our theoretical models.

3. THE THEORETICAL INDIVIDUAL-COLLECTIVE D IALECTIC IN MANAGEMENT SCIENCES

This brings us to the dynamic of those "groups" as the result of the interaction between the individuals who construct and constitute them (Latour, 2006). In management sciences, collectives described as micro-social are generally not taken into account (Desjeux, 1996): there are only individuals, their specific interests and the sum of those interests. For example, in neoclassical economic theory, the company is an agent and the concept of organisation is ignored. From a financial point of view, it is therefore a matter of optimising the utility function of the investor acting via financial markets in connection with the optimisation of the "corporate" function. Here, we are in a "market" universe where everything goes through and depends on goods and services markets on the one hand, and the financial markets on the other, in accordance with the hypothesis that the sum of individual interests (with each optimising its utility function) is equal to the general interest, i.e. in the terms of the dominant paradigm: collective (social) welfare.

This may seem simplistic but the simplism has great factual and day-to-day power even if, along with those who are interested in collective action (as it is indeed a matter of collective actions bringing into play two agents, one with a need for finance and the other with a financing surplus), we can only emphasis the theoretical and philosophical poverty of the operating hypotheses of those markets (above and beyond the apparent sophistication bestowed by the sophistication of the tools used, especially mathematical tools).

We want to break with the ontological hypothesis which asserts that all collective phenomena can be reduced to the sum of individual actions alone, where the conflicts which may result are dealt with by means of contracts (Hart, 1995). It must be understood that there are principles for the co-ordination of economic action based on interpersonality (Orléans, 2004; Amable and Palombarini, 2005; Salais and Storper, 1993) which are necessary for the realisation/construction of the "collective" (customs, rules, laws, institutions, etc.).

Here it should be noted that this focus on interpersonality may bring to mind the point of view adopted by the Latin sociologist (Maffesoli, 1996, p. 197) who calls for the revenge of the South and "Southern values" based on the importance of the community and social ties compared with "Northern values" based on the pre-eminence of the individual and trade. More precisely, Viard (1997, p. 48) states that "the model of liberalism is that of a society founded by colonists on the dream of absolute mobility as a figure of absolute freedom and on the old commercial culture imported from Great Britain. But, whereas that culture banks on the responsibility of each individual on his or her way through life - in harmony with protestant culture, we in France and, more widely, in Southern Europe remain members of a community which is fundamentally responsible for our destiny, in harmony - in this case - with the dominance of catholic values". Although the market and trade may always have been at the heart of Mediterranean societies, money was never the most important value. Trade in things is first and foremost trade between people and the economy remains subordinate to the human (Fabre, 1998).

We feel we should question this polar figure based on the individual versus the "collective". At the heart of the interaction, calling into question Montesquieu's invisible hand (Hirschman, 1980, p.14) which has the effect that in seeking honour "each pursues the common good while believing that he is pursuing his own particular interests", a central question is raised: what of the meaning of the world and of social responsibility? The reappearance of the need for meaning for which some (re)mobilise the divine, in an attempt to reduce the opposition between individual interests and the general interest, is in fact only a reflection of the absence of any perceived collective meaning. If Ricoeur (1997) can analyse ideology as the expression of a meaning permitting each individual's action the opposite of which is practice while specifying that it shuts him or her up in the past, it is because, at the same time, he identifies utopia as the means of escaping from the framework that is fixed by ideology: "what is at stake in a utopia is the fact of imagining another way of exercising power" (as above, p. 256).

Drawing only on Regulation Theory (Théorie de la Régulation, Boyer and Saillard, 2002) or Economics of Conventions (L'Economie des Conventions, Eymard-Duvernay, 2006), one of the crucial questions concerns the role of the individual and his/her place in the social dynamic (Boyer in Eymard-Duvernay, 2006; Amable and Palombarini, 2005; Raveaud, 2004; Orléans, 2004; Gomez, 1998; Favereau, 1993; Revue Economique, 1989). More widely, from the theory of transactions (Coase, 1937; Williamson, 1975) to agency theory (Jensen and Meckling, 1976), the problems of co-ordinating economic action are a source of debates and proposals but this questioning usually remains within the paradigm of methodological individualism (Birnbaum and Leca, 1991; Gomez, 1998; Defalvard, 1992; Hodgson, 2007).

4. COLLECTIVE, COORDINATION AND FINANCE: THE CREATION OF SHAREHOLDER VALUE

To question the place of the individual with respect to the collective in management sciences, the operation of financial markets is shown as an archetypal model. Indeed, markets place investors on one side and, on the other, projects which are generally supported by companies. We cannot examine one (the investor) without talking about the other (the company) because, once financing has been found, a relationship is formed between the investor, who is now a shareholder, and the company. This relationship is mediatised twice over, on the one hand by the market in the background (valorising the action) and, on the other, by the manager implementing the strategy "sold".

In his article of 2001, Jensen clearly explains the complexity of this relationship, emphasising the operational limits of the common interpretation/utilisation that is made of the maximisation of shareholder value and stakeholder theory. In other words, he puts forward a critical view of the dominant entrepreneurial model built around the polar figure of the manager and of the shareholder into which he wishes to "introduce" the other economic agents concerned by the company's activity. Indeed, on the one hand, we have/had the assertion that maximising the value for the shareholder, with all the control problems that would generate, was the best way - in market economy - to achieve collective welfare; on the other hand, there is the assertion of the necessity (need) of allowing for the interests of all stakeholders in the firm, from customers to all suppliers and including employees, in order to do so. Complementarity is provided by Jensen's assertion of the necessity of understanding the maximising of value from a collective point of view – even if it depends on an individual actor – and that collective and social welfare is only achieved if, firstly, "all the values" supported by each stakeholder are maximised and, secondly, that maximisation is effected over the long term. Financial markets are then the other, and even speculation is necessary. However, an operational problem arises if we want managers to maximise value, understood in this way, in as much as there is no reason why the objectives of the various stakeholders should be convergent, a priori. This criticism is as applicable from the point of view of the maximisation of value (how to manage several goals at once) as from the point of view of the stakeholder theory (how to define a common goal).

In fact, although Jensen (2001) acknowledges the relevance of stakeholder theory, he nevertheless considers that it is not capable of overcoming the impossibility of managing several different goals, more often than not divergent, and that is why he reasserts the maximisation of shareholder value as a long-term common goal. This implies the need for agreement. It is, in fact, a matter of defining collaborative procedures allowing the stakeholders to define, on the one hand, common goals (with the plural suggesting the necessity of also prioritising those goals subject to the creation of shareholder value) and, on the other hand, the ways in which they can be achieved along with the monitoring of the evaluation of the performance of the organisation under the manager's responsibility. In other words, being entrepreneurial and investing imply co-ordination. This co-ordination can be described in three possible ways, dated historically according to the types of capital ownership. "Firstly, it may include the workers in the case of paternalistic industrial relations (social responsibility inherent in the paternalistic model). Secondly, it may entail the maintaining of the ownership of their work and tools by the workers themselves, as may be observed in the case of craftsmen (the craftsman's community). Thirdly, it may be focused on only equipment and financial capital, as is the case nowadays. A depletion of those forms may be observed, however, as expressed by the search for new paths of development associating all the actors." (Salais et alii, 1999, page 230 and following)

In this context, the "agreement" is at the heart of the problem, as it is central to the organisation's performance. How can agreement be obtained, bearing in mind that it is necessary to obtain prior agreement of the parties on all organisational issues and on how to play them out and, therefore, on the conditions for the drawing up of the "rules" of the game. (Paranque, 2004).

This preoccupation concerning collective, social welfare is characterised by "problems of information, anticipation and evaluation" (Salais et alii, 1999, page 193). Here again, it is a matter, on both the collective and individual levels, of reaching agreement not only on a reality to be constructed but also to act together in that perspective: "What is at stake in these negotiations is the interpretation model to be adopted to 'construct reality' which is presented to them [the agents] as problem to be solved," (as above, pages 197-198). In other words, this necessary negotiation is the expression of a convention sanctioning the "agent's agreement on their description of the world and so [allowing] them to co-ordinate their projects" (as above, p. 236), and their creation "depends on social processes for the creation of models representing reality" (as above, p. 239). What is fundamental is not so much the capacity to process information as the capacity to produce it or, in other words, to know how to act and make decisions. This capacity is always the fruit of a previous history and of anticipations born of a given context, in this case the management of the risks associated with the allocation of resources.

We propose three examples to illustrate the key issue of this agreement. This issue of shared meaning is a product of history and situations encountered, faced and confronted by the relevant actors. It is not simple to modify these links. Two figures have emerged since the Industrial Revolution: the manager versus the shareholder and the customer (or, more recently, the consumer). These polar figures reflect another polarity, one of the terms of which is masked by the all-powerful reign of trade which succeeded (?) in pushing the production sphere out of the dominant paradigm and, along with it, any reflection on the source of the value, so reducing that value to trade and/or the purely symbolic. The emergence of the shareholder was accompanied by that of its alter ego – the manager – as from the end of the 19th century, as asserted at the beginning of the 20th century by Berle and Mean (Jensen et alii, 1984). What is of interest for us is that, from the outset[4], questions were posed regarding the governance of the capital structures represented by modern firms open to the financial markets and the expression of democracy in its management. Dunlavy (2006) shows that there was already a great diversity in the exercise of power among shareholders and that, as from 1790 in the United States, questions were posed regarding the organisation of rights with regard to the appropriation of the resulting wealth and also the exercise of power between "one man, one vote" and "one share, one vote". In other words, what appears to be self-evident today, was the object of social construction the outcome of which was not obvious in view of the challenges of democracy. These debates are still echoed in discussions on the all-powerfulness of financial markets, and their impact on people's daily lives.

In Africa, the "tontine" (a system for the financing of individual projects by the community) was so successful that it became necessary to modify its organisation. This entailed switching from the yard where members of the tontine gathered to a financial co-operative. The term "co-operative" clearly reflects the desire to remain anchored in and to the community, the problem being the change in social relations. This made itself felt on both the financial and social levels. The beneficiary gets a cheque which changes his or her relationship with the others and with the credibility of the collective commitment: what is the connection between receiving bank notes from an identified, known person integrated in a network of social and cultural ties and going to a teller's window for cheque? Is it necessary to modify the social bond (or link) to use so-called modern tools? Here again, social depths become decisive in the process of socialisation. How then can we think about supporting economic development when seeking to replace that type of regulation with that of the financial markets?

Since the year 2000, the Moroccan public authorities have encouraged the export of carpet manufacturers by developing the adoption of ISO or AFNOR type standards. Hitherto, this manufacture was based on corporations with implicit rules applicable both to the "validation" of quality and to the profession's organisation. Quality is thus "guaranteed" and built on relations of proximity and reputation. So where is the need for technical standards? More fundamentally, we note that those standards are based on individual rules which may dismantle existing solidarity on which the current quality of products recognised by the market resides? Furthermore, is it possible to envisage that the credibility achieved by such

---

[4]. See Marx, 1978, page 102.

practices could be perceived by the financial markets, with their scores, rankings and net present value (NPV)?

Literature on loan relations clearly shows the difficulty in understanding the demand and offer of credit solely through trading relations. In asymmetrical information situations, where information is not accessible to all in the same conditions or where the capacities to acquire and process information differ from one person to another or from one category of agents to another, individuals' decisions and forecasts will depend on their cognitive capacities and thus on the degree of uncertainty they are faced with (special issue of Revue Economique, 1989; Simon, 1976; Knight, 1921; Rivaud-Danset and Salais, 1992; Rivaud-Danset 1995, 1996; Moureau and Rivaud-Danset, 2004). Indeed, the elements required to draw up a statistical calculation, needed in order to allocate a probability of the occurrence of an event defining the risk, may not be available or may not exist. We may therefore be rational but our capabilities are limited, both by the imperfect nature of the market and by our social position (an investor will have less knowledge of a company than its manager, for example), by the impossibility of envisaging every possible future, by how other agents will behave by or how we ourselves will deal with future changes we are confronted with. Owing to this situation of incompleteness, formal rules (such as laws and contracts) and informal rules are drawn up in an attempt to reduce the uncertainty and so facilitate the co-ordination of persons. The market (prices) is then just one item, and one convention, among others (special issue of Revue Economique, 1989; Salais, Chatel and Rivaud-Danset, 1998).

The challenge is therefore knowing whether financial markets can be adapted to diverse situations or if, on the contrary, it is the actual modes of controlling performance (and thus its definition) which should be re-assessed? This question is all the more crucial (Belletante, Levratto and Paranque, 2001) in that, while the role of financial markets is to allow an optimal allocation of capital (and thus risk management with regard to the time required to make investments, and return on investment), the great majority of companies are confronted with managing their need for financial flexibility (Hicks, 1988).

Even though the shareholder has asserted himself since the 1970s (Jensen et alii, 1984) to reign undividedly as from the 1980s with the liberalisation of the financial markets, he hides the figure of the manager, i.e. the actual decision-maker, in the background. In splitting the function of the capitalist, his role is reduced to being the holder of securities in an imaginary way, instead of exercising the capacity of increasing the value of capital via the appropriation of surplus labour. However, the shareholder, unlike the manager who fulfils the function of capitalist without ownership and thus the related risk, bases his wealth on forecasts of gains justifying the mobilising/immobilising of capital. The constraint is then that those forecasts must be validated, at some time or other, through a reality check represented by selling/buying, in which value is realised, so that the surplus labour (surplus value) is appropriated/appropriable. In a certain sense, the shareholder must "consummate" his forecasting. But, in order to be completed, that forecasting must pass via the monetary form of trade in which the goods or service produced find a purchaser who pays. In other words, if there is no consumer/customer/purchaser, value and forecasts cannot be realised. In this context, the manager is the figure at the interface of three worlds: capital, work and the consumer, which may leave room for another reference figure based on the practices and uses associated with those goods and services.

5. Collective, Co-Ordination and Marketing: Co-Creation of Linking Value

At the beginning of the 21st century, marketing is faced with many questions and, even, many cases of being called into question, largely in relation to difficulties in identifying and analysing consumer behaviour. It appears that the central question can be stated in the following manner: "Is it possible to push the boundaries of marketing beyond the level of individual analysis in order to enhance our understanding of consumer behaviour?" Gainer and Fischer (1994, p. 137) suggest that: "Our neglect of non-individual level phenomena stems from the biases of our dominant perspective and theories. The goal of most consumer behaviour studies has only been to explain how individual cognition, perception or traits influence individual behaviour." When the analytical unit considered is not the individual, it is often an abstract aggregation of homogeneous individuals based on a marketing construction (segment, lifestyle) or a concrete institutional aggregation (inhabitants of a single region, consumers in a single professional category). The emotional links that individuals may have woven between them (and their influences on consumer behaviours) does not appear to have been a preoccupation of marketing research until recent years. In fact, marketing undertakes to group homogeneous individuals together on the basis of an egalitarian logic, even though community phenomena link heterogeneous individuals by an affinity-based logic. Community phenomena are therefore generally overlooked by consumer behaviour analyses.

Today however, carried along by an interest in social changes grouped together under the term of postmodernity and, in particular, the phenomenon of neo-tribalism, some marketing researchers are trying to allow for the community dimension in their analyses (Cova, 1997) in order to build a widened conceptual framework, like the Consumer Culture Theory or CCT (Arnould and Thompson, 2005). The increase in literature on the subject in the last five years, especially in well-known magazines in the field, such as the Journal of Marketing and the Journal of Consumer Research, confirms the subject's pertinence (Algesheimer, Dholakia and Hermann, 2005; Muniz and O'Guinn, 2001; Schouten, McAlexander and Koenig, 2007; Thompson and Sinha, 2008).

In fact, tribal marketing is much more than an nth panacea of a marketing discipline in the throes of redefinition. It has taken centre stage at the beginning of this new century when the classification of consumers into segments with homogeneous characteristics seeking the same "consumer benefit" is looking increasingly problematic. In its place, tribal marketing proposes to bring into play the concepts of tribe and linking value in order to decipher the fuzzy sets of consumers in a society with confused points of reference. It therefore fits into the whole trend described as interpretive which focuses on the actual experience of consumers to observe it and interpret it from as many points of view as there are different theories and methods for doing so. One of the pertinent viewpoints today is the ethnosociological view which useful tempers the psychosocial view put forward by Moscovici, in particular, and adopted by most practicians: where social psychology is interested in the effect of A on B (A being an individual or a group) in the power of A over B, in the contamination of B by A or the imitation of A by B, ethnosociology will, for its part, focus on what makes the glue between A and B, or, better still, the being-together AB, or the shared emotion between A and B, etc.. Consequently, tribal marketing is distinguished less by its territory than by its own specific view, which is more holistic than individualistic.

Tribal marketing therefore pays little heed to segments, niches and lifestyles which constitute the basis of marketing management. It is barely interested in these fictitious groupings of individuals with homogeneous but disconnected characteristics. On the contrary, the analytical unit it adopts consists of heterogeneous but interlinked persons: individuals who, through shared emotions and experiences, build (themselves) and strengthen their ties which smack of community, i.e. so-called postmodern tribes. Today, there are a great many examples: rapper tribes, roller rider tribes (inline roller skaters), biker tribes, Warhammer or World of Warcraft game enthusiast tribe, and other urban tribes (Cova and Pace, 2006; Cova et alii, 2007). In a tribal approach to marketing, there is less of a tendency to develop products and services which "serve" an individual, an average consumer or a segment of homogeneous consumers than products and services which link a number of persons or consumers in a single community, a single community feeling or a single tribe. This is done by bringing into play the concept of linking value. The linking value of a product or service is the value of that product or service, or even of any gesture, in the (even ephemeral) construction or strengthening of links between people. This value of the use of an item – the use of an item in the service of a link – is rarely included in the concept of value of use, which tends to recognise the immediate utilisation of the item by an individual and to exclude the fact that it acts in the service of social ties. This particular use of products or services is different enough from other uses to distinguish it from them. The more a product or service supports the creation, development or maintaining of links in a tribe, the greater will be its linking value owing to an effect described as network externality. The same product or service therefore has a different value according to the group in which it is implemented.

Marketing therefore tries to account for the postmodern future of our societies by recombining what was separated by the economics of the modern world. Whereas the neoliberal economic model excluded social networks (Godbout, 2007), advances in these disciplines are re-introducing them in their new models in order to better understand the operation of markets: "Such a model must necessarily make room for social networks which are different from both the market and the State or its bureaucracy. Among these networks, it is useful to distinguish between organised forms (associations) and the innumerable links that we have with one another, with our family and our neighbours, direct links that are not channelled by intermediaries. It is this entire world that the (neoliberal) model tends to forget." (Godbout, 2007, p. 96).

6. ACTING TOGETHER AND THE FINANCIAL MARKETS

In order to construct a complete model, we must understand how to act together: we therefore need common codes and rules; there are no parts which, added together, make a whole, but interactions which create new properties, i.e. capacities to act. We must build this relationship with the world together, and not impose it on others. This process of construction, however, entails returning to the question raised at the beginning of this article. Indeed, constructing meaning is by no means obvious; it cannot be done to order especially if, as in our case, it is wished that the construction should be as conscious as possible. In marketing for example (Carù and Cova, 2006), operational difficulties very soon arise, occurring when all that is done is to take the qualities of the whole without being able to link them to the parts which, in this case, are the behaviour of the consumer immersed in the concrete situation of consumption and, so, in interaction with one or more environments, and the identification of the determinants on the individual level in order to draw commercial applications from them. Nevertheless, it is still the case that understanding and managing the co-ordination of economic action remain a crucial issue owing, in particular, to its intrinsic characteristics: complexity and, its corollary, diversity are at the heart of the "process". By construction, the decision I make at instant "t" as a manager modifies the "world" in which I am acting and, thus, the conditions in which others exercise their decisions.

It is here that the Mediterranean can be of some help in constructing a relationship with the world and, notably, an economic relationship incorporating social ties. The Mediterranean sea is, in fact, described as "corrupting" (Horden and Purcell, 2000) as, it is claimed, it goes too far in facilitating interactions between the various regions bordering it and so is profoundly detrimental to social order: the Mediterranean corrupts because it establishes contact between the peoples on its shores. In fact, this sea is more "connecting" than "corrupting". In addition to the mosaic of colours drawn from cultures and biographies, there is the mosaic of time: linear, circular, cumulative, long, short, night, day, and caravans... Work is on this as it represents a relationship with the worlds concerned, interactions and thus social ties. So Mediterranean is an heuristic as say as say Gipouloux is his very fascinating book "La Méditerranée asiatique" – "asian Mediterranean" (2009) -.This debate is part of the heritage of common thought propounded in the 13th to 14th century by Thomas Aquinas who said that the good of the part must be subordinated to the good of the whole (Béraud and Faccarello, 1992, p. 26): "The specific finality of the species is incarnated in the good of society which cannot be reduced to the sum of individuals' goods any more than society may be reduced to the sum of individuals." But, at the same time in Great Britain, William of Ockham and John Duns Scot would reverse the sequence: society could not be independently made up of individuals who constituted it through their interactions (as above, p. 28). The key word is "interaction". Recognising this enables us to appreciate the diversity resulting from complexity, i.e. of the multitude of forms of co-ordination, i.e. answers to needs/questions. "Things" do not exist as such but, primarily, as the expression of interactions.

Our feeling is that it is necessary to start by looking at social relations, i.e.: interactions (Ricœur, 1997) – or relations persons are born of – rather than individuals. The approach adopted, which breaks with simple methodological individualism, considers that no collective phenomenon can be reduced to just the product of individual actions (Sève, 2005, p. 173), contrary to the recourse, in economics and finance, to the function of individual utility in which each one, by optimising that utility, allows everyone to achieve collective welfare via the market[5]. As regards methodological individualism, we consider that, in order for the "sum of individual optimisations" to form an organised whole – which makes sense – there is a need for co-ordination principles and regulations for that "whole" to emerge. In other words, a connection between persons is not the same thing as a collection of individual functions. Indeed, for "optimisation" to occur – besides the problems of cognitive capacity and information (Simon, 1976; Vecchi de, 2006) – there must be a capacity to think, but this is

---

[5]. See the analysis by Ricœur: page304 in his chapter on Habermas.

necessarily the result of a collective/organised educative process (Sève, 2005, pages 58, 160, 164 note 138 and p. 194,).

Financial markets, like all institutions, are built on interaction: "the whole is not, strictly speaking, made up of parts but, rather, organised in a set which can be broken down into members, organs, functions or moments. (…) In other words, the whole is then considered (…) as a fundamentally emergent global reality" (as above, p. 132 note 104 and p. 134, underlined by the author). But, if we acknowledge the complexity of that dynamic, the question of anticipation is then posed. Indeed, this can no longer be based on an expectation of simple, deterministic causality as a decision is made at a moment "t" on a trajectory resulting from previous decisions which modify the environment in which we are immersed at "t", and that decision will itself modify the conditions for the exercise of future decisions. In short, it is uncertainty that is dominant.

In fact, it is an approach in terms of creation of linking value that appears best able to take into account this dialectic dynamic of interactions, in order to define the field of the possible from which the achievable can only emerge through action (practice). It is through this approach that mankind creates reality. That reality may differ from one person to another, it is not with regard to its objective dimension but rather through the process of producing the action itself – the "praxi" (Ricoeur, 1997) – i.e. the way in which we define the conditions of our social co-ordination. Diversity is thus also a culture, a culture of roots (link with time), a culture of obstacles (living, economic, social, geographical and institutional conditions) and thus of chronos, as the relation to others is inscribed in a culturally marked time.

In finance, the requirement for a long horizon is reflected not only in debates which are echoed in the media but also by academic writers, not to mention the development of financial products (socially responsible investment, ethics, sustainable development, etc.). This temporal dimension to be (re)-conquered is also an interpellation on the questions of co-ordination and common meaning. In this sense, it is a matter of apprehending the organisational forms specific to the goals pursued by "citizens-actors-agents-persons" who express themselves, in the words of Armand Hatchuel[6], within "areas of innovation and struggle framed by public regulation" in the shape of firms and markets.

7. CONCLUSIONS

In the field of management sciences, while it may no longer be possible to think of the firm in accordance with the canonical neoclassical model, in which it is merged into/reduced simply to the individual producer encountering other producers in the market, it is even more difficult to think of it outside of and without financial markets, as it is to ignore their impact (before their role) on the real economy through the arbitrage they facilitate in terms of the allocation of capital to one project rather than another. Financial markets cannot exist outside the city with its challenges which primarily arise from debate within its walls. So what forms of organisation are appropriate in order to take up these challenges? How can we build new identities based not only on acquired skills but also on the recognition of skills to be acquired

---

[6]. La lettre de la régulation, n° 47, janvier 2004, p.2.

and mobilised? These are all questions raised by a re-examination of the individual-collective dialectic.

REFERENCES

Algesheimer, R., Dholakia, U.M. and Hermann, A. (2005), The Social Influence of Brand Community: Evidence from European Car Clubs, *Journal of Marketing*, Vol. 69, N° 3, pp. 19-34.

Amable B. and Palombarini S. (2005), L'économie politique n'est pas une science morale, Raisons d'Agir, Cours et Travaux, Paris .

Arnould E.J. and Thompson C.J. (2005), Consumer culture theory (CCT): twenty years of research, *Journal of Consumer Research*, Vol. 31, March, pp. 868-882.

Munoz F. (1965), Bakounine la liberté, Jean Jacques Pauvert Ed, Paris .

Baudrillard, J. (1992), L'illusion de la fin, ou la grève des évènements,Galilée. Paris.

Bauman, Z. (2007) , Le présent liquide, Paris, Seuil.

Béraud A. and Faccarello G. (1992), Nouvelle Histoire de la Pensée Economique, (sous la direction de), La Découverte. Paris .

Birnbaum P. and Leca J. (1991), Sur l'individualisme, (sous la direction de), Presse de la Fondation Nationale des Sciences Politiques, Références. Paris .

Bourguignat H. and Briys E. (2009), L'arrogance de la Finance, La Découverte. Paris .

Boyer R. (2004), Une théorie du capitalisme est-elle possible ?, Odile Jacob. Paris .

Boyer R. and Saillard Y. (2002), Théorie de la régulation : l'état des savoirs, La Découverte. Paris .

Carù, A. and Cova, B. (2006), How to Facilitate Immersion in a Consumption Experience: Appropriation Operations and Service Elements, *Journal of Consumer Behaviour*, Vol. 5, N°1, pp. 4-14.

Cecconi O. (1983), Désir et Pouvoir, Presse Universitaire de Lyon–AEH, Lyon.

Cefaï D. (2007), Pourquoi se mobilise-t-on? Les théories de l'action collective, La Découverte. Paris .

Coase R. (1937), The nature of the firm : Origin, Meaning, Influence, in Williamson O.E. and Winter S.G. (1991), The Nature of the Firm, Oxford University Press. Oxford.

Cova, B. (1997), Community and Consumption: Towards a Definition of the Linking Value of Products or Services, European Journal of Marketing, Vol. 31, N° 3/4, pp. 297-316.

Cova, B. et Pace, S. (2006), Brand community of convenience products: new forms of customer empowerment - the case "my Nutella The Community". *European Journal of Marketing* Vol. 40, N° 9/10, pp. 1087-1105.

Cova, B., Pace, S. et Park, D. J. (2007), Global brand communities across borders: the Warhammer case, International Marketing Review, Vol. 24, N°3, pp. 313-329.

Defalvard H. (1992), Critique de l'individualisme méthodologique revu par la théorie des conventions, *Revue Economique*, Vol. 43, n° 1, janvier :127-144.

Desjeux, D. (1996), Scale of Observation: A Micro-Sociological Epistemology of Social Science Practice, *Visual Sociology,*Vol. 11, N° 2 : 45-55.

Dunlavy, Colleen A., (2006), Social Conceptions of the Corporation: Insights from the History of Shareholder Voting Rights, Washington and Lee Law Review, Vol. 63, no. 4 :1347-1388. Available at SSRN: http://ssrn.com/abstract=964377.

Eymard-Duvernay F. (2006), L'économie des conventions, méthodes et résultats, (sous la direction), La Découverte. Paris .

Fabre, T. (1998), La Méditerranée entre la raison et la foi, Actes Sud/Babel. Arles.

Favereau O. (1993), Objets de gestion et objet de la théorie économique, Revue Française de Gestion, novembre décembre : 6-12.

Feyerabend P. (1979), Contre la méthode, Seuil, Sciences. Paris .

Feyerabend P. (1989), Adieu la raison, Seuil. Paris .

Gipouloux F. (2009), La Méditerranée asiatique, CNRS édition., Paris .

Godbout, J.T. (2007), Ce qui circule entre nous. Donner, recevoir, rendre, Seuil. Paris.

Gomez P. Y. (1998), MCO et modèles positifs de l'organisation : une esquisse critique, Cahiers de recherche de l'EM Lyon, http://www.ifge-online.org/ifge,professeur-pierre-yves-gomez_institut-fr-4-23.html.

Goux J.F. (1995), Économie monétaire et financière, théorie, institution, politiques, Economica, 2e édition. Paris .

Hallyn F. (1987), La structure poétique du monde : Copernic, Kepler, Seuil, Des Travaux. Paris .

Hart O. (1995), Firms, Contracts and Financial structure, Clarendon Press, Oxford.

Hicks J. (1988), La crise de l'économie keynésienne, Fayard. Paris .

Hirschman A.O. (1980), Les passions et les intérêts, Presse Universitaire de France. Paris .

Hodgson G. M. (2007), Meanings of Methodological Individualism, *Journal of Economic Methodology*, 14:2, June : 211-226.

Horden, P. and Purcell, N. (2000), The Corrupting Sea, A study of Mediterranean History, Oxford, Blackwell.

Jensen M. C. (2001), Value Maximization, Stakeholder Theory, and the Corporate Objective Function, october, téléchargeable sur http://ssrn.com/abstract=220671; also publishing in Andriof J. and al., Unfolding Stakeholder Thinking, Greenleaf Publishing, 2002; *Journal of Applied Corporate Finance*, volume 14, n° 3, 2001; European Financial Management Review, n°7, 2001 et in Beer M. and Norhia N., Breaking the Code of Change, HBS Press, 2000.

Jensen M. C. and Meckling W. H. (1976), Theory of the Firm: Managerial Behavior, Agency Costs and Ownership Structure, The Journal of Financial Economics, Vol. 3 : 305-60

Jensen, Michael C., Smith, Jr. and Clifford W., (1984), The Theory of Corporate Finance: A Historical Overview, in The modern theory of corporate finance, New York: McGraw-Hill Inc.: 2-20, 1984. Available at SSRN: http://ssrn.com/abstract=244161 or DOI: 10.2139/ssrn.244161

Knight F. (1921), Risk, uncertainty and profit, Houghton Mifflin Company. Boston.

Latour, B. (2006), Changer de société – Refaire de la sociologie, La Découverte. Paris.

Lipovetsky, G. (1983), L'ère du vide : essais sur l'individualisme contemporain. Paris, Gallimard.

Lipovetsky, G. (2006), Le bonheur paradoxal, Gallimard. Paris.

Lyotard, J.F. (1979), La condition postmoderne, Ed Minuit. Paris.

Maffesoli, M. (1988), Le Temps des Tribus : le déclin de l'individualisme dans les sociétés de masse, Méridiens Klincksieck. Paris.

Maffesoli, M. (1996), Eloge de la raison sensible, Grasset. Paris.

Maffesoli, M. (2007), Le réenchantement du monde : une éthique pour notre temps, La Table Ronde. Paris.

Moureau N. and Rivaud-Danset D. (2004), L'incertitude dans les théories économiques, La Découverte. Paris .

Muniz, A. M. *Jr. and O'Guinn, T.C. (2001), Brand Community,* Journal of Consumer Research, Vol. 27, March, pp. 412-432.

Onfray M. (2005), Traité d'athéologie, Grasset. Paris .

Orléans A. (2004), Analyse économique des conventions, (sous la direction de) Presse Universitaire de France, Quadridge, 2ème édition. Paris .

Paranque B., Rivaud-Danset D. and Salais R. (1997), Evaluation de la performance et maîtrise du risque des entreprises industrielles françaises, Revue Internationale PME, Volume 10, pp. 156-172.

Paranque B. (2004), Toward an Agreement, Euromed Marseille Ecole de Management WP, n 11-2004, available at http://ssrn.com/abstract=501322 .

Piaget J. (1972), Epistémologie des sciences de l'homme, Gallimard, La Pléiade. Paris .

Piaget J. (2005), L'épistémologie génétique, Presse Universitaire de France, Que sais-je ?, 6ième édition. Paris .

Raveaud G. (2004), Causalité, holisme méthodologique et modélisation « critique » en économie, Document de travail, 04-01, IDHE UM CNRS 8533. Paris .

Redondi P. (1983), Galilée hérétique, Gallimard. Paris .

Revue Economique (1989), Numéro spécial : L'économie des conventions, n° 40, mars.

Ricœur P. (1997), L'idéologie et l'utopie, Seuil Essais. Paris .

Rivaud-Danset D. (1995), Le rationnement du crédit et l'incertitude, Revue d'Économie Politique, 105, mars-avril : 223-247.

Rivaud-Danset D. (1996), Les contrats de crédit dans une relation de long terme, Revue Économique, n° 4, juillet : 937-962.

Rivaud-Danset D. and Salais R. (1992), Les conventions de financement. Premières approches théorique et empirique, Revue Française d'Économie, Vol. VII 4 : 81-120.

Salais R. and Storper M. (1993), Les Mondes de Production – Enquête sur l'identité économique de la France, École des Hautes Études en Sciences Sociales, Paris.

Salais R., Baverez N. and Reynaud B. (1999), L'invention du chômage, Presse Universitaire de France, Quadrige. Paris .

Salais R., Chatel E. and Rivaud-Danset D. (1998), Institutions et conventions : la réflexivité de l'action économique, Raison Pratique, École des Hautes Études en Sciences Sociales, Paris.

Sève L. (2005), Emergence, complexité et dialectique, Odile Jacob. Paris .

Schouten, J.W., McAlexander, J.H. et Koenig, H.F. (2007), Transcendent Customer Experience and Brand Community, *Journal of the Academy of Marketing Science*, Vol. 35, N°3, pp. 357-368.

Simon G. (1979), Kepler, astronome ou astrologue, Gallimard. Paris .

Simon H.A. (1976), From substantive to procedural rationality, in Methods and appraisals in economics, Lastis ed., Cambridge University Press. Cambridge .

Thompson, S.A. et Sinha, R.K. (2008), Brand Communities and New Product Adoption: The Influence and Limits of Oppositional Loyalty, *Journal of Marketing*, Vol. 72, N°6, pp. 65-80.

Vecchi (de) D. (2006), La pragmaterminologie. Démarche terminologique appliquée aux organisations, Working Paper, Université Paris 7, Etudes Culturelles des Langues Appliquées (EILA), supervisor : Professeur John Humbley.

Viard, J. (1997), Pourquoi des travailleurs votent FN et comment les reconquérir, Seuil, Paris.

In: After the Crisis: Rethinking Finance
Editor: Thomas Lagoarde-Segot

ISBN 978-1-61668-925-4
© 2010 Nova Science Publishers, Inc.

Chapter 3

IRELAND AND THE CRISIS

Ciarán mac an Bhaird [*]

ABSTRACT

The growth of the Irish economy in the years 1995-2007 was dramatic and unparalleled by Western economies, earning Ireland the moniker "The Celtic Tiger". Emerging from conditions of high unemployment, very high rates of graduate emigration, and enormous government debt in the 1980s, the transformation of the Irish economy in two decades was remarkable and lauded by economists and commentators. High growth rates were facilitated by a number of factors, including the presence of a large number of multinationals producing goods for export, benign global economic conditions, low interest rates, low taxation, a lax regulatory regime, and government policy which embraced the tenets of the 'free market'. With the onset of the financial crisis, however, came another rapid transformation in the shape of the Irish economy. From being one of the fastest growing Western economies in the late 1990s, in 2009 Ireland suffered the greatest contraction of any OECD country since the Second World War. The reasons for this dramatic reversal of fortune were attributable not only to the global financial crisis, but also to government policies and the structure of the Irish economy. In this chapter, the remarkable rise and fall of the Irish economy is described and analysed. Influences on the performance of the Irish economy in this period, including benign global economic conditions, government policy, and the structure of the Irish economy are examined. Proposals on how best to initiate recovery are also assessed, particularly the narrow focus of discourse which largely concentrates on attempts to 'fix' the current system, without considering alternative approaches.

1. INTRODUCTION

This chapter seeks to address the main themes of this book by considering the case of Ireland in the aftermath of the global financial crisis. As one of the most globalised, open

---

[*] I am grateful for comments and suggestions received from William Kelly.Figures quoted are sourced from Central Statistics Office and Economic and Social Research Council databases, unless otherwise indicated.

economies in the world, Ireland benefited greatly from a worldwide economic expansion during the Celtic Tiger years. Increased demand from booming global economies, as well as a surge in supply of foreign direct investment (FDI), primarily from US multinationals, contributed to Ireland having the highest sustained growth rates in its history. Was it inevitable, therefore, that the Irish economy would suffer commensurately during the global financial crisis? Given that "....small states have a greater exposure to exogenous shocks than larger states because of their vulnerability to external economic, political, strategic and environmental shocks" (Read, 2004: 369), did it necessarily follow that the Irish economy would suffer a decline as dramatically low as growth during the Celtic Tiger years had been remarkably high? Did the liberalisation of the Irish financial sector facilitate and hasten contagion of the global financial crisis to Ireland? Were the effects of the crisis exacerbated by the actions of financial institutions and other actors in the Irish economy? Were policies enacted by the government effective in dealing with the crisis, or did they aggravate the problems even further?

The Irish circumstances present an interesting case study through which to view the financial crisis for a number of reasons: the performance of the Irish economy over the past two decades embodies the extremes of a boom / bust cycle which has been experienced by the majority of Western economies. In addition to being a salutary illustration of the boom / bust cycle, it is a small, open economy, and a member of the European Monetary Union (EMU), thus lacking autonomy over exchange rate and interest rate policy. Additionally, the Irish financial sector has experienced significant structural change and liberalisation over this period (Kelly and Everett, 2004). One would expect, therefore, that the Irish economy was particularly vulnerable to contagion from the financial crisis. This chapter explores elements of the Irish economy over recent decades, and examines contributory endogenous and exogenous factors for the current economic position. A primary conclusion is that, whatever the effects of the international financial crisis, the present predicament of Ireland's banking sector and fiscal position can, to a large extent, be attributed to endogenous policy decisions in government and private institutions. This chapter proceeds as follows: firstly, the performance of the Irish economy over the past two decades is considered by employing commonly-used variables. A number of potential endogenous and exogenous contributing factors are considered, including policy decisions and the global economic environment. Secondly, the Irish property boom and related banking crisis are described, and policy responses to the crisis are detailed and examined. The chapter concludes by considering a number of salient long-standing deficiencies in bank-based systems which have been highlighted by the crisis. Policies and strategies that could be implemented to ensure that the economy is better prepared to cope with future exogenous shocks and to best build capacity for future development are briefly considered.

The geographical characteristics of the Republic of Ireland, an island nation of almost 4 million people on the periphery of Europe, have implications for its advancement and development. A lack of large deposits of natural resources, combined with a very small domestic market for goods and services offers few alternatives to seeking greater integration with the global economy. Ireland pursued a policy of import substitution and protectionism from the 1930s to the 1950s, resulting in stagnation of national income, balance of payments crises, and high rates of emigration(Bew and Patterson, 1982, Ó Gráda, 1997,). Policies pursued in subsequent decades were in marked contrast, as Ireland progressively became one of the most open economies in the world (Ireland was ranked as the world's most globalised economy from 2002 to 2004 in the Kearney/*Foreign Policy* index). An early endeavour in trade policy was characteristic of a desire for greater integration in the global economy, as the Industrial Development Agency (IDA) embarked on a policy of actively seeking FDI. Providing incentives in the form of grants, capital facilities and lower rates of taxation, the agency was particularly successful in attracting US multinationals over the following six decades. This aspect of trade policy has received much attention in media and academia (e.g. Burnham, 2003), and its beneficial effects in terms of economic growth and wealth generation are touted as incontrovertible evidence of the benefits of globalisation, liberalisation and *laissez-faire* economics. The success of this policy was not attributable to one single factor, but to a combination of policies, institutions, and a favourable external environment as explained in the following brief analysis.

2. IRELAND'S ECONOMIC 'MIRACLE'

Irish economic circumstances in the mid-1980s were extremely unenviable, characterised by high rates of unemployment (over 18 percent in 1985), high rates of emigration (including a large proportion of university graduates), substantial government debt (almost 130 percent of GNP in 1985), and high rates of inflation (over 17 percent in 1982). Indeed, Irish public finances were in such poor shape that the intervention of the International Monetary Fund (IMF) was considered as the solution. An extraordinary transformation occurred over the following two decades, as the Irish economy experienced a period of remarkably high, sustained growth rates as measured by growth in Gross National Product (GNP)[1]. This period of exceptional growth raised Ireland from being one of the poorest economies in the European Union to the second richest, receiving approval and acclaim from economists and commentators, earning Ireland the moniker 'The Celtic Tiger'. This economic 'miracle' has been the subject of many books and papers, and the common consensus is that the Irish economic boom can be categorised in two parts: by a period of export-led growth from the early 1990s to 2001, and secondly, by a huge expansion in the domestic property sector from 2002 to early 2007. Commentators have frequently examined the policies and conditions that laid the foundations for this phenomenon, with the aspiration of emulating and replicating it (Acs et al., 2007). Politicians were quick to claim credit for devising and implementing policies which brought about the economic boom, and whilst they were a contributory factor in creating the conditions for increased investment and economic activity, the simultaneous occurrence of advantageous external economic conditions were an essential element of the sudden increase in growth. Commonly cited endogenous factors in creating the underlying conditions for the economic boom include a young, well-educated English speaking population, membership of the European Union, a low corporate tax rate[2], grants and incentives provided by the IDA, wage moderation resulting from central wage bargaining, and a high rate of immigration. Whilst these factors undoubtedly contributed to economic

---

[1] Whilst this approach has been described by some commentators (e.g. Kirby, 2002) as a somewhat simplistic, one-dimensional approach adopted by neoclassical economists, it is beyond the scope of this chapter to address sociological factors, provision of and access to welfare, education and health, etc. It is, however, important to note that spending on welfare, education, and health increased dramatically during the economic boom.
[2] At 12.5 percent, the Irish corporate tax rate is one of the lowest in the OECD, and its effectiveness results from the double-taxation agreement with a number of countries, including the US.

growth by attracting FDI by exporting multinationals, Honohan and Walsh (2002) stress that the most important factor was an increase in the proportion of the population at work, particularly increased participation of females in the workforce. This, rather than increased productivity, was the primary reason for the growth in output and subsequently economic growth. Additionally, financial liberalisation and a decrease in restrictions in banks' activities contributed significantly to economic growth (Kelly and Everett, 2004), although Honohan (2006) finds little evidence that Irish finance made a leading contribution to this period of export-led growth.

Favourable exogenous factors also played an important part in the economic boom. Increased growth and demand in destination economies for Ireland's exports(Kennedy, 2001), sustained lower interest rates, a high immigration rate (Honohan and Walsh, 2002) and large inflows of FDI were significant factors in the expansion of the Irish economy during this period. Gallagher et al. (2002) state that the primary driver of growth in the Irish economy during the Celtic Tiger years was attributable to foreign owned firms in electronics, pharmaceuticals, and financial services. An indication of the success of this policy is that, by 2002 Ireland was the largest exporter of software in the world with a commercial software sector comprising 600 companies, many of them foreign, employing 15,000 people and generating €5 billion in export revenue. Whilst Irish growth rates were remarkably high in relation to OECD countries, the Irish economy was essentially converging with European norms (Honohan and Walsh, 2002, Ó Gráda, 2002), and by 2001 capacity for convergence was reduced. Furthermore, a diminishing supply of labour, combined with increased energy and wage costs meant that it was not possible to maintain the growth rates achieved during these years (Kennedy, 2001, Whelan, 2009), and before long a slowdown was inevitable.

The Irish economic boom did not end abruptly in 2001, and GNP continued to grow by an annual rate of 4.5 percent in the period 2001 to 2007. It was important to note, however, that the composition of GNP changed dramatically during this period. The most important component of this period of growth was expansion of the construction sector resulting from a domestic housing boom. Whilst the volume of exports fell from €93.6 billion in 2002 to €82 billion in 2003, the value of output from the construction industry was 80 percent higher in 2005 than it had been in 2000, increasing from €17.6 billion to €32 billion.

Table 1 Average annual growth rates, unemployment rate

	1987-1993	1994-2000	2001-2007	2008	2009 (forecast)	2010 (projected)
GNP	3.4%	8.7%	4.5%	-2.8%	-10%	-1.5%
GDP	3.9%	9.5%	4.5%	-3%	-7.25%	-0.25%
Unemployment rate	15.3%	9.5%	4.2%	6.3%	11.75%	13.75%

Source: CSO and ESRI.

3. IRELAND'S HOUSING BOOM

By the year 2001 Irish incomes, as measured by GNP per capita, had increased significantly. Notwithstanding increased personal wealth, Irish housing stock was very low by European standards – the lowest in the EU(Somerville, 2007). Low interest rates, higher incomes, a greater number of people employed, as well as increased immigration resulted in a greater demand for housing. A supply side response resulted in an explosion in activity in the construction sector, and it became an increasingly significant component of the Irish economy. In 2006 construction output represented 24 percent of total GNP, compared with an average ratio of 12 percent in Western Europe. By the second quarter of 2007 construction accounted for over 13 percent of all employment (almost 19 percent when those indirectly employed are included), and generated 16 percent of tax revenues. This increase in construction activity resulted in a doubling of the number of house completions, from 46,500 units in 1999 to over 93,000 units in 2006. Despite the increase in supply, the average price of houses soared, increasing fourfold in the years 1996 to 2007. House price inflation was partly driven by low interest rates, but also by a considerable increase in bank lending. This led to a vicious circle – as house prices increased, banks were prepared to lend increased amounts secured on collateral which was regularly being valued upwards, continuously relaxing lending conditions and providing more attractive terms. Growth in lending by financial institutions in the Irish economy was inexorable[3]. Whilst the international credit boom saw an increase in bank lending to an average of 100 percent of GDP by 2008, in Ireland bank lending grew to 200 percent of national income(Kelly, 2009). This included an increase, not only in mortgage lending, but also a large increase in lending to property developers. This is reflected in the growth rates of two institutions specialising in lending to the property sector: Irish Nationwide Building Society and Anglo Irish Bank had average annual growth rates of 20 percent and 35 percent respectively (Honohan, 2009a). Whilst growth in credit largely fuelled the huge increase in house prices (Kelly, 2009), government policy was also a contributory factor. Tax incentives were extended to entice investment in the property sector, and capital gains tax was cut from 40 percent to 20 percent. These measures remained in place, despite indications of oversupply.

Whilst the construction industry, the banking sector, the media and politicians were all of the view that growth in the housing market would continue apace, in early 2007 it became apparent that a slowdown was imminent with the accumulation in the number of unsold units[4]. Most interest groups insisted that a "soft landing" would cushion the blow. Few signalled the wider implications for the banking sector (apart from Kelly (2007), for example), although the dramatic fall in their share prices from early 2007 indicated that investors were nervous about the risk[5]. The risk to Irish banks stemmed from two sources: firstly, their assets were disproportionately concentrated in property development[6]; secondly, their liabilities were increasingly sourced in the interbank market. Up to the mid-1990s, Irish banks' liabilities were largely comprised of deposits. The huge expansion in bank lending after 1997 was substantially funded through borrowing in the interbank market. Had Ireland an independent currency, the risk of large scale foreign borrowing to fund the property boom

---

[3] Michael Soden, ex chief-executive of Bank of Ireland remarked that, while it took Bank of Ireland over 100 years to grow its loan book to €100 billion in 2001, this was doubled to €200 billion by 2008.

[4] The 2006 Census revealed that there were 266,000 empty housing units in the country.

[5] Between May 2007 and December 2008, the index of Irish bank shares fell by 94 percent, with shares in Anglo Irish Bank falling by 98 percent (Honohan, 2009). The fall in bank share prices comprised a two stage decline: from May 2007 to August 2008, the decline was relatively greater for Irish banks; from September 2008 to December 2008, the decline was universal, affecting bank share prices worldwide.

[6] By 2008 80 percent of the loan book of Anglo Irish Bank was secured against property in the UK and Ireland; 71 and 60 percent of the loan books of Bank of Ireland and Allied Irish Banks respectively were secured against property.

might have been signalled by adverse exchange rates. However, because of membership of the EMU, this warning sign (what Honohan (2006) referred to as 'the canary in the mine') was not signalled. This model of funding was facilitated by the global expansion of credit, ensuring adequate liquidity in the interbank market. Circumstances changed dramatically in the wake of the bankruptcy of Lehman Brothers. As institutions became increasingly nervous about advancing funds to the interbank market on which the Irish banks had become extremely dependent, problems arose for their funding model. In late September 2008 one Irish bank was reportedly unable to roll over its foreign borrowings, and lacked adequate collateral to raise funds from the ECB. Worried about potential contagion effects, the chief executives of the two main Irish banks approached the Minister for Finance for assistance on the night of 29 September 2008. The following day the Irish government took the markets by surprise by moving to guarantee the liabilities of six banks and building societies. This initial guarantee exposed the state to a potential loss of €400 billion, and although it was unlikely that a liability of this amount would come to pass it attached the banks' financing problems to the state, raising concern about the Irish government general debt. It subsequently emerged that the Irish banks faced, not a short-term liquidity problem but a long-term solvency problem. Unable to raise funds on the financial markets, they turned to the government for assistance once more. Because of the wide-ranging nature of the initial guarantee, the Irish government had to make ever-increasing interventions to stabilise the banking sector. In January 2009 Anglo Irish Bank was nationalised, and Bank of Ireland and Allied Irish Banks were advanced €7 billion in return for preference shares. In April 2009, the government announced the establishment of the National Asset Management Agency (NAMA) to acquire the impaired property development loans of the banks. The underlying philosophy for the establishment of the agency is to remove impaired assets from the banks' balance sheets and facilitate access to funding[7], in the hope of restoring liquidity to the real economy. This plan has received much criticism, not least because bond holders and subordinated debtholders are secured at the expense of the taxpayer. Even with this cash injection, most commentators are of the view that the two main banks will require further recapitalisation over the course of 2010 (Honohan, 2009b). Economists opposed to the 'bad bank' model adopted by the state voiced concern that it would ultimately result in the state overpaying for impaired loans and that alternative mechanisms should be implemented by the government, such as temporary nationalisation or purchasing equity stakes for the taxpayer (Lucey et al., 2009a,b).

Whilst the unsustainability of the vast growth in bank lending, allied with a huge property bubble appears obvious in hindsight, why did this not seem apparent at the time, and why were steps not taken to rectify the situation? Just as the banking crisis can be partly explained by financial contagion, the property bubble can be explained by the social contagion of boom thinking (Shiller, 2009). Additionally, it was in the short-term interests of a lot of sectors to perpetuate the bubble, even though it meant value destruction in the long-term. As property prices rose, almost all sectors of the economy were affected. The Irish economy was highly concentrated: a large portion of taxation revenue, employment and wealth was generated by the property sector; the increase in property related taxes facilitated reductions in income taxes and increases in government spending; the media, particularly newspapers, generated a significant proportion of advertising revenue from the property boom; a significant proportion

---

[7] NAMA is to acquire loans of €77 billion for a consideration of €57 billion, even though the estimated market value is €47 billion. (NAMA, 2009).

of the Irish stock exchange was based on property values - furthermore, the valuation of companies whose main business had no connection to the property sector were valued on the speculative value of their sites (for example, Greencore, a food company). The Irish economy lacked diversification, and became increasingly dependent on the property bubble.

The role of the financial regulator came in for much scrutiny in the wake of the crisis. Commentators queried inaction by the regulator given the phenomenal rate of growth of the Irish banks and the concentration of growth in lending to the property sector. (Honohan (2009a) states that regulators employ an annual real growth rate of 20 per cent in the balance sheet as a warning sign of increased risk for a bank. Two Irish banks crossed this threshold on a number of occasions during this period). Whilst it appeared that the banks were growing too fast too quickly the financial regulator stated that "...Irish banks are resilient and have good shock absorption capacity to cope with the current situation" (Neary, 2008a). Claiming that banks had adequate capital to absorb losses on property loans, and that over-exposure to the property market was not a weakness of the Irish banking sector (Neary, 2008b), it appeared that whilst the regulator was applying capital adequacy rules, the systemic risks were not fully evaluated or appreciated. Additionally, stress testing conducted in 2006 was based on an overly optimistic estimation of the rate of default or non-performing loans (Honohan, 2009a). As the risk posed to the banking sector did not stem from Irish banks' use of exotic derivatives or hedging ('areas of significant ignorance' (Strange, 1997)), the problem did not arise from a lack of understanding of complex financial instruments and transactions. Rather, it was an inadequate appreciation of the increasing exposure of Irish banks to the property sector, in particular the large amount of loans advanced to the development sector, and the inadequacy of collateral provided. Whilst there were instances of irregular transactions in a number of cases, it appears that, by and large the crisis stemmed from an underappreciation of risk combined with inaction.

4. THE IRISH BUDGETARY POSITION

Rapid expansion of the property sector in 2002 resulted in a remarkable increase in government revenues from stamp duty and capital gains tax. Property-related taxes increased from 4 percent of total government revenue in 1995 to 16 percent in 2007. Enriched with windfall taxes from the construction boom, the government implemented a procyclical fiscal policy(Barry, 2009). In the period from 2002, increases in spending on social transfers and public pay far outpaced the rate of growth in GDP. The government also cut income tax rates repeatedly, with the result that income taxes as a percentage of total tax revenue declined from 37 percent in 1994 to 27 percent in 2006 (Lane, 2007). Additionally, the tax base was narrowed as rises in exemption levels were raised, placing those on low incomes, comprising almost 50 percent of PAYE workers, outside the tax net. Consequently, the income tax burden was exceptionally light - Whelan (2009: 8) estimates that the average tax rate for a single income married couple with two children on the average wage was 6.7 percent, compared with an EU-15 average of 23.7 percent and an OECD average of 21.1 percent. Whilst income tax cuts were popular, the transformation in composition of tax revenues was highly significant. By 2007 government revenues were greatly dependent on windfall taxes from the housing market. When activity in the sector came to a "shuddering halt" (Lenihan,

2008) tax revenues plummeted. The slowdown in the construction sector was accompanied by increased business closures in the traded sector, resulting in rising unemployment with consequent increased transfer payments and lower tax receipts. The deterioration in the budgetary position was immediate. After a decade of almost uninterrupted surpluses, the deficit in the general government balance soared to 7.5 percent of GDP in 2008 and 12.9 percent of GDP in 2009, levels not seen since the 1980s. The budgetary position was exacerbated by government policy in stabilising the banking sector. Re-financing the Irish banks entailed not only an increase in gross government debt, but also increased costs of raising finance on international debt markets. In March 2009, the yield premium over Germany which Ireland paid on its bonds rose to 3 percent in the wake of government assistance to the banks. (This spread has narrowed to 1.5 percent above German rates in recent months, as the perceived riskiness of Irish government debt recedes).

Steps taken in five successive budgetary measures since June 2008 have resulted in a stabilisation of the general government deficit[8], and whilst general government debt is projected to rise to 75 percent of GDP, it remains lower than that of many Eurozone countries[9]. Notwithstanding a number of contractionary budgets, competitiveness problems persist in the Irish economy. Combined with the imperative of restoring the general government balance and the general government debt within the limits of the Stability and Growth Pact (SGP), the fiscal 'correction' required remains substantial.

5. DISCUSSION

The global financial crisis, similar to the economic boom that preceded it, had a significant impact on the Irish economy. Notwithstanding additional contributory factors, the financial crisis triggered an emergency in the Irish banks, exposing serious structural problems in an increasingly undiversified economy. Even more importantly, the global financial crisis highlighted a major deficiency in the way in which banks seek to overcome agency-related costs of adverse selection and moral hazard when advancing loans to firms and households. Whilst banks typically employ four main lending techniques in seeking to overcome these costs, including financial statement lending, business credit scoring, relationship lending, and asset-based lending (Baas and Schrooten, 2006), the latter is by far the most frequently employed technique. Empirical evidence highlights the pervasiveness in use of collateral-based methods in most bank-based economies (Coco, 2000, Bartholdy and Mateus, 2008). This approach leads to the inefficient allocation of resources as debt is advanced on the basis of collateral rather than profitability. This method of lending results in underinvestment, and is further exacerbated by the reluctance of firms and households to apply for debt finance because of a perception that they will be refused because of inadequate collateral (Kon and Storey, 2003). Some authors suggest that the introduction of stricter capital adequacy laws under the Basel II proposals will promote the use of asset-based lending techniques even further (Tanaka, 2003), and increase the procyclicality in boom and

---

[8] The general government deficit is projected to stabilise at 12.8 percent in 2010.

[9] Ireland was well positioned at the onset of the crisis, as general government debt had been steadily decreasing since the early 1990s. In 2007, general government debt stood at 25 percent of GDP. Public liability is even lower when the assets of the National Pensions Reserve Fund are taken into account. .

bust cycles(Caprio et al., 2008). A related problem for institutions advancing debt finance secured by collateral is the valuation of collateralised assets. As revealed demonstrably in the Irish case, the procyclical nature of asset valuation amounts to a one-way bet, and in the absence of adequate appraisal of risk can lead to large-scale losses, amplified by the provision of high Loan To Value (LTV) mortgages.

A further disadvantage with the use of collateral-based lending techniques is that they favour investment in property, which is an unproductive use of capital. This is intensified in the Irish case, as property has long been a preferred investment for Irish investors. Concentration of investment in property resulted in a general lack of diversification in the Irish economy, and the neglect of alternative, wealth generating sectors. This was encouraged by government policies which rewarded investment in property (Rae and Van Den Noord, 2006). In order to encourage more productive use of private investment, the government should create a level playing field by reducing incentives to invest in the property market, and create additional incentives to invest in research and development and/or business enterprise. The requirement for greater expenditure on research and development is particularly applicable in the Irish case, which at 1.43 per cent of GDP is lower than the average for Eurozone countries, and considerably lower than Germany, France and the Scandanavian countries (Eurostat, 2009).

A related issue is the need for greater development of human capital and social cohesion, which is a source of comparative advantage and international competitiveness for small island states (Read, 2004). A widely-touted reason for the attraction of FDI to Ireland was the presence of a 'highly educated workforce'. This may no longer be true, however. At the Global Irish Economic Forum at Farmleigh in September 2009, Craig Barrett (ex CEO of Intel corporation) insisted that Ireland needed to invest in its education system; to spend more on research and development, and to place a greater emphasis on producing top-class science graduates. This is even more important in Ireland presently, because we cannot compete with more labour-intensive developing countries producing low-cost exports as we have in the past.

The primary obstacle to revitalising the real economy at present is the lack of liquidity in the financial system. NAMA was established to remove impaired loans from the balance sheets of Irish banks, encouraging them to resume lending, thereby stimulating activity in the real economy. There is an inherent difficulty in achieving this aim, however. Even if the banks emerge from NAMA adequately capitalised, and with balance sheets cleansed of non-performing loans, there is no guarantee that they will advance loans and credit facilities to business and personal customers. Banks are under no obligation to lend money, and it is both difficult and unwise to compel them to do so. Indeed, banks have a fiduciary duty to their shareholders to maximise their earnings. They must, therefore, seek to earn the highest return for their investment. If securities provide a higher return than commercial and domestic lending, then directors are duty-bound to invest in the former rather than the latter. Recent experience in Germany is salutary in this regard. The German finance minister, Peer Steinbruck, expressed disappointment that, despite assisting financial institutions to recapitalise, banks are investing capital in securities rather than lending to small businesses. Because of structural difficulties in their balance sheets, Irish banks have to either raise increased funding and/or significantly reduce their loan books. Failure to attract funds from institutional investors means that the banks are dependent on the state for badly-needed capital, and this source is limited. All evidence indicates that the main Irish banks will have to reduce their loan books, and this means even lower levels of lending. This outcome is potentially detrimental for the SME sector and the real economy. Surveys conducted by small firm organisations in the past six months reveal that SMEs are finding it increasingly difficult to secure debt funding from financial institutions. Firms are experiencing a 'credit squeeze' because of reduced lending facilities, which have been exacerbated by rising bad debts and by creditors taking longer to pay. This is not to suggest that banks should expand lending activity just to satisfy an increased volume of credit applications. Provision of finance to the real economy should be improved through the development of alternative means of financing, such as provision of sources of private equity and venture capital. This ensures, not alone a diversity of sources of capital, but also a source of knowledge, advice and investment expertise. Additionally, it promotes investment in intangible activities and sectors, which are typically not favoured by the banking sector.

6. CONCLUSION

Many commentators wish for a return to the halcyon days of the Celtic Tiger, which were characterised by extraordinary rates of growth, soaring incomes, 'negative' real interest rates, decreasing personal taxation, and 'full' employment. As Ireland has now converged with Eurozone economies, we should beware of a return to high rates of growth vastly out of sync with our European partners. Most would welcome a return to positive, more sober growth rates. Economists contend that export-led growth is the means to achieve this aim and improve the present fiscal predicament. The main obstacle to this approach, however, is the lack of competitiveness of the Irish economy. The commonly-held view is that this should be achieved by reducing prices and wages by approximately 30 percent to promote growth in the traded sector, although this may involve significant job losses. An alternative view is that competitiveness may be achieved by leaving the EMU (Mc Williams, 2010), thus adopting a (vastly devalued) independent currency. Whilst this option is appealing for its immediate competitiveness benefits, it would have long-term economic costs and political implications. Firstly, it would likely cause a 'run' on bank assets, as depositors rushed to withdraw euro deposits. Secondly, it would significantly increase Irish foreign debt holdings, greatly indenturing future generations. Thirdly, it would create a myriad of political problems (Eichengreen, 2007). On balance, 'going it alone' is not a practicable or a wise course of action at present.

Ireland's vulnerability as a small open economy suggests that it will continue to experience disproportionately greater instability in its growth trajectory. Experience over the past two decades has shown that membership of a monetary union can amplify rather than reduce economic shocks. Whilst membership of EMU facilitated the Irish banking crisis through lower interest rates and enabling banks to borrow large amounts on the interbank markets, policies enacted by government and private institutions rendered the Irish economy vulnerable to the global financial crisis. It may be argued that the adoption of different policies or alternative systems would have resulted in different outcomes or have an ameliorating effect, although it is impossible to say. Recent experience highlights the consequences of short-term decisions in times of economic abundance. To achieve a more stable economic environment requires long-term strategic planning for sustainable development, and creation of a capacity to enable swift response to minimise the effects of negative external economic shocks.

REFERENCES

Acs, Z., O'Gorman, C., Szerb, L. and Terjesen, S. (2007) "Could the Irish Miracle be Repeated in Hungary?". *Small Business Economics*, 28, 123-142.

Barry, F. (2009) "Politics and Economic Policymaking in Ireland". Working Paper, Trinity College Dublin.

Bartholdy, J. and Mateus, C. (2008) "Financing of SMEs: An Asset Side Story". Paper presented at the Société Universitaire Européenne de Recherches Financiéres. Paris.

Bew, P. and Patterson, H. (1982) Sean Lemass and the Making of Modern Ireland. Dublin: Gill and MacMillan.

Burnham, J. B. (2003) "Why Ireland Boomed". The Independent Review, 7, 537-556.

Caprio, G., Demigurc-Kunt, A. and Kane, E. (2008) "The 2007 Meltdown in Structured Securitization : Searching for Lessons, not Scapegoats". Policy Research Working Paper Series. The World Bank.

Coco, G. (2000) "On the Use of Collateral". *Journal of Economic Surveys*, 14, 191.

Eichengreen, B. (2007) "The Breakup of the Euro Area". Paper presented at the NBER Summer Institute, July 12, 2007.

Eurostat (2009) Available at http://epp.eurostat.ec.europa.eu/tgm/table.do ?tab=tableandinit=1and language=enandpcode=tsiir020andplugin=0). [Accessed 7 December 2009].

Gallagher, L., Doyle, E. and O'Leary, E. (2002) "Creating the Celtic Tiger and Sustaining Economic Growth: A Business Perspective". In D. McCoy et al, (Eds), Quarterly Economic Commentary, Economic and Social Research Institute, Spring, pp. 63.

Honohan, P. (2006) "To What Extent has Finance Been a Driver of Ireland's Economic Success?". Quarterly Economic Commentary, Economic and Social Research Institute, Winter 2006, 59-72.

Honohan, P. (2009a) "Resolving Ireland's Banking Crisis". *The Economic and Social Review,* 40, 207-231.

Honohan, P. (2009b) Introductory Statement to the Joint Oireachtas Committee on Economic Regulatory Affairs. 15 December, 2009.

Honohan, P. and Walsh, B. (2002) "Catching Up With the Leaders: *The Irish Hare".* Brookings Papers on Economic Activity, 1.

Kelly, J. and Everett, M. (2004) *"Financial Liberalisation and Economic Growth in Ireland".* Central Bank and Financial Services Authority of Ireland.

Kelly, M. (2007) "Banking on Very Shaky Foundations". Irish Times, 7 September, 2007.

Kelly, M. (2009) "The Irish Credit Bubble". Working Paper WP09 / 32, School of Economics, University College Dublin.

Kennedy, K. A. (2001) "Reflections on the Process of Irish Economic Growth*". Journal of the Statistical and Social Inquiry Society of Ireland*, 30, 123-139.

Kirby, P. (2002) "The Celtic Tiger in Distress. *Growth With Inequality in Ireland".*Basingstoke, Hampshire ; New York, NY :, Palgrave.

Kon, Y. and Storey, D. J. (2003) "A Theory of Discouraged Borrowers". Small Business Economics, 21, 37-49.

Lane, P. (2007) "Fiscal Policy for a Slowing Economy". In T. Callan (Ed.) Budget perspectives 2008, Dublin: Economic and Social Research Institute, October 2007.

Lenihan, B. (2008) Address to the European Construction Industry Federation. Dublin Castle, 20 June 2008.

Lucey, B. et al., (2009a) "Nationalising Banks the Best Option". *The Irish Times.* April 17, 2009.

Lucey, B. et al., (2009b) "Nama Set to Shift Wealth to Lenders and Developers". *The Irish Times.* August 26, 2009.

McWilliams, D. (2010) "Should we Divorce the Euro?". Sunday Business Post, January 10, 2010.

NAMA (2009) "Draft Business Plan". October 14, 2009. Available at http://www.nama.ie/Publications/2009/Business_Plan_13OCT09.pdf [Accessed 15 December, 2009].

Neary, P. (2008a) Address at the Institute of Directors. Dublin: 19 September, 2008.

Neary, P. (2008b) Interview with Mark Little. RTÉ 1 Television, Prime Time, broadcast October 2, 2008.

Ó Gráda, C. (1997) "A Rocky Road: The Irish Economy Since the 1920s". Manchester, U.K.: Manchester University Press.

Ó Gráda, C. (2002) "Is the Celtic Tiger a Paper Tiger?". Working Paper 200202, School of Economics, University College Dublin.

Rae, D. and Van Den Noord, P. (2006) "Ireland's Housing Boom: What has Driven it and Have Prices Overshot?". Working Paper 492, Economics Department, Organisation for Economic Co-operation and Development.

Read, R. (2004) "The Implications of Increasing Globalization and Regionalism for the Economic Growth of Small Island States". World Development, 32, 365-378.

Shiller, R. (2009) "The Subprime Solution: How Today's Global Financial Crisis Happened, and What to Do About It". Princeton: Princeton University Press.

Soden, M (2008) Interview with Marian Finucane. RTÉ Radio 1 broadcast, 6 December 2008.

Somerville, R. A. (2007) "Housing Tenure in Ireland". *Economic and Social Review*, 38, 107-134.

Strange, S. (1997) Casino Capitalism. Manchester: Manchester University Press.

Tanaka, M. (2003) "The Macroeconomic Implications of the New Basel Accord". CESifo Economic Studies, 49, 217-232.

Whelan, K. (2009) "Policy Lessons from Ireland's Latest Depression". Working paper WP09/14, Centre for Economic Research, University College Dublin.

In: After the Crisis: Rethinking Finance
Editor: Thomas Lagoarde-Segot

ISBN 978-1-61668-925-4
© 2010 Nova Science Publishers, Inc.

Chapter 4

THE GLOBAL MORTGAGE CRISIS LITIGATION FALLOUT

William V. Rapp

ABSTRACT

This chapter is an analysis on the legal recourse investors in subprime mortgage vehicles might have against originators, packagers and investment vehicle organizers in the subprime mortgage process based on the resulting bubble and the economic aftermath of its collapse. It does this by reviewing major sources of litigation and then looking through the lens of a major civil case involving two financial giants, Barclay's Bank and JP Morgan Chase the current owner of Bear Stearns. This approach is used because if a large well-financed plaintiff investor with a credible claim cannot make a good legal case against a participant controlling all aspects of the mortgage origination to investment chain it will be even more difficult with respect to smaller participants or those that worked with different or multiple participants in the chain on an arms-length-basis. Indeed the evidence indicates that only direct claims against specific players have a reasonable chance of success. Further, the case offers an excellent perspective concerning how even sophisticated investors to their regret got caught up in the intricacies and complexities of the global mortgage backed securities market and its related financial products. As part of this analysis the paper also addresses the origins of the subprime crisis and the cascading errors in judgment especially lapses in evaluating and documenting mortgage credit.

1. INTRODUCTION

In the aftermath of most bubble collapses a proliferation of scams and legal controversies emerge as investors realize their greed or naivete' has been exploited legally and illegally (Kindleberger and Aliber 2005)[1]. This naturally results in a surge in lawsuits as such investors

---

[1] See Kindleberger, C. and Aliber, R. (2005), Manias, Panics, and Crashes. John Wiley. Chapter 9, "Frauds, Swindles and the Credit Cycle", 143-175.

try to recover some of their money from everyone involved in promoting and exploiting the rapid rise in asset prices. The current global financial crisis resulting from the Mortgage Meltdown has been no exception. This chapter will review some of these legal controversies by examining the recourse to the courts of two types of investors: one, investors in subprime mortgage vehicles and two, investors in banks and other lenders that lent and promoted such loans and securities and whose stock prices subsequently declined dramatically or became worthless. The analysis includes an assessment of which suits appear to have the best chance of success and those that have ended in frustration. This review is also an excellent way to understand how the bubble developed and how some investors became involved directly or indirectly in the Bubble's evolution and ultimate collapse.

The former situation will be addressed by primarily examining the cases an investor might have against integrated originators, packagers and investment vehicle organizers in the subprime mortgage process based on the Bubble's development and the economic aftermath of its collapse. This approach is used because if a plaintiff investor cannot make a legal case against a defendant who was a participant controlling all aspects of the mortgage origination to investment chain it will be even more difficult with respect to those participants that worked with several different players in the chain on an arms-length-basis.

This is because one frustration potential investor litigants have is that those that sold them the subprime mortgage investments can generally point down the mortgage chain and claim they were also deceived until the investor arrives at a mortgage originator that is in many cases bankrupt such as New Century Financial, Lehman Brothers, or Washington Mutual. Still, several large integrated players are viable targets if investors can implicate the holding companies or substantive subsidiaries regarding the management and actions of the investment vehicles they or their subsidiaries created.

Further these remaining integrated participants are generally large sophisticated financial institutions with access to detailed economic, regulatory and financial information that if available would have suggested caution with respect to advising investors of potential risks. If cautionary flags were raised the integrated providers should have been among the first to recognize these warning signals both from their own portfolios and from available industry and government data.

The chapter will examine this idea from two aspects. The first will seek to differentiate and compare the potential causes for civil action by investor plaintiffs with the three areas where there have actually been investor settlements by financial institutions. These are violation of pension management obligations under ERISA, misrepresentations or failure to disclose the actual risks related to managed accounts that specified a certain level of prudence and risk and decisions based upon long-term reputation considerations. The second aspect will be to specifically apply this comparative template to the *Barclays. Ltd versus Bear Stearns* case where Barclays Bank tried but failed to implicate the Bear Stearns holding company and thus access the deep pockets of JP Morgan Chase[2] for reimbursement of the roughly $400 in losses Barclays sustained in a hedge fund Bear Stearns Asset Management [BSAM] created and managed that has subsequently gone bankrupt.[3]

---

[2] JP Morgan acquired the Bear Stearns Companies, formerly a NYSE listed company and the holding company for various Bear Stearns entities, on May 31, 2008 as a going concern and is now liable for any of its obligations.

[3] The Bear Stearns High-Grade Structured Credit Strategies Enhanced Leverage Master Fund, Ltd. [henceforth the Enhanced Leverage Fund] filed for bankruptcy in NY October 10, 2007. The bankruptcy case was terminated May 30, 2008. See PACER 1:07-cv-08746-RWS. Barclays, however, filed suit against Bear Stearns and

The chapter will then address the second major area of litigation, the class action suit against large subprime mortgage lenders by "injured" shareholders. This section will examine derivative action cases against firms such as Countrywide Financial or Accredited Lending, which represents the other major part of the post collapse litigation story, though some suits have been complicated by SEC or state actions against these defendants for violating securities laws or predatory lending.

As noted above the mortgage meltdown aftermath has brought numerous civil and criminal actions. For example, mortgage fraud in the US, including Federal and state prosecution, has grown dramatically.[4] This reflects the huge increase in the US mortgage market's size and its increasing complexity, both of which have opened many opportunities for fraudsters across a range of activities and institutions. Yet plaintiffs seeking remedies often end up in civil court.[5] As explained in more detail below plaintiffs' lawyers and their clients have been active in making claims to try and recover some of the billions of dollars in losses that investors have sustained. While this paper only explores some of these legal developments, to fully grasp even these situations, one must first understand the critical changes that have occurred in global financial markets for US mortgage related securities and their legal underpinnings. The paper will then show how US banking and security laws changes have complicated the situation for any legal causes of action and why a focus on integrated participants and derivative call class action suits are thus a good place to analyze possible theories of recourse.

---

related parties in Federal Court in the Southern District of New York on December 19, 2007. While the initial complaint did not specify actual damages subsequent amended complaints stated Barclays' losses were about $400 million. See Barclays Bank Plc. v. Bear Stearns Asset Management Inc., Ralph Cioffi, Matthew Tannin, Bear Stearns and Co, Inc., and the Bear Stearns Companies, Case No. 07 Civ. 11400 (LAP) [henceforth Barclays v. BSAM]. Available at 2008 WL 4499468.

[4] A former Federal Prosecutor notes suspicious activity reports related to mortgage fraud increased over 1000% between 1997 and 2005 and pending FBI mortgage fraud investigations rose from 436 in fiscal 2002 to 1210 in fiscal 2007 [see Grant, J. (2008) "FBI opens subprime fraud inquiries." Financial Times.]. Further the FBI in its 2008 Mortgage Fraud report notes that Suspicious Activity Reports [SARs] for "mortgage fraud filings from financial institutions increased 36 percent to 63,713 during Fiscal Year (FY) 2008 compared to 46,717 filings in FY2007" [available at www.fbi.gov/publications/fraud/mortgage_fraud08.htm]. While estimated losses are in the billions of dollars only a small number of SARs lead to prosecutions by Federal or state law enforcement. Thus many result in civil claims instead or in conjunction with criminal cases. See Pierson, H. (2007) "Mortgage Fraud Boot Camp: Basic Training of Defending a Criminal Mortgage Fraud Case." The Champion, National Association of Criminal Defense Lawyers, 14. See also Gibeaut, J. (2007) "Mortgage Fraud Mess." ABA Journal, available at http://www.abajournal.com /magazine/mortgage_ fraud_mess where it is cited that US mortgage fraud reports have really jumped since the 1990s along with the housing boom. The most common types of fraud involve "property flipping" or other illegal schemes to get the proceeds from mortgages or property sales through misleading appraisals or false documentation. The SEC is also looking at insider trading related to unexpected write-downs by publicly traded companies with assets tied to mortgage-backed securities. See Grant, supra. The SEC also filed a complaint against Cioffi and Tannin in an action related to the Barclays v. Bear Sterns case available at www.sec.gov.

[5] The number of fraud reports in 1996 were 1,318; 1997 - 1,720; 1998 - 2,269; 1999 - 2,934; 2000 - 3,515; 2001 - 4,696; 2002 - 5,387; 2003 - 9,539; 2004 - 18,391; and 2005 - 25,989. It rose again in 2006 with the FBI reporting on a fiscal year basis a rise to 35,700 from 22,000 in fiscal 2005 and from 7000 in fiscal 2003 and now to 63,713 in 2008 indicating an exploding trend. [See Bajaj, V. (2008) "F.B.I. Opens Subprime Inquiry." NY Times.] Comparing these growing number of reports with the number of investigations noted in footnote 4, much less the actual prosecutions, indicates the growth potential in various civil actions. Further there are many possible causes of action other than fraud that plaintiffs seeking financial recovery and other remedies can pursue.

2. Explanation of Structure and Evolution of US Mortgage Market[6]

2.1. Traditional Mortgages between Lenders and Borrowers

The US residential mortgage market is a multi-trillion dollar market that dramatically increased from 2002 onwards to the market collapse in 2007-2008. As of June 2007 residential and non-profit mortgages outstanding amounted to $10.143 trillion up from $5.833 trillion as of September 2002.[7] The number of firms and organizations participating in this huge market proliferated as well. Twenty-five years ago a local bank or local savings and loan [SandL] issued the typical home mortgage to a local borrower and the bank or SandL would hold that mortgage subject to local real estate laws and land registry regulations on its books to maturity or until the home was sold or the mortgage refinanced.

2.2. Securitization

But starting in the 1980s and expanding into the 1990s and the first years of this century, that all changed. Banks and SandLs discovered the benefits of securitization and balance sheet turnover. They realized mortgages and other regular payment credit instruments such as auto loans and credit cards had steady cash flows that if bundled could provide even large institutional investors with a large apparently steady income stream that could be capitalized and sold. They were securitized.

This meant banks and SandLs rather than holding the loans in their investment portfolios[8] would bundle them and sell them to investors while retaining the servicing function for which they deducted fees.[9] This innovation meant the bank or SandL could now turn over their balance sheet on a rapid basis since they did not have to wait until a loan was repaid or their capital increased to make new loans and thus expand their revenues from the loan servicing and origination fees. This process increased their return on capital, earnings per share, and

---

[6] Opportunities for mortgage fraud and misrepresentation leading to civil action on these and other legal grounds exist in the commercial real estate sector too as some cases show. But residential mortgages are where the market, technical changes, and number of players is largest and the players are both sophisticated and unsophisticated ranging from large financial institutions to public entities to individual homeowners and investors.

[7] Source Federal Reserve Bank, *available at* https://www.federalreserve.gov/datadownload/Review.aspx?rel=Z1andseries=dd6e0a09170055cee26a1e11b50710fcandlastObs=10andfrom=andto=andfiletype=csvandlabel=includeandlayout=seriesrowandtype=package. This compares with $2.3 trillion in single-family mortgage debt in 1989 and $3.5 trillion in that year for all mortgage debt. *See* Korngold, G. and Goldstein, P. (2002) *Real Estate Transactions*. Foundation Press, 359. Thus US residential mortgage debt took about 12 years to double before the boom but only 5 years during it, indicating the rapid rise in housing asset prices and the use of debt to expand the bubble.

[8] Any statistically steady stream of payments can be discounted to determine a present value that then sets the price of an obligation that can be sold to investors who receive the future cash flows. This process is called asset securitization. Home mortgages are attractive to securitize due to the long payment periods and underlying assets.

[9] *See* for example the business model description of Countrywide Financial Corporation, *2006 10K*, pp 3-17 *available at* http://about.countrywide.com/SECFilings/Form10K.aspx.

shareholder value[10] benefiting shareholders and corporate officers with stock options.

As this new system evolved, however, and became national or even international rather than local[11], other financial intermediaries emerged that specialized in specific functions within the overall mortgage packaging and sale to investors business chain. For example, mortgage brokers realized they could sell a New York mortgage to a California or Washington SandL that might price it more aggressively on rate and term than a local New York bank. This situation could arise due to the other lender's lower funding costs, its desire to diversify lending risks across more markets, or an interest in expanding its servicing portfolio where it had economies of scale. Indeed the reasons could be a combination of all these factors. The broker could thus help a borrower find the best rate within an increasingly competitive and integrated national market for residential mortgages that ultimately squeezed out the small local bank or SandL.

Further as the market expanded, economies of scale in specialization at different points in the mortgage financing and investment chain emerged. The development of the Internet and personal computer power only increased such considerations as technological progress created significant cost improvements in sourcing and processing mortgage applications and approvals on-line. In the same way that a prospective home buyer could now virtually tour several houses in an afternoon without leaving home they could compare mortgage rates from several sources while the lenders could quickly scan a buyer's credit score and outstanding loans from many different sources. Similarly huge increases in computing power and telecommunications introduced economies of scale in servicing these mortgages and the ultimate investors.[12]

Under this new and evolving structure it was quite possible that no federally insured bank or SandL would ever be involved in the loan or that any one investor would even hold the actual mortgage as security. A mortgage broker could find a lender such as GMAC or GE Credit Services or Merrill Lynch instead of a traditional bank or SandL.[13] These lenders in turn would bundle the mortgages into pools of cash flows usually in the form of a trust and either themselves or via investment banks such as Lehman Brothers or Bear Stearns[14] place them with investors. But rather than selling these pools as a whole or percentages of the pool to an insurance company, hedge fund, or structured investment vehicle [SIV], they sold pieces of the mortgage pool's cash flow tailored according to the investor's individual and often unique requirements. Thus long-term investors might only want the final monthly payments

---

[10] In the 1980s under the Basle agreements and The Resolution Trust Corporation Act [see footnote 20 below], banks and SandLs became subject to more stringent capital requirements relative to the loans on their books. This gave them an incentive to no longer hold loans to maturity or payoff. Rather it made sense to package and sell these loans to long-term investors such as insurance companies. *See* Chapter on Citibank in Rapp, W. (2004) *Information Technology Strategies*. Oxford University Press, 214-246.

[11] *See* Countrywide, *supra* note 9, relative to their UK operations.

[12] *See* Rapp, *supra* note 10.

[13] In 2005 GMAC Bank was the country's 6th largest prime mortgage lender with $314 billion outstanding while Lehman Brothers Bank was the 9th largest subprime lender with $142 billion outstanding. *See* Gramlich, E. (2007), *Subprime Mortgages*, Urban Institute Press. Bear Stearns' bank was called EMC Mortgage.

[14] A recent client study byYoshinobu Yamada, a bank analyst at Merrill Lynch, indicates Bear Stearns and Lehman Brothers before their collapse were the number one and two underwriters respectively of sub-prime mortgage backed securities. *See* Yamada, Y. and Kubo, T. (2008) *Japanese Major Banks*. Merrill Lynch Japan Securities, Tokyo.

of the mortgage pool while another, shorter-term investor, might desire only the first three years' interest payments.

The longer dated monthly payments would then be sold to a different investor group. Thus, in many situations no one investor owned an entire mortgage and none were involved in the loan administration or the handling of the security.[15] The power of large computer systems supported the servicing of these many different structures and favored those firms that could source and service in volume and so could spread the system costs over a large number of mortgages, customers and structured investments. This led to a factory mentality in creating the pools including the supporting legal documentation, a practice that has apparently carried over to foreclosure activity in the current economic downturn and housing crisis.[16]

Because the initial lenders only expected to hold the mortgages[17] for a short period they frequently funded the initial mortgage loan using commercial paper. In addition to GMAC and GE, several specialized mortgage lenders used this technique, including those that focused heavily on the sub-prime mortgage market.[18] The Countrywide Financial Corporation [CFC] perhaps the largest mortgage lender in the US did this extensively with its commercial paper backed by its mortgage loans.[19] It did this even though a subsidiary was a federally insured SandL. It continued this funding practice up until 2006, probably to avoid the more stringent capital requirements the government had imposed on SandLs in 1989 as part of The Resolution Corporation Trust Act.[20]

The collapse of the sub-prime market, though, forced Countrywide to change its business model. In 2006 it applied for changed status to a Federally Regulated Savings and Loan Holding Company.[21] However, even this did not save it since it was ultimately absorbed by Bank of America. Nevertheless, the size of the mortgage financing market, its rapid growth and its increasing complexity have combined with the current meltdown and the billions in losses by financial institutions and investors, to create many opportunities for legal actions including both criminal prosecutions for mortgage fraud and numerous civil causes of action seeking a legal remedy and some restitution of the lost billions.[22]

Not surprisingly these points of legal altercation are generally at the intersections that represent handoffs of the loans and mortgages in some form between institutions such as mortgage broker to lender or between lender and packager or packager and investor since these points have usually been accompanied by contractual documentation representing the

---

[15] For a deal based view of this process see Sloan, A. (2007) "House of Junk." Fortune,117-124.

[16] See Morgenson, G. and Glater, J. (2008) "The Foreclosure Machine." NY Times .

[17] See Countrywide's 10K for description of their business model, supra note 9.

[18] In their 2005 annual reports GM and GE indicate this kind of activity. Indeed GM indicated $4 billion in mortgage servicing rights on its balance sheet. Examples of GMAC's mortgage activities are available at http://www.gmacmortgage.com/index.html. The ABA Journal has published several articles on the sub-prime mortgage meltdown and the related collapse in the US housing market. These are available at http://www. abajournal.com/ topics/real+estate+property+law. They include discussions of mortgage fraud, see Gibeaut, J. supra note 4, or Neil, M. (2007) "N.Y. Lawyer Stole $24M, Gets 10 Years." ABA Journal. However they also note the increase in related litigation and the fact some law firms are setting up special practices to sue banks or to pursue owner claims. See for example Weiss, D. (2007) "Judges Crack Down on Law Firm 'Foreclosure Mills'." ABA Journal, or Weiss, D. (2007) "Suits Follow Mortgage Meltdown." ABA Journal, orNeil, M. (2007) "More Law Firms Seek to Sue Banks." ABA Journal.

[19] See Countrywide's 10K, supra note 9.

[20] Financial Institutions Reform, Recovery, And Enforcement Act Of 1989, P.L. 101-73 or FIRREA

[21] Id., pp 17-24.

[22] See footnotes 4 and 5.

warranties and responsibilities of the party doing the handing off[23] or the offering to the one receiving or accepting the securities. These contractual obligations then become the basis for recovery. However the cookie cutter approach used produced these securities on mass production basis that is now creating some problems.[24] This is why this chapter will focus on those institutions that handled through different subsidiaries the entire process from origination to bundling the mortgage backed securities to selling pieces of the pools to final investors or to a hedge fund or SIV that they managed and whose equity they then marketed to final investors.

3. CAUSES OF ACTION

So while litigation situations may in fact exist at all points in the mortgage origination and investment chain, it is easier to pinpoint possible knowledge of potential problems and risks when only one holding company is involved and when various actions are primarily against or between related financial institutions acting as the originators, packagers, security purchasers and ultimate investor marketers to those that invested in their mortgage related products.[25]

That is the market developments described above have combined with changes in the legal regime regulating financial institutions to significantly complicate the steps a plaintiff's lawyer must take in developing a complaint or pursuing a particular course of action. Slicing loan pools into several tranches or pieces with varying rights to specific mortgage payments coupled with the multiplicity of documentation at each point in the chain have combined with the split between servicing and loan ownership to make it unclear who controls the pool or the underlying loan and mortgage and its payment stream as well as who was responsible for the final loss to investors by failing to properly assess the credit risks when the underlying mortgages defaulted. Indeed in several cases the servicing agent holds the mortgage in trust for the pool, while the pool is controlled by the super senior tranche for a diverse group of investors with conflicting interests.[26] This is why focusing on the integrated players reduces complexity and simplifies claims and possible recourse.

---

[23] Facilitating these handoffs and reducing the possible causes of action were changes in UCC Article 9 that legalized the automatic transfer of security interests in mortgage loans to subsequent investors while simultaneously eliminating or substantially reducing a borrower's defenses against the initial lender being extended to purchasers.

[24] *See* Morgenson, G. and Glater, J. *supra* note 16, and also Bajaj, V. (2008) "If Everyone's Finger-Pointing,Who's to Blame?" *NY Times*.

[25] "A wave of lawsuits is beginning to wash over the troubled mortgage market and the rest of the financial world. Homeowners are suing mortgage lenders. Mortgage lenders are suing Wall Street banks. Wall Street banks are suing loan specialists. And investors are suing everyone." Bajaj, V. "If Everyone's Finger-Pointing," *supra* note 24. This article also notes two important legal issues underpinning these cases. Whether lenders and packagers alerted borrowers and investors to the risks involved and how much they were legally required to disclose.

[26] The mortgages are bundled into pools and then the cash flows from the pool are separated into tiered tranches each with its own documentation and rights to the cash flow including proceeds from the sale of the property after foreclosure. The super senior tranche sits on top and as recently reported can force liquidation wiping out more junior tranches. *See* van Duyn, A. and Mackenzie, M. (2008) "Tranche warfare breaks out over CDOs." *Financial Times* and Mackenzie, M. (2008) "Super-senior CDO investors begin to flex their muscles." *Financial Times*.

For example, an integrated player such a Citicorp could originate mortgage loans in its commercial bank Citibank and then package them for sale to its Smith Barney Solomon subsidiary who would then sell the pool to a Citicorp structured and managed SIV or hedge fund. Citicorp commercial bankers and investment bankers could then market investments in the SIV or hedge fund that had invested in the pool of mortgage backed securities that were in turn often leveraged to a wide range of their clients. Citibank would also provide the loans or leverage to the SIV or hedge fund to support their balance sheets and "improve" yields. Alternatively they could market the SIV's short term paper supported by the mortgage-backed investment portfolio. If this seems like double leverage, it was, thus increasing the downward consequences of a collapse in value from any defaults or decrease in the value the underlying real estate.

Therefore senior managers at the corporate holding company level in such integrated operations were in an excellent position to monitor and control all aspects of the chain from mortgage origination through to the sale of mortgage backed securities or SIV investments to the final investor. In some cases they advertised this capability as a way to convince potential investors that because they could directly monitor all aspects of the process they could better control quality, even though given their large reported losses, we now know this was not true.[27] Still because they did cover the entire chain, from a plaintiff's perspective one only needs to look for a remedy to a defined group of related entities facilitating claims, discovery and litigation. In addition as will be seen in the *Barclays v. BSAM* case because dealings between related entities require certain corporate declarations regarding independent valuation and pricing of the traded securities the paper trail or lack thereof can become a cause of action too.

4. CHANGES IN THE APPLICABLE LEGAL REGIME

As cited above almost every financial boom and bust is followed by a series of scandals.[28] As a consequence since the population is usually hurt by the collapse in asset values and especially the ones involving fraud, there is usually political pressure to punish those whose are perceived as having caused the problem as well as to prevent future abuses even though the real reason for the boom is generally the public's greed followed by panic as the bubble runs out of liquidity to further support much less inflate asset prices. Therefore these episodes are frequently followed by "barn-door closing" legislation. The Federal Reserve, the SEC and Sarbanes-Oxley resulted from the financial crises of 1907, the crash of 1929 and the collapse of the Internet Bubble respectively.

Therefore in looking for statutory grounds for their suits plaintiffs might want to focus on the legislation that responded to similar situations in the past. The most recent one involving real estate was the Congressional response in 1989 and 1990 to the SandL crisis and the junk

---

[27] In its suit against BSAM as will be detailed below Barclays stressed in its claims how BSAM promoted its expertise as part of an integrated corporate-wide Bear Stearns mortgage-backed securities operation as giving it an important competitive edge in monitoring and controlling risk regarding these securities even in a volatile market.

[28] As cited in footnote 1, the classic study in this regard is Kindleberger, C. and Aliber, R. (2005) Manias, Panics and Crashes. John Wiley and Chapter 9 on "Frauds, Swindles, and the Credit Cycle".

bond scandals[29] that resulted in Congress substantially increasing and broadening penalties for crimes impacting financial institutions by enacting FIRREA [Financial Institutions Reform, Recovery and Enforcement Act] that included the establishment of the Resolution Trust Corporation and amendments that strengthened the penalties for mail, wire and bank fraud.

5. SETTLEMENTS

However, so far FIRREA has played a relatively small role in the cases that have settled. These cases fall into three groups, misrepresentation, statutory violations and public relations and indicate some of the situations and legal arguments used where financial institutions have actually compensated investors. Examining these may thus show ways that investors that are thinking of suing integrated providers could make their case.

5.1. Misrepresentation of Risk

CDO investments and the associated risks. Merrill settled for $13.9 million, though The City of Springfield Massachusetts sued Merrill Lynch for misrepresenting the quality of some subprime that did not prevent the Massachusetts Attorney General from launching a fraud action against Merrill too.[30] A key issue in this and similar cases is "whether the lenders and securities underwriters fully disclosed the risks to borrowers who took out subprime loans or to investors [*such* as Springfield] who bought securities backed by them".[31] Therefore a

---

[29] For an excellent and very readable assessment of this period, see Bruck, C. (1989) The Predators' Ball: The Inside Story of Drexel Burnham and the Rise of the Junk Bond Raiders. Penguin Books.

[30] Davis, P. and Wighton, D. (2008) "CDO case may not be foretaste of suits to come." Financial Times. In the same article the authors quote a former head of a Wall Street concerning the potential litigation as stating that "This is going to go on for years". See Anderson, J. (2008) "Massachusetts Accuses Merrill of Fraud." NY Times. One reason the Attorney General sued Merrill Lynch despite its settlement with Springfield is because the case was "part of a larger investigation into Merrill's sales of similar investments to other Massachusetts towns and cities." Id.. Attorney General Gavin in his complaint "argued that the city had not been properly warned of the risks associated with the investments. By the end of 2007, the $13.9 million of securities was worth $1.2 million." Id.. Merrill Lynch trying to limit any wider legal damage from the settlement claimed the Springfield situation was unusual "because the central issue was the firm's sales practices, not whether the city was a suitable buyer for the securities." Id.. However, this distinction between not having responsibility for a security's market performance and not properly advising of the inherent risks may still open a wide line of attack for certain plaintiffs since upon review Merrill found no one in Springfield had ever authorized the specific purchase of CDOs but only triple-A rated investments. Thus the fact the securities were triple-A rated may not help Merrill in similar suits if the risky chinks in those ratings were not fully explained to the various investors.

[31] Hamilton, W. (2008) "Lawyers smell opportunity as subprime suits start to boom." Los Angeles Times. The author notes, "First came the subprime mortgage boom. Next was the bust. Now, surely as day follows night, come the lawsuits. All large-scale financial scandals spawn mountains of lawsuits, but the subprime financial stands out because of the complexity of the system that funneled more than $1 trillion from investors around the world through Wall Street and mortgage lenders to borrowers with dicey credits. As losses mount on those loans, the scene of the blame game is shifting to the courts. Subprime borrowers are suing loan brokers and lenders accusing them of deceptive practices. Wall Street companies that bought now delinquent subprime loans are trying to force lenders to buy them back. Investment bank shareholders are going after those companies' managers, saying they took excessive risks by loading up on bonds backed by subprime mortgages. And investors are suing managers whose subprime laden funds have suffered hefty losses."

bank defendant's best defense is that these were sophisticated investors that understood the dangers and they just like the banks that sold the securities failed to foresee the collapse of the housing market and the collateral damage it would spread to the financial markets.[32] So the amount of actual disclosure and the legally required disclosure will be critical elements in determining the strength of similar complaints. In this case Merrill apparently felt their position was weak because they were actually managing Springfield's account and the management guidelines required that the investment be relatively riskless.[33] Furthermore, Springfield had never specifically authorized any investment in mortgage-backed securities. However, other suits will be case by case and are likely to be very circumstance and fact specific.

5.2. Statutory Violation

ERISA [Employee Retirement Insurance Security Act] is an example where if plaintiffs can prove a statutory violation some recourse seems available. Under ERISA managers of pension funds have a fiduciary responsibility to act in the interests of their clients. Under a pending case State Street Global Advisors, a subsidiary of State Street bank has set aside $618 million to "settle claims that the firm invested in risky mortgage-related securities" including those brought by five pension plans.[34] The pension clients claim State Street told them the funds "would be invested in risk-free debt securities (e.g. Treasuries) but were used instead to acquire 'high risk' investments and mortgage-backed securities".[35]

The applicable law here seems to be 29 U.S.C.A. §1104, covering the fiduciary duties of plan administrators. Here the act requires under subsection (a) a prudent man standard of care where "subject to sections 1103(c) and (d), 1342, and 1344 of this title, a fiduciary shall discharge his duties with respect to a plan solely in the interest of the participants and beneficiaries and (A) for the exclusive purpose of: (i) providing benefits to participants and their beneficiaries; and (ii) defraying reasonable expenses of administering the plan; (B) with the care, skill, prudence, and diligence under the circumstances then prevailing that a prudent man acting in a like capacity and familiar with such matters would use in the conduct of an enterprise of a like character and with like aims; (C) by diversifying the investments of the plan so as to minimize the risk of large losses, unless under the circumstances it is clearly prudent not to do so; and (D) in accordance with the documents and instruments governing the plan insofar as such documents and instruments are consistent with the provisions of this subchapter and subchapter III of this chapter." It would appear State Street now recognizes CDOs backed by subprime mortgages do not meet this prudent man test.

---

[32] *Id.*.

[33] *See also* Bajaj, V. "If Everyone's Finger-Pointing." *supra* note 24. Further in 2009 State Street announced it was increasing the amount it had reserved to settle such ERISA related claims.

[34] *See* Bajaj, V. "If Everyone's Finger-Pointing," *supra* note 24. The article notes however these cases will be difficult since the plaintiffs have to prove intent to defraud.

[35] Id.

5.3. Public Relations

Citibank and several other major banks used SIVs to take mortgage-backed securities off their balance sheets especially if they were not easily placed with third party investors. The banks structured the SIVs and sold equity investments in them to final investors. The SIVs then purchased bundled mortgage securities from the bank using loans or repurchase agreements [Repos] thus leveraging the potential return on the investors' equity.[36] In this way the banks got the debt and the mortgages off their balance sheet while reducing their capital requirements. However, they retained the servicing fees on the mortgages and management fees for arranging and managing the SIVs.[37]

When the mortgage market collapsed lenders to the SIVs demanded payment such that SIVs would have to sell the securities at a big loss if they could be sold at all and the investors would be wiped out. Citi and other large banks that had created SIVs where now faced with a choice of alienating their investor clients that they had assured the investments were "safe" or walking away and facing both litigation and client loss. They decided to settle the matter by either taking the mortgages and related debt back onto their balance sheets or guaranteeing the SIVs' debt. In the former case Citi and other large banks with SIVs and hedge funds paid off the investors while in the latter case the Repo lenders did not dump the securities and investors continued to get their return until the mortgages were paid off. In this way the banks have unwound the SIVs and settled their claims with the SIVs' lenders and investors. This was partly based on reputation considerations but also an evaluation that by holding the mortgages to maturity ultimate losses could be minimized.[38]

Though there are some similarities as to structure, these three settlement situations can be distinguished, though, from the *Barclays v. BSAM* case and highlight some of the difficulties facing plaintiffs seeking remedies for their losses. In both the Merrill Lynch and State Street cases the plaintiff was dealing directly with the corporate entity against which it had made a claim. In other words there was privity in the relationship and there was no need to either pierce the corporate veil or prove any vicarious liability. Further even in the Citibank case the investors were only one step removed from the bank and appear to have dealt with the bank in making their investment decision.

In the Bear Stearns case, while Barclays has a good claim against BSAM, Barclays ultimately wants access to the deep pockets of the holding company, The Bear Stearns Companies that JP Morgan Chase acquired, and not just Bear Stearns Asset Management the entity that stood in a Citibank relationship to Barclays as the one structuring and marketing

---

[36] An SIV might raise a billion dollars in equity from investors. It would then use that money to buy mortgage-backed securities. It would then either sell those securities to lenders under repurchase agreements [Repos] using that money to buy more securities, which they would also borrow against until they might have $20-25 billion in securities of which only 1 billion was equity. Another approach was for the SIV to issue commercial paper backed by the securities and a line of credit from the bank that established the SIV or hedge fund. As we will see in the Enhanced Fund case BSAM used a variation of the Repo model to leverage the money contributed by Barclays and the two feeder funds. Since the Repo lenders own the securities they can always sell them to recover their loans and there is no incentive for them to get the best price. Thus in a quick sale any equity value of the security over the Repo loan can disappear and the net asset value of the fund or NAV with it.

[37] In its complaint Barclays asserted that it was these multiple fees that accounted for a large portion of BSAM's net earnings and in turn Cioffi's and Tannin's compensation that provided the scienter for the alleged fraud.

[38] For detailed review *see for example* Citigroup Inc. (2008) "Securitizations And Variable Interest Entities." *Form 8-K, Current Report*, section 23.

the investment. Further in the Citibank case because Citi settled partly for reputation reasons the issue of responsibility and piercing the corporate veil of the SIV was never tested. This is important because in both the Merrill Lynch and State Street Bank cases the investors [Springfield and the pension funds] had their accounts with Merrill and State Street. However in Barclays' situation BSAM was managing an independently incorporated hedge fund in which Barclays was the sole shareholder. Thus there was no account or client relationship, though as discussed below Barclays still asserts a relationship "approaching privity" and that BSAM owed Barclays a fiduciary duty.

Before examining the Barclays' case in more detail, though, we should briefly examine to what extent BSAM and its parent the Bear Stearns Companies knew or should have known that the mortgage backed securities it was purchasing for the Enhanced Leveraged Fund were high risk or below market value. This is because a critical element indicated by the Merrill, State Street, and Citibank SIV settlement situations is that they implicitly acknowledged they had not properly informed their clients of the risks or had made investments knowing those investments exceeded their clients' risk guidelines. Otherwise a good defense would be that everyone was fooled and at the time the investments were made or the fund structured there was no reason to know these securities were so risky.

6. AVAILABLE INFORMATION

The Bear Stearns Companies was a financial holding company listed on the New York Stock Exchange and it was an integrated mortgage-backed securities company with its own mortgage company, EMC Mortgage, an investment bank, Bear, Stearns and Company, that bundled and packaged mortgage securities pools that it then sold to investors including hedge funds. Further some of these hedge funds it managed itself through BSAM. Thus the holding company and its subsidiaries were or should have been fully familiar with publicly available information about the mortgage-backed securities market, with information available directly from regulators and with proprietary information available from its own operations including changes in underwriting standards and data on past due and delinquent loans, foreclosures, and reset schedules. Indeed it used its knowledge and integrated status as part of its overall marketing approach to Barclays and others, such as investors in the two feeder funds that invested in the two hedge funds at issue in the case.

From this perspective the guidance provided as early as February 2003 to all banks by the Federal Reserve Board on behalf of itself and other regulators, including the Office of the Comptroller of the Currency, the Federal Deposit Insurance Corporation, and the Office of Thrift Supervision, is very instructive. In a supervisory guidance letter the Fed advised the banks about its concerns as to their "valuation and hedging of mortgage servicing assets (MSAs) and similar mortgage banking assets."[39] It also provided "guidance on sound risk management practices regarding valuation and modeling processes, management information systems, and internal audit as applied to mortgage banking activities."[40]

---

[39] Board of Governors of the Federal Reserve System (2003) "Risk Management and Valuation of Mortgage Servicing Assets Arising from Mortgage Banking Activities." SR 03-4, available at www.federalreserve.gov.
[40] Id.

This memo and its attached Interagency Advisory suggested a "need for enhanced rigor in the specification and documentation of the underlying assumptions, models, and modeling processes used to value MSAs," including "incorporating available market data in their valuations."[41] "In general, management should ensure that detailed policies, procedures and limits are in place to monitor and control mortgage banking activities, including loan production, pipeline (unclosed loans), and warehouse (closed loans) administration, secondary market transactions, servicing operations, and management (including hedging) of MSAs." In this regard "[m]anagement information reports should provide comprehensive and accurate information on the institution's mortgage banking operations and MSAs."[42] In its Interagency Advisory even at this early date these regulatory agencies indicated that it was sending this message to the banks because while it recognized exposure to mortgage-banking assets was relatively small at that time it was concerned by its growth in response to historically low interest rates and the many borrowers "attracted to new lending products by innovative, low-cost lending programs, widespread use of automated underwriting, and increased competition among banks, thrifts, and other financial institutions." The regulators believed this "high volume of mortgage activity exposes institutions to a number of risks."[43]

They identified these risks as including earnings volatility and erosion of capital from revaluation of MSAs.[44] Other risks included the mortgage loans' actual cash flow performance, documentation risk, timely impairment identification, interest rate risk, hedging strategies, and tracking loan quality. There were also related system monitoring and flagging of risks since it does little good to be concerned about cash flows if an organization's systems are not properly structured to capture and highlight this information. Such information systems should also be tied to the organization's accounting and reporting requirements.

In sum, the regulatory agencies believed and were clearly stating that "institutions engaged in mortgage-banking activities should fully comply with all aspects of their primary federal regulator's policy on interest rate risk. In addition, institutions with significant mortgage-banking operations or mortgage-servicing assets should incorporate these activities into their critical planning processes and risk management oversight. The planning process should include careful consideration of how the mortgage banking activities affect the institution's overall strategic, business, and asset/liability plans. Risk management considerations include the potential exposure of both earnings and capital to changes in the value and performance of mortgage banking assets under expected and stressed market conditions. Furthermore, an institution's board of directors should establish limits on investments in mortgage banking assets and evaluate and monitor such investment concentrations (on the basis of both asset and capital levels) on a regular basis."[45]

This view was reinforced by further Interagency guidance in May 2005.[46] Of particular

---

[41] Id.

[42] Id. The document also states explicitly that its guidance applies to state member banks, bank holding companies, Edge Corporations, and foreign banks both agencies and branches.

[43] Id.

[44] Mortgage servicers capitalize their expected income stream from service contracts and so prepayments or re-financings due to lower interest rates affect these values as would delinquencies and foreclosures. See for example GMAC supra note 13.

[45] "Interagency Advisory On Mortgage Banking." supra note 33.

[46] See Board of Governors of the Federal Reserve System (2005) "Interagency Advisory On Accounting And Reporting For Commitments To Originate And Sell Mortgage Loans." SR 05-10 and "Credit Risk Management Guidance For Home Equity Lending." SR 05-11 available at www.federalreserve.gov.

concern were agreements called *forward loan sales commitments* under a *mandatory delivery contract* where certain institutions had committed to delivering a "certain principal amount of mortgage loans to an investor at a specified price on or before a specified date. If the institution fails to deliver the amount of mortgages necessary to fulfill the commitment by the specified date, it is obligated to pay a 'pair-off' fee, based on then-current market prices, to the investor to compensate the investor for the shortfall."[47] Further one was not allowed to offset these contracts through netting arrangements with other contracts that committed to the purchasing institution delivery of the equivalent mortgages. Thus, the regulators wanted to make sure these exposures were properly recorded in the company's financial accounts.

This was because as shown in the following Table 1 mortgage loan demand began to decrease sharply in the fourth quarter of 2003 through the first quarter of 2005. Thus mandatory delivery could pressure originators to reduce loan quality to meet their obligations rather than pay a fee. The regulators logically wanted to measure this pressure especially since it is also shown in the "Supply and Demand for Residential Mortgage Loans" table that lending standards began to decrease in the first quarter of 2004. Taken together with the rapid growth in Home Equity Lines of Credit [HELOCs] during this period,[48] a clear mortgage lending pattern was emerging as the mortgage market responded to higher interest rates as the Fed tightened credit.

Higher rates meant homeowners were less interested in refinancing, especially those with prime credit. Thus new loans were generally to homebuyers. To continue to deliver a certain principal amount to their clients originators were therefore pressured to reduce credit standards and to extend larger loan to value [LTV] credit than was warranted. They were also induced to lend to people that would not normally qualify [subprime loans]. The logical result was an expanding trend in subprime loans. Lenders also expanded the number and amount of HELOCs.[49]

The regulators saw in these trends, especially the last, the following risks:

- "Interest-only features that require no amortization of principal for a protracted period;
- Limited or no documentation of a borrower's assets, employment, and income (known as 'low doc' or 'no doc' lending);
- Higher loan-to-value (LTV) and debt-to-income (DTI) ratios;
- Lower credit risk scores for underwriting home equity loans;
- Greater use of automated valuation models (AVMs) and other collateral evaluation tools for the development of appraisals and evaluations; and
- Increase in the number of transactions generated through a loan broker or other third party." [50]

Unfortunately as seen in the Mortgage Loan Table the trend of deteriorating mortgage demand and declining credit standards continued through the third quarter of 2006.

---

[47] "Interagency Advisory On Accounting And Reporting For Commitments To Originate And Sell Mortgage Loans." *op. cit.*.

[48] "Credit Risk Management Guidance For Home Equity Lending." *supra* note 46.

[49] *available at* www.federalreserve.gov

[50] *Id.*.

Table 1. Supply and Demand for Residential Mortgage Loans

"Net Percentage of Domestic Respondents Reporting Stronger Demand for Mortgage Loans"[51]

Year - Quarter	All	Prime	Nontraditional	Subprime
1999 - 1	10.00	n.a.	n.a.	n.a.
1999 - 2	8.90	n.a.	n.a.	n.a.
1999 - 3	-33.40	n.a.	n.a.	n.a.
1999 - 4	-41.20	n.a.	n.a.	n.a.
2000 - 1	-63.50	n.a.	n.a.	n.a.
2000 - 2	-42.60	n.a.	n.a.	n.a.
2000 - 3	-39.70	n.a.	n.a.	n.a.
2000 - 4	-32.70	n.a.	n.a.	n.a.
2001 - 1	0.00	n.a.	n.a.	n.a.
2001 - 2	46.10	n.a.	n.a.	n.a.
2001 - 3	24.50	n.a.	n.a.	n.a.
2001 - 4	-1.90	n.a.	n.a.	n.a.
2002 - 1	28.90	n.a.	n.a.	n.a.
2002 - 2	5.60	n.a.	n.a.	n.a.
2002 - 3	27.50	n.a.	n.a.	n.a.
2002 - 4	40.00	n.a.	n.a.	n.a.
2003 - 1	7.40	n.a.	n.a.	n.a.
2003 - 2	17.00	n.a.	n.a.	n.a.
2003 – 3	46.30	n.a.	n.a.	n.a.
2003 – 4	-18.60	n.a.	n.a.	n.a.
2004 – 1	-38.50	n.a.	n.a.	n.a.
2004 – 2	-5.80	n.a.	n.a.	n.a.
2004 – 3	-7.70	n.a.	n.a.	n.a.
2004 – 4	-24.50	n.a.	n.a.	n.a.
2005 – 1	-27.50	n.a.	n.a.	n.a.
2005 – 2	-18.30	n.a.	n.a.	n.a.
2005 – 3	20.40	n.a.	n.a.	n.a.
2005 - 4	-22.20	n.a.	n.a.	n.a.
2006 - 1	-44.00	n.a.	n.a.	n.a.
2006 - 2	-23.10	n.a.	n.a.	n.a.
2006 - 3	-58.50	n.a.	n.a.	n.a.
2006 - 4	-60.40	n.a.	n.a.	n.a.
2007 - 1	-37.00	n.a.	n.a.	n.a.
2007 - 2	n.a.	-18.90	-15.90	-18.80
2007 - 3	n.a.	-10.00	-21.30	-43.80

---

[51] Source: Federal Reserve.

Table 1. (Continued)

Year - Quarter	All	Prime	Nontraditional	Subprime
2007 - 4	n.a.	-51.00	-45.00	-50.00
2008 - 1	n.a.	-60.30	-69.20	-71.50
2008 - 2	n.a.	-24.50	-29.70	-66.60
2008 – 3	n.a.	-30.50	-46.90	-28.60

Unfortunately as seen in the Mortgage Loan Table the trend of deteriorating mortgage demand and declining credit standards continued through the third quarter of 2006. Thus the overall situation during the period in which Barclays was negotiating its deal with Bear Stearns was known to both the regulators and the industry.[52] Indeed the regulators had put the industry at the highest level on notice as to their concerns. In terms of product development for example the regulators noted that "risk management personnel should be involved in product development, including an evaluation of the targeted population and the product(s) being offered. For example, material changes in the targeted market, origination source, or pricing could have a significant impact on credit quality and should receive senior management approval."[53]

In terms of origination and underwriting they stated, "[c]onsistent with the agencies' regulations on real estate lending standards, prudently underwritten home equity loans should include an evaluation of a borrower's capacity to adequately service the debt," and "consider a borrower's income and debt levels and not just a credit score."[54] Consistent with these statements the regulators saw heightened need for "strong collateral valuation management policies, procedures, and processes." This should include establishing "criteria for determining the appropriate valuation methodology for a particular transaction based on the risk in the transaction and loan portfolio. For example, higher risk transactions or non-homogeneous property types should be supported by more thorough valuations. The institutions should also set criteria for determining the extent to which an inspection of the collateral is necessary."[55]

"Loans in excess of the supervisory LTV limits should be identified in the institution's records. The aggregate of high LTV one- to four family residential loans should not exceed 100 percent of the institution's total capital. Within that limit, high LTV loans for properties other than one- to four family residential should not exceed 30 percent of capital."[56] Further firms "should consider stress tests that incorporate interest rate increases and declines in home values. Since these events often occur simultaneously, the agencies recommend testing for these events together."[57]

Finally to put teeth into their guidance the regulators state that "[p]ortfolios of high-LTV loans to borrowers who exhibit inadequate capacity to repay the debt within a reasonable time may be subject to classification. ... Those institutions engaging in programmatic subprime

---

[52] According to Barclays' complaints filed with the Court found at 2008 WL 4499468 their negotiations with BSAM began in March 2006 and closed on July 31, 2006.

[53] "Credit Risk Management Guidance For Home Equity Lending." supra note 46.

[54] Id.

[55] Id.

[56] Id.

[57] Id.

The Global Mortgage Crisis Litigation Fallout

home equity lending or institutions that have higher risk products are expected to recognize the elevated risk of the activity when assessing capital ... adequacy." [58]

In addition the Federal Reserve publishes a quarterly bank Supervisory Report that includes a report on residential mortgage lending. The following Table 2 reporting stronger or weaker loan demand and whether loan standards were being tightened or loosened was included as part of this Report. Looking as this data one can readily see that weaker loan demand and the relaxing of credit standards were very closely tied. This is why between 2005 and 2007 each quarterly supervisory report continually increased its focus on residential mortgage lending often asking special questions related to residential mortgage lending as part of the survey. These reports clearly indicate falling lending standards between the end of 2003 and the end of 2006 coupled with a lower general demand for residential mortgage loans. Thus when in 2006 Barclays and BSAM negotiated their agreement, it represented the weakest part of this period in terms of credit standards.

Based on this publicly available information[59] it was clearly apparent to those in the industry that mortgage lending criteria were deteriorating and that investing in mortgage-backed securities directly or indirectly was becoming increasingly risky with pressures rising on originators to keep the flow going even if this meant a rising proportion of questionable subprime loans. This was the financial environment in which BSAM concluded its deal with Barclays. Nevertheless, if Barclays' factual presentation in its complaint is reasonably correct neither side was really ignorant of the deterioration in the mortgage-backed securities market.[60] Rather to address Barclays' natural concerns given the perceived market and security risks, BSAM presented itself as an integral part of the Bear Stearns mortgage investment operation and that given Bear Stearns integrated operation and position as the leading underwriter of subprime mortgages[61] it had greatly superior monitoring and risk control management systems compared to the competition.[62]

Therefore BSAM through Cioffi and Tannin stated that Barclays should feel very comfortable with BSAM's proposal that Barclay's be the sole shareholder and swap provider in the Enhanced Fund. This is because BSAM's asset management capabilities as demonstrated in its other large hedge fund, the High Growth Fund, showed it could produce higher returns with little risk despite the evolving adverse market conditions for mortgage-backed securities. In other words BSAM in conjunction with other Bear Stearns entities had taken the Fed's best guidance and done it one better.

Further, this stated prudential market approach specifically excluding risks like squared CDOs was negotiated by Barclays and BSAM and written into the Enhanced Fund's investment guidelines, which is an Exhibit in Barclays' amended complaint.[63]

---

[58] Id.

[59] In October 2005 FDIC's President Dan Powell publicly warned about no doc loans with teaser rates. Even earlier in September 2003 a FDIC analyst wrote "Evaluating the Consumer Lending Revolution" noting easing trends in consumer lending, including home mortgages, available at http://www.fdic.gov/bank/analytical/fyi/2003/091703fyi.html.

[60] Barclays Bank Plc V. Bear Stearns Asset Management Inc., Ralph Cioffi, Matthiew Tannin, Bear Stearns and Co. Inc., and The Bear Stearns Companies Inc. [2008 WL 4499468].

[61] Supra note 13.

[62] Barclays Bank Plc V. BSAM, et al [2008 WL 4499468].

[63] Id.

Table 2. Weaker or Stronger Loan Credit Standards for Residential Mortgages

"Net Percentage of Domestic Respondents Tightening Standards for Mortgage Loans"

Year - Quarter	All	Prime	Nontraditional	Subprime
1999 - 1	2.00	n.a.	n.a.	n.a.
1999 - 2	0.00	n.a.	n.a.	n.a.
1999 - 3	-1.90	n.a.	n.a.	n.a.
1999 - 4	-2.00	n.a.	n.a.	n.a.
2000 - 1	-1.90	n.a.	n.a.	n.a.
2000 - 2	-5.60	n.a.	n.a.	n.a.
2000 - 3	0.00	n.a.	n.a.	n.a.
2000 - 4	0.00	n.a.	n.a.	n.a.
2001 – 1	0.00	n.a.	n.a.	n.a.
2001 – 2	3.80	n.a.	n.a.	n.a.
2001 – 3	3.80	n.a.	n.a.	n.a.
2001 – 4	3.80	n.a.	n.a.	n.a.
2002 – 1	1.90	n.a.	n.a.	n.a.
2002 – 2	1.90	n.a.	n.a.	n.a.
2002 – 3	3.90	n.a.	n.a.	n.a.
2002 – 4	10.00	n.a.	n.a.	n.a.
2003 – 1	11.10	n.a.	n.a.	n.a.
2003 – 2	5.70	n.a.	n.a.	n.a.
2003 – 3	1.90	n.a.	n.a.	n.a.
2003 – 4	0.00	n.a.	n.a.	n.a.
2004 – 1	-1.90	n.a.	n.a.	n.a.
2004 – 2	-7.80	n.a.	n.a.	n.a.
2004 – 3	-5.80	n.a.	n.a.	n.a.
2004 – 4	1.90	n.a.	n.a.	n.a.
2005 – 1	-7.80	n.a.	n.a.	n.a.
2005 – 2	-2.10	n.a.	n.a.	n.a.
2005 – 3	0.00	n.a.	n.a.	n.a.
2005 – 4	-3.70	n.a.	n.a.	n.a.
2006 - 1	0.00	n.a.	n.a.	n.a.
2006 – 2	-9.40	n.a.	n.a.	n.a.
2006 – 3	-9.30	n.a.	n.a.	n.a.
2006 – 4	1.90	n.a.	n.a.	n.a.
2007 – 1	16.40	n.a.	n.a.	n.a.
2007 – 2	n.a.	15.10	45.50	56.30
2007 – 3	n.a.	14.30	40.50	56.30
2007 – 4	n.a.	40.80	60.00	55.50
2008 – 1	n.a.	52.90	84.60	71.50
2008 – 2	n.a.	62.30	75.60	77.70
2008 – 3	n.a.	74.00	84.40	85.70

Source: Federal Reserve.

7. MAKING THE CASE FOR DAMAGES, COMPENSATION OR RESCISSION

Since JP Morgan Chase has little concern at this point in time in preserving Bear Stearns' reputation whatever that might be, my focus in examining the Barclays' case is on the claims and remedies available to it under Contractual Misrepresentation and the Securities Statutes. While Barclays' initial claims against BSAM and other Bear Stearns entities[64] were based entirely on allegations of fraud and misrepresentation in entering and implementing their contractual obligations, subsequently the SEC and Department of Justice [DOJ] instituted civil and criminal proceedings against two senior BSAM managers for violations under the 1933 and 1934 Security Acts.[65] This opened the possibility for Barclays to amend its complaint to include a private right of action under these statutes as well.However, while Barclays did amend its complaint to include statements that note these government actions so as to support its case in terms of stating a claim, it did not revise or add to its causes of action any private right of action for violation of the US Securities Laws.[66] There are several possible reasons for this that will be examined below in the Statutory Violations' section.

7.1. Contractual Misrepresentation

Barclays filed its complaint in Federal Court in the Southern District of New York on December 19, 2007 against BSAM et al with respect to consequences impacting it from the bankruptcy of the Enhanced Fund.[67] But the initial private placement relationship between Barclays and BSAM had begun in March of 2006 and given the adverse market situation for mortgage backed securities recognized at that time by both parties it took several months to close the Enhanced Fund deal at the end of July 2006. Still Barclays did not include the Enhanced Fund as a defendant in filing its case, probably because the Fund had already filed for bankruptcy in October two months before Barclays filed its suit in Federal Court. This

---

[64] See Barclays Bank Plc V. BSAM, et al [2007 WL 4718847].

[65] SEC (2008) "SEC Charges Two Former Bear Stearns Hedge Fund Managers With Fraud." Release 2008-115Washington, D.C. available at www.sec.gov. Further, CBS/AP reported on June 19, 2008 the Cioffi and Tannin were arrested by the FBI. See CBS News (2008) "Bear Stearns Pair Surrenders to Feds." CBS Interactive Inc. available at www.cbs.com. Further, just because one is integrated does not mean one has good services across all product lines and services. On September 9, 2008 EMC Mortgage, Bear Stearns' Mortgage Lender and Servicing unit reached a $28 million settlement with the FTC to "redress consumers who have been injured by the illegal practices alleged in the complaint." The settlement bars EMC from misrepresenting amounts due, requires them to rely on reliable evidence to support claims, bars them from charging unauthorized fees especially for property inspections, and prohibits them from initiating foreclosure actions or violating FDCPA, FCRA or TILA. See Federal Trade Commission (2008) "Bear Stearns and EMC Mortgage to Pay $28 Million to Settle FTC Charges of Unlawful Mortgage Servicing and Debt Collection Processes." FTC File No. 062 3031. available at ftc.gov.

[66] See Barclays Bank Plc V. BSAM, et al Third Amended Complaint, July 15, 2008 [2008 WL 4499468].

[67] Barclays Bank Plc v. BSAM, et al. This complaint was later amended in April, June and July of 2008. See 2008 WL 4499468. Interestingly in the initial complaint Barclays does not try to pierce the corporate veil or claim vicarious liability of the holding company for the top employees of BSAM but rather includes the parent Bear Stearns Companies as being an aider and abetter and part of BSAM's scheme to defraud. However, it preserved the possibility of such a vicarious liability claim in its factual representations by stating top BSAM officials reported to a senior manager in the parent, and he later fired and replaced them at BSAM after the Enhanced Fund's meltdown. In its First Amended Complaint filed April 22, 2008 it identified the senior Bear Stearns Companies' manager as the co-President Warren Spector.

was just as well since one suit that was filed against the Fund was ultimately terminated in bankruptcy court in May 2008 with no benefit to the claimant.[68]

Rather Barclays sued BSAM, Ralph Cioffi, Matthew Tannin, Bear Stearns and Co. Inc., and The Bear Stearns Companies Inc.[69] In its complaint it first stated its right to be in Federal Court based on subject matter jurisdiction under 28 U.S.C. §1332 and on meeting the diversity test and the $75,000 minimum claim requirement under the Federal Rules of Civil Procedure. However, to survive a motion to dismiss Barclays' complaint needed to state a cause of action by setting forth facts that if true would meet the required elements of its allegations of fraud and conspiracy.

This would include stating facts indicating that Cioffi and Tannin knowingly with scienter or motivation took explicit actions or actus rea in violation of their fiduciary obligations to Barclays that were deceptive and material on which Barclays' justifiably relied and but for these misrepresentations and deceptive acts Barclays would not have lost millions of dollars. Further Barclays needed to assert that BSAM is liable under the doctrine of vicarious liability for Cioffi's and Tannin's acts. Finally it had to present evidence the other Bear Stearns entities and especially the holding company knew about and facilitated these actions because their timely intervention could have presented the loss.

It addressed these requirements in its initial December 2007 filing and three amended complaints dated April 22, 2008, June 6, 2008 and July 15, 2008. These filings contained the following major factual allegations, claims and representations:

BSAM held itself out both as an entity and as part of an integrated operation as having superior knowledge for evaluating mortgage backed securities and managing the risks inherent in such a portfolio through superior selection and hedging techniques including a proprietary computer modeling system that enabled it to track and monitor the over 2000 securities in the Enhanced Fund's portfolio.Barclays' complaint quotes Bear Stearns' 2006 Annual Report as stating "Our vertically integrated mortgage franchise allows us access to every step of the mortgage process, including origination, securitization, distribution and servicing." It also quotes a BSAM SEC filing describing its risk management approach:

> "The proprietary and third-party surveillance systems used by BSAM were designed to ensure that all assets are reviewed real time and those showing signs of potential credit deterioration or poor performance are designated for further review. BSAM's surveillance systems track over 80,000 securities on a daily basis and monitor the performance of all of our CDO holdings as well as perform in-depth analysis on all the underlying collateral backing such holdings. ... [This real-time system is] designed to be early warning in nature, as opposed to systems that provide alerts only after an asset begins to deteriorate."

Unfortunately Barclays discovered over the next year that this system was not able to monitor and evaluate the Enhanced Fund portfolio as it added more unique out-of-market securities. Thus Barclays alleges in their complaint that the negotiated reporting requirements were not met. Rather Barclays was forced to rely on statements from Tannin and Cioffi as to

---

[68] See1:07-cv-08746-RWS, In Re: Bear Stearns High-Grade Structured Credit Strategies Enhanced Leverage Master Fund, Ltd. Date filed: 10/10/2007; Date terminated: 05/30/2008, available at PACER Service Center.

[69] There are many repetitions of claims and events cited in the various documents filed by the parties in this case as well as in the SEC filings. However they still run more than 600 pages. Therefore the review and analysis presented here synthesizes and highlights what seem to be the major facts and issues.

the Fund's actual performance. The complaint then explains that these verbal and e-mail reports were intentionally misleading. For example Barclays claims it was told hedges were working despite turbulent markets when in fact they were not; particularly after a volatile February market performance Barclays was told the Fund was up almost 5% due to superior asset selection and market hedging when in fact the Fund barely broke even. Then in May BSAM reported to Barclays a 2% positive return when in fact the Fund had tanked 38%. By the end of June there was nothing at all left.

Barclays claims indicate that the scienter for BSAM, Cioffi, and Tannin to reach the initial agreement with Barclays on the Enhanced Fund involved liquidity problems in the High Growth Fund because it was difficult to get Repo credits for several securities. Yet these troubles in the High Growth Fund were withheld from Barclays because BSAM, Cioffi and Tannin needed to form the Enhanced Fund where Barclays would be providing liquidity so that they could use Barclays money to buy illiquid securities from the High Growth Fund for the Enhanced Fund. For this reason Barclays claims BSAM, Cioffi and Tannin also made misrepresentations about the High Growth Fund's performance as an illustration of what they would be able to do with respect to the new Enhanced Fund.

Further the Enhanced Fund and the High Growth Fund provided a large percentage of BSAM's annual earnings and because of this Cioffi and Tannin received millions of dollars in compensation. If the High Growth Fund had fallen this would have had a material adverse effect on BSAM, Cioffi, and Tannin. Indeed this was another reason why BSAM, Cioffi and Tannin misrepresented material information to Barclays about the High Growth Fund's performance when making their pitch for Barclays participation in the Enhanced Fund. It is also why they did not report to Barclays the Enhanced Fund's actual performance during the first part of 2007 since they needed Barclays to keep increasing its participation in the Enhanced Fund like a Ponzi scheme to provide liquidity to both that Fund and the High Growth Fund. And due to these alleged misrepresentations Barclays did increase its participation from $50 million when the Deal was signed in July 2006 to over $500 million in March 2007.

Other material information Barclays claims was withheld was that Bear Stearns the Investment Bank [BSandCo] had put a moratorium on Repos with BSAM relative to the High Growth and Enhanced Funds due to failure to follow regulatory procedures. This situation exacerbated both Funds' liquidity problems. BSAM also did not follow the negotiated investment guidelines presented in the Appendix and in fact bought prohibited CDO squared obligations made up of other CDOs as well as stock in a company called Everquest whose assets were made up of CDOs from the High Growth Fund or pools that BSAM and Bear Stearns had bundled but were not able to place with third party investors.

Importantly Barclays claimed if it had realized any aspect of these and similar facts up until June 2007 the Swap Agreement would have been breached and Barclaywould have exercised its termination clause under the swap agreement with BSAM and if this had been done any time before mid-June 2007 they would not have lost money. However, because they relied on BSAM's, Cioffi's and Tannin's duty to them and trusted that they were operating truthfully Barclays was not able to take this action.[70] Further, Barclays argues that because

---

[70] According to the SEC complaint against Cioffi and Tannin, there were two key contractual arrangements regarding the Enhanced Fund. One was the Asset Management Agreement between BSAM and the Fund incorporated in the Caymans and the second was the Swap Agreement between Barclays and BSAM.

Cioffi and Tannin knew this, they withheld critical data concerning the Enhanced Fund's performance and this was also true for Bear Stearns co-president Spector when he inserted himself into the situation in May 2007. This is their "but for" assertion.

Based on these and other alleged facts and representations in their amended complaint, Barclays stated the following causes of action for which it has sought judicial remedies:[71]

- FIRST - Fraud and Deceit as to Defendants BSAM, Tannin and Cioffi
- SECOND - Fraudulent Concealment as to Defendants BSAM, Tannin and Cioffi
- THIRD - Aiding and Abetting Fraud and Fraudulent Concealment to Defendant Bear Stearns
- FOURTH - Aiding and Abetting Fraud and Fraudulent Concealment Bear Stearns Companies
- FIFTH - Civil Conspiracy Commit Fraud and Fraudulent Concealment BSAM, Tannin, Cioffi
- SIXTH - Civil Conspiracy Commit Fraud and Fraudulent Concealment BSAM, Tannin, Cioffi, Bear Stearns
- SEVENTH - Civil Conspiracy Commit Fraud and Fraudulent Concealment BSAM, Tannin, Cioffi, and Bear Stearns Companies
- EIGHTH - Negligent Misrepresentation as to Defendants BSAM and Tannin
- NINTH - Negligent Misrepresentation BSAM and Tannin During Management andOperation of Structure
- TENTH - Promissory Estoppel as to Defendant BSAM
- ELEVENTH - Breach of Fiduciary Duties Owed Barclay by BSAM, Cioffi and TanninDuring Management and Operation of Structure
- TWELFTH - Aiding and Abetting Breach Fiduciary Duties Owed Barclays by Bear Stearns
- THIRTEENTH - Aiding and Abetting Breach Fiduciary Duties Owed Barclays by Bear Stearns Companies
- FOURTEENTH - Gross Negligence and Negligence With Regard Barclays by BSAM, Cioffi, and Tannin During Management and Operation of Structure

In evaluating these causes of action the ones involving just BSAM, Cioffi and Tannin [1, 2, 5, 8, 9, 10, 11, and 14] seem strong and might get stronger depending on evidence produced in the SEC and DOJ actions. However, the ones involving Bear Stearns or the holding company that is the real target appear more problematic unless co-President Spector can be shown to have knowingly facilitated the fraud in which case the holding company could be brought in under vicarious liability. However, as discussed in the Statutory Violations section below neither he nor the company was named in the SEC complaint. Further, there is evidence presented in the SEC complaint that other BSAM employees as well as employees of BSandCo were fooled by Cioffi and Tannin as well. Thus it should be difficult to pierce the corporate veil and to prove an integrated corporate holding company wide conspiracy to defraud Barclays.[72]

---

[71] Third Amended Complaint Barclays v. BSAM et al at 116-143.

[72] Defense counsels for the holding company, the investment bank, BSAM, Cioffi and Tannin filed a motion April 8. 2008 to postpone discovery for the case pending resolution of the merger between JP Morgan and the Bear

7.2. Statutory Violations

On June 19, 2008 the SEC brought charges of violating sections 10(b) of the 1934 Securities Exchange Act and 17(a) of the 1933 Act against the two former senior managers of BSAM, Ralph Cioffi and Matthew Tannin "for fraudulently misleading investors about the financial state of the firm's two largest hedge funds and their exposure to subprime mortgage-backed securities before the collapse of the funds in June 2007."[73] The SEC's allegations and complaint generally support Barclays' claims.

In addition the Department of Justice at the same time announced Cioffi's and Tannin's criminal indictments on "conspiracy and fraud charges."[74] Thus Barclays would be able to use the information and evidence from the SEC and DOJ cases to support its claims against the two former officers and subsequently against BSAM based on vicarious liability. But it is less clear whether these cases help Barclays extend its claims to Bear Stearns the investment bank or to the holding company, The Bears Stearns Companies Inc., or add anything to its claims based on violations of US Securities Laws or more particularly a private right of action for violation of Section 10(b).[75]

This is because in its investigation and charges against Cioffi and Tannin the SEC identified no other person or entity in its complaint including BSAM, though by listing BSAM as well as other Bear Stearns entities as related parties the SEC preserved the right to

---

Stearns holding company arguing senior management time and legal resources. The court denied their request. However, it did agree in setting the calendar that the case would probably not come to trial for two years. Thus at this point it appeared about have half way through the first part of the litigation process given appeals, etc. The defense counsel for just the companies then filed a motion October 6, 2008 to bar a jury trial and to strike references to any government actions from Barclays' Third Amended Complaint and especially any material from the complaint the SEC filed against Cioffi and Tannin. It is instructive that this time Cioffi and Tannin were not involved in the motion since it was filed subsequent to Cioffi's and Tannin's arrest and the SEC's complaint. It thus illustrates the difficulty BSAM faced because while due to vicarious liability what happens to Cioffi and Tannin affects BSAM it cannot assert Cioffi's or Tannin's evidential exclusion rights such as that using the SEC's claims is too prejudicial. Indeed as the SEC case proceeds due to BSAM's vicarious liability, the investment bank and the holding company might feel they need separate counsel to make sure the corporate veil is not pierced and they are not perceived as a single integrated operation. The October submission also indicated that the companies had moved to dismiss but that the court had not yet granted their motion.

In retrospect it was unlikely the court would grant the companies' motion to bar a jury trial or to strike the SEC allegations from Barclays' Third Amended Complaint. This is because taking the plaintiff Barclays' allegations as true BSAM, Cioffi and Tannin from the beginning misrepresented the situation in the High Growth Fund and their ability to successfully manage such a portfolio in a volatile market. Thus the initial Swap Agreement was entered into fraudulently and one cannot use the terms of a fraudulent contract to bar a plaintiff's legal remedy. Therefore the clause in the Agreement forgoing a jury trial in the case of a contractual dispute would not govern. As to striking the references to all government actions the motion argues that one cannot use references to cases that have not yet been adjudicated to support a claim. However, as with hearsay this would only be true if the truth of the matter asserted or adjudicated were required to support the claim. My understanding of how Barclays is using the SEC complaint is similar to someone actually speaking being the evidentiary issue rather than the words spoken. That is Barclays is indicating to the court that another court based on similar facts and circumstances found that the requirements to state a claim had been satisfied or in the DOJ case a grand jury had found the evidence sufficient to indict Cioffi and Tannin on probable cause. Of course we now know as is covered in the Epilogue that Barclay's withdrew their claim and Cioffi and Tannin were found not guilty by a jury, though civil litigation is continuing.

[73] SEC (2008) "SEC Charges Two Former Bear Stearns Hedge Fund Managers With Fraud." 2008-115. *available at* www.sec.gov. Only the government can proceed under 17(a) but an implied private right of action under 10(b) is well established. *See* Superintendent of Ins. v. Bankers Life and Cas. Co., 404 U.S. 6, 13 n.9 (1971).

[74] Id.

[75] Id.

do so in the future. Thus the SEC-DOJ investigation has so far found "no smoking gun" tying other Bear Stearns entities or personnel to the "fraudulent acts and misrepresentations made by Cioffi and Tannin in connection with the high-profile collapse of two now-defunct hedge funds which they managed; the Bear Steams High-Grade Structured Credit Strategies Fund ('High Grade Fund') and the Bear Steams High-Grade Structured Credit Strategies Enhanced Leveraged Fund ('Enhanced Leverage Fund')."[76]

Indeed in its complaint the SEC notes that at certain times while they were perpetrating their fraudulent acts Cioffi and Tannin made statements that fooled others within both BSAM and the Bear Stearns investment bank that were responsible for marketing the two funds. This hardly supports Barclays' theory of a knowing scheme perpetrated by Bear Stearns as an integrated operation to defraud or harm either Barclays or the investors in the two feeder funds.

With respect to the private action under 10(b) a brief review of the current state of suits under this statute to which investors in the feeder funds as well as those filing the shareholder derivative action suits covered in the next section will probably limited, indicates that Barclays cannot use this statute to get closer to the holding company and is probably better off with its direct claims for fraud and breach of contract under common law than any claims as a private right of action under 10(b) even relative to BSAM. Indeed this is probably why it did not add such a private right of action to its claims even after the SEC/DOJ filings.

Because from a strategic standpoint Barclays' main objective was to access the Bear Stearns Holding Company and in turn the deep pockets of JP Morgan, it remained best to start with the question as to whether a private right of action under §10(b) would support their claim of a scheme involving the holding company. In this regard there are two key Supreme Court cases that control. One is *Central Bank v. First Interstate Bank* where the court ruled that to aid and abet a violation of 10(b) for deceit and manipulation the plaintiff has to show the aider and abetter actually and knowingly participated as a primary actor in the activity.[77] That is it is not sufficient just to show the aider and abetter facilitated the fraud, deception or manipulation. Rather it must have been a primary actor in the deception or manipulation so it would itself be liable under §10(b). This would also be true under the bright line test put forward by the Second Circuit in *Wright v. Ernst and Young LLP.*[78] Since Barclays' complaint basically argues the holding company's knowledge, assistance and facilitation,[79] of BSAM's, Cioffi's and Tannin's fraud, using the Securities Laws will not get Barclays closer to its objective of involving the holding company in its claim.

More recently the Supreme Court in *Stoneridge Inv. Partners, LLC v. Scientific Atlanta, Inc.* specifically rejected the scheme complaint in §10(b) cases.[80] The violation of a Securities

---

[76] Securities And Exchange Commission v. Ralph R. Cioffi and Matthew Tannin, filed Southern District of New York, June 19, 2008 available at www.sec.gov ¶110 "Moreover, the BSAM and BSandC sales forces did not know that Cioffi had transferred nearly half of his original investment out of the Enhanced Leverage Fund. On the contrary, based upon statements by the defendants, the sales forces affirmatively represented to investors during March and April that the funds' managers were adding to their investments." and ¶114, "Relying on his assertions, the BSAM and BSandC sales forces repeated Tannin's claim."

[77] 511 U.S. 164 (1994)

[78] 152 F.3d 169 (2d Cir. 1998) – Here the 2d circuit held Ernst andYoung had to have "directly or indirectly communicated misrepresentations to investors." Barclays presented no evidence that The Bear Stearns Companies or its co-president Warren Spector did that with respect to Barclays.

[79] See Barclays' Third Amended Complaint 4th Cause of Action at 122, 7th Cause of Action at 128 and 13th Cause of Action at 139.

[80] 127 S.Ct. 1873 (2007)

Law complaint in this instance has also lost traction because the SEC and DOJ did not extend these violations by Cioffi and Tannin to other Bear Stearns entities.[81] On top of this fact, due to changes passed by Congress in the 1990s Security Law, defendants have several more tools to counter a private §10(b) suit than they did before, including a scienter requirement and a right to stay discovery during any motion to dismiss.[82] In fact the latter could have actually created untoward delay for Barclays since the defendants have filed motions to dismiss.[83] For these reasons it is not surprising Barclays declined to pick up the 10(b) private right of action but stuck with its more traditional common law approach based on fraud.

Since no other statutory remedy appears to have been available to Barclays, any statutory violation option for them seems to have been foreclosed.

8. EPILOGUE

On February 11, 2009 Bloomberg News reported "Barclays Drops Suit Against Bear Over Fund's Collapse." The report stated "Barclays submitted a notice yesterday to dismiss the suit without the ability to renew it." ... "It dropped the case against all defendants," including Cioffi and Tannin. Barclays and JP Morgan declined to comment further. While it is not possible to break the wall of silence it is logical that despite its strong case against BSAM , Cioffi and Tannin these defendants did not have the resources to make Barclays whole and the expense of pursuing the case only made sense if Barclays could access the deep pockets of JP Morgan Chase. As noted above this was problematical and so the decision to dismiss.[84]

Then in November 2009 a jury acquitted Cioffi and Tannin of the criminal charges brought by the DOJ. However, the SEC's civil complaint continues as well as does that of investors in the two feeder funds.[85]

9. CASE CONCLUSION

While it is clear the current mortgage crisis and its aftermath will continue to involve numerous suits and claims along the whole mortgage origination, packaging, and investment chain for several years, the *Barclays v. BSAM* case illustrates that the likelihood of success will be greatest when there is a direct fiduciary or similar contractual relationship between the plaintiff and the defendant as in the Merrill Lynch Springfield settlement or the claims of Barclays directly against BSAM as a single entity. This would also be true for any claims based on violation of Federal or state statutes as in the State Street settlements. Thus attempts

---

[81] See SEC v. Cioffi and Tannin.

[82] PSLRA or Private Securities Litigation Reform Act of 1995. See Nagy, D., Painter, R. and Sachs, M. (2008) Securities Litigation and Enforcement, 2d Ed., Thomson-West, 9-10.

[83] See "Introduction" of motion to bar jury trial and strike certain references to government actions filed October 6, 2008, available at 2008 WL 4499468.

[84] Weidlich, T. (2009) "Barclays Drops Suit Against Bear Over Fund's Collapse." available at www.bloomberg.com/apps/news?pid=20601103andsid=aWVopdweC040

[85] Since civil suits' "preponderance of the evidence" is a weaker standard than "reasonable doubt" for criminal offenses Cioffi's and Tannin's ultimate liability in this case is yet to be fully determined.

to extend liability and claims to third parties even when owned by the same company in an integrated operation appear problematic.

At the same time this situation argues that from a contractual standpoint going forward potential investors who have been sold on the risk management benefits and access to the market expertise of using an integrated mortgage chain operation, such as Barclays was by BSAM, should alter their contractual demands. The new approach would require that related parties such as the investment bank and the holding company be included as contractual parties with their contributions and oversight responsibilities clearly delineated along with their liabilities in cases of fraud or deception.

This procedure would have the benefit of forcing holding companies to pay close managerial attention to how parts of their mortgage chains are operated and make sure more stringent credit and risk management practices are implemented as the regulators have repeatedly requested.[86] If applied across the board this should also reduce the risk associated with massive defaults as lenders and bundlers become more prudent in their activities.

10. Class Acrion Suits and Corporate Related Actions[87]

10.1. Insider Trading

The SEC filed a complaint against Countrywide Financial Corporation's former CEO, Angelo Mozilo, for insider trading related his sales CFC stock sales between 2005 and 2007 prior to when Countrywide applied for Federal Holding Company status and started reporting a sharp increase in problem loans.[88] His likely defense will be the sales were part of a preplanned selling program. However, the question then is when that program was actually

---

[86] See section above on Available Information.

[87] Complicating these securities related actions are cases brought by state and local governments against various lenders for predatory lending targeted against minorities with massive foreclosures negatively impacting local finances and blighting whole neighborhoods. See for example Powell, M. (2009) "Memphis Accuses Wells Fargo of Discriminating Against Blacks." NY Times. where the City Of Memphis is suing Wells Fargo for such activities having "filed a lawsuit accusing one of the nation's largest banks, Wells Fargo, of singling out black homeowners for high-interest subprime mortgages."
Further states, such as Illinois and Ohio, filed suits against lenders such as Countrywide and more recently have filed suits against loans servicers. See Harris, A. (2008) "Countrywide Settles Fraud Cases for $8.4 Billion." bloomberg.com/apps/news? pid=newsarchiveand sid=aEasVHGtwC9A or Harris, A. (2009) "Ohio Attorney General Sues Barclays Unit Over Loans." bloomberg.com/apps/news?pid=20601087andpos=7 andsid=aX40ie3WgH.s

[88] "Securities and Exchange Commission today [June 4. 2009] charged former Countrywide Financial CEO Angelo Mozilo and two other former executives with securities fraud for deliberately misleading investors about the significant credit risks being taken in efforts to build and maintain the company's market share. Mozilo was additionally charged with insider trading for selling his Countrywide stock based on non-public information for nearly $140 million in profits." Available at www.sec.gov/news/press/2009/2009-129.htm. Further, "[t]he SEC alleges that Mozilo along with former chief operating officer and president David Sambol and former chief financial officer Eric Sieracki misled the market by falsely assuring investors that Countrywide was primarily a prime quality mortgage lender that had avoided the excesses of its competitors." This complaint was filed in Federal Court in Los Angeles."The SEC's complaint alleges that each of the defendants violated Section 17(a) of the Securities Act of 1933, Section 10(b) of the Securities Exchange Act of 1934 and Rule 10b-5 thereunder, and aided and abetted violations of Sections 13(a) of the Exchange Act and Rules 12b-20, 13a-1, and 13a-13 thereunder. The complaint further alleges that Mozilo and Sieracki violated Rule 13a-14 under the Exchange Act."

put in place and the size difference between those plans and prior ones.[89] Under §16 of the Securities Exchange Act of 1934 all officers must report sales of securities and under20A if it can be shown that this was done "while in possession of material, non-public information" the SEC can pursue civil penalties under §21A(2) that can amount to "three times the amount of the profit gained or loss avoided as a result of such unlawful, purchase, sale or communication."

The SEC has issued more detailed Rules and Regulations in terms of their administration of the 1934 Act regarding insider trading, which is covered primarily in Rules 10b5-1 and 10b5-2. Under these Rules it is an affirmative defense to an allegation of insider trading, 10b5-1(c)(1)(i)(A)(3), if the person had "adopted a written plan for trading securities." However, this must be done "before becoming aware of the information" and the plan "did not permit the person to exercise any subsequent influence over how, when, or whether to effect purchases or sales; provided, in addition, that any other person who, pursuant to the contract, instruction, or plan, did exercise such influence must not have been aware of the material nonpublic information when doing so." Any deviation or alteration in the plan including any subsequent hedging arrangements voids this defense. Thus given SEC complaint Mr. Mozilo must show he did not know Countrywide's business model was in jeopardy when he established the plan and neither did the people who were implementing the plan know when they sold the stock. Further there should have been no change in the plan during the period.

This position is in question, however, given the basis of the SEC complaint combined with evidence presented in an earlier and separate derivative suit that shareholders in Countrywide are pursuing against CFC and its officers and directors led by the Arkansas Teacher Retirement System also brought in Federal Court in Los Angeles claiming as in the SEC complaint that they turned a blind eye to deviations from mortgage underwriting standards.[90] As part of their case the "plaintiffs contend that the officers and directors dumped shares even as the company spent $2.4 billion to repurchase its own stock in late 2006 and early 2007".

In his defense as one of those officers Mozilo has claimed as noted above with respect to the SEC complaint that he had complied with the securities laws under a planned selling program. But the federal judge noted in denying the defendants motions to dismiss that Mozilo had revised the program several times, each time increasing the shares to be sold. Indeed in her opinion judge Pfaelzer wrote: "Mozilo's actions appear to defeat the very purpose of 10b5-1 plans". As the trial case proceeds,[91] the shareholders through discovery may find more smoking guns as seems to have been confirmed by the SEC complaint (Morgenson 2008). Given the SEC inquiry Mozilo may thus face stiff penalties in addition to shareholder claims.[92]

---

[89] Morgenson, G. (2008) "Lenders Who Sold and Left." NY Times. Also see relative to suspected securities fraud Hernandez, R. (2008) "Countrywide Said to Be Subject of Federal Criminal Inquiry." NY Times.

[90] Morgenson, G. (2008) "Judge Says Countrywide Officers Must Face Suit by Shareholders." NY Times. The total amount of Mozilo's stock sales during the relevant 3-year period was $474 million.

[91] On December 9, 2009 the federal judge certified all classes in the suit. See securities.stanford.edu /1038/CFC_01/.

[92] Complicating the matter is another derivative suit pursued in Delaware Chancery Court where an agreed settlement on class certification was initially postponed due to issues related to claims of common fraud but then approved August 2009. See delawarelitigation.com/2009/08/articles/chancery-court-updates/chancery-

10.2. Improper Disclosure of or Failure to Report Material Facts[93]

In a class action *Michael Atlas v. Accredited Home Lenders Holding Co.* (WL 80949 [2008]), the plaintiffs lead by the State of Arkansas's Teacher Retirement Plan alleged that Accredited and certain directors concealed the firm's "true financial condition and made materially false and misleading statements regarding the company's operations and income."[94] Particularly they cited the firm's assertions that underwriting standards for subprime borrowers were especially conservative and reserve policies for possible delinquent loans or repurchase obligations were more than adequate. Further the plaintiffs alleged that Accredited did not write down to fair value properties gained by foreclosure. Since Accredited's statements seem to have erroneously and artificially its inflated income, the plaintiffs asserted they had a course of action. In turn the Federal Court in Southern California agreed and denied Accredited's motion to dismiss noting a "prior auditor's refusal during the class period to approve the company's 2006 financial statements before the deadline for filing its form 10-K, and the new auditor requiring the company to restate to increase its allowance for loan losses by over $30 million."[95]

Nevertheless these cases do not fall all one way. While in *Atlas* the court agreed with the plaintiffs that they had met their burden of showing a cause of action and thus the case could proceed, in 2007 another class action suit, *Claude A. Reese v. IndyMac Bancorp*, No. 07-CV-01635, where the plaintiffs also claimed the company had overly touted its business prospects, "the court dismissed the case without prejudice, finding among other things –

court-approves-class-action-settlement-involving-countrywide-and-attorneys-fees-for-plaintiffs-attorneys-based-on-therapeutic-disclosures/.

[93] Several mortgage lenders and underwriters have been accused of taking inadequate reserves or not properly accounting for returned mortgages pools or those held in portfolio even while delinquencies and foreclosures have been rising and could reach epidemic proportions nationwide. See article on New Century by Bajaj, V. and Cresswell, J. (2008) "A Lender Failed. Did Its Auditor?", NY Times. This is particularly troublesome because some legal obstacles are starting to emerge to the foreclosure mills that certain law firms have organized to deal with these problems. One Federal District Court ruled "that the plaintiff-lenders failed to show Article III standing because they did not prove that each was the holder of the note and mortgage on each property when the foreclosures were filed. The court refused to accept documents showing an intent to convey the rights in the mortgages – as opposed to proof of ownership." Further, the FTC may bring "unfair and deceptive marketing actions" against some lenders that marketed "non-traditional" mortgages and the Department of Justice's Civil Rights Division could bring enforcement actions against lenders who aimed higher cost and riskier products at a protected class. Mintz, S. (2008) "Subprime Mortgage Meltdown Spurs Wave of Litigation." Litigation News. Further the US Trustee Program that is a unit of the Justice Department overseeing the integrity of the bankruptcy system is bringing cases against lenders and indirectly their law firms for abusing the bankruptcy system. In one case in Georgia they are specifically suing Countrywide. These abuses arise from legal "foreclosure mills" that get "paid by number of motions filed in foreclosure cases." Volume and speed are their metrics. However some judges have begun to sanction firms for filing faulty motions. See Morgenson, G. and Glater, J. "The Foreclosure Machine," supra note 15. Revenues come from: eviction and appraisal charges, late fees, title search costs, recording fees, certified mailing costs, document retrieval fees, and legal fees. Fidelity National Default Solutions is one of the biggest foreclosure service companies with revenues of $448 million in 2007. Two smaller law firms Wilson Castle Daffin and Frappier in Houston and McCalla, Raymer, Padrick, Cobb, Nichols and Clark in Atlanta are actively pursuing this business. The former had estimated 2007 foreclosure related fees of roughly $11 million and the latter had over $10 million from Countrywide alone, Id. However, some possible improper fee sharing arrangements between some law firms and the foreclosure-servicing firms have come to light, Id. Such situations bring into question whether lenders and underwriters have correctly estimated the time and effort needed to handle foreclosures and have adequately accounted for the likely recoveries or related costs.

[94] See Brejcha, B. and Richmond, K. (2008) "The Subprime Crisis: Investigating and Defending Disputes." ABA On-Line Journal.

[95] WL 80949 (2008)

absent significant insider sales during the class period – that the complaint did not satisfy the heightened scienter requirements of *Tellabs*."[96]

While many actions remain in early stages some have made it through a court adjudication and settlement process. *Atlas v. Accredited Home Lenders Holding*, which is a derivative class action suit, is one and it did involve a large sophisticated financial loan originator and packager as well as some large sophisticated investors.[97] Accredited is a mortgage banking company originating, servicing and selling pools of primarily sub-prime mortgage loans that rode the US housing and mortgage securitization boom. In turn it established a REIT [Real Estate Investment Trust] subsidiary that bought mortgage backed securities. The REIT in turn sold and publicly listed its preferred shares with Accredited owning all the common stock. The company's officers and directors as well as the officers and directors of the REIT were sued in Federal Court in Southern California in a derivative action by their shareholders with the lead plaintiff being the Arkansas Teacher Retirement System. The defendants in turn made a motion to dismiss which was not granted.

The Court, however, did divide the case in two by finding that while the officers and directors of the parent company whose stock was listed in 2003 may have made false statements there is not sufficient evidence that the directors of the REIT made any false statements. Therefore the derivative suit against the REIT directors by the REIT preferred shareholders was dismissed. However, the court found the following allegations against particularly the officers of parent were persuasive enough to survive the motion to dismiss and thus the derivative class action case could still proceed. These claims included allegations very similar to those made in other shareholder actions against corporate participants in the great subprime mortgage meltdown that have had their balance sheets, income statement and stock prices hammered. Thus this case may represent somewhat of a template for those that are coming or in process.[98]

1) The plaintiffs alleged the defendants intentionally made false Statements in order to conceal Accredited's real financial condition and made materially false and misleading statements regarding the company's operations and income, the purpose being to artificially inflate the firm's stock price. Once the real situation was apparent the stock price plummeted. A major problem was that Accredited borrowed funds in the wholesale financial markets to fund their mortgage loans unlike the traditional SandL's that used retail saving's deposits. These loans were in turn supported by securitized pools of subprime mortgages where Accredited had agreed as part of their financing arrangements to buy back loans and mortgages that became impaired. Therefore just as a bank will provide reserves on its balance sheet for expected loan losses it was an important aspect of Accredited's business model to take reserves against such possible buybacks. But accounting rules require such increases in reserves to be charged against earnings. This would naturally affect the stock price.

2) As part of the securitization process and their funding arrangements the company had to make certain representations and warranties concerning the underwriting standards they were using in making the loans. The suit alleged as these standards deteriorated

---

[96] Id.

[97] Id.

[98] *See for example* report on New Century and its accounting for reserves, footnote 93.

the firm continued to make the same representations and warranties implying that there would be no need to change the size of the reserves for returned mortgages. These warranties were also false and thus misleading as to the company's real financial condition.

3) When a mortgage lender forecloses on a property the lender now owns the property and must carry it as an asset while trying to sell it. But frequently it will not be able to sell it for the amount of the original mortgage. There are also carrying costs in terms of property taxes, insurance and utilities while the firm looks for a buyer. There also brokers' fees to be paid. All these considerations imply that a reserve be established for such owned real estate reflecting the amount of impairment in asset values. In this case the plaintiff's argue the defendants intentionally under-reserved.

After considering these arguments and the supporting evidence the court found the plaintiffs had shown enough that their claims could not be dismissed except against the non-officer directors of the REIT and the case could proceed.[99]

11. CONCLUSION

11.1. Summary

This paper has examined some of the legal causes of action related to the subprime mortgage meltdown. Since the related securities were sold globally some of these suits have involved foreign parties suing in both US and foreign courts. In this way the US housing bubble fueled by the aggressive securitization of mortgages organized and distributed by a number of large financial institutions has created its own corresponding legal bubble in both class action and direct party claims as various claimants look for their share of the remaining cash flow or restitution by others not in bankruptcy and with deep pockets.

Yet it is clear many of the large financial firms that created the problem have taken huge hits and in many respects did not fully understand the risks they were assuming or selling to others. Therefore from a legal point viewpoint in terms of a defense against potential plaintiffs this "honest belief" in a security's value and the absence of intent to defraud may prove the best defense in various legal actions. Also arguing for this legal strategy is the higher defendant intent and participation bar that plaintiffs must hurdle as set by the Supreme

---

[99] There were also claims related to an acquisition and alleged violation of US securities laws. However, these claims appear on the whole to be particular to this case whereas the allegations related to failure to disclose material information or the disclosure of deliberately misleading information related to appropriately accounting for reserves are quite similar to those arising in other derivative class action suits involving mortgage lenders and underwriters. So the reserve issue and its impact on income, net equity, and the stock price are likely to be at the center of many such suits. Therefore the court's treatment of these allegations in this case could be an indicator of how this and other courts will treat defendants' motions to dismiss or for summary judgment in the cases to come.

By way of a conclusion to the suit, "on August 4, 2009, Judge Marilyn L. Huff preliminarily approved the settlement. The Final Settlement Hearing [was] scheduled on November 2, 2009. On November 4, 2009, Judge Marilyn L. Huff signed the Final Order Approving Settlement and Plan of Allocation and Granting Plaintiffs' Motion for Award of Attorneys' Fees and Other Expenses. The Court grant[ed] the attorneys' fees in the amount of $5,317,936.16, and reimbursement of litigation expenses in the amount of $728,255.35." A brief litigation calendar and history is *available at* securities.stanford.edu/1037/LEND_01/.

Court in recent cases. Thus most suits will probably be decided case by case. What is clear from all this, however, is that lawyers and the law have been and continue to be very heavily involved in every step of the subprime crisis and its related financial fallout.

11.2. Lawyer Involvement

Even traditional direct mortgage lending involved extensive documentation in terms of land records, building certificates, zoning, easements, loans, recordings and mortgages. The securitization boom then added several more complex contractual layers to this basic legal structure for real estate, particularly residential, to bundle the mortgages and then slice and dice the cash flows. Further to get the assets and attendant liabilities off their balance sheets or to offset default risk, the financial institutions created new vehicles and financial instruments such as CDOs [collateralized debt obligations], SIVs [structured investment vehicles], and CDSs [credit default swaps]. All these financial innovations required extensive legal documentation that lawyers supplied. This work generated millions in fees.

In sum lawyers provided documentation and legal structures for every part of the subprime paper generation process from origination and securitization to structuring complex mortgage backed trust certificates on the upside to foreclosure mills on the downside. One might even assert that without lawyers and their ability to structure and document complex transactions the subprime mortgage boom and bust might not have been possible. It is clear lawyers are also heavily involved in dealing with the aftermath since they are the ones pursuing or defending various civil actions on behalf of their clients or criminal prosecutions on behalf of the government and defendants.[100] They are and will continue to be involved in writing the laws and regulations designed to deal with the consequences flowing from the subprime collapse such as massive foreclosures and increased bankruptcies. They will also be called upon to draft laws and regulations seeking to prevent similar future meltdowns.

Unfortunately as is true with many booms and busts everything happens in a rush on the upside and accelerates even faster on the downside. Therefore in many cases the documentation was done at a rush and on the cheap due to the pressure on fees and the incentive to maximize revenues with lawyers perhaps telling themselves it was OK because US housing prices had always trended up. Thus the stability of the supporting cash flows and the underlying value of a house as an asset guaranteed the documentation would never be tested. The underlying loans would just be rolled over or refinanced. This may also have been true when filing corporate disclosure documents with the SEC such as 10Ks. However, as the housing market began to collapse and more loans fell behind in terms of monthly payments or went into default, the chinks in the legal armor became apparent. As the *Financial Times* recently reported "many deals suffer from poorly worded documentation and there are cases where the trustee does not know how to proceed." This has complicated lawsuits as holders of different tranches with different rights fight about a decreasing cash pie.[101]

---

[100] For the expanding scope of criminal actions see footnotes 4 and 5.

[101] Mackenzie, M. "'Super-senior' CDO investors begin to flex their muscles." *supra* note 26. He quotes Janet Tavakoli of Tavakoli Structured Finance as opining that "[a] lot of senior note holders did not do their job and ask for clarity on the documentation of deals."

However, some trustees have moved to protect cash flows. Deutsche Bank and Wells Fargo have already sued to ensure payments to credit holders of trusts they administer.[102] In addition as explained in footnote 93 some lawyers representing lenders in foreclosure actions have come up short in front of judges demanding documentation that shows their clients actually hold registered mortgages on the properties for which they seek foreclosure.

Yet it somehow seems wrong that lawyers should benefit through the cost of litigation or foreclosure on the downside from their or other lawyers' errors or slipshod work on the upside where they were also compensated. Lawyers under Model Rule 1.3 Comment [2] in order to act diligently on behalf of their clients are supposed to manage their time as part of their responsibilities to properly and diligently represent their clients.

Exposing clients to financial losses or litigation by not taking documentary precautions relative to what were certainly possible risks in the supporting cash flows for various structured assets probably does not meet the hurdle for malpractice but it certainly raises questions the profession should be asking itself. Indeed the ethical issues for the profession related to this mess along with many of the related cases will be with us for years to come. Further given the scope and complexity of the underlying securities and contractual arrangements, the related legal actions are likely to persist even through the next boom and bust whatever that is. Therefore it might be appropriate for the ABA to initiate a discussion on the proper role for lawyers in facilitating and professionally exploiting such events on both sides of the bubble. On the other hand this may just evolve as governments and central banks begin to explore regulatory approaches to controlling asset bubbles, a process that is already under way. In this manner the lawyer as policeman versus the lawyer as facilitator should be part of the conversation.

REFERENCES

Anderson, J. (2008) "Massachusetts Accuses Merrill Of Fraud." *NY Times.*
Bajaj, V. (2008) "F.B.I. Opens Subprime Inquiry." *NY Times.*
Bajaj, V. (2008) "If Everyone's Finger-Pointing, Who's To Blame?" *NY Times.*
Bajaj. V. and Cresswell, J. (2008) "A Lender Failed. Did Its Auditor?", *NY Times.*
Board Of Governors Of The Federal Reserve System (2003) "Risk Management And Valuation Of Mortgage Servicing Assets Arising From Mortgage Banking Activities." SR 03-4, *available at* www.federalreserve.gov.
Board of Governors of the Federal Reserve System (2005) "Interagency Advisory On Accounting And Reporting For Commitments To Originate And Sell Mortgage Loans." SR 05-10 *available at* www.federalreserve.gov.
Board of Governors of the Federal Reserve System (2005) "Credit Risk Management Guidance For Home Equity Lending." SR 05-11 *available at* www.federalreserve.gov.
Brejcha, B. and Richmond, K. (2008) "The Subprime Crisis: Investigating and Defending Disputes." *ABA On-Line Journal.*
Bruck, C. (1989) *The Predators' Ball: The Inside Story of Drexel Burnham and the Rise of the Junk Bond Raiders.* Penguin Books.

---

[102] van Duyn, A. and MacKenzie, M. *supra* note 26.

CBS News (2008) "Bear Stearns Pair Surrenders to Feds." *CBS Interactive Inc.available at* www.cbs.com.

Citigroup Inc. (2008) "Securitizations And Variable Interest Entities." *Form 8-K, Current Report*, section 23.

Countrywide Financial, *2006 10K*, 3-17. *at*about.countrywide.com/SECFilings /Form10K.aspx.

Davis, P. and Wighton, D. (2008) "CDO Case May Not Be Foretaste Of Suits To Come."*Financial Times*.

FDIC (2003) "Evaluating The Consumer Lending Revolution." *available at* http://www.fdic.gov/bank/analytical/fyi/2003/091703fyi.html.

Federal Trade Commission (2008) "Bear Stearns And EMC Mortgage To Pay $28 Million To Settle FTC Charges Of Unlawful Mortgage Servicing And Debt Collection Processes." FTC File No. 062 3031. *available at* ftc.gov.

General Electric, *2005 10K. available at* www.sec.gov.

General Motors, *2005 Annual Report. available at*http://www.gmacmortgage.com/index.html

Gibeaut, J. (2007) "Mortgage Fraud Mess." *ABA Journal*.

Gramlich, E. (2007), *Subprime Mortgages*. Urban Institute Press, Washington, D.C.

Grant, J. (2008) "FBI Opens Subprime Fraud Inquiries." *Financial Times*.

Hamilton, W. (2008) "Lawyers Smell Opportunity As Subprime Suits Start To Boom." *Los Angeles Times*.

Harris, A. (2008) "Countrywide Settles Fraud Cases For $8.4 Billion." *Available at* bloomberg.com/apps/news?pid=newsarchiveandsid=aEasVHGtwC9A

Harris, A. (2009) "Ohio Attorney General Sues Barclays Unit Over Loans." *Available at* bloomberg.com/apps/news?pid=20601087andpos=7andsid=aX40ie3WgH.s

Hernandez, R. (2008) "Countrywide Said To Be Subject Of Federal Criminal Inquiry."*NY Times*.

Kindleberger, C. And Aliber, R. (2005), *Manias, Panics, And Crashes*. John Wiley, NJ.

Korngold, G. And Goldstein, P. (2002) *Real Estate Transactions*. Foundation Press, NYC, 359.

Mackenzie, M. (2008) "Super-senior CDO Investors Begin To Flex Their Muscles." *Financial Times*.

Mintz, S. (2008) "Subprime Mortgage Meltdown Spurs Wave of Litigation." *Litigation News*.

Morgenson, G. (2008) "Judge Says Countrywide Officers Must Face Suit By Shareholders." *NY Times*.

Morgenson, G. (2008) "Lenders Who Sold And Left." *NY Times*.

Morgenson, G. And Glater, J. (2008) "The Foreclosure Machine."*NY Times*.

Neil, M. (2007) "N.Y. Lawyer Stole $24M, Gets 10 Years." *ABA Journal*.

Neil, M. (2007) "More Law Firms Seek To Sue Banks." *ABA Journal*.

Pierson, H. (2007) "Mortgage Fraud Boot Camp: Basic Training Of Defending A Criminal Mortgage Fraud Case." *The Champion*, National Association Of Criminal Defense Lawyers, 14.

Powell, M.(2009) "Memphis Accuses Wells Fargo of Discriminating Against Blacks." *NY Times*.

Rapp, W. (2004) *Information Technology Strategies*. Oxford University Press, NYC, 214-246.

SEC (2008) "SEC Charges Two Former Bear Stearns Hedge Fund Managers With Fraud." Release 2008-115, Washington, D.C. *available at* www.sec.gov.

SEC (2009) "Securities and Exchange Commission Today Charged Former Countrywide Financial CEO Angelo Mozilo And Two Other Former Executives With Securities Fraud." *Available at* www.sec.gov/news/press/2009/2009-129.htm.

Sloan, A. (2007) "House Of Junk." *Fortune*, 117-124.

Van Duyn, A. And Mackenzie, M. (2008) "Tranche Warfare Breaks Out Over CDOs." *Financial Times*.

Weidlich, T. (2009) "Barclays Drops Suit Against Bear Over Fund's Collapse." *available at* www.bloomberg.com/apps/news?pid=20601103andsid=aWVopdweC040

Weiss, D. (2007) "Judges Crack Down On Law Firm 'Foreclosure Mills'." *ABA Journal*.

Weiss, D. (2007) "Suits Follow Mortgage Meltdown." *ABA Journal*.

Yamada, Y. And Kubo, T. (2008) *Japanese Major Banks*. Merrill Lynch Japan Securities, Tokyo.

In: After the Crisis: Rethinking Finance
Editor: Thomas Lagoarde-Segot

ISBN 978-1-61668-925-4
© 2010 Nova Science Publishers, Inc.

Chapter 5

FROM FINANCE TO GREEN TECHNOLOGY ACTIVIST STATES, GEOPOLITICAL FINANCE AND HYBRID NEOLIBERALISM

Federico Caprotti

ABSTRACT

This chapter considers financial and world markets as stages on which geopolitical, international relations, conflicts and tensions are being articulated in a post-Cold War world. The aim of this chapter is to explore the ways in which the financial crisis has exposed the webs of political and financial interdependency among states, and the mechanisms of power projection which can be deployed through financial markets and financial actors such as state investment vehicles. Particular emphasis will be placed on, firstly, the increasing financial interdependency of states which share significant banking overlaps, due to regulatory environments and financial firms functioning and spreading risks across boundaries, resulting in the potential political tool of 'offloading risk' across state boundaries. This will be carried out with a case study of Iceland's economic collapse in 2008, and the resulting effect on relations with the United Kingdom, Scandinavian countries and Russia. Secondly, the role of 'state financial actors' will be analysed: these are actors such as state investment and private equity firms which are strategically deployed to ostensibly take advantage of economic opportunities outside state boundaries. This chapter argues that such firms can be seen both in terms of economic actors, *and* as power-projection. Thirdly, this chapter argues that the state should today be seen as a geopolitical actor in financial markets, and that the financial crisis has provided clear opportunities for states to involve themselves in innovative rounds of policy-making, most notably financial re-regulation, as explored elsewhere in the book, and the boosting of green technology investment and international emissions standards negotiations through the inclusion of the 'green economy' in states' response to the crisis through 'green' stimulus programmes. Examples of this will be drawn from the USA, China, and South Korea.

1. INTRODUCTION

The years between 2007 and 2010 have seen startling, systemic changes in the global economy. World-leading finance houses have been nationalised or have rapidly imploded; the 'credit crunch' and restrictions in liquidity have led to global recession; and political fractures have arisen as wealthy states have been brought to the brink of national bankruptcy or, in less extreme cases, have been forced to plunge into long-term, large-scale debt. The title of this book suggests that the current financial crisis requires us to 'think otherwise'. It does, indeed, seem as though many commentators, pundits and scholars are attempting at all costs to think outside the box, or at least to try and place the crisis in boxes or categories which make it easier to understand and grapple with this rapid and dramatic turn of events (Montgomerie and Williams, 2009). Some have suggested that the crisis has emphasised not only fractures in financial markets, but in neoliberalism itself: thus, the financial crisis is seen as paralleled by a 'crisis of neoliberalism' (Chorev and Babb, 2009). In the following, I want to suggest that the crisis has, in many ways, engendered an evolution of neoliberalism, and that evidence of this can be found in the changed role of the state and the new geopolitical spatialities of finance.

The lens through which the financial crisis is analysed in this chapter is one which sees neoliberalism – in governance, policy, and finance – as a *process*. The chapter takes issue with depictions of neoliberalism as monolithic on the one hand, or as a system in the throes of terminal crisis as a result of the 'credit crunch' on the other. Rather, neoliberalism is understood as having passed through a process of transition during 2007-10, a period of change which rooted in earlier events (Konings, 2009). It is argued that changed neoliberal forms of economic and financial governance have emerged from the crisis in the credit markets, and that actually existing neoliberalism can today be described as 'hybrid neoliberalism'. This is characterized, first and foremost, by a financial and geopolitical landscape populated by what I have called 'activist states': those states which have started acting in ways akin to activist investors (such as value hedge funds and private equity firms) as a response to the crisis. The nationalization of banks in various countries can therefore be seen in the light of states increasingly acting like investors, taking significant stakes in specific financial firms, and taking on the mantle of activist investors in influencing corporate decision-making, strategy, and direction.

The role of activist states is explored in the next section. The following section then explores the new geopolitical configurations found in a landscape in which activist states are increasingly prominent. In order to do this, the section focuses on the case of the collapse of Iceland's banking sector in late 2008, and the resulting formation of interactions between activist states (Iceland, other Nordic countries, the UK, the Netherlands, and Russia) in its aftermath. Particular attention is given to the fact that: a.) in the their new roles as majority shareholders in financial firms, activist states also have to operate in *cross-border* fashion, mimicking the range of international activities found at the inter-firm level in globalised markets; and b.) activist states are also increasingly becoming active in taking stakes not only in private firms, but in *other states* as well, as is the case with loans and guaranteed currency swaps arranged with other states. In so doing, activist states invest in other states, and reap potential economic, and certain geopolitical dividends. The activist state can therefore be described as a player in the geopolitical arena of finance.

Finally, the last section focuses on one other characteristic of the crisis: the large-scale deployment of stimulus programs and packages by a variety of countries, from the US to South Korea. This could again be seen as a symptom of a 'crisis' affecting former light-touch neoliberal economic governance. However, the section argues that stimulus packages can be seen as strategic decisions by activist states: stimulus funds are tools through which these states take stakes *in their own economies*, and become capital allocators. Resultantly, states target those sectors which are seen as holding promise for initiating or powering recovery from crisis, and delivering positive returns on invested tax monies in the medium term. The section focuses on the large amounts of stimulus funding allocated to green technology by a wide range of states, as a result of the recent development of new policy and economic drivers for what has been called the 'low carbon economy'. Investing in green technology as part of recovery programs can therefore be interpreted as a targeted, opportunistic strategy focused on recovery and the creation of potentially profitable and market-leading sectors within the domestic economy. Thus, activist states can be understood, in a hybrid neoliberal framework, as strategic and active investors in private firms, other states, *and* specific sectors within their own economies.

2. GEOPOLITICAL FINANCE, HYBRID NEOLIBERALISM AND THE ROLE OF THE ACTIVIST STATE

In 2010, the financial and geopolitical landscape is different, structurally and contextually, from its composition in the years before the crisis. Individual states – even those rhetorically averse to market interventions, like the US and the UK – have entered the market as owners of newly nationalized banks and finance houses; the regulatory competency of financial institutions from the Bank of England to the Federal Reserve has been questioned; and renowned finance houses, once the spearheads of neoliberal capitalism, have gone bust and disappeared from the market altogether. The following briefly analyses what has been built on the ashes of the financial crisis, and specifically how finance and the state have re-engaged, so that the state is now an active player in world markets, and markets are now arenas of geopolitical tension and conflict as a result of the state's rediscovered industrial-financial role. Specifically, the section argues that neoliberalism has not entered a period of crisis as a result of recent events (Torbat, 2008); rather, the reformulation of state and institutional roles in the international economy has led to what may be termed a 'hybrid neoliberalism': an evolution of neoliberalism in which market logic is not only regulated and lightly directed by government, but increasingly incorporated into the sphere of state-run economic activities. This has been made possible through the development of a new role for the state: governments, by taking stakes in key financial firms, have started acting in much the same way as activist investors.[1]

---

[1] For an early discussion of the state as an activist investor, see Caprotti (2009).

2.1. Hybrid Neoliberalism

In the late 1990s and 2000s, much scholarly effort was expended in attempting to conceptualize financial policy in light of a wider neoliberalization of the economy and of government institutions, functions and remits. It is useful here to provide a broad, workable definition of neoliberalism as an economic-political system which calls for: a roll-back of state functions, the deregulation of national and international economic transactions, and 'the privatization of state-owned enterprises and state-provided services; the use of market proxies in the residual public sector; and the treatment of public welfare spending as a cost of international production, rather than as a source of domestic demand' (Jessop, 2002: 107). These trends were prevalent throughout the period ranging from the 1970s to the current financial crisis. However, some of the underlying assumptions and tenets of neoliberalism – chief among these the reduction of the role of the state in market and financial regulation – have been questioned as a result of the crisis. In particular, government ownership of formerly private finance houses has highlighted tensions in established understandings of the finance-state nexus under neoliberalism.

Finance is key to analyses of neoliberalism. Indeed, it is the 'close connection with the internationalization of capital and the globalization of markets' (Duménil and Lévi, 2005: 17) which has seen finance placed as a driving force behind the development of neoliberalism. This has not occurred in a political vacuum: from monetarist policies in 1980s Britain, to French institutional views of neoliberal policies as tools with which to adapt a national economic system to the demands of the new global economy, institutions have played a key part in bringing about neoliberalization (Fourcade-Gourinchas and Babb, 2002; Jessop, 2002; Peck, 2001). Institutional involvement has been ramified at a variety of scales, so that scholars now speak of neoliberalization and the neoliberal economy at scales which range from the national and global, to the local. For example, analyses of local-scale neoliberalism have tackled place-specific policies such as Urban Development Projects (UDPs) in Europe (Swyngedouw, Moulaert and Rodriguez, 2002), rural support programs in Mexico (Klepeis and Vance, 2003), and the welfare state (Larner, 2000). Nonetheless, finance can be seen as a key driver behind neoliberalization, in tandem with the state.

What can be said, then, of the 'crisis' of neoliberalism engendered by the re-enmeshment of the state with private financial firms and the markets? A key question is whether the financial crisis has caused a crisis of neoliberalism (Torbat, 2008), or whether we are witnessing a readjustment (or stabilization) of neoliberal forms of government (Bakker, 2005). As Peck (2004: 394) has argued, 'neoliberalism cannot be reduced to a simple process of replacing states with markets because, in practice, 'privatized' or 'deregulated' markets still have to be managed and policed (often by a new breed of neoliberal technocrats)'. Likewise, the recent financial crisis has not heralded a replacement of markets with state intervention and ownership. Rather, the resulting policy and financial landscape has become hybridized, with states increasingly involved in running financial corporations, and negotiating across borders in order to organize new ways of communication and interaction between these new state-owned entities. The market has not disappeared: instead, the state has been forced into the market as a new player.

2.2. The Rise of the Activist State

The state has become the *activist state*. What is an activist state? As described above, it is a state acting in the same, or similar, ways as an activist investor. In general, an activist investor is understood to be those individuals or firms which acquire significant equity holdings in a company, in order to gain influence over the target firm and force changes in its direction, strategy, management, or operations (Engelen, Konings and Fernandez, 2008). Activist investors are most commonly hedge funds, institutional investors, groups of individual investors, or an individual investor with access to large amounts of capital (Smith, 1996). Such investors target firms where value can be realized through changes in management, board makeup, investment policies, and strategic decisions; these changes are made possible through the shareholder activism which becomes possible when control of a substantial amount of equity is achieved (Ryan and Schneider, 2002).[2] Although the overall effect of activism on share values and earnings are debated (see Karpoff, 2001), what interests us here is the notion of the activist investor as an institution or group of social actors who decide to actively participate in influencing a firm's direction by directly engaging with ownership structures and channels. It is in this light that this chapter argues that the state has, in the aftermath of the financial crisis, effectively become an activist state; this has had repercussions economically, socially and geopolitically.

The financial crisis has heralded the era of the activist state. Since 2007, governments have been proactively changing the ways in which they interact with financial firms and with systems of financial regulation and governance. The crisis has caused national governments to take increasingly significant stakes in private firms and corporations. The stated motivation is the preservation of these companies from failure, taking pre-emptive action to stabilize domestic markets and thus avoiding shocks stemming from problems of liquidity and credit. Nonetheless, some states have gone even further, and individual members of government have taken steps, such as public exhortations for changes in management practices, previously left to leading or 'celebrity' activist investors in industry, such as Carl Icahn, a well-known private equity investor, or Daniel Loeb, head of $5.5 billion hedge fund Third Point LLC. This was the case, for example, with UK prime minister Gordon Brown's public calls for changes in 'bonus cultures' and risk/reward structures in banks in the City of London in February 2009 (Griffiths, 2009), and his threat of a 'bonus tax', in December of the same year, if measures were not voluntarily taken by finance houses (Elliott and Wintour, 2009). Other activist states, most notably France and Germany, publicly backed these calls (Traynor, Clark and Treanor, 2009), which resulted in Goldman Sachs announcing a suspension in bonuses for its top 30 executives at the end of the year.

Examples of governments intervening in the market by placing financial firms under state ownership abound. For example, the British government has nationalized Bradford and Bingley, Royal Bank of Scotland and HBOS, a large UK mortgage and savings firm (Vina and Stirling, 2008; Kennedy, 2008). Northern Rock, an early casualty of the crisis, was nationalized in 2007. In the US, the overall bailout package announced by the government was of over $700 billion. In Denmark, Roskilde Bank was bought out for $7.2 billion by the

---

[2] For example, activist investors may propose changes to management or strategy through the instrument of shareholder proposals. Activist investors have also been known to use public relations channels to influence firms' decision-making processes.

Danish Central Bank in summer 2008; another Danish bank, Trelleborg, avoided nationalization by being bought out by Sydbank earlier in the year (McLaughlin and Levring, 2008). Some of the bailouts and state ownership deals reflect the cross-border nature of banking, especially in markets such as the EU: for example, the Dexia bank, which operated across Belgium and France, was taken over by the governments of France, Belgium and Luxembourg in a $9.2 billion bailout (EUbusiness, 2008). In Germany, Hypo Real Estate, the country's second-largest commercial property lender, was bailed out by the state in 2008, and fully nationalized in late 2009.

It seems apparent that there exists an emerging landscape of state actors as activist shareholders in financial firms. The concept of the 'activist state' has already been applied to countries actively involved in delivering social and health policies (Ramesh and Holliday, 2001; Biehl, 2004). Extending the concept of the 'activist state' to encompass those states which are acting in ways similar to activist investors allows for an acknowledgement of the myriad interlinkages between the financial industry, other economic sectors, and the diverse communities of citizens which constitute the modern state. Finance – as the recent crisis has painfully brought home to millions of mortgage holders, savers and the energy poor – is deeply involved in everyday material life. It therefore comes as no great surprise that states are, through buyouts and bailouts, becoming involved in financial firms, and that some of these firms – Goldman Sachs and Morgan Stanley being the leading examples – are taking steps to re-regulate, utilizing tighter regulatory controls. It may be argued that this has happened before in specific markets, for example with Spain's boosting of European regulations on Structured Investment Vehicles (SIVs) after the Spanish domestic banking crisis (Tett, 2008). However, the difference in 2010 is, firstly, that multiple states have taken unilateral steps to re-regulate. As José Viñals, deputy director of the Banco de España stated in a recent panel given to the IESE and Harvard Business Schools:

> "[T]he global banking system is continuously evolving within what is known as the "new global financial landscape". This is characterised by several features: free international capital flows, global financial markets and global banks, faster transmission of risks from one area to another, and potential cross border contagion effects. In this context, some new products of increasing complexity, many of them derivatives, are being introduced. We are also observing new players such as hedge funds, private equity funds, conduits, SIVs, etc, whose actions are less and less transparent and subject to little or no regulation"(Viñals, 2008: 4-5).

This has occurred through state-owned investment vehicles which often behave like private equity firms – such as Temasek Holdings of Singapore, the Abu Dhabi Investment Authority, or the China Investment Corporation in the People's Republic of China. Furthermore, institutional investors retain major holdings in financial firms (Gillan and Starks, 2003). However, what is new about state activism in finance after the recent crisis is the level of direct involvement by states in financial firms, without the need for intermediary investment vehicles or firms. The activist state is now a player in its own right on the global financial landscape. The following examines the geopolitical ramifications of this new role.

3. ACTIVIST STATES: GEOPOLITICAL FINANCE

The increasing involvement of activist states in global finance in a period of hybrid neoliberalism has led to a reformulation of relations between the state, finance, and various governmental entities. The financial landscape transcends national boundaries. However, through activist states' new-found financial roles, the state itself *also* transcends national boundaries. Thus, the state is now engaged, through financial activism, in relations with financial firms and, as a consequence, other states in the cross-border arena of finance. This leads to conflicts and tensions, not only over financial policy and capital flows, but over jurisdiction, impacts, risk and governance (Swyngedouw, 2000). Activist states have, resultantly, found themselves in a new sphere of geopolitical conflicts and cleavages in which finance, politics, international relations, and transnational policy-making intersect in often unpredictable, multi-scalar ways.

In order to explore these interactions, this section presents the case of Iceland's banking crisis, perhaps the most prominent geopolitical conflict to have taken place on the global financial landscape between 2007 and 2010; the section also provides an analysis of the tensions resulting from the implosion of Iceland's economy following the crisis. It is argued that the fragmenting of political relationships, and the formation of alliances, around the case of Iceland's economic woes during the crisis, is emblematic of a changed political and economic environment. In this new, hybrid neoliberal environment, states such as Iceland find themselves having to engage in power struggles not only directly with other states, but with other states *through* the vehicles of nationalized financial firms, and with *foreign* firms through both the traditional state apparatus, and newly nationalized financial firms. The resulting picture is one of financial and geopolitical complexity.

3.1. The Case of Iceland: When Finance and Geopolitics Collide

Until the new millennium, Iceland did not seem a promising location for banking or finance. Indeed, until 2000, the island's most established industries were tourism and fishing, while banking and other sectors were heavily controlled by government.[3] However, by 2000 Iceland responded to increasing pressures to neoliberalize its economy, including a minimization of the nexus between the state and finance. Between 2001 and 2003, the Icelandic banking sector was deregulated, the Central Bank was made effectively independent, and Iceland's banks – Kaupthing, Landsbanki and Glitnir – expanded (Central Bank of Iceland, 2002). The expansion was rapid: by 2007, the Icelandic financial sector was worth approximately eight times Iceland's GDP, and the country's banks accounted for 75% of Iceland's stock market value just before the onset of the crisis (Bhaskar and Gopalan, 2009). By the second quarter of 2008, Iceland's external debt was valued at $718 billion, with approximately 80% of this amount originating in the banking sector (Central Bank of Iceland, 2008a).

In short succession in late September and early October 2008, Iceland's banks faltered and then failed. This was due to a culmination of factors stemming from the wider, global

---

[3] Iceland's first bank, Landsbanki Islands (National Bank of Iceland), was established in 1885 (Central Bank of Iceland, 2002).

crisis, including currency fluctuations, and the maturation of large tranches of bank debt in short space of time. In late September, Glitnir was nationalized; the following week, both Glitnir and Landsbanki were placed under the control of a government institution, the Financial Supervisory Authority (FME). Kaupthing, the country's largest bank, was nationalized barely a week later, on 9 October 2008 (Bonsignore, 2008). Within the short space of a month, Iceland found itself having to transition from a new neoliberal economy, to an activist state in a hybrid neoliberal environment. The neoliberal tenets on which the Icelandic financial revival had taken place since 2000 collapsed with unprecedented speed, leaving the state to confront realities of debt, stringent repayment deadlines, and management of new cross-border relations.

The collapse of Iceland's main banks, and their subsequent nationalization, had serious repercussions internally as well as externally. It is not possible to examine the effects of the crisis, especially in domestic terms, in the short space of this chapter. However, it can briefly be noted that as a direct result of collapse, the Icelandic krona (ISK) decreased in value by more than 35% against the euro between January and the end of September 2008 (Central Bank of Iceland, 2010).[4] The situation had not improved by 2010. In early January 2008, one US dollar could buy 61.49 krona; by the first week of 2010, one dollar was worth 124.85 krona.[5] Furthermore, the collapse of Iceland's banking sector meant that, in the short term, trading in the krona was suspended for several weeks in late 2008. In employment terms, the number of jobseekers in the country increased dramatically as a result of layoffs in banking and other industries, such as airlines and newspapers. At the end of August 2008, before the start of the crisis, the number of registered unemployed in Iceland was 2,136. By November 2008, after the collapse of the banks, the number had risen to over 7,000, or 3.3% of the workforce.[6] By November 2009, unemployment had risen to 7.6% of the workforce: a peak of 9.1% was reached in April 2009.

The failure of Iceland's banks, and their nationalization, placed the state in a situation whereby the FME, and other institutions, had to: a.) effectively negotiate with non-Icelandic creditors; b.) interact with other countries (notably, the UK) in discussing retail banking deposit protection schemes; and, c.) interpret national economic policy for domestic and international interlocutors. In terms of relations with foreign creditors, the situation was complicated by the wide variety of creditors, from individuals to government-backed institutions. Iceland's banks had expanded operations aggressively abroad. This enabled them to access markets previously untapped by the country's banks. For example, in the UK, Kaupthing and Landsbanki owned operations under the Kaupthing Edge and Icesave brand names.[7] In the UK, Icesave had 300,000 customers with $6.4 billion in deposits; it also owned Heritable Bank, which operated in the UK and had 22,000 customers and $862.5 million in deposits. Kaupthing Edge had 160,000 depositors with over $4 billion in savings in the UK.

As a result of the Icelandic banking collapse, Heritable was taken over by ING Direct UK, a subsidiary of Dutch ING Group (Stevenson, 2008); ING also took over the $4 billion

---

[4] For historical exchange rate information on the Icelandic krona, see the exchange rate database at Central Bank of Iceland (2010).

[5] Rates current as of 4 January 2008 and 4 January 2010; values given are mid rates (Central Bank of Iceland, 2010).

[6] This is not a historically high figure; a 4% rate of unemployment was also reached in Iceland in 2003 (Central Bank of Iceland, 2008b).

[7] Kaupthing's trading name in the UK was Kaupthing Edge; however, deposits were held by its Kaupthing, Singer and Friedlander subsidiary.

in deposits held by Kaupthing Edge's 160,000 UK savers. Deposits were, as a result, covered by the Dutch deposit compensation scheme, which ensured that UK customers of Icelandic banks would be adequately protected from further market shocks (O'Sullivan, 2008). However, this still left Icesave's 300,000 UK customers, and a total of $6.4 billion in deposits under contention. The UK and Dutch governments guaranteed savers' deposits, thus ensuring that Icesave's UK customers were 'bailed out'. However, this measure rested on an understanding that the Icelandic government, which now effectively owned Icesave, would repay the British and Dutch governments' outlay. This resulted in a dispute between three different activist states, with the UK and the Netherlands disputing Iceland's non-repayment of the loan into 2010 (Jagger and Sherman, 2010).

Furthermore, Icelandic banks' UK customer base was not only restricted to individuals. Indeed, the high interest rates offered by the banks to aid their entry into the UK market also attracted local authorities in Britain, which deposited in excess of $1.6 billion in Kaupthing Edge and Icesave. The range of savings and their risk exposure varied widely: for example, Kent county deposited $24 million with Glitnir, $27 million with Landsbanki, and $28.8 million with Heritable, while Flintshire county council, in north Wales, only had a total of $6 million invested in Landsbanki (The Guardian, 10 October 2008). Local and regional authorities were not the only entities affected: for example, Transport for London, the institution which runs London's public transport system, including its buses, trains and subways, had invested $64 million with Kaupthing Edge, whilst London's Metropolitan Police Authority had $48 million invested in Icelandic banks.[8]

3.2. The Northern Hedge Fund: Geopolitics and Activist States

The collapse of the Icelandic banks elicited a state response, as seen above, through the strategy of nationalization. However, this was a domestic strategy which did not reflect, nor could it impinge on, these same banks' international network of branches, subsidiaries, capital holdings and debt obligations. While Iceland acted as an activist state in nationalizing banks and taking control of their strategic direction, the particularly acute situation of Icelandic finance in 2008 required activism on a variety of levels and by several different actors. The Icelandic government's bank nationalization highlighted the need for other countries to directly engage, through a political and diplomatic process, with banks *and* the Icelandic state. This effectively meant that activist states – the UK perhaps foremost among these – became involved in negotiations centred on firm-state relations. This became starkly apparent when the British government used anti-terrorism legislation in October 2008 to freeze Landsbanki holdings in the UK. Ostensibly, the move was a measure aimed at protecting the $3.3 billion in deposits held in the UK under Icesave.[9] Indeed, as Kirstin Baker, the head of financial stability resolution at the British treasury,[10] wrote in a letter to Iceland's finance minister on 25 May 2009:

---

[8] For a full list of UK local and regional authorities invested in Icelandic banks, see The Guardian, 10 October 2008.
[9] Approximately $1.7 billion was also deposited in Icesave by retail customers in the Netherlands (Valdimarsson, 2009).
[10] Formally known as Her Majesty's Treasury, or HM Treasury.

'The primary reason for the Treasury making the freezing order was its belief that the Icelandic Government was likely to take discriminatory action to use Landsbanki assets to protect Icelandic depositors and that this would be of severe detriment to UK depositors and other UK creditors." (Baker, 2009)

However, the use of anti-terrorism legislation to freeze firm assets was not simply an economic measure aimed at protecting retail depositors. Since the Icelandic government effectively owned and operated the banks in question by October 2008, the freezing of Landsbanki's assets under the stated legislation was an action by an activist state (the UK) which directly affected another activist state (Iceland). In short, the UK's legislation acted on Landsbanki's British subsidiary Icesave; Landsbanki was under state control, therefore the British treasury's action was directly aimed at the Icelandic state. Resultantly, what can be identified is a geopolitical interaction between two activist states, acting through traditional political means (legislation in the case of the UK), with effects on firms (Icesave and Landsbanki), and on other activist states (Iceland). This highlights the generation of geopolitical tensions which has resulted from the development of activist states during and after the economic crisis.

Furthermore, in the case of the Icelandic banking collapse, geopolitical tensions were ramified through a network of state actors not confined to the UK and Iceland. On the one hand, Iceland's retail depositors were protected from bank failure by the country's own deposit protection scheme, the Icelandic Depositors' and Investors' Guarantee Fund.[11] Furthermore, an attempt was made to temporarily boost liquidity through use of Iceland's reciprocal swap facilities with the central banks of other Nordic states (Sweden, Norway and Denmark), for a total of $2.2 billion (Central Bank of Iceland, 2008c). Strikingly, the Icelandic government explored the option of taking a loan from Russia in order to shore up its debts and ensure liquidity. A delegation headed by Sigurdur Sturla Palsson, the chief of the Central Bank of Iceland's international department, visited Moscow in mid-October 2008 to initiate loan negotiations (Nicholson and Meyer, 2008).[12] The estimated $5.5. billion loan was significant for several geopolitical reasons. Firstly, the loan was a response to international negotiations which placed Iceland in a difficult position in terms of securing sufficient loans to ensure liquidity and a (low) level of currency stability. Iceland's request for a $2.1 billion loan from the International Monetary Fund (IMF) in late November 2008 was aimed at:

"[containing] the negative impact of the crisis on the economy by restoring confidence and stabilizing the exchange rate in the near-term; [promoting] a viable domestic banking sector and [safeguarding] international financial relations by implementing a sound banking system strategy that is non-discriminatory and collaborative; [safeguarding] medium-term fiscal viability by limiting the socialization of losses in the collapsed banks and implementing an ambitious multi-year fiscal consolidation program" (IMF, 2008).

---

[11] For a full list of reciprocal deposit protection agreements, treaties and membership of multilateral and bilateral financial committees in the case of Iceland, see the Financial Supervisory Authority of Iceland's Cooperation statement (Financial Supervisory Authority, 2010). For details of Iceland's deposit protection scheme, see the website of the Icelandic Depositors' and Investors' Guarantee Fund (2010).

[12] The delegation arrived in Moscow on 13 October 2008; talks began the following day (Nicholson and Meyer, 2008).

The request for an IMF loan was an emergency measure, but it was needed to forestall risks of potential defaults on state debt (Mason, 2010). However, the IMF loan issue became geopolitically conflictual when further refinancing was needed: an IMF-led $10 billion program for Iceland was agreed to in December 2009, but had stalled by January 2010. The governments of the UK and the Netherlands effectively blocked loan disbursement because of disagreements over Iceland's compensation to the UK and the Netherlands of $5.7 billion which had been used by these respective governments to cover UK and Dutch depositors in the failed Icesave (Northedge, 2010).[13] Thus, Iceland's involvement with a supranational body such as the IMF was conditioned by other activist states, leading to political tensions and conflicts in an arena which was no longer purely political, but which included a spectrum of actors from individual retail depositors, to banks, to government institutions and ministers.

Secondly, financial tensions overflowed into geopolitical fractures. Iceland is a member of NATO. The island state was a US military ally during the Cold War, and acted as a crucial location for NATO defence strategy: Iceland housed Keflavik air base, operational throughout and after the Cold War, until its closure in 2006. The base was crucial in providing opportunities for the projection of air power close to Russia, and for air defence and early warning systems. It is therefore striking that Iceland was enticed to, or explored options to secure loans from Russia in 2008. As Brad Setser, writing for the US-based think-tank Council on Foreign Relations, argued, 'During the cold war, the US would never have allowed Russia to bail out a military ally. And Russia hasn't traditionally thought of Iceland as part of its near-abroad either' (Setser, 2008). However, it seems evident that, in exploring loan options, both Iceland and Russia were acting not like former Cold Warriors, but like activist states. The Icelandic state was, by late 2008, the owner of formerly private banks and, as a result, of their foreign assets. However, its liquidity and debt problems provided potential opportunities for another activist state – Russia – which could explore the possibilities inherent in allocating surplus capital from its reserves in a strategic investment in Iceland. As Setser (2008) argued, 'no nation resembled a high-living hedge fund quite as much as Iceland. Its big banks and big firms had enormous international liabilities and enormous international assets — at least in relation to Iceland's small economy. And for a while, Iceland used the profits from its intermediation to live very well, running a large current account deficit.' In a similar way, Russia's reserves enabled it to consider taking a stake in Iceland and its asset holdings.

Following negotiations, no agreement was reached on the Russian loan to Iceland; however, it remains the case that in a landscape of activist states, large countries such as Russia with significant amounts of reserves can effect intervention not only by taking control of private firms, but by gaining influence over other activist states. This seamlessly blends economic and financial influence with political power. The case of Iceland has shown that in the post-crisis financial and geopolitical landscape, activist states are locked into complex relationships which comprise overlapping economic, political, diplomatic and ideological spheres; furthermore, as a result of the crisis, these same states have taken on new roles and acquired novel spheres of action, over formerly private firms as well as within the traditional political remits of other states.

---

[13] For full details of the IMF's involvement in the Icelandic financial crisis, see IMF (2009).

4. Hybrid Neoliberalism and Capital Allocation: The Case of Green Technology

So far, this chapter has argued that the financial crisis has generated a complex, changed landscape of political and financial actors and international linkages. This landscape of hybrid neoliberalism is characterised by the partial reformulation of the state as an economic actor in its own right. Indeed, the chapter has argued that the state can, post-2007, be described as an activist investor. This description applies to those states – like the UK, Iceland, France, and the US – which have seen themselves pushed towards gaining partial or complete control of previously private economic and industrial activities. The complexities, tensions and conflicts inherent in this shift are too numerous and far-reaching to be examined here, and to be analysed at this point in time, when the crisis is not yet over. However, it is clear from the example of Iceland's financial crisis that activist states interact geopolitically as well as financially *across* as well as *within* their own borders, reflecting the trans-border character of trade and commerce today. Thus, finance becomes a geopolitical tool, and activist states gain influence *inside* other states' territories through direct ownership of formerly private firms and their subsidiaries, or alternatively through investing in other states by enabling liquidity.

Therefore, the activist state within a hybrid neoliberal landscape is becoming increasingly involved in economic activities and in acting effectively as an activist investor in private firms, and in other states. However, what this section argues is that there is a third, important facet or sphere of activity pertaining to activist states. These states are not only investors and shareholders; they are capital allocators. As such, activist states work within their own domestic economies to utilize tax revenue and budgets (many of these financed or secured through sovereign debt held by other activist states) so as to promote sectors of economic activist seen as promising, undervalued, or potentially profitable. This characteristic is not traditionally associated with neoliberal forms of financial and economic governance; much of the literature points towards a shrinkage of the neoliberal state in terms of economic direction and policy. The assumption in economic policy in neoliberal states such as the US (Harvey, 2007: 88) and the UK (Hay, 2001), as well as in several emerging economies (Chwieroth, 2007), seems to have been that states are inefficient administrators of economies; 'light touch regulation' has been the norm. However, this section argues that, in light of the economic stimulus programmes which have been organized and implemented in several states, the activist state has become a capital allocator and thus has centralised economic activity to some extent. This does not mean that neoliberalism has collapsed, or that it is somehow 'in crisis'. Rather, the argument is that states' capital allocation activities are another characteristic of what I have termed hybrid neoliberalism. This argument fits with a view of neoliberalism which, 'like globalization, should be thought of as a contingently realized *process*, not as an end-state or 'condition'' (Tickell and Peck: 165).

The following provides an example of the role of the activist state as capital allocator by focusing on the case of economic stimulus and recovery programmes, and specifically those programmes focused on green technology. Green technology funding has been selected for analysis here over, say, programmes to aid automobile manufacturers, for two main reasons. Firstly, one of the characteristics of neoliberalism over the past decade has been the increasing incorporation of the 'environment', and the externalities of industrial activities, within a market logic and market mechanisms (McCarthy and Prudham, 2004): this can be seen in arenas ranging from Emissions Trading Schemes (ETS) (Bailey and Maresh, 2009), to wetland mitigation banking (Robertson, 2004) , to environmental policy, governance and trade (Eckersley, 2004: 81-2; McCarthy, 2004). The 'low carbon economy', as well as the 'green collar economy', have become clarion calls in government and industry for investment in technologies, industrial processes and services which will be able to reap economic opportunities from a 'low carbon' future of more stringent and comprehensive environmental regulation (Bailey and Wilson, 2009). Therefore, by examining the state's allocation of stimulus funds to green technologies, the following focuses on a specific aspect of hybrid neoliberalism in the centralised allocation of capital to 'desirable' sectors of economic activity. Secondly, within the context of the recent financial crisis and the stimulus programmes which have been elaborated as responses to economic slowdown, 'green stimulus packages' have been prominent across a wide range of states and markets. The financing of green technology by activist states as a response to the financial crisis can therefore be seen as a key example of the trend towards active capital allocation in an era of hybrid neoliberalism.

The green economy is already here: green technology firms alone were worth $284 *billion* globally in 2008. By the end of the third quarter of 2009, and notwithstanding the financial crisis, cleantech venture investment – funding for new technologies and companies – had increased 182% from the first quarter, with $965 million invested in new ventures in the US alone (Sims, 2009). The years since Kyoto entered into force in 2005 have seen a meteoric rise both in the amounts invested in the green economy, and in the number of companies receiving investment for clean technologies. While the 'green economy' is not necessarily a 'low carbon economy', the existence of a rapidly developing economy focused on green technologies and services and processes aimed at sustainability is a reality. The speedy rise in investment amounts in green and renewable energy technologies in the first decade of the twenty-first century is a reflection, in part, of a changing policy landscape which has seen agreements and regulations stemming from the Kyoto Protocol and, now, the aftermath of the 2009 Copenhagen Climate Conference. However, the private capital flowing into green technologies has also been attracted by clear, market-based economic opportunities as well as government-led incentives (Kiernan, 2008).

Green stimulus programmes have been part and parcel of state-backed stimulus packages globally. In the US, the American Recovery and Reinvestment Act of 2009 (ARRA) provided for $787 billion in nominal funding for economic recovery.[14] The measures included under ARRA range from federal tax cuts, welfare provisions, and expansions in spending on infrastructure, education, and health care. The green technology allocation amounts to around $80 billion, aimed at infrastructure, mass transit, renewable energy, energy efficiency, and research and innovation (Croston, 2010).[15] In the UK, the green stimulus package designed by government is an $870 million tranche of the overall $4.8 billion national recovery package (Adam, 2009). In China, the overall green stimulus package size was set at $221 billion, out of a total stimulus fund comprising $586 billion (Qi, 2009). South Korea's green stimulus fund was was valued at $37 billion – or 81% of the state's overall economic recovery package (Watts, 2009).

---

[14] Full ARRA details are available at US Government Printing Office (2009). Recovery impact information is available on the website of US Recovery (2010).

[15] For example, $2.5 billion is allocated for energy efficiency research and development, and $6 billion in loan guarantees for renewables firms (Merchant, 2009).

Furthermore, activist states are becoming involved in directly funding actual, material green technology projects; mostly, these activities have taken the shape of investments in infrastructure and business hubs or clusters focused on technology development and innovation. Cleantech hubs and green energy research centres are being set upglobally. For example, China has invested heavily not only in existing renewable energy sources, but in the provision of infrastructure for clean energy development. A case in point is Cleantech hubs and green energy research centres are being set upglobally: for example, China has also invested heavily not only in existing renewable energy sources, but in the provision of infrastructure for clean energy development. A case in point is the foundation of Xuzhou Cleantech Park (Xuzhou Cleantech Park, 2010), a joint enterprise between the Jiangsu provincial government, Tsinghua Holdings, cleantech investment fund Tsing Capital, and US cleantech investment network firm Cleantech Group LLC. These moves are paralleled, albeit on a smaller scale, by similar projects being set up in the EU – such as the Cleantech Cluster being mooted for Cambridge, in the UK, as a way of promoting transition from the existing ICT cluster in the region – and in the Gulf, such as Abu Dhabi's Masdar eco-city and Masdar Clean Tech Fund. These small-scale examples point towards state investment in green technology as a way of allocating capital to industries which are seen to be promising sectors of economic activity in providing engines of growth out of the current crisis – although questions remain as to the results of such 'state entrepreneurial' policies (McKendry, 2008).

Clearly, the 'green' tranches of economic stimulus packages globally are significant both in terms of values, and in terms of size relative to overall stimulus package values. This points to another facet of the workings of activist states in a hybrid neoliberal environment: namely, that states are increasingly re-engaging with their domestic economic environments, and are doing so with the aim of boosting sectors which can lead economic recovery, and eventually provide excellent tax returns in the future. The clean technology sector is a good example of this: it has seen increased investment*during* the crisis across a range of asset classes. It is, furthermore, a sector branded as being central to the 'low carbon economy'; as such, it has also benefited from green stimulus packages, and can be seen as a strategic value investment made by activist states. As a result, I argue that state funds aimed at green technology – and other sectors – ought to be seen not in light of a 'crisis of neoliberalism', but in terms of a hybrid neoliberalism whereby the activist state actively invests and takes value-oriented positions in firms, other states, and specific sectors of the domestic economy.

5. CONCLUSION

As seen above, the financial, political and economic world we are entering in 2010 is radically different, in many ways, to the world before the crisis. The liquidity bubble and the era of cheap and easy credit have given way to a landscape characterized by uncertainty, risk aversion, and economic contraction. Fear and insecurity have replaced confidence and hubris (Thompson, 2009), and the past few years have seen established, legacy firms – from Bear Stearns to Lehman Brothers – reduced to ashes as the crisis snowballed. This situation has posed clear challenges for policymakers, economists, workers, and scholars alike. 'Taking action' or, more accurately, reacting to the crisis, has been the hallmark of policies and firm strategies during recent years. Likewise, scholars have attempted to reconceptualise the economic and political system which is emerging from these years of turmoil. What this chapter has argued is that, whilst still in the depths of the crisis, what seems apparent is that the nexus between economy and politics has shifted somewhat, as neoliberalism has changed, or transitioned, into a 'hybrid neoliberalism' in which the state has re-engaged with the economy in market-oriented ways. The financial and political landscape which is taking shape today is one which sees activist states interacting politically and economically, acting like activist investors as they gain economic influence, through market mechanisms, over formerly private firms, other states, and whole sectors of domestic economies, as seen in the case of green technology above. The future is, as always, unclear; however, what seems to be emerging from the murk of the past few years is a hybrid geopolitical and financial landscape of political and financial state actors; it remains to be seen how the interactions between and *within* activist states will influence the economic and policy landscape into the 2010s.

REFERENCES

Adam, D. (2009) "UK Economic Rescue Plans 'Must Be Greener', MPs Say.' The Guardian, 16 March 2009. Available at: http://www.guardian green-stimulus-falls-short (Accessed 4 January 2010).

Bailey, I. and Maresh, S. (2009) "Scales and Networks of Neoliberal Climate Governance: the Regulatory and Territorial Logics of European Union Emissions Trading." Transactions of the Institute of British Geographers, 34(4): 445-461.

Bailey, I. and Wilson, G. A. (2009) "Theorising Transitional Pathways in Response to Climate Change: Technocentrism, Ecocentrism, and the Carbon Economy." Environment and Planning A, 41(10): 2324-2341.

Baker, C. (2009) "Review of the Landsbanki Freezing Order 2008". Iceland: Prime Minister's Office website. A copy of the letter is available at: http://www.island.is/media. pdf (Accessed 4 January 2010).

Bakker, K. (2005) "Neoliberalizing Nature? Market Environmentalism in Water Supply in England and Wales." Annals of the Association of American Geographers, 95(3): 542-565.

Bhaskar, R. and Gopalan, Y. (2009) "The Financial Crisis in S, M and L: Three Very Different Countries Respond Similarly." The Regional Economist, 2(2009), available at: http://www.stlouisfed.org/publications/re/articles/?id=1252 (Accessed 4 January 2010).

Biehl, J. (2001) "The Activist State: Global Pharmaceuticals, AIDS, and Citizenship in Brazil." Social Text, 22(3): 105-132.

Bonsignore, T. (2008) "Kaupthing Nationalised as Iceland Crisis Intensifies." Citywire, 9 October 2008. Available at: http://www.citywire.co.uk/selector/-/news/ratings-update/content.aspx?ID=317007 (Accessed 4 January 2010).

Brett, A. S. (2007) "Two-Tiered Health Care: A Problematic Double Standard." Archives of Internal Medicine, 167(5): 430-432.

Caprotti, F. (2009) "Financial Crisis, Activist States and (Missed) Opportunities." Critical Perspectives on International Business, 5(1): 78-84.

Central Bank of Iceland (2002) "History." Available at: http://www.sedlabanki.is/? PageID=192 (Accessed 4 January 2010).

Central Bank of Iceland (2008a) "External Debt." Available at: http://www.sedlabanki.is/?pageid=552anditemid=a55be3a0-9943-484e-a8de-46d23f17ba25andnextday=4andnextmonth=12 (Accessed 4 January 2010).

Central Bank of Iceland (2008b) "Economic Indicators: September 2008." Available at: http://www.sedlabanki.is/lisalib/getfile.aspx?itemid=6451 (Accessed 4 January 2010).

Central Bank of Iceland (2008c) "Central Bank of Iceland Draws on Swap Facility Arrangements." Press release, 14 October 2008. Available at: http://www.sedlabanki.is/?PageID= 287andNewsID=1904 (Accessed 4 January 2010).

Central Bank of Iceland (2010) "Exchange Rate." Available at: http://www.sedlabanki.is/Default.aspx?PageID=183 (Accessed 4 January 2010).

Chorev, N. and Babb, S. (2009) "The Crisis of Neoliberalism and the Future of International Institutions: A Comparison of the IMF and the WTO." Theory and Society, 38(5): 459-484.

Chwieroth, J. (2007) "Neoliberal Economists and Capital Account Liberalization in Emerging Markets." International Organization, 61(2): 443-463.

Croston, G. (2010) "Stimulus Package Has Green for Clean Energy." Entrepreneur website. Available at: http://www.entrepreneurgoinggreen/article200500.html (Accessed 10 January 2010).

Duménil, G. and Lévi, D. (2005) Costs and Benefits of Neoliberalism: a Class Analysis. In: Epstein, G. A. Financialization and the World Economy. Edward Elgaer: Northampton, MA: 17-45.

Eckersley, R. (2004) The Green State: Rethinking Democracy and Sovereignty. MIT Press: Cambridge, MA.

Elliott, L. and Wintour, P. (2009) "Darling Announces One-Off Shock Tax to 'Break Bonus Culture'." The Guardian, 7 December 2009. Available at: http://www.guardian /2009/ dec/07/alistair-darling-shock-tax-bankers (Accessed 4 January 2010).

Engelen E., Konings M. and R. Fernandez (2008) "The Rise of Activist Investors and Patterns of Political Responses: Lessons on Agency". Socio-Economic Review, 6: 611-636.

EU business (2008) "Dexia Gets EUR 6.4 Billion Three-State Bailout." EUbusiness, 30 September 2008. Available at: http://www.eubusiness.com/news-eu/1222760822.41 (Accessed 4 January 2010).

Financial Supervisory Authority (2010) "Co-Operation." Available at: http://www.fme.is /?PageID=206 (Accessed 4 January 2010).

Fourcade-Gourinchas M. and Babb, S. L. (2002) "The Rebirth of the Liberal Creed: Paths to Neoliberalism in Four Countries." American Journal of Sociology, 108(3): 533-79.

Friedman, T. L. (2006) The World is Flat: A Brief History of the Twenty-First Century. Macmillan: London.

Gillan, S. and Starks, L. T. (2003) "Corporate Governance, Corporate Ownership, and the Role of Institutional Investors: a Global Perspective." Journal of Applied Finance, 13(2): 4-22.

Griffiths, P. (2009) "Brown Vows to Shake Up Banks' Bonus Culture." Reuters, 10 February 2009. Available at: http://uk.reuters.com/article/idUKLNE51300Q20090210 (Accessed 4 January 2010).

Harvey, D. (2007) A Brief History of Neoliberalism. Oxford University Press: Oxford.

Hay, C. (2001) The "Crisis" of Keynesianism and the Rise of Neoliberalism in Britain. In: Campbell, J. L. and Pedersen, O. K. (Eds.) The Rise of Neoliberalism and Institutional Analysis. Princeton University Press: Princeton, NJ.

Icelandic Depositors' and Investors' Guarantee Fund (2010). Website available at: http://www.tryggingarsjodur.is/AboutUs/ (Accessed 4 January 2010).

International Monetary Fund (IMF) (2008) "IMF Executive Board Approves US$2.1 Billion Stand-By Arrangement for Iceland." Press release, 19 November 2008. Available at: http://www.imf.org/external/np/sec/pr/2008/pr08296.htm (Accessed 4 January 2010).

International Monetary Fund (IMF) (2009). "Iceland and the IMF." Available at: http://www.imf.org/external/country/ISL/index.htm (Accessed 4 January 2010).

Jagger, S. and Sherman, J. (2010) "Britain Threatens to Freeze Iceland Out of EU as Loan Payback Vetoed." The Times, 6 January 2010. Available at: http://www.timesonline.co.uk/tol/news/world/europe/article6977152.ece (Accessed 6 January 2010).

Jessop, B. (2002) Liberalism, Neoliberalism, and Urban Governance: a State-Theoretical Perspective. In: Brenner, N. and Theodore, N. (Eds.) Spaces of Neoliberalism: Urban Restructuring in North America and Western Europe. Blackwell: Malden, MA.

Karpoff, J. M. (2001) "The Impact of Shareholder Activism on Target Companies: A Survey of Empirical Findings." Social Science Research Network, 18 August 2001. Available at: http://papers.ssrn.com/sol3/papers.cfm?abstract_id=885365 (Accessed 4 January 2010).

Kennedy, S. (2008) "Bradford and Bingley Nationalized by UK Government: Santander Taking on Branch Network." Market Watch, 29 September 2008. Available at: http://www.marketwatch.com/news/story/bradford--bingley-nationalized-uk/story.aspx?guid={FF8C6FD0-EE03-4E97-BA71-B2DF0C182C34}anddist=msr_2 (Accessed 4 January 2010).

Kiernan, M. J. (2008) Investing in a Sustainable World: Why Green is the New Color of Money on Wall Street. AMACOM: New York, NY.

Klepeis P. and Vance, C. (2003) "Neoliberal Policy and Deforestation in Southeastern Mexico: An Assessment of the Procampo Program." Economic Geography, 79(3): 221-240.

Konings, M. (2009) "Rethinking Neoliberalism and the Subprime Crisis: Beyond the Re-regulation Agenda." Competition and Change, 13(2): 108-127.

Larner, W. (2000) "Neoliberalism: Policy, Ideology, Governmentality." Studies in Political Economy, 63(2000): 5-25.

Mason, R. (2010) "Iceland in Emergency Talks to Secure Scandinavian Loan Payment." The Telegraph, 7 January 2010. Available at: http://www.telegraph.co.uk/finance6947648/Iceland-in-emergency-talks-to-secure-Scandinavian-loan-payment.html (Accessed 10 January 2010).

McCarthy, J. (2004). "Privatizing Conditions of Production: Trade Agreements as Neoliberal Environmental Governance." Geoforum, 35(3): 327-341.

McCarthy, J. and Prudham, S. (2004) "Neoliberal Nature and the Nature of Neoliberalism." Geoforum, 35(3): 275-283.

McKendry, C. (2008). "Competing for Green: Neoliberalism, Environmental Justice, and the Limits of Ecological Modernization." Presentation at the 49th Annual Conference of the International Studies Association, March 26 - 29, 2008. Available at: http://www.allacademic.com//meta/p_mla_apa_research_citation/2/5/4/0/9/pages254091/p254091-1.php (Accessed 4 January 2010).

McLaughlin, K. and Levring, P. (2008) Danish Central Bank Buys Out Ailing Roskilde Bank. Reuters, 25 August 2008. Available at: http://uk.reuters.com/article/ idUKLP5 6732520080825 (Accessed 4 January 2010).

Merchant, B. (2009) "$60 Billion for Green in the Stimulus Bill: Where the Money Will Go." Tree Hugger, 2 June 2009. Available at: http://www.treehugger.com/files/2009/02/green-stimulus-bill-60-billion.php (Accessed 4 January 2010).

Montgomerie, J. and Williams, K. (2009) "Financialised Capitalism: After the Crisis and Beyond Neoliberalism." Competition and Change, 13(2): 99-107.

Nicholson, A. and Meyer, H. (2008) "Iceland Starts Talks With Russia on $5.5 Billion Loan." Bloomberg, 14 October 2008. Available at: http://www.bloomberg.com/apps/news?pid =20601085andsid=a6cr3RnsK34Iandrefer=europe (Accessed 4 January 2010).

Northedge, N. (2010). "Iceland's Voters Set to Remain Out in the Cold." The Independent, 10 January 2010. Available at: http://www.independent.co.uk/news/business/analysis-and-features/icelands-voters-set-to-remain-out-in-the-cold-1862955.html (Accessed 10 January 2010).

O'Sullivan, A. (2008) "ING Buys Up Bust Kaupthing's UK Savings." This Is Money, 8 October 2008. Available at: http://www.thisismoney.co.uk/savings-and-banking/a rticle.html?in_article_id=454063andin_page_id=7 (Accessed 4 January 2010).

Peck, J. (2004) "Geography and Public Policy: Constructions of Neoliberalism." Progress in Human Geography, 28(3): 392-405.

Peck, J. (2001) "Neoliberalizing States: Thin Policies / Hard Outcomes. Progress in Human Geography, 25(3): 445-455.

Qi, Z. (2009) "$30b Set Aside For Green Stimulus to Double Alternative Fuel Use." China Daily, 25 May 2009. Available at: http://www2.chinadaily.com.cn/bizchina/2009-05/25/content_7937667.htm (Accessed 4 January 2010).

Ramesh, M. and Holliday, I. (2001) "The Health Care Miracle in East and Southeast Asia: Activist State Provision in Hong Kong, Malaysia and Singapore." Journal of Social Policy, 30(4): 637-651.

Recovery website (2010). Available at: http://www.recovery.gov (Accessed 4 January 2010).

Robertson, M. M. (2004) "The Neoliberalization of Ecosystem Services: Wetland Mitigation Banking and Problems in Environmental Governance." Geoforum, 35(3): 361-373.

Ryan, L. V. and Schneider, M. (2002) "The Antecedents of Institutional Investor Activism." The Academy of Management Review, 27(4): 554-573.

Schwartz, N. D. and Dougherty, C. (2008) "Europeans Handle Crisis Together and Separately." International Herald Tribune, 7 October 2008. Available at: http://www.iht.com/articles/2008/10/07/business/07euro.php (Accessed 4 January 2010).

Setser, B. (2008) "Russia, Global Lender of Last Resort? Will Russia Bail Out the Hedge Fund of the North…" Council on Foreign Relations, 7 October 2008. Available at: http://blogs.cfr.org/setser/2008/10/07/russia-global-lender-of-last-resort-will-russia-bail-out-the-hedge-fund-of-the-north/ (Accessed 4 January 2010).

Sims, S. (2009) "US Cleantech Venture Capital Continues to Gain Momentum in Q3 2009 With 46% Increase to $965 Million." Reuters, 29 October 2009. Available at: http://www.reuters.com/article/idUS122316+29-Oct-2009+PRN20091029 (Accessed 4 January 2010).

Slater, S. and Croft, A. (2008) "Santander Buys BandB Deposits as Nationalization Looms." Reuters, 29 September 2008. Available at: http://www.reuters.com/article /innovatio nNews/idUSTRE48Q1Z520080929 (Accessed 4 January 2010).

Smith, M. P. (1996) "Shareholder Activism by Institutional Investors: The Role of CalPERS." The Journal of Finance, 51(1): 227-252.

Stevenson, R. (2008) "ING Scoops Up Iceland Online Deposits in UK." Reuters, 8 October 2008. Available at: http://www.reuters.com/article/idUSTRE4974P320081008 (Accessed 4 January 2010).

Swyngedouw, E. (2000) "Authoritarian Governance, Power, and the Politics of Rescaling." Environment and Planning D: Society and Space, 18(1): 63-76.

Swyngedouw, E., F. Moulaert and Rodriguez, A. (2002) Neoliberal Urbanization in Europe: Large-Scale Urban Development Projects and the New Urban Policy. In: Brenner, N. and Theodore, N. (Eds.) Spaces of Neoliberalism: Urban Restructuring in North America and Western Europe. Blackwell: Malden, MA.

Tett, G. (2008) "Time for Central Bankers to Take Spanish Lessons." The Financial Times, 29 September 2008. Available at: http://www.ft.com/cms/s/0/1f50c5d4-8e65-11dd-9b46-0000779fd18c,dwp_uuid=86c92008-1c23-11dd-8bfc-000077b07658.html (Accessed 4 January 2010).

Thompson, G. (2009) "What's in the Frame? How the Financial Crisis is being Packaged for Public Consumption." Economy and Society, 38(3): 520-524.

The Guardian (2008) "Icelandic Bank Failure: Which Councils Are Affected?" The Guardian, 10 October 2008. Available at: http://www.guardian 2008/oct/ 10/localgovernment-iceland (Accessed 4 January 2010).

Tickell, A. and Peck, J. (2005) Making Global Rules: Globalization or Neoliberalization? In: Peck, J. and Yeung, W. (Eds.) Remaking the Global Economy. Sage: Thousand Oaks, CA.

Torbat, A. E. (2008) "Global Financial Meltdown and the Demise of Neoliberalism." Global Research, 13 October 2008. Available at: http://www.globalresearch.ca/index. php?context= vaandaid=10549 (Accessed 4 January 2010).

Traynor I., A. Clark and J. Treanor (2009) "France and Germany Back UK Bonus Tax." The Guardian, 10 December 2009. Available at: http://www.guardian /dec/10/france-germany-back-uk-bonus-tax (Accessed 4 January 2010).

US Government Printing Office (2009). "Public Law 111 - 5 - American Recovery and Reinvestment Act of 2009."Available at: http://www.gpo.gov/fdsys/pkg/PLAW-111publ5/content-detail.html (Accessed 4 January 2010).

Valdimarsson, O. R. (2009) "Iceland to Repay Landsbanki's Foreign Depositors." BusinessWeek, 31 December 2009. Available at: http://www.businessweek.com/ globalbiz/content/ dec2009/gb20091231_146432.htm (Accessed 4 January 2010).

Vina, G. and Stirling, C. (2008) "Royal Bank of Scotland, HBOS Set to be Taken Over by Government." Bloomberg, 12 October 2008. Available at: http://www.bloomberg. com/apps/news?pid=20601102andsid=aw6Y9TU3RioIandrefer=uk (Accessed 4 January 2010).

Viñals, J. (2008) "The Role of the Banco de España in Spanish Banking." Panel Presentation at IESE and Harvard Business Schools, 11 January 2008. Available online at: http://www.bde.es/prensa/intervenpub/subgoberna/Sub110108e.pdf (Accessed 4 January 2010).

Watts, J. (2009) "South Korea Lights the Way on Carbon Emissions with its £23bn Green Deal." The Guardian, 29 April 2009. Available at: http://www.guardian /environment /2009/apr/21/south-korea-enviroment-carbon-emissions (Accessed 4 January 2010).

Weir, M., Orloff A. S. and T. Skocpol (1988) Understanding American Social Politics. In: Weir, M.., Orloff A. S. and T. Skocpol (Eds.) The Politics of Social Policy in the United States. Princeton University Press: Princeton, NJ.

Xuzhou Cleantech Park (2010). "China Xuzhou Cleantech Park." Available at: http://cleantechpark.com/English/touzi.asp (Accessed 4 January 2010).

In: After the Crisis: Rethinking Finance
Editor: Thomas Lagoarde-Segot

ISBN 978-1-61668-925-4
© 2010 Nova Science Publishers, Inc.

Chapter 6

GLOBALIZATION AND ECONOMIC CRISIS: DOES INFORMATION REALLY MATTER?

Leonardo Baccini, Soo Yeon Kim and Fabio Pammolli [*]

ABSTRACT

On 24 September 2008, the WTO Director-General Pascal Lamy warned that, as the Great Depression illustrates, "protectionism and economic isolationism do not work". By this logic, defecting from trade cooperation in a time of economic turmoil does not lead to a Pareto optimum equilibrium. However, during a period of economic crisis beggar thy-neighbor policies are commonly employed by governments as short-term instruments to tackle falling growth rates and rising unemployment rates. Moreover, economic crisis generates uncertainty regarding the responses of other countries, which in turn encourages defection in the form of discriminatory trade practices. In other words, each country has a dominant strategy to implement protectionism during an economic crisis. The historical record supports this argument. For instance, during the Great Depression governments reverted to protectionist policies as a response to pressures from sectors hurt by economic crises. We argue that the current era of globalization is distinguishable from its earlier counterparts by the presence of an extensive network of international institutions. Whereas economic crisis induces uncertainty in the conduct of commercial relations, institutions serve as conveyors of information that help to mitigate the information problem that prevails in prisoner's dilemma settings. Specifically, globalization increases the flow of information among countries alleviating the coordination problems and enabling the detection of potential free-riders. We suggest that this mechanism may explain why the current crisis is not replicating the pattern of the Great Depression. We test our argument on globalization and economic crisis using a newly-compiled dataset in large-N studies.

---

[*] The authors are grateful to Ju-Hyung (Josh) Lim for excellent and timely research assistance on this project and to Paul Ingram for providing data on the categorization of governmental organizations.

1. Introduction

The global economic crisis is widely regarded as the most serious setback for the international economy since the Great Depression and one which has brought a host of governance issues to the fore, ranging from reform of banking regulations to reform of the International Monetary Fund. The impact of the crisis has not been limited to the financial sector in which it originated but has extended to virtually all areas of international economic interactions. Among the casualties has been international trade, which saw a historic and steep drop in the months following the outbreak of the crisis. The "great trade collapse" (Baldwin 2009) reflects the trade policy choices of countries that are deeply integrated into the global trading system but have shifted their orientation in favor of protectionist measures in an effort to cushion the blow of the crisis to their national economies. Measures such as import restrictions, export subsidies, anti-dumping measures, and state aid, to name a few, are examples of "beggar-thy-neighbor" policies adopted by states threaten to lead to an unraveling of liberal global trade. While many countries have appealed to such measures, not all have done so, and this pattern of state choices informs the main question underlying this paper: what explains the trade policy choices of countries in times of crisis?

In addressing this question, this paper highlights the political context of international commercial exchange and focuses on the role of international institutions, especially international economic organizations, as purveyors of information in times of crisis. The network of international institutions or organizations that span a wide range of issues are a distinct feature of the political landscape of the last century since the Great Depression and are important in understanding governance in this globalization era. We advance the argument that international institutions mitigate the uncertainty inherent to sustaining the optimal outcome of liberal trade and in times of crisis, when the uncertainty problem is especially acute, institutions provide information and transparency regarding state choices in trade policy and, in doing so, take on an important role in the continuation of a liberal trading system. The main hypothesis of our empirical analysis tests this argument by analyzing the impact of membership in international organizations on the use of protectionist trade policies.

We carry out a quantitative analysis using data provided by Global Trade Alert, which monitors and provides real-time information on government measures taken during the current global crisis that are likely to affect international trade. We analyze the impact on the propensity and intensity of protectionism of membership in international organizations, controlling for other factors that may also affect the implementation of protectionist measures. The analysis distinguishes between the effects of membership in international economic and political organizations and also between interventionist and non-interventionist organizations. This paper finds that membership in international economic organizations and participation in preferential trade agreements reduce the likelihood and extent of adopting protectionist trade measures.We also find that neither membership in international political organizations nor the institutional capacity for enforcement distinguishing interventionist and non-interventionist organizations has any significant impact on the adoption of protectionism. Rather, our findings suggest strong support for the informational function of international economic institutions and its role in preventing the rise of protectionism in times of crisis.

Immediately below we provide the theoretical framework of our paper, including the major points of comparison between the Great Depression and the current crisis and our main argument on the role of institutions in international trade. The research design section discusses case selection, model specification, and data. The subsequent section reports the findings of the analysis and we conclude with a discussion of the implications of the paper for understanding trade policy choices in times of crisis.

2. INSTITUTIONS, INFORMATION, AND TRADE POLICY IN TIMES OF CRISIS

The 1930s Depression era saw the "Contracting Spiral of World Trade," as reported by the League of Nations' Economic Survey for 1932-1933 (Eichengreen and Irwin 1995, 4-5), as countries turned their backs on the liberal trading order and appealed instead to "beggar-thy-neighbor" policies that sought to shield national economies from the economic crisis. By 1932, the volume of world trade had fallen by 40 percent (Irwin 1993, 112). World trade disintegrated as countries put in place higher tariffs, the most notable example of this being the adoption of the famous Smoot-Hawley tariff of 1930 in the United States. Countries imposed import quotas, subsidies, licensing requirements as well as exchange controls. Bilateralism was rampant in this period (Culbertson 1937, Snyder 1940), as bilateral trade agreements were concluded to balance trade on a case-by-case basis and to preserve hard currency or gain political advantage. Trade became increasingly concentrated in blocs through arrangements such as the Ottawa Agreement of 1932 that created Imperial Preference in Great Britain's trade with its dominions or through currency blocs linking one large economy with a set of smaller economies (Feinstein, Temin, and Toniolo 1997; Pomfret 1988, Chapter 3). Exchange controls and clearing arrangements to stabilize exchange rates promoted intra-bloc trade while actively discriminating against those outside the bloc. Thus the 1930s was, according to Douglas Irwin, a "disaster in the field of commercial policy" (1995, 324), and the trade and exchange rate policies pursued in this period dismantled what little remained of the system of liberal trade that had been in decline since the late 19th century.

The record of international trade during the Depression era prompts comparison to the possible consequences for international trade of the current global economic crisis, widely recognized as the most serious economic crisis in the seventy years that have passed since then. Concerns about the consequences of the global economic crisis for international trade is what prompted figures such as Pascal Lamy, director-general of the WTO, to urge countries not to adopt protectionist trade policy as a way to insulate national economies from the effects of the crisis, warning that, as the Great Depression illustrates, "protectionism and economic isolationism do not work" (2008).[1] Indeed, the current global crisis, as Baldwin notes, led to "the great trade collapse," a "sudden, severe, and synchronized" fall in global trade between the third quarter of 2008 and the second quarter of 2009, when global trade flows were 15% below their previous year's levels (2009).[2] Though not as great in magnitude as that of the Great Depression, "the treat of trade collapse" was steeper, falling in the span of nine months

---

[1] "Lamy warns against protectionism amid financial crisis," 24 September 2008. http://www.wto.org/ english/ news_e/sppl_e/sppl101_e.htm.

[2] http://www.voxeu.org/index.php?q=node/4304. Accessed 7 January 2010.

what took 24 months during the Great Depression. Overall, this was the steepest decline in global trade on record and greatest in magnitude since the Great Depression.

In understanding the link between economic crisis and trade policy in this globalization era, and especially the prospects for sustaining a liberal trade system in a time of global economic crisis, we direct attention to a key variable in the political environment of international trade: international institutions. We argue that the current era is distinguishable from that of the Great Depression by the presence of an extensive network of international institutions that provide governance functions in the international economy.3 Even in the case of preferential trade agreements, which have seen a rapid rise in recent years, their configuration, in contrast to the trade and currency "bloc" formation of the 1930s that was also highly regionalized, is more akin to a "spaghetti bowl" (Bhagwati, 1995) with numerous overlapping memberships in trade agreements that are not solely regional but often link states in different regions. The trading system of the interwar years was a "nonsystem" (Irwin 1995, 324), lacking any institutional mechanism comparable to what exists now to promote the reduction of the trade barriers. In contrast, the great power politics that has shaped the course of global trade since the end of World War II has centered on a "constitutional order" founded on strategic restraint on the part of the winning state—the United States—and institutional binding of less powerful states (Ikenberry 2001). While earlier eras of globalization were driven largely by private economic actors, the globalization of the post-World War II era has proceeded within a vast and extensive network of state-led institutions that have managed political and economic relations among countries. It is this expressly political aspect of the international economy that is the focus of this paper on how states fashion trade policy in times of crisis.

3. INSTITUTIONS AND INFORMATION

The protectionist policies of the interwar Depression era demonstrate the dominant tendency of states to "defect" from a liberal trading order as a response to heightened uncertainty in times of economic crisis. Government policies responded with protectionism not only in the Great Depression of the interwar years but also in the earlier Great Depression of 1873 when prices of agricultural goods fell on the international market, threatening the gold standard in affected countries (Frieden 2006, 8-9). The turn to protectionism as a response to economic crisis illustrates prominently the collaboration problem inherent in maintaining a liberal trading system, represented in the classic single-shot Prisoners' Dilemma. In the absence of a central authority such as a hegemon or an institutional mechanism to enforce the optimal outcome of liberal trade, actors lefts to their own rational devices will "defect" from this outcome by pursuing protectionist policies without regard to its impact on the international system. Such defections have the effect of devolving throughout the international economy as countries retaliate in response to others' "beggar-thy-neighbor" policies, thus reducing aggregate welfare, precluding the gains that can accrue from liberal trade, and leaving everyone in a worse position than before such policies were

---

[3] Eichengreen and Irwin (2009) argue that the current global crisis differs from the Great Depression in terms of the policy instruments available to governments. Baldwin and Evenett (2009) consider the prospects for WTO-consistent protectionism.

adopted. In the case of the Great Depression, this global crisis coincided with the decline of Pax Britannica, in which the age of golden age capitalism led by Great Britain and its adherence to the gold standard saw a decline that began in the late 19th century that was reinforced after World War I. As Kindleberger argues in his classic volume on the Great Depression, the international trading system lacked a strong central actor to uphold a liberal trading order (1973[1986]), and by the time of the Great Depression international trade centered in Europe had degenerated into a network of discriminatory trading blocs.

Whereas economic crisis induces uncertainty in the conduct of commercial relations, institutions serve as conveyors of information that help to mitigate the information problem that prevails in prisoner's dilemma settings. International institutions promote cooperation among participants and thus mitigate the collaboration problem of liberal international trade in several ways. In trade, institutions such as the World Trade Organization (WTO) create expectations of repeated interaction and thus render participants more aware of the "shadow of the future" and the long-term costs of defection. International institutions also reduce transaction costs as they provide negotiating fora through regular meetings and a set of common rules for behavior. Most relevant to this paper, institutions provide transparency and information regarding participants' policies, and for international trade cooperation, such characteristics enable countries to pursue reciprocity strategies when cheating occurs and to enforce the institution's rules.

Institutions are one type of international regime, defined in the classic volume on the subject as "principles, norms, rules, and decision–making procedures around which actor expectations converge in a given issue-area" (Krasner 1983, 1). In the area of commercial exchange, institutions transform trade from a single-play Prisoners' Dilemma to an iterated game in which the "shadow of the future" figures strongly in the behavioral choices of actors. In doing so, institutions reduce uncertainty about the behavior of participating actors and the risks of making agreements. Institutions reduce uncertainty by providing information about participant behavior and preferences. Indeed, as a mechanism to redress market-failure problems, Keohane (1984) emphasizes that the most important of an institution's functions may informational (92), that is, in providing transparency regarding the preferences and behavior of participating actors.

In addition, the informational function of institutions takes place within a set of mechanisms that include formal legal procedures and rules that "lock in" state commitments and create strong expectations about future behavior. By providing mechanisms for resolving disputes, formal channels of communication and consultation, and rules for decision-making, institutions allow for greater communication among participants, making it difficult for participants to renege on their institutional obligations without incurring great political costs. Institutions also create transgovernmental "connections, routines, and coalitions" that promote the continuity of state policies consistent with institutional obligations and also generate an institutional "spillover" process that may reinforce policy orientations outside an institution's particular scope (Ikenberry 2001, 66-68).

In spite of the importance of an institution's informational function in reducing uncertainty, the uncertainty problem of international cooperation is greatly exacerbated in times of economic crisis, as the crisis is attended by a lack of information about how actors will address its effects on individual economies and some are increasingly pressured from within to "defect" from a liberal trading order and enact protectionist trade policy. Heightened uncertainty in times of economic crisis, therefore, threatens to unravel the current liberal trading order. We advance the argument that institutions are important in preventing states from pursuing protectionist policies in times of economic crisis and to maintaining a liberal trading system. Institutions continue to reduce uncertainty through two key functions. First, institutions continue to function as conduits of information and thus enhance transparency in the preferences and behavior of institutional participants. Second, institutions, as they "lock in" particular policies, tend to exhibit "stickiness" even in times of crisis and high uncertainty, thus making it difficult for sudden policy changes to occur.

4. MEMBERSHIP IN INTERNATIONAL ORGANIZATIONS AND TRADE POLICY IN THE CURRENT GLOBAL CRISIS

We test our argument on the informational function of institutions by analyzing the impact of membership in international organizations on states' trade policies during the current global economic crisis. As noted above, the main difference between the current economic crisis and the Great Depression is the network of international institutions installed after the end of World War II that have constituted the broader political environment in which globalization has proceeded. Indeed, international organizations have flourished since the end of World War II. The Allied victory after World War II led to the creation of the United Nations to "govern" the area of international security, the Bretton Woods institutions to promote international cooperation in monetary relations, and the General Agreement on Tariffs and Trade, though far less formal than its intended parent the International Trade Organization, to promote multilateral trade liberalization. Numerous international organizations followed that were devoted to a diverse range of issue areas. In this paper, we focus our attention on political and economic international organizations and their impact on state behavior during this economic crisis. Our main hypothesis is that countries with more memberships in international organization are less likely to enact trade politics that "defect" from a liberal trading order. In testing our hypothesis, we differentiate between political and economic international organizations, which we argue differ in their relative impact. While political organizations are important in the non-economic arena, we expect that international organizations devoted to economic issues are far more relevant in their informational function in times of crisis and thus more effective in preventing the adoption of protectionist trade policies.[4] In addition, we also distinguish between interventionist and non-interventionist international organizations, in which the former are characterized by the institutional capacity to enforce organizational obligations.

5. MODEL AND CASE SELECTION

To test our hypothesis that the network of international organizations decreases the probability of states implementing protectionist policies, we implement a cross-sectional analysis using a newly-compiled dataset including 167 countries on which there is available data. We include in our sample the European Union (henceforth, the EU) as a single actor in

---

[4] For a similar distinction see Mansfield and Pevehouse (2008).

addition to each EU member country. We have selected this coding procedure in view of the fact that, in our data, protectionist policies are implemented by both the EU as a whole and by each EU member country acting individually.[5] Since we are not able to distinguish which EU country is involved in the push to implement a specific policy, we think this is the most appropriate way to code EU protectionist policies without inflating our dependent variable in relation to EU member countries.[6]Moreover, we cannot ignore the fact that the EU is a customs union with a common commercial policy. For instance, EU member countries alone are not allowed to sign trade agreements with third countries; only the EU as single actor is allowed to engage in this behaviour.The operationalization of variables presents two main challenges. On the one hand, we need a reliable and systematic way to capture states' defection from trade cooperation in the current crisis. On the other hand, we need to categorize IGOs in relation to both their function, *i.e.* economic vs. political IGOs, and their structure, *i.e.* institutionalized vs. non-institutionalized IGOs. The former categorization allows us to test the claim that economic IGOs are more effective than political IGOs at inhibiting state defections. The latter categorization helps us to see if IGOs impact states' behaviour during the crisis by increasing information or by locking in state commitments, or both. Below we describe these variables as well as other control variables included in our models in detail.

5.1. Dependent Variable

Our dependent variable captures the number of protectionist measures taken by states during the current economic downturn that are likely to affect foreign commerce. We label this variable Protectionism. Data comes from Global Trade Alert (henceforth, GTA), which is co-ordinated by the *Centre for Economic Policy Research*, an independent academic think-tank based in London, UK. GTA monitors a large number of countries in the world, drawing upon expertise from independent research institutes in seven regions.In addition, GTA identifies those trading partners that are likely to be harmed by protectionist measures, as well as the type of measures implemented, e.g. bail out measures, export subsidies, etc. Moreover, this data is up-to-date, since GTA provides real-time information, and is freely accessible.[7]

We collected data on protectionist measures that were implemented between January 2008 to the 26th of December 2009. We ended up with 604 protectionist measures.[8] In line with our theoretical framework we are interested in measuring beggar-thy-neighbor policies implemented by countries during the current crisis. Accordingly, our dependent variable

---

[5] If a EU member country were to implement a protectionist policy that discriminates against at least one other EU member, such member would veto said policy in the EU Commission.

[6] We speculate that it is quite unlikely that each EU member country has an interest in every protectionist policy implemented by the EU as a single actor. For instance, a protectionist policy concerning milk and milk products, such as the one issued by the European Commission on 2 January 2009, is likely to have been lobbied only by those countries that have significant dairy industries. Countries that have no interest in a specific sector back, or at least fail to oppose, a protectionist policy to gain support in other sectors that they care about. This issue-linkage mechanism has little to do with our theoretical framework, *i.e.* defection as result of (the fear of) defection by trade partners, and would bias results against our argument.

[7] Data are available at www.globaltradealert.org.

[8] GTA marks each measure in red if it certainly discriminates against foreign commercial interests; in amber if it is likely to discriminate against foreign commercial interests; in green if it involves liberalization. We dropped "green measures" from the analysis.

captures every protectionist measure that includes nationalistic provisions distorting the market and harming trading partners exporters, investors, and workers. For instance, in December 2009 the Canadian government announced that it would provide up to 173 million Canadian dollars in loans to Bombardier Inc. to complete and deliver an order to Sweden's Scandinavian Airlines.[9] This measure affected several Bombardier's competitors in Brazil, France, Germany, Japan, Spain, United Kingdom, and the US. Similarly, in September 2008 Germany notified rescue aid for Delitzscher Schokoladen GmbH, a company active in the manufacture and trade of cocoa, chocolate, and sugar confectionery.[10] This measure discriminates against the foreign commercial interests of the other EU member countries.

Figure 1 shows the five countries that implemented the largest number of unfair trade practices in our sample. There are three main considerations to take into account here. First, the biggest countries cheat the most. This is not surprising since big countries have a large number of trade partners, operate commercially in almost every sector, and often have a high level of bargaining power internationally. Second, large developing countries take the lead in cheating. In particular, BRIC countries are responsible for almost a third of the total number of measures implemented during the period under investigation.

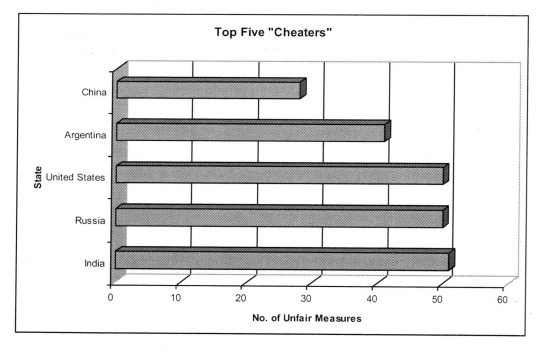

Figure 1 Countries with the largest number of protectionist measures implemented during the current crisis (position from 1st to 5 th).

This result is a testament to the increasing power of these states. Third, and somewhat surprisingly, European countries cheated less than other large and powerful states in this new

---

[9] Bombardier Inc. is Canada's largest aircraft producer and the third-largest civilian aircraft producer in the world. It employs approximately 17,000 people in Canada.
[10] Delitzscher Schokoladen GmbH was originally established in 1894 and its main customers are numerous German food retail chains as well as European and international trade companies.

round of protectionism. The EU as single actor is in 8th position, even Brazil and Canada cheated more than the EU. Germany is the only European country placed in the first ten positions (ranking 10th).[11] Finally, these three features are consistent with trade-damaging measures tracked by the WTO, adding plausibility to the reliability of our dependent variable.[12]

As the figure shows, the majority of unfair measures concerns anti-dumping provisions. Specifically, countries impose definitive antidumping duties on imports to protect strategic sectors. This finding is in keeping with the trade literature. As Prusa argues, "anti-dumping laws have nothing to do with economically harmful practices; rather, anti-dumping is just a cleverly designed form of protectionism" (2005: 683-684). Tariff increases, safeguard measures, and state aid to troubled industries represent, respectively, 23, 16, and 10 percent of the total amount of measures. Surprisingly, there are only five cases of subsidies granted to sectors that face difficulties: i) subsidies for the fruits and vegetables sector (France); ii)wage subsidies for firms in financial distress (Poland); iii) interest rate subsidies for the construction sector (UK); iv) subsidies for electric cars and batteries (US); v) "black liquor" subsidies to the paper industry (US).[13]

5.2. Main Explanatory Variables

Our main independent variable is the number of IGOs joined by each country. IGO membership captures the amount of information available to each state during the current crisis. Data comes from International Governmental Organization (IGO) Data (Pevehouse, Nordstrom, and Warnke, 2004), which is available up to 2000. The total number of IGOs in our sample is 383. European states are the most integrated in IGOs (Pevehouse et al. 2004, 113). As Figure 3 shows, among the countries in our sample, France, Spain, Italy, Germany, and Netherlands joined the largest number of IGOs. Conversely, the least integrated countries in IGOs are usually either small, autocratic developing countries or controversial states, such as Taiwan, whose independence is contested in diplomatic circles (Figure 4).In order to test their impact on trade cooperation, we differentiate among types of IGOs in two ways. First, different IGOs have different functions. Building upon Ingram et al.'s (2005) categorization, we divide IGOs into two groups: economic IGOs and political IGOs. There are 109 of the former, whichinclude organizations such as the WDO, the IMF and NAFTA. There are 278 of the latter, which include organizations that deal with military, political, and social issues.[14] Second, we divide IGOs into interventionist and non-interventionist organizations (Ingram et al., 2005). The former contain mechanisms for mediation, arbitration, and adjudication and other means to coerce state decisions, e.g. withholding of loans or aid, as well as means of enforcement of IGO provisions. The latter have no institutional capacity to coerce member

---

[11] Italy and UK are in the first 20 position, respectively 19th and 20th position. However, they are below countries such as Kazakhstan, Australia, Turkey, South Africa, Japan, and South Korea.

[12] See The Economist , January 2nd-8th 2010, page 26.

[13] Several measures are categorized by GTA as "State aid in the form of direct grants, loans, interest rate subsidies, and guarantees". In drawing Figure 3, we include them in the category "state aid".

[14] We took a conservative approach in selection organizations into the variable Economic IGOs. For instance, in contrast to other studies (Cao, 2009), we do not include into economic IGOs organizations that rules on standardization. The rationale for this decision is that we assume that standardization IGOs has little to do with trade issues.

states' policy choices. There are 39 interventionist IGOs, whereas there are 344 non-interventionist IGOs

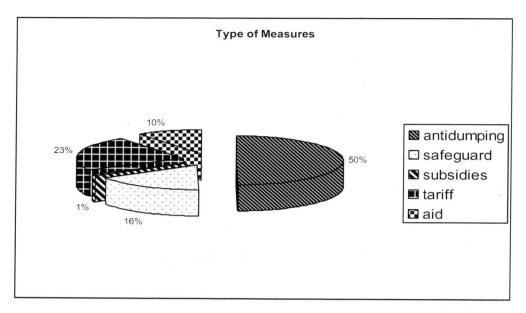

Figure 2 Type of protectionist measures (2009).

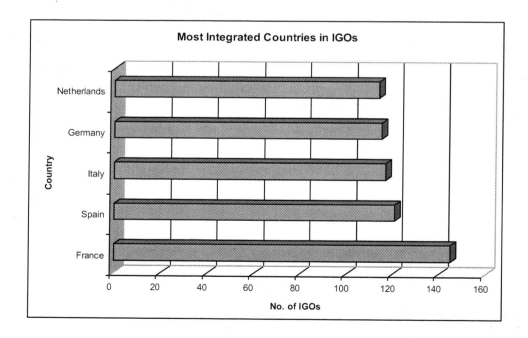

Figure 3 Most Integrated Countries in IGOs.

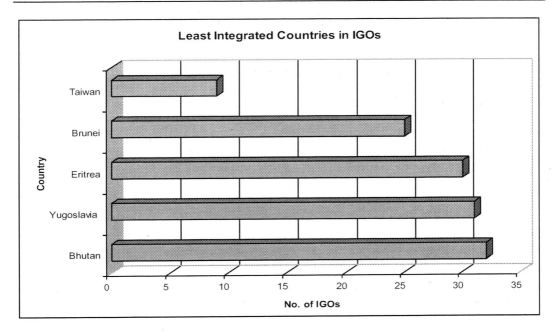

Figure 4. Least Integrated Countries in IGOs.

Finally, to further assess the impact of international institutions on trade cooperation we measure the number of preferential trade agreements (henceforth PTAs) to which each country in the sample belongs. PTAs are bilateral and plurilateral arrangements among countries that decide to decrease tariffs, e.g. the European Union, NAFTA, Asean Pact. During the past 20 years, PTAs have dramatically proliferated. Thus, PTAs are currently among the most important instruments of international economic policy (Limao, 2007). Due to their emphasis on trade liberalization and their enforcement mechanisms, PTAs should be the perfect candidates to show whether or not international institutions convey information among countries during the current crisis. Data on PTAs comes largely (but not solely) from three different databases, namely the list of regional trade agreements notified to the World Trade Organization (henceforth, WTO), the Tuck Trade Agreements Database, and the McGill Faculty of Law Preferential Trade Agreements Database. Excluding partial-scope agreements, agreements that envisage no preferential treatment, and agreements no in force, we find that 257 preferential trade agreements were signed up to 2007. Note: only a small number of PTAs are included in the variable Economic IGO previously described, e.g. NAFTA and Mercosur. For instance, bilateral trade agreements that count for 80 percent of the total number of PTAs signed are not included in the variable Economic IGOs. Thus, despite their high correlation ($\rho = .69$), these variables capture different concepts.

5.3. Control Variables

Since other factors are likely to influence the chances of a country implementing protectionist measures, we include a series of characteristics of states under analysis. Doing so is vital to avoid overestimating the effect of the main explanatory variables, as parallel policy choices may be a result of correlated unit-level factors or exogenous shocks that are common to various countries. We hence include several economic and political control variables in our model. Concerning economic variables, we include the variable GDP growth from IMF (2008). Indeed, the magnitude of the economic downturn is expected to affect the trade policy of countries during the current turmoil. Furthermore, we include per capita GDP to measure the level of development of a country. The more developed a country is, the easier it should find dealing with a crisis without relying on protectionist policies. Indeed, a developed country is in a better position to compensate societal groups that face losses arising from the economic downturn. This data is collected by the IMF (2008). Moreover, we include the variable Trade Openness (trade/GDP) to capture the importance of trade for a country. The prediction of this variable sign is ambivalent. On the one hand, open countries are more to lose from a race to increase tariffs and so it should be less likely to implement beggar-thy-neighbor policies. On the other hand, more globalized countries have been hit harder by the crisis and so they are more likely to protect those sectors harmed by the economic downturn. Data for these two variables is from the WDI (2008) for total trade and the IMF (2008) for GDP. Finally, we include the logarithm of population for each country (Population). As previously shown, big countries are more likely to implement protectionist measures. Data comes from The World Bank (2009).

Table 1 Descriptive statistics of the control variables in the dataset

Variable	Mean	Std. Dev.	Min.	Max	Number of Obs.
Protectionism	3.51	8.23	0	51	167
ΔGDP	4.19	3.68	-14.06	16.40	167
Ln(GDP Per Capita)	1.69	1.20	.10	4.51	167
Trade Openness	.33	.76	.01	5.38	167
Ln(Population)	15.76	1.76	11.18	20.87	167
Type of Regime	3.42	2.15	1	7	167
Government Effectiveness	2.47	.98	.29	4.7	167
IGOs	64.77	21.07	9	145	167
Econ. IGOs	9.67	3.42	2	23	167
Political IGOs	55.10	18.71	6	125	167
Interventionist IGOs	10.15	2.34	3	17	167
Non-Interventionist IGOs	55.10	18.71	6	129	167
No. of PTAs	7.71	9.17	0	27	167

Two control variables capture domestic political conditions. We use the seven-point Freedom House (2007) scale to measure the type of regime of each country (Type of Regime). The advantage of the Freedom House index over others is that it covers all of the countries in our dataset and provides values for up to and including 2007. To ease the interpretation, we invert the values provided by Freedom House so that 1 is the value for a completely oppressive regime and 7 the value for a completely free regime (Democracy).[15] This variable controls for the claim that democracies behave differently from autocracies in the international system (Fearon, 1997; McGillivray and Smith, 2008). Moreover, the variable

---

[15] Results do not change if we replace Freedom of House with Polity IV, another widely used indicator of the type of regime.

Government Effectiveness measures the credibility of the government's commitment to the policies that have been formulated and implemented. The prediction is that high government effectiveness should increase the capability of executives to deal with the crisis and therefore decrease the need to implement unfair policies. Data comes from Kaufmann, Art, and Mastruzzi (2006) and has been built using 33 data sources provided by 30 different organizations. Univariate summary statistics and data sources for all of these variables are available in Table 1.[16]

5.4. Method

In order to test the previous hypotheses, we consider the possibility of selection effects, i.e. unobserved factors that control whether or not a country implements "unfair trade policies", which could introduce systematic bias. For example, only large countries or export-oriented countries might employ beggar-thy-neighbor policies, resulting in a flawed interpretation of the relative significance of these variables. The sample of unfair trade practices is not random if there is a selection process that predetermines whether countries take these practices in the first place. To deal with these issues, we use the following specification of Heckman selection model known as the HECKIT model (Grier, Minger, and Brian., 1994; Heckman, 1979).

$$Y_i = \alpha_1 X_i + \alpha_2 V_i + \varepsilon_1 \tag{1}$$

$$Z_i = \gamma + \beta_1 U_i + \varepsilon_2 \tag{2}$$

Y is the dependent variable of the outcome equation, X and V are matrices including respectively the main explanatory variables and the control variables of the outcome equation. All these variables have been described above. Moreover, Z is the dependent variable of the selection equation. Specifically, Z scores 1 if a country implemented at least one protectionist policies in the period under investigation; 0 otherwise. 82 countries in our sample score 1. U is the matrix containing the specification of the selection equation: ln(GDP) to control for the salience and size of the country, Trade Openness, and GDP growth.[17]Finally, γ is the constant, α_1, α_2, and β_1 are vectors of parameters, and ε_1 andε_2 are *i.i.d.* error terms with a constant mean and infinite variance.

In sum, we endogenize the probability of a country to implement at least one protectionist provisions using some economic variables. The estimated probability of selection is then used as a regressor in the second stage for analyzing the impact of IGOs on the number of unfair measures implemented by states. The econometric logic of the Heckman model allows conditioning the estimated mean function in the second stage on the selection process in the first stage. Moreover, it takes into account that for each state the probability of implementing at least one unfair trade policy affects the likelihood of cooperating or defecting during the crisis. Finally, since the data are organized as a cross-section, to control for potential

---

[16] In relation to the EU we summed Population and GDP (see below), whereas we averaged the remaining variables. In addition, the EU had 24 bilateral trade agreements in force in 2007.

[17] We use GDP instead of Population in the selection equation so that at least one variable that is included in the selection equation does not appear in the outcome equation (a so-called exclusion restriction).

heteroskedasticity across countries, we employ the robust Huber-White sandwich in every estimation.

6. RESULTS

Table 2 shows the results of the main models. Model 1 contains a general measurement of IGO membership, i.e. without differentiating among types of IGOs. Model 2 distinguishes between Economic IGOs and Political IGOs. Model 3 distinguishes between Interventionist IGOs and Non-Interventionist IGOs. Finally, Model 4 includes the variable Number of PTAs.[18] Model 1 shows that there is no evidence that countries that joined a high number of IGOs are more likely to cooperate, i.e. to not implement unfair measures. The reason we get this result is clear from Model 2. Indeed, on the one hand, countries that joined a large number of economic IGOs are less likely to implement protectionist policies during this economic crisis. On the other hand, countries that are members of a large number of political IGOs are more likely to pursue uncooperative behaviors. The latter finding may be explained by the fact that big countries are usually members of a large number of political IGOs.[19]

Table 2. Heckman Model: The impact of IGOs and PTAs on protectionist policies

Covariates	Model 1	Model 2	Model 3	Model 4
Outcome Equation				
IGOs	.01 (.06)			
Econ. IGOs		-.91** (.39)		
Political IGOs		.15** (.07)		
Interventionist IGOs			.65 (.69)	
Non-Interventionist IGOs			-.03 (.05)	
No. of PTAs				-.19** (.08)
ΔGDP	-.09 (.31)	-.09 (.28)	-.06 (.32)	-.17 (.26)
Ln(GDP Per Capita)	-.51 (1.27)	-.34 (1.12)	-.67 (1.30)	-.13 (1.13)
Trade Openness	9.47 (8.15)	8.51 (6.69)	10.55 (9.64)	7.02 (8.87)
Population	1.63*** (.49)	1.43*** (.44)	1.51*** (.53)	1.70*** (.45)

[18] As mentioned above, Economic IGO and No. of PTAs are highly correlated. Thus, we do not include them in the same model to avoid multicollinerarity. Results do not change if IGO or Political IGO is included into Model 4 (they turn out to be not statistically significant), i.e. a missing variable problem does not seem an issue.

[19] The correlation between Population and Political IGO is .50.

Covariates	Model 1	Model 2	Model 3	Model 4
Outcome Equation				
Type of Regime	1.42	.95	1.69*	1.69**
	(.90)	(.73)	(.90)	(.84)
Government	-4.11**	-3.01**	-4.74**	-3.39*
Effectiveness	(1.63)	(1.29)	(1.89)	(1.67)
Selection Equation				
ΔGDP	-.01	-.004	-.01	-.01
	(.04)	(.04)	(.04)	(.04)
Ln(GDP)	.60***	.59***	.61***	.58***
	(.12)	(.11)	(.14)	(.09)
Trade Openness	.31*	.29*	.34*	.28**
	(.18)	(.16)	(.20)	(.14)
Constant	-2.04***	-2.00***	-2.08***	-1.97***
	(.43)	(.40)	(.48)	(.36)
ρ	-.84**	-.81***	-.85**	-.80***
	(.16)	(.13)	(.17)	(.12)
λ	-9.18**	-8.48***	-9.36**	-8.41***
	(3.81)	(3.15)	(4.11)	(2.91)
Observations	167	167	167	167
Censored Obs.	84	84	84	84
(Uncensored Obs.)	(83)	(83)	(83)	(83)
Log likelihood	-374.13	-371.84	-373.26	-373.27

Notes: robust standard errors are in parentheses.
***Significant at 1%, **significant at 5%, * significant at 10%.

Thus, as the next section will show, India, Russia, and the US are driving this result. Furthermore, there is no evidence that IGOs structure impacts the probability of cooperation in trade (Model 3). Finally, countries that are members of a large number of PTAs are less likely to pursue beggar-thy-neighbor policies (Model 4).

These results confirm the hypothesis that networks of IGOs reduce the probability of defecting by cooperation during this severe economic downturn. Not every IGO has this effect, rather only those that have an economic scope or are constituted by trade agreements. We claim that the explanation lies with the capability of IGOs to convey information, thereby mitigating the prisoner dilemma trap. Our results seem to suggest that only economic IGOs are able to convey such information. Moreover, the fact that the structure of IGOs is not statistically significant (and the sign is actually positive) seems to imply that information matters more than enforceability in relation to IGOs. Specifically, the crucial element here is that economic IGOs membership and PTA membership allow countries to collect large amounts of information. In turn, this helps to overpass the coordination problem that is particularly severe in a period of economic crisis. Conversely, there is no evidence that IGOs constrain countries' behaviors due to the presence of sanctioning mechanisms.

The results of our main variables are not only statistically significant, but they are also substantively large. Table 3 shows that Economic IGOs has the largest impact on the dependent variables among all the covariates. Specifically, moving from the minimal value to the maximum value of this variable decreases the number of protectionist measures by 18. Bearing in mind that the maximum value of the dependent variable is 51, the magnitude of this result is quite impressive. For instance, since European countries are members of several Economic IGOs, this contributes to explaining why they are behaving better than other big countries in terms of trade policies during the current crisis. Moreover, although the variable No. of PTAs has the smallest impact on the dependent variable among the statistically significant covariates of Model 4, moving from the minimal value to the maximum value of this variable decreases the number of protectionist measures by 5. This result is noteworthy, considering that the average number of unfair trade policies is 3.5 (see Table 1). In sum, international organizations play an important role in reducing unfair trade policies, though other economic and political variables are admittedly (and not surprisingly) more important.

Regarding the control variables, almost every control covariate that is statistically significant has the predicted sign, adding plausibility to our results. Specifically, the size and salience of a country strongly affect the probability of implementing protectionist policies (even controlling for the selection effect). Moreover, effective governments are less likely to cheat. The only exception is the variable Type of Regime, which is positive, though statistically significant only in Model 3. Thus, democracies are actually more likely to implement protectionist trade policies according to our analysis. This finding goes against the claim that democratic regimes comply more than autocratic regime internationally. A possible explanation of this result is that democratic leaders are sensitive to interest groups and to voters who usually ask protection during economic downturn (Henisz and Mansfield, 2006).In addition, India and the US that are two of the leading "cheaters" may also drive this result. Finally, regarding the selection equation, GDP is by far the strongest predictor, always positive and statistically significant, whereas the positive sign of Trade Openness shows that the more open a country is, the more likely it is to implement at least one protectionist policy.

To conclude, a note on the econometric model that we decided to implement is necessary. Results demonstrate the superiority of the Heckman model over competing specifications. Specifically, since ρ, which measures the correlation between the errors of the first and second stage, differs significantly from 0, a Heckman model is the only efficient and unbiased estimator in light of the theoretical framework developed in this paper.

Table 3 Predicted values: The effect of Economic IGOs and PTAs on protectionist policies compared with the other statistically significant variables

Variable (Model 2)	[min, max]	[μ-σ, μ+σ]	Variable (Model 4)	[min, max]	[μ-σ, μ+σ]
Economic IGOs	-19	-5	No. of PTAs	-5	-3
Political IGOs	+18	+6			
Population	+14	+5	Population	+16	+6
			Democracy	+10	+7
Gov. Effect.	-13	-6	Gov. Effect.	-15	-7

7. ROBUSTNESS CHECKS

To check the robustness of the empirical results, we made a series of changes to the base models. First, and most importantly, since our dependent variable is a count variable, an OLS regression may be inconsistent due to the fact that the dependent variabledoes not havea normal distribution, i.e. the distribution is skewed to the right (Wooldridge, 2002: 52-53).[20] Thus, we estimate Model 2 and Model 4 using a count data regression to check if our main results still hold. To take into account the selection bias problem, we first run a probit model and we obtain the probability of states implementing at least one protectionist measures (GDP Growth, ln(GDP), Trade Openness as explanatory variables). Then, we get the linear predictions to calculate the "inverse Mills ratio" (the λ coefficient in Table 3), and use it in the second stage regression in which we implement a negative binomial regression.[21] As Table 4 shows, results are very similar to those presented in Table 3, confirming the validity of our previous findings.

Table 4. Negative binomial regression with sample selection

Covariates	Model 2	Model 4
Econ. IGOs	-.08***	
	(.03)	
Political IGOs	.004	
	(.01)	
No. of PTAs		-.02***
		(.009)
ΔGDP	-.02	-.02
	(.03)	(.03)
Ln(GDP Per Capita)	-.08	-.02
	(.07)	(.07)
Trade Openness	2.21***	2.00*
	(.81)	(1.04)
Population	.23***	.24***
	(.03)	(.09)
Type of Regime	.03	.10*
	(.06)	(.06)
Government Effectiveness	-.16	-.21
	(.10)	(.16)
λ	-2.27***	-2.07***
	(.35)	(.62)
Observations	83	83
Log likelihood	-205.71	-206.83

---

[20] Since the mean of our dependent variable is not very close to zero, "a normal approximation and related regression may be satisfactory" (Cameron and Trivedi, 1998: 2).

[21] A likelihood ratio test shows that we have a problem with over dispersion data. Thus, the ordinary Poisson cannot be used here.

Moreover, we implement other robustness checks using our original Heckman model (Table 5 and Table 6).[22] First, to avoid an omitted variables bias we include in the outcome equation other variables that may impact the probability of implementing protectionist policies. In particular, we add the number of veto players (Henisz, 2000) and a dummy for countries that are islands (CEPII, 2007). The former variable proves to be an important determinant of trade policy during economic downturn (Henisz and Mansfield, 2006), whereas islands usually have *ad hoc* trade policies compared to non-island countries (Rose, 2004). We also include a dummy for WTO membership, since this is (by far) the most important trade organization. None of these variables are statistically significant nor do they change the results of the main variables.[23] Furthermore, we use the dyadic version of the variable No. of PTAs (Dyadic PTAs). Specifically, we count the number of trade partners that each country share an trade agreement with, e.g. by being member of the EU Germany has a bilateral trade agreement with 26 countries. We do this as another way to operationalize the network of PTAs in the international system. With this specification, PTAs have an even stronger impact in reducing the number of protectionist policies (Table 6). Finally, we dropped India, Russia, and United States from the analysis to check if our results are driven by these three countries, which are responsible for a large number of protectionist measures. In addition, we use the natural logarithm of the variable Protectionism to both decrease the impact of outliers and obtain a more normally distributed dependent variable. Even with these two changes we get comparable results in the sign and level of significance of our main variables. Note that Political IGOs is not statistically significant in these two last regressions. Thus, our intuition that big countries drive the result of this variable is confirmed by this further analysis. In addition, Type of Regime is not statistically anymore in Model 2 and is statistically significant at (only) 10 percent level in Model 4, raising the suspicious that India and the US were driving the result of this variable in previous analysis.

Table 5. Robustness Checks of Model 2: Heckman Model

Covariates	Adding new variables	Dropping India, Russia, and the US	Taking the ln of Protectionism
Outcome Equation			
Econ. IGOs	-1.00**	-.58**	-.05**
	(.39)	(.29)	(.026)
Political IGOs	.18**	.08	.01
	(.08)	(.06)	(.01)
ΔGDP	.07	-.12	-.04**
	(.30)	(.15)	(.02)
Ln(GDP Per Capita)	-.24	-.25	-.02
	(1.13)	(.45)	(.06)
Trade Openness	11.72	1.33	.33
	(7.90)	(2.33)	(.31)
Population	1.49***	.87***	.18***

---

[22] Since our main results are produced by Model 2 and Model 4, even in this case we limited the robustness checks to these models.

[23] We also added some of other variables, such as Type of Regime and Government Effectiveness, in the selection equation without any remarkable effects on the main explanatory variables.

Covariates	Adding new variables	Dropping India, Russia, and the US	Taking the ln of Protectionism
	(.43)	(.20)	(.03)
Type of Regime	1.39**	.50	.05
	(.66)	(.39)	(.04)
Government	-1.98	-1.03	-.16*
Effectiveness	(1.25)	(.87)	(.09)
Veto Players	-3.41		
	(5.01)		
Island	-1.10		
	(2.11)		
WTO	-4.45		
	(4.31)		
Selection Equation			
ΔGDP	-.01	-.01	-.00
	(.04)	(.04)	(.03)
Ln(GDP)	.58***	.53***	.55***
	(.10)	(.07)	(.07)
Trade Openness	.27*	.20	.24**
	(.15)	(.12)	(.12)
Constant	-1.94***	-1.78***	-1.89***
	(.36)	(.34)	(.31)
ρ	-.80***	-.64***	-.89***
	(.13)	(.12)	(.05)
λ	-8.14***	-4.01***	-.70***
	(2.91)	(1.10)	(.10)
Observations	167	164	167
Censored Obs.	84	84	84
(Uncensored Obs.)	(83)	(80)	(83)
Log likelihood	-370.69	-328.94	-152.09

Table 6. Robustness Checks of Model 4: Heckman Model

Covariates	Adding new variables	Including dyadic PTAs	Dropping India, Russia, and the US	**Taking the ln of Protectionism**
Outcome Equation				
No. of PTAs	-.19**		-.14**	-.02**
	(.09)		(.06)	(.008)
Dyadic PTAs		-.14***		
		(.04)		
ΔGDP	-.06	-.15	-.15	-.05**
	(.27)	(.27)	(.14)	(.02)
Ln(GDP Per	-.10	-.52	-.16	-.01
Capita)	(1.15)	(1.17)	(.44)	(.06)
Trade Openness	9.58	6.21	.12	.22
	(6.95)	(7.41)	(2.06)	(.30)

Table 6.(Continued)

Covariates	Adding new variables	Including dyadic PTAs	Dropping India, Russia, and the US	**Taking the ln of Protectionism**
Population	1.85***	1.83***	.96***	.18***
	(.47)	(.48)	(.24)	(.02)
Type of Regime	2.08***	1.30	.92*	.10*
	(.79)	(.81)	(.52)	(.05)
Government	-2.80	-3.61***	-1.10	-.16
Effectiveness	(1.82)	(1.42)	(.99)	(.10)
Veto Players	-1.74			
	(5.26)			
Island	.24			
	(2.69)			
WTO	-3.62			
	(3.86)			
Selection Equation				
ΔGDP	-.01	-.01	-.01	-.01
	(.04)	(.04)	(.04)	(.03)
Ln(GDP)	.58***	.60***	.53***	.54***
	(.09)	(.13)	(.07)	(.07)
Trade Openness	.28*	.29	.18	.22*
	(.14)	(.19)	(.12)	(.12)
Constant	-1.95***	-1.98***	-1.75***	-1.84***
	(.35)	(.43)	(.33)	(.30)
ρ	-.80***	-.83**	-.60***	-.87***
	(.13)	(.18)	(.13)	(.05)
λ	-8.37***	-8.60**	-3.76***	-.66***
	(3.02)	(3.87)	(1.09)	(.10)
Observations	167	167	164	167
Censored Obs.	84	84	84	84
(Uncensored Obs.)	(83)	(83)	(80)	(83)
Log likelihood	-372.65	-370.69	-329.85	-152.28

Notes: robust standard errors are in parentheses.
***Significant at 1%, **significant at 5%, * significant at 10%

8. CONCLUSION

Nassim Nicholas Taleb and George Soros disagree on a variety of economic, political, and philosophical issues, but not on the seriousness of the current global economic turmoil. The former thinker defines the current crisis as "vastly worse" than that of the 1930s because of the interdependence of the financial systems and economies worldwide.[24] The latter states

---

[24] See at http://georgewashington2.blogspot.com/2009/05/taleb-global-crisis-vastly-worse-than.html [consulted on January 12, 2010].

that "the world faces the worst finance crisis since WWII".[25] The two experts are not alone in this comparison. Several other scholars and policy makers, as among them Bernanke, Stiglitz, and Volker, have recently drawn comparisons between the two crises. Similarly, there is an emerging consensus that the outbreak of protectionism feared at the beginning of the crisis has been avoided thus far (Calì, 2009; Evenett, Hoekman, and Cattaneo, 2009). To be clear, protectionism has indeed increased since the beginning of the crisis, as shown by Evenett (2009), but not nearly as much as expected, and nowhere near the level to which this practice ascended in the 1930s.

We started from these two basic observations related to the current crisis and the Great Depression, *i.e.* the similarity in terms of magnitude and the dissimilarity in terms of trade policy response, to propose a simple explanation on why the protectionism spiral of the 1930s did not reappear in 2009. We claimed that the presence of numerous IGOs, characterizing the current international system, decreases uncertainty among countries. In turn, this helps states to solve the coordination problem that is particularly severe during such a downturn. Specifically, by receiving assurance that other countries are not going to defect, each state has a low incentive to implement beggar-thy-neighbor policies in the first place, making cooperation possible even in tough times.

In this respect, our argument is similar in spirit to that developed by Helen V. Milner (1988) in *Resisting Protectionism: Global Industries and the Politics of International Trade.* Comparing trade policy formulation in 1920s and 1970s, Milner argues that the growth of economic ties among companies reduces their interest in protection by increasing its costs. Similarly, we have developed the *macro* version of this claim. We have argued that the presence of IGOs generates ties among countries and in turn, decreases their interest in protectionism by raising the quality and the quantity of information available to states. The empirical analysis carried out in this study seems to confirm this claim.

By focusing on only one element, we are aware that our study does not provide a complete understanding of all factors influencing trade policy during the current crisis. This was not our goal. Indeed, although we took into account in our empirical model other possible explanations affecting protectionist measures, we do not examine directly the influence of public opinion, ideology, domestic political structures, or the role of specific interest groups. Our aim herein was to apply a theory that is firmly grounded in the international relations literature, *i.e.* international organizations increase information among states (Abbott and Snidal, 1998; Keohane and Nye, 1977; Morrow, 1994), to an extreme case, *i.e.* a very serious economic crisis, to see if these were any evidence that the theory holds. It did and this is indeed good news for the global economic system.

The take away point from this study is that globalization is often, and often rightly, blamed for every disease of the world economy, but it is something of a double-edged sword for crises. On the one hand, globalization, through interdependence, makes crises more frequent and makes the diffusion of crises faster and wider.[26] On the other hand, globalization, through the presence of international organizations, produces ties among countries, helping to mitigate the severity and the duration of crises. In this sense, our results

---

[25] Statement reported by Reuters on January 22, 2008.

[26] The crisis problem was one of the dominant features of the 1990s: the EMS crisis of 1992-3, the Tequila crisis of 1994-5, the Asian crisis of 1997-8, the Brazilian crisis of 1998-9, and the Russia-LTCM affair.

are in line with the findings of the empirical study *Is the Crisis Problem Growing More Severe?* carried out by Bordo et al. (2001).

A final note on the results obtained by the categorization of IGOs implemented in this study: we have showed that the impact of IGOs on reducing protectionist policies is only true for economic organizations, whereas it is missing for political organizations. Indeed, economic organizations provide the information that is relevant in setting trade policy. Moreover, the fact that the structure of IGOs *does not* affect the probability of implementing protectionist policies tells us that enforcement mechanisms and the credibility of commitments have no sway in this regard. This does not come as a surprise given the well-known anarchic feature of the international system. When crucial interests of countries are at stake (as in the case of a serious crisis), international organizations are not able to constrain country behaviors. Thus, information is more effective than (the threat of) sanctions in extreme events such as an economic depression.

REFERENCES

Abbott, Kenneth W. and Snidal, Duncan. (1998) "Why States Act through Formal International Organizations" Journal of Conflict Resolution, 42(1): 3-32.

Baldwin, Richard. (2009) "The Great Trade Collapse: What Caused it and What Does it Mean?"In Richard Baldwin, ed. The Great Trade Collapse: Causes, Consequences, and Prospects. VoxEU.org Ebook. http://www.voxeu.org/index.php?q=node/4304.

Baldwin, Richard and Simon Evenett. (2009) "The Crisis and Protectionism: Steps World Leaders Should Take," In Richard Baldwin, ed. The Great Trade Collapse: Causes, Consequences, and Prospects. VoxEU.org Ebook. http://www.voxeu.org/index.php?q=node/2656.

Jagdish Bhagwati. (1995), "U.S. Trade Policy: The Infatuation with Free Trade Areas" in Jagdish Bhagwati and Anne O. Krueger. The Dangerous Drift to Preferential Trade Agreements, The AEI Press: pp. 1-18.

Bordo, Michael, Eichengreen, Barry, Klingebiel, Daniela, and Martinez-Peria, Maria Soledad. (2001) "Is the crisis problem growing more severe?" Economic Policy, 32 (04): 51-82.

Cali, Massimiliano. (2009) "Protectionism and the crisis: some good news" Overseas Development Institute: Opinion November 2009: 138-39.

Cameron, Adrian Colin and Trivedi, P. K.. (1998) Regression analysis of count data. Cambridge: Cambridge University Press.

Cao, Xun. (2009) "Networks of Intergovernmental Organizations and Convergence in Domestic Economic Policies," International Studies Quarterly, 53(4): 1095-1130.

Culbertson, William Smith. (1937) Reciprocity: A National Policy for Foreign Trade. New York: McGraw-Hill.

Eichengreen, Barry and Douglas A. Irwin. (2009) "The Slide to Protectionism in the Great Depress: Who Succumbed and Why?" NBER Working Paper 15142.

_____. (1995) "Trade Blocs, Currency Blocs and the Reorientation of World Trade in the 1930s," Journal of International Economics, 38: 1-24.

Evenett, Simon J. (2009) "What Can Be We Learned From Crisis-Era Protectionism? An Initial Assessment," Business and Politics, 11(3): 1-26.

Evenett, Simon J., Hoekman, Bernard M., and Cattaneo, Olivier (2009) "The Fateful Allure of Protectionism: Taking stock for the G8" CEPR-World Bank e-book.

Fearon, James D. (1997) "Signaling Foreign Policy Interests: Tying Hands versus Sunk Costs," Journal of Conflict Resolution, 41(1): 68-90.

Feinstein, Charles H., Peter Temin, and Gianni Toniolo. (1997) The European Economy Between the Wars. Oxford: Oxford University Press.

Frieden, Jeffry A. (2006) Global Capitalism: Its Fall and Rise in the Twentieth Century. New York: W.W. Norton and Company.

Global Trade Alert. (2009) Available at www.globaltradealert.org.

Grier, Kevin B., Munger, Michael C., and Roberts, Brian E. (1994) "The Determinants of Industrial Political Activity, 1978-1986", American Political Science Review, 88(4): 911-26.

Heckman, James J. (1979) "Sample Selection Bias as a Specification Error," Econometrica, 47(1): 153-61.

Henisz, Witold J. (2000) The Institutional Environment for Economic Growth. Economics and Politics, 12(1): 1-31.

Henisz, Witold J., and Edward D. Mansfield. 2006. Votes and Vetoes: The Political Determinants of Commercial Openness. International Studies Quarterly 50 (1):189-212.

Ikenberry, John G. (2001) After Victory: Institutions, Strategic Restraint, and the Rebuilding of Order after Major Wars. Princeton: Princeton University Press.

Ingram, Paul. (2005) Interorganizational Learning. In The Blackwell Companion to Organizations, edited by Joel A. C. Baum. Oxford: Blackwell Publishing.

Irwin, Douglas A. (1995) "The GATT in Historical Perspective," AEA Papers and Proceedings, 85(2): 323-328.

_____. (1993) "Multilateral and Bilateral Trade Policies in the World Trading System: An Historical Perspective." In Jaime DeMelo and Arvind Panagariya, eds. New Dimensions in Regional Integration.Cambridge: Cambridge University Press.

Kaufmann, Daniel, Kraay Art, and Mastruzzi, Massimo (2006) Worldwide Governance Indicators (WGI) Dataset. The World Bank.

Keohane, Robert and Nye, Joseph S. Jr. (1977) Power and Interdependence World Politics in Transition. Little, Brown.

Kindleberger, Charles P. (1973[1986]) The World in Depression, 1929-1939. Berkeley: University of California Press.

Keohane, Robert O. 1984. After Hegemony: Cooperation and Discord in the World Political Economy. Princeton: Princeton University Press.

Krasner, Stephen D. (1983) "Structural Causes and Regime Consequences: Regimes as Intervening Variables," In Stephen D. Krasner, ed. International Regimes. Ithaca: Cornell University Press.

Limao, Nuno. (2007) "Are Preferential Trade Agreements with Non-Trade Objectives a Stumbling Block for Multilateral Liberalization?" Review of Economic Studies, 73(3): 821-55.

Mansfield, Edward D. and Pevehouse, Jon C. (2008) "Democratization and the Varieties of International Organization," Journal of Conflict Resolution, 52(2): 269-94.

McGillivray, Fiona and Smith, Alastair. (2004) "The Impact of Leadership Turnover on Relations Between States," International Organization, 58(3): 567-600.

Milner, Helen V. (1988) Resisting Protectionism: Global Industries and the Politics of International Trade. Princeton: Princeton University Press

Morrow, James, D. (1994) "Modeling the Forms of International Cooperation: Distribution Versus Information", International Organization, 48(3): 387-423.

Pevehouse, Jon C., Timothy Nordstrom, and Kevin Warnke. (2004). "The COW-2 International Organizations Dataset Version 2.0," Conflict Management and Peace Science, 21(2):101-119.

Pomfret, Richard. (1988) Unequal Trade: The Economics of Discriminatory International Trade Policies. Oxford: Basil Blackwell.

Prusa, Thomas J. (2005) "Anti-dumping: A Growing Problem in International Trade," The World Economy, 28(5): 683-700.

Rose, Andrew K. "Do We Really Know That the WTO Increases Trade?" American Economic Review, 94(1): 98-114.

The Economist. (January 2nd-8th 2010) "Counting their blessing," pp. 24-26.

Snyder, Richard C. (1940) "Commercial Policy as Reflected in Treaties from 1931 to 1939," American Economic Review, 30(4): 787-802.

Wooldridge, Jeffrey M. (2002) Econometric Analysis of Cross Section and Panel Data. Cambridge: The MIT Press.

In: After the Crisis: Rethinking Finance
Editor: Thomas Lagoarde-Segot

ISBN 978-1-61668-925-4
© 2010 Nova Science Publishers, Inc.

Chapter 7

TOWARDS A NEW POLITICAL ECONOMY OF CENTRAL BANKING

Roy Allen and Kristine Chase

ABSTRACT

One century before the global financial crisis of 2007, a similar 'global' financial meltdown in 1907 helped the United States overcome significant political, economic and social barriers to create the U.S. Federal Reserve. For the most part, the Fed represents, still, the political economy of that time. Since the 1970s, however, it is increasingly apparent that a true central bank must be 'central' to the entire world, if one assumes that recent globalization of the world's economy is a permanent condition.Key developments since the 1970s that, collectively, challenge the older nation-state-oriented ecology of central banking include: dramatic advances in information-processing technology; expanded use of derivatives and other new transactions instruments; a decline of formal state-influenced banking institutions relative to competitive global institutions; and the extraordinary size and borderless use of the global money and credit pyramid. In this chapter we propose a new and broadened concept of a central bank, one that recognizes how a central bank must operate within the new ecology of the 21st century.Promising research areas are suggested that might help frame a new political economy of central banking. The 2007 global financial crisis, and central bank responses to it, provides a rich case study for these purposes, and it is referred to throughout the text.

1. INTRODUCTION

One century before the global financial crisis of 2007, a similar "global" meltdown in 1907 helped the United States overcome significant political, economic and social barriers to create the Federal Reserve (Fed). The Fed represents still the political economy of that time – central banking has always been subject to the forces of political economy. Critics of the Fed today are using the same arguments, and the Fed is using the same policies as those devised in 1907: today's Fed reflects an at least century-old political economy. It is now apparent, however, that a "true" central bank must be "central" to the entire world, if one assumes that the globalization of the world's economy is a permanent economic state.

In this chapter we thus propose a new and broadened concept of a central bank, one that recognizes the emergence of "stateless money" as only one of many forms of wealth, that supports a more sustainable balance between real and financial transactions and that allows both state and non-state actors influence over its actions. This new concept of central banking is developed in three stages. First, we look carefully at the meaning of important terms within a political-economic framework: central bank, money, financial transactions. Second, we consider the "ecology" of central banking today, looking at the impact of information technology, new transactions instruments and globalization of the money and credit pyramid. This context provides a rich opportunity to use heterodox frameworks to consider central banking from new and enriching perspectives. Third, we compare this new concept with current central banking – its historical role and institutional framework. We also compare our approach with those of other well-known critics of central banking, both outside and inside the current system.

2. ISSUES, CONCEPTS AND FRAMEWORKS FOR CENTRAL BANKING

2.1. What is a "Central Bank"?

Though traditionally a central bank has been denoted by its role as "lender of last resort", modern central banks are best defined through a broader functional definition: a central bank is that institution within an economy that performs certain functions within one economy. These have expanded to include acting as the:

- Lender of last resort for financial intermediaries;
- Regulator of financial intermediaries;
- Depository for the government's Treasury;
- Investment banker for the Treasury;
- Institution "responsible" for monetary policy;
- Source of important economic and financial research and data analysis;
- Facilitator and protector of the payments system;
- Institution "responsible" for the value of the currency;
- Representative of the government in international economic negotiations.

Not all central banks in all countries perform all these functions, and the development of this list has strong historical legacies, some of which we will discuss later in this chapter. Clearly, this list developed organically, with existing institutions assuming ever-broadening functions over time. Further, as we note below, the ecology of the financial system is putting significant pressure on the boundaries of the above list. In particular, the advent of truly global financial markets along with the development of new financial instruments has brought into question the meaning of many of the terms in the above list.

In this section we consider, albeit briefly, what might be workable meanings for "financial intermediary", as well as "money and monetary policy" in today's world. This provides the foundation for considering, in Section 4 below, what a central bank would look like, if developed to match the needs of the world's financial markets today. This means taking a fresh look at the functions that should be centered in a single state-based institution, at structures that recognize the increased role of non-official actors in the financial system, and at how the world economic system can recognize and best manage the "stateless money" that is now dominating world commerce.

2.2. Financial Transactions and Financial Intermediaries in Today's Global Economy. State-Based Financial Intermediaries

Traditionally, a financial intermediary (FI) is an institution (state- or non-state based) that issues its own securities in the process of a financial transaction.[1] The transaction itself involves money and documentation changing hands in opposite directions. Since it would appear that nothing "real" has occurred in the transaction, commentators throughout history have assumed that financial transactions and financial intermediaries are either an unnecessary or an undesirable part of the economy. Needless to say, we do not agree: financial intermediaries perform the important role of facilitating savings and investment, as well as channeling funds from surplus holdings to those real needs that require financial assets. In fact, the financial intermediary system has become so essential to the health of the global economy (as evidenced by the impact of its crash on real wealth recently) that states have, over time, expanded control, creating what we argue are "state-based financial intermediaries" (SBFI) whose basic structure and management are significantly controlled through active regulation. While this regulation has at times been partially relaxed, the historical role of "crashes" and "panics" has been to increase state oversight.[2]

Thus, we define SBFIs are those financial intermediaries that have as their regulator either the central bank or an agency that performs one of the typical central bank functions. For the United States, epicenter of the most recent "panic", SBFIs include all the depository financial intermediaries (many of which have as their principal regulator an agency other than the Federal Reserve System.) While these are almost entirely for-profit enterprises, their activities are significantly controlled to attempt to insure an outcome that addresses social in addition to economic goals. Specifically, risk-assumption and asset composition are channeled for both private and public ends. From a broader perspective, these institutions are treated in some ways as a "public utility". This treatment varies between nations, but the basic strands of regulation are the same globally. While the latest crash highlighted the imperfections of our current regulatory system, it further reinforced the public demand for increased oversight and strengthened the case for a public role in these institutions.

---

[1] Some intermediaries, known as broker/dealers, buy and sell securities issued by other institutions. For purposes of this paper, we will assume that this function is subsumed to the broader definition.

[2] The DIDMCA of 1980 in the US reduced many restrictions on the operation of depository FIs, but it did not change the basic concept of state control and oversight.

2.3. The Growth of Non-State-Based Financial Intermediaries

Because securities (or "financial instruments") are simply "promises to pay" and can be invented to fulfill any particular need, a network of non-state based, or "non-official" FIs has always been in existence. The growth of the global economy has increased creation of instruments and their supporting institutions at a near-geometric rate, and created what has been termed most recently the "shadow-banking system". Within this shadow banking system are a wide range of non-SBFIs that include mutual funds, insurance companies, hedge funds, finance companies, off-shore banks, non-financial corporations that have developed financial instruments, etc. The principal attribute of all of these institutions is that, though they produce and sell securities, they are not regulated in any significant way by the central bank or its corollary organizations. In the U.S. the Securities and Exchange Commission (SEC) does have the oversight of certain types of securities (though not all by any means), but this oversight is limited to making sure that the truth is told about a security. The SEC does not have any central bank authority.

It is within the non-SBFIs that the growth in financial transactions has occurred, as documented in section 3 below. This growth has fueled a global expansion of credit and real output, but has been outside the traditional purview of central banks. These intermediaries do not have a formal lender of last resort, they do not have a payments structure that reflects systematic consideration of counterparty risk and satisfaction of claims, and their activities have not been regulated to reflect the social costs and benefits that come from the public utility aspects of the financial industry. As we note below, any design of a "true" central bank, de novo, must bring under its umbrella the non-SBFIs. The current legacy central banking system, developed ad hoc over several centuries, does not match the reality of FIs today. We note, though, that this is not the same as advocating an overall increase in regulation – some of the functions listed above may need to be redesigned or reassigned to other governmental institutions. Our point is more that the design of the central bank needs to reflect the economic, political and social background of the real financial system.

2.4. Money and Monetary Policy in Today's Global Economy

The classic definition of money has not changed over many centuries. Money in any economy is that "good" that is used as a medium of exchange, unit of account and store of value. Economies for centuries have chosen the good to act as money (the monetary good) on the basis of "what works" – i.e. the choice is based on functionality and has been extremely fluid over time. In today's world, almost all of the money that is in use represents debt: a promise to pay a certain amount in the future. This promise is fulfilled simply by exchanging the monetary good for another, with a trust that one unit of the monetary good can be exchanged for another unit of a monetary good (though not necessarily the same monetary good.)

In today's world, with global trade having eclipsed trade within economies, there has arisen a need for a global monetary good, one that people trust across state boundaries. At the same time, there is a desire for a single monetary unit of account, since this facilitates trade and reduces the risk involved in exchange rate movements. Further, the advent of global financial institutions has created a demand for a global store of value, so that accounts that exist internationally can all be in one monetary good.

Given that there is no world central bank, let alone central government, the world effectively has created "stateless money", a monetary good largely denominated in dollars, but not subject to the control by the U.S. Federal Reserve. This monetary good is created every time a financial intermediary, be it a SBFI or non-SBFI, creates debt or financial obligations denominated in dollars. Given the lack of reserve requirements for most of the FIs, the ease of the internet in making transactions and the desire of creditors to be paid in "trusted monies", the world monetary system has extended the reach of what used to be the realm of national central banks. Cohen (2004) refers to this phenomenon as the "deterritorialization" of the global monetary system.[3] In many ways, it is the ultimate free market solution to the problem of global money, but it comes with all the volatility inherent in market solutions. The world has long recognized the public utility aspect of the financial system (as the history of central banking and government control shows), but it also is faced with a multi-faceted conundrum: how do we encourage the development of new financial frameworks that match the globalization of commerce, while at the same time both minimizing volatility and yet allowing independent nations to pursue social and economic programs that often diverge. As Cohen states, "At issue is a classic collective-action dilemma. How can the preferences of multiple states be managed to minimize the risks of currency instability or conflict?"[4]

Before we can address possible solutions to this conundrum, we need to take a look at the world in which central banking exists today – one that has a very new ecology and clearly requires a new political-economic framework. This new financial ecology is dominated by instantaneous communication as well as new types of financial instruments whose long-term stability is yet to be determined. Further, as already noted, market-based rather than state-based institutions have come to dominate global finance and the sheer scale of financial transactions has grown at a geometric rate over the last two decades.

3. THE NEW ECOLOGY OF CENTRAL BANKING

3.1. What is Different Today?

New Technologies and Transactions Instruments

No industry spends more on information technology than financial services: $500 billion globally in 2009, compared to (in descending order) $433 billion spent on information technology by the global manufacturing sector, $390 billion spent by governments, $211 billion spent by retail and wholesale trade, $202 billion spent by communications companies, etc.[5] Why? As noted earlier, a financial transaction can loosely be defined as any business arrangement where money changes hands but the only other thing that changes hands is documentation. Both money and documentation are moved by information technologies; therefore financial market activity is enhanced by advances in those technologies. Expanding use and performance of electronic and regular mail service, telephones, computers, fax

---

[3] Cohen (2004), p. 211.
[4] Ibid.
[5] The Economist, (5 December 2009), "Banks and Information Technology," p. 83.

machines, image processing devices, communication satellites, fiber optics, the internet and so on creates better opportunities and profits in finance.

Since the micro-processor revolution that began in the 1970s, banks and competitive financial intermediaries have become, increasingly, digital technology firms. New technologies which have enhanced the opportunities in boundary-less electronic finance include automatic transfer machines (ATMs), telephone and on-line banking, and ever more innovative debit, credit and smart cards. The average retail user of money still depends mostly on paper money and plastic cards, but the multinational corporation or financial institution or trader relies mostly on satellite and fiber optic routing. The large wholesale amounts are transferred electronically. In 1995 the US Federal Reserve estimated that the *value* of US electronic transactions had risen to $544 trillion, check transactions were $73 trillion, and currency and coin transactions were $2.2 trillion—however, the physical number or *volume* of currency and coin transactions was estimated at 550 billion, check transactions at 62 billion, and electronic transactions at 19 billion.

By 2000, networks which handled staggering amounts of money included the Clearing House Interbank Payments System (CHIPS) run by private banks out of New York. CHIPS mostly handles foreign exchange and other large-value, wholesale-level international transactions, and the net settlement of its transactions is in dollar reserves through the Federal Reserve Bank of New York. Transfers through CHIPS increased from $16 trillion in 1977 to more than $310 trillion in 1997. The Federal Reserve's Fedwire is its electronic facility, which transfers reserve balances among private banks through dedicated wire and is the favored system for large domestic transfers. Transfers through Fedwire increased from $2.6 trillion in 1977 to more than $225 trillion in 1997. On a daily basis, CHIPS and Fedwire now move more than $2 trillion. Retail systems such as credit and debit cards transfer an additional several hundred billion dollars per day. By 1997, these daily recorded flows amount to half the entire broad money (M3) stock of the US, and more than one-third of the US gross domestic product for the whole year.[6] Compared to the US, Europe uses even more electronic transfers: for example, its GIRO credit transfer system sends money directly from the buyer's account to the seller's and accounts for 19 percent of transactions, whereas indirect and debit-based checks account for only 2 percent.

Derivatives and other new exotic 'off-balance-sheet' contracts, which are based on underlying balance sheet assets such as stocks, bonds, and commodities, have also added to international finance. As of 2009, the Bank for International Settlements puts the "notional value" of derivatives worldwide at $604.6 trillion.[7] This notional value does not appear on anyone's balance sheet, but as in the case of credit default swaps (CDSs)—which have a notional value of $36 trillion within that total—and other 'insurance-like' products, this estimate reflects the value of all guaranteed debt. Of course the rise of CDSs, subprime mortgage securities, collateralized debt obligations, and other more recent bundled derivative securities played a key role in the current global crisis. Ultimately, risk from these holdings was concentrated as much as spread, bad judgments were magnified, and credit was leveraged far beyond profitable levels.

---

[6] Solomon (1997), p. 7.

[7] "Over the Counter, Out of Sight," The Economist, 12 Nov 2009.

The Global Money and Credit Pyramid

Changes in communications have always affected the structure of finance, but these new technologies and transactions instruments of the last few decades are responsible for the truly global nature of today's financial markets. New international opportunities have occurred for centuries, but only recently has inter-dependence become so pervasive to merit the word 'global'. The growth of 'offshore financial markets' along with the complicated securitization of derivatives and other products since the 1970s makes the global money and credit pyramid increasingly difficult to measure. But, it is likely that non-US-owned savings in dollars of almost $300 billion per year were made available for new uses in the global economy in the late 1990s compared to less than $150 billion per year in the early 1990s. Sixty percent of the world's money supply in recent decades has been provided by the US dollar, and more dollars circulate outside the US than inside.

By the end of the 1980s, global financial markets were generating a *net* international flow of funds of more than $3 trillion each month, that is, the flow of funds between countries which reconciles end of the month balance of payments data. The *gross* monthly flow was several orders of magnitude higher than this net flow, and it is increasingly impossible to measure given the often unregulated use of electronic funds transfers. Of the $3 trillion net monthly flow by the end of the 1980s, $2 trillion was so-called stateless money, which is virtually exempt from the control of any government or official institution, but available for use by all countries.[8]

Eurodollars (dollars held in accounts outside the US), and many of the other new money and financial accounts and forms that have been created since the 1970s, often do not have reserve requirements in the banking system; therefore quasi-money and loans can be created based upon these accounts almost without limit. The rise of 'offshore finance' has encouraged this process, because offshore accounts usually do not have reserve requirements. Offshore finance can be defined as 'markets where operators are permitted to raise funds from non-residents and invest or lend that money to non-residents free from regulations and taxes'. Once money is raised, then without a reserve requirement it can be loaned, deposited, re-loaned, re-deposited, re-loaned, etc. in offshore markets without limits imposed by the banking system.

Offshore markets are generally categorized into three types: 'spontaneous' offshore sites, as in the UK and Hong Kong; 'International Banking Facilities' (IBFs) as in New York and Tokyo; and 'tax havens' as in the Cayman Islands and Switzerland. London became an offshore site 'spontaneously' after the new Thatcher government abolished foreign currency exchange controls in 1979. In the UK, minimum reserve requirements were then abolished in August 1981 for onshore banks. The Bank of England wanted to maintain them, but the commercial banks lobbied successfully to abolish them so that they could compete in the Eurocurrency business with non-British institutions. This is an excellent example of the growth of the market framework vs. SBFIs.

IBFs, which are more stringently licensed and controlled, were allowed in the US after 1980 in order to compete with London and the tax havens of the Caribbean. The net worth of assets held in offshore markets has been difficult to estimate, but through the 1990s and until the current crisis as late as December 2008, it has been estimated at $6 trillion or

---

[8] 'The Globalization of the Industrialized Economies', *Barron's*, 4 May 1987, p. 45.

approximately 20 percent of world GDP.[9]As early as the 1990s, according to some estimates, "as much as half of the world's stock of money either resides in, or is passing through, tax havens" (Kochen, 1991, p.73). The nine tax havens of the Caribbean have been home to half of the world's insurance companies, and 15 percent of the world's merchant shipping companies. In addition, individual private savings of $500 billion was held in tax havens in 1993—an amount of money approximately equal to the entire savings of the world's 'super-rich' (Norton, 1993). Thus, Lord Rees-Mogg (1993) warned:

The world has never seen anything quite like this before. Governments are unlikely to recover their control of finance ... Any future attempts to restore capital controls or regain taxing power are quite implausible ... American and European welfare systems which depend on high tax may become insolvent. In the new world 'tax the rich' has ceased to be an option; the rich are not going to sit around waiting to be taxed.

Formal Vs. Competitive Institutions

"Non-state," or "non-official," or "shadow" banking institutions were just as present and just as responsible for the financial crisis in 1907 as they were in 2007.As Minsky (2008) points out, the rapid growth and influence of these less secure, less regulated financial intermediaries, and the leveraged credit boom that they facilitate, are typical drivers of the "financial fragility" boom that precedes a crisis.The dominant shadow banking institutions prior to the 1907 panic were the so-called 'Trusts' and the investment bank-brokerages, which had come into existence and grown dramatically in the previousthree decades.Unlike national banks, these "competitive" institutions (although there was some joint ownership with banks) could hold stock equity and their reserves and interest rates were largely unregulated.In the decade before 1907, Trust assets quadrupled to equal nearly three fourths the total assets of national banks.Adding in assets of various private banks, investment banks, insurance companies, and others, the shadow financial system had grown at least as large as the national commercial banking system in 1907—just as it would in 2007.

When the 1907 crisis hit, J. P. Morgan brought together the Presidents of these shadow banks as well as official Banks into his office and negotiated solutions, which typically involved forcing a majority of institutions to pool their rescue funds and serve as lenders of last resort (LOLR) for the most distressed.Similarly in the current crisis, U.S. Treasury Secretary Henry Paulson and Fed Chairman Ben Bernanke did the same with financial executives in October 2008, in the context of the $700 billion 'TARP' rescue fund provided by Congress.To start, this rescue provided $125 billion to the nine largest banks, $180 billion to the insurance company AIG and another $125 billion to regional banks. Subsequently, further Federal Reserve money went to other segments of the shadow banking system: commercial paper, mutual funds, hedge funds, credit card companies, and even foreign banks holding US currency.

What is different today, compared to the period leading up to the creation of the Federal Reserve, is not the existence and influence of competitive banking institutions, but instead the more difficult regulatory job of identifying who they are (or at least who their counterparties and clients are), where they are, and given their global nature, the difficulty of 'bringing them together in one room' in the event of a crisis. The securitization and multiple reselling of risky assets, as discussed in the previous section, began to compound this problem in the

---

[9] 'Harbours of Resentment', Financial Times, 1 December 2008, p. 11.

1990s.For example, unlike the Latin American debt crisis of the 1980s, which involved large, well-identified loans from U.S. and other money-center banks, during the 1994-95 Mexican debt crisis securitized stocks and bonds were the vehicles for much of the foreign investment into Mexico.Selling of these liquid securities was thus immediate when the crisis revealed itself, and selling could not be slowed by negotiations between government officials, the IMF, and large financial institutions.When the Mexican finance minister presented his economic crisis management program at the Federal Reserve Bank of New York on 21 December 1994, various mutual fund and hedge fund managers were present, who represented only a subset of the exposed investors.If Mexican officials had wanted to renegotiate terms with its creditors, they would have had trouble even identifying them.

This early 1994-5 example of what we might call the "non-identification of troubled assets" problem faced by central banks, due to securitization and globalization, was of course a central problem in the current crisis.For example, Iceland's three major banks, Kaupthing, Landsbanki, and Glitnir, after deregulation in 2001, became major players in the transactions-based global economy, and essentially acted as a giant hedge fund for domestic and international clients until their failure in late 2008.During this period, the debt levels of non-financial corporations in Iceland increased from 50 percent of GDP to 300 percent, and international real estate and other systemic risks contained in these highly leveraged portfolios was not identified by the too-small-by-comparison central bank until it was too late.

3.2. The Current Crisis: Stabilization in an Unstable World

Author Allen has attempted to correlate changes in the money and credit pyramid and related institutions with changes in GDP and employment in the 'real' economy, including in light of the current crisis and the long boom which preceded it (Allen, 2009, Allen and Snyder, 2009).His primary results are:

- As discussed in section 3.1, advances in information processing technologies and related innovations since the early 1970s increased the profitability of financial market participation and arbitrage across the global system.Government deregulation of national financial markets to allow international competition and participation also encouraged the expansion and globalization of financial markets, especially during the 'explosive 1980s'. This government deregulation, based upon the free market belief system and related ideologies, was championed by President Ronald Reagan in the US in the early 1980s along with Prime Minister Margaret Thatcher in Britain among others.
- Also as discussed in section 3.1, the new global financial markets allowed a remarkable expansion of no-reserve banking and money and wealth creation.Offshore markets, new financial products and other ways to securitize and market the ownership of tangible property supported the 'long boom' from the early 1980s through 2006, but unsustainably so, thus resulting in a dramatic contraction in this money and credit pyramid starting in 2007. The current global crisis demonstrates many of the common 'boom–bust' patterns of previous large-scale

crises, although the current crisis played itself out in a more systematically-linked global ecology.

- Allen's econometric research (Allen, 1989, 2009) indicates that significant portions of new money creation through reserve banking, securitization of assets and other processes, as well as use of the expanded 'float' of purchasing power that is based upon core monies, can be allocated to people over time and space arbitrarily through 'pure social agreement' within the new financial infrastructure. Wealth and transaction capital can be created, reallocated and destroyed without necessarily involving (in the first round of system-adjustment) the 'good old' political economy of tangible merchandise, stocks of production capital, non-financial services, GDP productivity of labor, etc.

These innovations and processes since the 1970s have helped coordinate and direct the global economy, and they have produced efficiencies and sustainable new wealth. They have also increased instabilities and the potential for loss, as per the current crisis.

3.3. The Call for New Political-Economic Frameworks

Recent research by Carmen Reinhart and Kenneth Rogoff (2007, 2008, 2009) reveals that large-scale financial crises have been a regular phenomenon for centuries. Based on historical data, the current crisis is not unusual in magnitude, and if anything 'we were overdue' based upon historical patterns. However, heightened awareness of the likelihood of crisis only began to surface in the mid-1990s. In 1996, the International Monetary Fund (IMF) indicated that approximately three-quarters of its more than 180 member countries had encountered 'significant' banking sector problems between 1980 and 1995, one-third of which warrant the definition 'crisis' (Lindgren et al., 1995). Then, in 1997, the East Asian financial crisis struck, which was followed by the Russian and Brazilian crises in 1998 and various others, such as the Argentine crisis in 2002.

These crises, even prior to the current situation, began to generate a flurry of policymaking activity. At the international level, initiatives at the IMF and elsewhere in 2000–05 came close to, but did not realize, a 'bankruptcy procedure' for countries, which was a stark contrast from the famous, and uninformed, quote of less than three decades ago (shortly before the 1982 Latin American debt crisis) from the Chairman of CitiCorp that 'countries don't go broke'. However, there was no agreement within the IMF's Executive Board regarding the best way to proceed. Its Director Anne Krueger had proposed various 'Sovereign Debt Restructuring Mechanisms' (SDRMs), which in some cases would require an Amendment of the IMF's Articles of Agreement in order to extend the IMF's role in resolving crises. She summarizes IMF discussions of the first SDRM proposals as follows:

"Many Directors believe that ... intermediate options could help address concerns about significantly extending the Fund's powers in a statutory approach ... Some Directors, however, expressed a strong preference for a contractual approach not requiring an Amendment of the Fund's Articles, and cautioned against any mechanism that would imply the creation of an international judicial body to oversee the restructuring process, either within or outside the Fund" (IMF, 2002).

The *ad hoc* rescue fund provided to Mexico after its crisis at the end of 1994 was unprecedented in size—approximately $50 billion—as well as in international political scope, given the ways that it involved the IMF, the US Treasury's Exchange Stabilization Fund (normally reserved for other purposes), the Bank for International Settlements, and a variety of independent countries. Mexico's oil export revenues could even be held by the Federal Reserve Bank of New York to guarantee US loans. *Ad hoc* financial bail-outs offered to Korea and Indonesia in 1997, and Brazil in 1998 were similarly large.

Complicating efforts by the IMF, central bankers and others to prevent and resolve country crises and to advance a better international financial architecture has been disagreement on how recent financial crises are related to recent 'globalization' of economic activity. When author Allen published the first edition of *Financial Crises and Recession in the Global Economy* in 1994, a member of the US Federal Reserve Board concluded that the author "grossly overstates [that financial globalization] is the principal cause and explanation of various events that Allen exaggeratedly refers to as crises."[10]

Scholarly journals were launched in recent decades to respond to these issues. For example, in the first edition of *Review of International Political Economy* (1994), the editors state:

> The creation of a global economic order has come to represent the defining feature of our age, as a major force shaping economies and livelihoods in all areas of the world. Globalization, of course, has many aspects ... The first of these is the emergence of a truly global financial market ... and the resulting increase in the power of finance over production.[11]

As authoritatively summarized by Kindleberger, over the long history of market capitalism, the start of an unsustainable financial boom or 'mania' is always linked to a sudden increase in money liquidity and lending. Unstable and exaggerated expectations, which are quite subjective, play a role:

> "The heart of this book is that the Keynesian theory is incomplete [in explaining economic instabilities and crises], and not merely because it ignores the money supply. Monetarism is incomplete, too. A synthesis of Keynesianism and monetarism, such as the Hansen-Hicks IS-LM curves that bring together the investment-saving (IS) and liquidity-money (LM) relationships, remains incomplete, even when it brings in production and prices (as does the most up-to-date macroeconomic analysis), if it leaves out the instability of expectations, speculation, and credit and the role of leveraged speculation in various assets" (Kindleberger, 1989, p. 25).

Given the increased importance, across a larger and more dynamic global political economy, of subjective expectations, leveraged investment as supported by new electronic and derivative money and credit forms, unregulated no-reserve-requirement offshore financial markets, etc., some current research is consistent with the innovative notion that monetary-wealth, or what Marx called 'unproductive finance capital' (as opposed to physical capital or capital goods such as machines and factories) may be a 'driver' of economic instabilities. As

---

[10] *Choice*, January 1995.
[11] *Review of International Political Economy*, 1994, p. 3).

elaborated by Philip Cerny among others, the new global financial markets may even be an 'infrastructure of the infrastructure'. Cerny's initial position, elaborated in debates that began in the early 1990s, was that 'a country without efficient and profitable financial markets and institutions will suffer multiple disadvantages in a more open world ... [and will] attempt to free-ride on financial globalization through increasing market liberalization' (Cerny, 1994, p. 338). Helleiner (1995) critiqued this position—of a determinist, autonomous, technology-driven financial globalization—by demonstrating that states, especially the US and the UK, have fostered and guided the entire process.

Reversing the causality of Karl Marx's (and many others') philosophical materialism, it may increasingly be true that autonomous, invisible financial processes can drive changes in the physical relations of production, as well as vice versa. As part of this process, central banks and other financial market participants can (usually haphazardly) increase or reduce wealth independently of any initial changes in the production of GDP or other 'real' economic prospects. The Chairman of the US Federal Reserve Alan Greenspan began allowing for this possibility in the late 1990s:

> "Today's central banks have the capability of creating or destroying unlimited supplies of money and credit ... It is probably fair to say that the very efficiency of global financial markets, engendered by the rapid proliferation of financial products, also has the capability of transmitting mistakes at a far faster pace throughout the financial system in ways that were unknown a generation ago, and not even remotely imagined in the 19th century ... Clearly, not only has the productivity of global finance increased markedly, but so, obviously, has the ability to generate losses at a previously inconceivable rate" (Greenspan, 1998).

Mainstream neoclassical general equilibrium theory has come under attack recently for failing to provide the theoretical basis for, as Greenspan states above, "the productivity of global finance to generate losses [or gains] at a previously inconceivable rate."Thus, surfacing in the literature is a revival of interest in evolutionary economics and complex adaptive systems approaches to understanding financial instability, especially models that privilege the role of subjective expectations and interactive knowledge among financial market participants.It is not easy to model a rapidly changing economy or one with non-normal (non-Gaussian) distributions of variables using the neoclassical model, which can accommodate growth fairly readily but structural change only with great difficulty.In a neoclassical model of an evolving economy based on past history, the parameter values are always becoming obsolete—slowly and steadily sometimes, or very quickly when there is a structural shift—as per the structural changes discussed in section 3.1.

The field of evolutionary economics has made efforts to incorporate capacity for structural change into its models. Schumpeter's idea that creative destruction is the essence of capitalism forms the basis of much modern thinking in evolutionary economics (Schumpeter, 1934). Schumpeter emphasized the role of liberal credit as a driver of speculative booms, and sudden credit contraction as a major contributor to the severity of the ensuing crash (Leathers and Raines, 2004). The version of evolutionary economics that appears most useful for analyzing financial crises is the 'Micro-Meso-Macro' framework of Dopfer et al. (2004). This framework centers around two novel concepts: rules, and meso units.

A rule is a pattern that agents follow in their everyday economic behavior: it may be cognitive, behavioral, technological, institutional, organizational, sociocultural, etc. Rules may be nested in other rules: we might talk about a motorcycle rule that includes engine rules, tire rules, etc. or a market rule that includes a double auction rule, a fixed-price rule, etc. Rules are carried out (actualized) by microeconomic agents (individuals, families, organizations, etc.). A meso unit is a rule plus its population of actualizations (e.g., the motorcycle meso is the motorcycle rule plus all agents who make, sell, repair, or drive motorcycles). An economic system (assumed to be complex adaptive) is a collection of meso units evolving over time. Macroeconomic behavior is the result of interactions among meso units. Economic evolution is the process by which new rules originate and diffuse through the population: very often this process takes the form of a logistic growth path in the new rule's meso unit. Structural change occurs when a new meso rule permanently alters the coordination structure of the meso units of the economic system. Over time, creative destruction occurs: new rules are constantly being originated; the successful ones develop strong mesos which displace previously dominant mesos; the weak ones disappear.

In this framework, a bubble or crisis in the financial sector would be analyzed as a structural change. Foster and Wild (1999b) have developed a promising econometric methodology for analyzing such structural shifts in terms of the logistic function, and for identifying early warning signals that the macro economy may be about to undergo a structural change. A high priority today is to analyze the international growth of money and credit over recent decades using these techniques.

For example, Figure 1 shows a structural change in the long-term trend GDP velocity of money (v) in the US, UK, and Canada in the early 1980s that marked the beginning of what author Allen (2009) has identified as the boom phase of this current financial crisis. In each of these countries, corresponding with the particular timing of the break in (v), governments dramatically abandoned financial market protectionism. Policymakers removed ceilings on interest rates, reduced taxes and brokerage commissions on financial transactions, gave foreign financial firms greater access to the home financial markets, allowed increased privatization and securitization of assets, and took other steps that allowed money to move more freely and profitably between international and national markets.In these key 'phase shift' years, there was a corresponding dramatic expansion in the transactions volumes of money-absorbing financial transactions (measured as the combined value of stock, bond and government securities transactions)—identified with econometric methods by Allen (1989, 2009, Chapter 2) as an inverse relationship between (v) and financial transactions volumes.As financial transactions boomed, supported by the money stock, the rate of use (or velocity) of that aggregated money stock for GDP markets (v) decelerated. In the US, the major structural break from trend in (v) along with other monetary-transmission relationships occurred in 1982 as participants responded to newly profitable forms of liberalized financial market participation with the aid of new information-processing technologies.[12] The major structural break in the UK occurred in 1985–86 as participants anticipated the UK's 'big-bang' of October 1986, which ended fixed commissions for brokers and separation of powers between brokers, and allowed a rush of foreign financial firms into the marketing of British stocks and government bonds and other securities.The major structural break in Canada's money supply and demand relationships also occurred in the mid 1980s when the Ontario government announced that it would open the highly restricted Canadian securities industry to unrestricted access by foreigners and Canadian financial institutions.

---

[12] Allen, 1989, p. 273

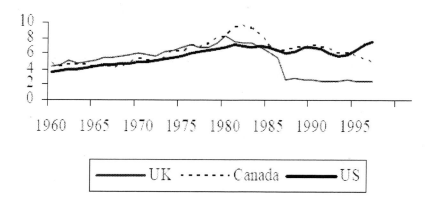

Figure 1. Structural declines in the income (GDP) velocity of money (M1) in the 1980s: using an evolutionary economics approach to identifying the start of the long boom that preceded the current crisis (Source: IMF).

4. CENTRAL BANKS: THEN AND NOW

4.1. The Roles of the U.S. Federal Reserve and the European Central Bank

Still Operating within Old Frameworks?

The two most powerful central banks today, the Federal Reserve (Fed) and the European Central Bank (ECB), were designed with respect to the political-economic problems of national financial systems over a century ago: the need for a state lender of last resort, the inflexibility and countercyclical nature of credit availability and the desire for a state-imposed and controlled money supply. As we shall see from a brief overview of their design, these two institutions are still operating as though the financial and political ecology of the global economy were the same as in 1900.

The Fed was created in 1913 as a response to the U.S. financial "panic of 1907", which precipitated the intervention of J. P. Morgan, as described earlier. Though it was certainly clear at the time that more than the SBFIs were involved and at risk, the legacy of almost eight decades of rapid U.S. economic growth without a central bank required the Fed to be created with relatively limited control. Further, the key central bank in the world at that time was the Bank of England, and the U.S. Congress saw its new creation as one purely for the narrow purpose "to furnish an elastic currency, to afford means of rediscounting commercial paper, [and] to establish a more effective supervision of banking in the United States."[13] As a massive compromise between agrarian and industrial/banking interests, power was located in the twelve regional Reserve Banks, rather than being centralized in Washington. Only ten years later did the Fed "discover" the ability to use open market operations to run policy, and only after the Depression did Congress create formal central control in the Federal Reserve System.

---

[13] Federal Reserve Act of 1913.

As originally envisioned, and ironically now resurrected, the key tool for the Fed would be the "rediscounting" of commercial, agricultural and industrial paper: essentially, the central bank's main function was to provide credit (the "elastic currency") to the real economy.[14] In fact, the Board, under "unusual and exigent circumstances", can authorize the regional banks to broadly discount paper of individuals, partnerships and corporations. Clearly, the recent and massive loans made by the Fed to financial and non-financial institutions are well within its charter. However, from the outset, there was little control over how the credit was used, and the general feeling was that the private market should have control. As Benjamin Strong, New York Fed President said in 1922, "the eligible paper we discount is simply the vehicle through which the credit of the Reserve System is conveyed to the members. But the definition of eligibility does not effect the slightest control over the use to which the proceeds are put."[15] Clearly, a framework was established that enabled credit to expand and contract with the economy, without microeconomic consideration of the type of credit extended, the terms at which it was made or the degree to which bubbles might be supported, or allowed to explode.

The ECB came to the central banking world almost a century later, replacing some, but not all, of the functions of the previously independent central banks of the eurozone nations. Though many of these nations did have some tradition of official intervention into microeconomic credit markets, and the European financial and political ecology was more aware of the "public utility" nature of the financial system, the ECB itself was patterned after the Fed. This is not surprising, given the feeling at the time that the Fed had done an excellent job at creating what Alan Greenspan called the "great moderation" in credit, interest rates and the real economy.[16]Thus, the ECB has as its four main functions:

- To define and implement the monetary policy of the Community;
- To conduct foreign-exchange operations….;
- To hold and manage the official foreign reserves of the Member States;
- To promote the smooth operation of payment systems.

As with the Fed, internal regulation of the financial system is left to other parts of the European Community.We thus can see that the basic framework of the two key players in the current global financial system suffers from a lack of coordination between the macroeconomic control of overall credit and the microeconomic operation of the individual private financial firms. Here, the meso and rule framework of evolutionary economics mentioned earlier (Dopfer et al., 2004) could be used to guide new research—this framework shows how the "micro" and "macro" are systematically codependent on the evolution of the "meso."

Further, in both the U.S. and Europe, significant numbers of these private financial firms are non-SBFIs – they form the shadow banking system that is outside of any significant state control.This is because they either are not regulated, or they operate across international borders and are able to avoid national regulations by careful choices in citing of operations. Further, the framework for the macroeconomic control remains strictly regional rather than

---

[14] Federal Reserve Act, Section 13.
[15] Chandler (1958) as cited in Meltzer (2003).
[16] Greenspan (2008)

global, with a continued legacy of concern over too much governmental control of credit allocation.

New Approaches are Needed by the Fed and ECB to Manage Financial Volatility

As noted above, the current political-economic framework for central banks is based on the clearly unrealistic assumption that the monetary good is produced exclusively within the SBFIs. These institutions must satisfy public-utility-like regulation, maintain reserves (though not in all countries) and provide transparency in their operations. These responsibilities impose significant costs on SBFIs, and rational managers of these firms have found that non-SBFIs are at a competitive advantage. The resulting growth of non-SBFIs has increased the market-driven risk in the financial system. The lack of transparency also leads to a lack of information about the new types of financial instruments and intermediaries, especially without a global central bank charged with gathering this information (let alone defining what is to be measured.) Further, as discussed next, the focus on traditional macroeconomic modeling within the world's central banks has prevented them, until recently, from recognizing the need for new theoretical frameworks.

Recently, given the new ecology of central banking discussed in section 3, the Federal Reserve has gotten interested in a complex adaptive systems approach to managing financial crises. In the world at large, complex systems abound: weather patterns, tectonic processes, disease contagion, power grids, etc. Their instability and potential for large, disruptive regime shifts are major social concerns. The ubiquity of such problems suggests that there may be common principles at work. A 2006 Federal Reserve conference on systemic risk (Kambhu et al., 2007) saw experts from fields such as civil engineering, disease control, ecology, national security and finance discuss their approaches to catastrophe control. The following composite picture emerged: an initial shock (possibly a seemingly insignificant one) leads to a coordinated behavior in the system with reinforcing (positive) feedbacks. A contagion begins, which spreads the original shock. When the pressure becomes too much the system makes a regime shift "from a stable state to an inferior stable state while shedding energy so that it cannot readily recover its original state, a process known as hysteresis" (ibid., p. 7).Research is focusing on factors that increase resistance to regime shifts and hysteresis, and on factors that can help the system recover. Some of this research may prove helpful in managing financial crises.

The emergence of a market-based global monetary system requires an approach that mirrors the new focus on the market as a complex adaptive system. Disciplines that this new field should draw on include (the already overlapping) economics, politics, international relations, political economy, and international political economy. Prominent contributors to these fields during the last century are also prominent contributors to the study of financial crises and the role of central banks, including John Maynard Keynes (1936), Charles Kindleberger (1989), and Hyman Minsky (2008).

Current models of financial crisis, while simulating many common patterns, do not yet explain sudden movements in exchange rates, interest rates, international investment flows, stock market and real estate values, and other key variables to levels beyond normal fluctuations. Thus, there is a revival of interest in what Keynes, in *The General Theory*, called 'animal spirits' such as 'spontaneous optimism' among entrepreneurs and others (Marchionatti, 1999). Essentially, Keynes argued that people may have a limited cognitive and informational basis for fully rational decision-making, and therefore, they may rely on less rational social conventions, vague beliefs, and other psychological factors. One implication is that:

> "The market will be subject to waves of optimistic and pessimistic sentiment, which are unreasoning and yet in a sense legitimate where no solid basis exists for a reasonable calculation" (Keynes, 1936, p. 154).

Given the growth in the market, any global central banking institution(s) will need to prepared for increased volatility, and for quick, equitable and workable responses to episodes where supplies of the monetary good and credit expand and contract suddenly and in large amounts. Further, unlike the well-researched national banking crises that have been resolved under domestic regulations, there is no comprehensive international law or policy that sets out the procedures for the international community to follow in international crisis episodes. Instead, the world has resorted to *ad hoc* responses, which increases uncertainty, generally have a longer response time, and likely are not viewed as equitable within the world's political system. Further, these *ad hoc* responses, as we noted above, often privilege exactly those institutions, the non-SBFIs, who suddenly are seen as "too big to fail." As Fed Chairman Bernanke recently said, in response to a question about supporting Goldman Sachs and Morgan Stanley, "I want to be very, very clear: too big to fail is one of the biggest problems we face in this country, and we must take action to eliminate too big to fail."[17]

4.2. Whither the International Economic Accounting System?

Though tangential to a consideration of an improved central banking system, it is important to note that the world's framework for financial accounting between nations and regions also is a "legacy system" ill-suited for measuring either trade or financial flows. Since it is often true that the measurement of something affects how we model it, and affects the types of policies we develop when problems arise, the current system for the Balance of Payments contributes to the world's difficulties in designing a system that supports real economic growth without excessive volatility.

First, the simple issue of terminology (i.e. the "Balance" of Payments) obscures the global importance of trade and financial flows and the reality that such flows will, in any market economy, likely be unbalanced and volatile. Second, economists have long known that the convention of pluses and minuses representing outflows and inflows, respectively, of the state-based monies does not even begin to capture the true flows of monetary goods today. The focus on net flows obscures the gross flows that support, emanate from, and measure the financial system.

The Mexican crisis of 1994-95 (noted earlier), is an excellent example. When the crisis hit, much of the transfer of Mexican monetary wealth into dollars and out of the country went, initially, into offshore financial markets. This data is mostly not reported in balance of payments statistics, but Brown estimates what was happening at least with 'LDC fuel exporters' and offshore dollar markets – Mexico can be presumed to account for the major

---

[17] Time (12/28/2009), p. 78.

share of these flow-changes between 1993 and 1994.18 In 1992 and 1993 the LDC fuel exporters did not accumulate or lose dollars reserves, but in 1994 there was a $20 billion loss (this portion of the data is fairly reliable as reported to the IMF). This loss in reserves occurred despite $20 billion in 'net financing in dollars' by LDC fuel exporters in 1993 and $25 billion in 1994 (still reliable data).

Where did these monetary reserves and credit supplies of dollars held by LDC fuel exporters go? Brown (Ibid) estimates that, from all sources (not just LDC fuel exporters) there was flow of hidden dollar income into offshore centers and tax havens of $50 billion in 1993 and $55 billion in 1994, and additional 'capital flight' into the dollar is estimated at $40 billion in 1993 and $50 billion in 1994 (unreliable data now). Industrial countries (excluding the US) were accumulating dollar reserves in this period (an additional $40 billion in 1993 and $80 billion in 1994); therefore they were not likely to be contributing dollars to offshore financial markets. Likewise, the US was receiving a massive inflow of dollars in all investment categories. Therefore, the LDCs, especially Mexico, probably accounted for a majority of the dollar flows into offshore markets, which in turn were mostly transferred to the US and other industrial countries.

A third problem of the current system is its reliance on an outdated framework for data-collection, reliant as it is on irrelevant distinctions between SBFIs and non-SBFIs in creating the global monetary good. Therefore we do not have reliable estimates of the true amount of financial flows. This means that central banks are devising policy without good information.

4.3. Proposals for Change

Proposals for a world monetary system have ranged from a reinstatement of the gold standard (which is essentially the creation of a world money, fixed in supply) and a cessation of any central bank control over money supplies, through ideas for fine-tuning of the current system, to calls for a single world central bank. Most proposals for a return to the gold standard are viewed with significant skepticism by the majority of political economists. These proposals rest on a desire for stability and the concern that central banks have mismanaged credit money systems. Nathan (2007) gives a thoughtful presentation of this view. More common are proposals for reform of the current system, leaving in place national central banks, but refining their responsibilities to address the obvious weaknesses in the current framework. Minsky (2008) states this position well:

> "Central banking is a learning game in which the central bank is always trying to affect the performance of a changing system. Central banking can be successful only if central bankers know how the institutional structure behaves and correctly assess how changes affect the system. Central bankers have to steer the evolution of the financial structure".[19]

Considerations of a single world central bank have a long and respected pedigree, starting at least as early as John Stuart Mill (1871) and continuing through to presentations at present-

---

[18] Brown, 1996, p. 119

[19] Minsky (2008), p. 359.

day major economics conferences (for example, see Rogoff (2001)). Though most acknowledge the utopian nature of this proposal, a single global central bank would be the logical end of a progression to ever-larger common currency areas such as the United States and Europe. It would reap the benefits of scale economies and would have the ability to consider policy in the context of the true world money supply. However, the world probably is not ready for the macroeconomic policy compromises that this would require, nor is it ready to subsume national interests to what would be an untested concentration of economic power.

Following Minsky, we propose that any new central banking system must match, and co-evolve with the political-economic framework that exists in the world today. In the evolutionary economics framework of Schumpeter and others mentioned earlier, institutions need to be subject to the processes of creative destruction just as are private entrepreneurs.This approach means that nations will not want to cede power over macroeconomic policy entirely to a supranational central bank unless the gains in political/economic stability and economic performance are seen to outweigh the loss from giving up policy flexibility and focus on the local economies. This is the trade-off the currently 16 nations in Europe have made in ceding power to the ECB, and is the same trade-off made in the United States in creating the Fed. Thus, we note a number of requirements for an effective global central banking system, one that recognizes the "new political economy of central banking."

- The basic "unit of control" should be the monetary good that the global markets have chosen. In today's world, this would mean that the world, as a whole, needs to cooperatively focus on the quantities of dollar- and euro-denominated debt instruments, along with any other currencies that competitively arise in proportion.Thus, in the current crisis, Fed Chairman Bernanke entered into currency swap arrangements with 14 other central banks in order to provide U.S. dollars to international markets—an unprecedented official step (both procedurally and in quantities of international liquidity supplied) toward globalization of central banking money and debt management.

- Central banks should revisit their guidelines for policy. First and foremost, the quantities that are tracked need to be expanded to include all "monetary goods" and not just narrowly defined domestic money supplies. For example, the Fed should reinstate its measurement of M3 (supplies of cash plus a wide range of bank instruments).As in Japan in its crisis after 1989, the acceleration of the current crisis in mid-2008 was associated with a collapse in the broad money supply (M3 in the US) — in both cases an early indicator of crisis that was not fully considered. Although the US Federal Reserve took the controversial decision to stop reporting M3 data after February 2006 on the grounds that the modern financial system made this data unmanageable and not useful, estimates compiled by Lombard Street Research show a decline in the US M3 growth rate from 19 percent in early 2008 to 2.1 percent (annualized) in the period May–June 2008.Not coincidentally, this decline was very similar to the decline in Japan's broad money supply (M2+CDs) from 10-12% growth in the late 1980s to 0% growth in the early 1990s preceding its 'lost decade(s?).' A continuing decline in estimated US M3 in July 2008 by $50 billion was the biggest one-month fall of US M3 since modern records began in 1959.

- The US M1 growth rate, which had fluctuated around 0 percent during 2006 and 2007 and the first half of 2008, was dramatically increased by the Federal Reserve (too little too late in the view of the authors) to approximately 5 percent in September 2008 and 15 percent by the end of 2008.Yet M1 has not served asa base for expanded supplies of broad money as these supplies are instead consumed by financial institutions in distress. Eurozone M1 growth had also fallen to near zero growth levels in mid-2008, and M4, the broadest measure of money in the UK, had actually dipped into negative growth territory. A temporary boom in US estimated M3 prior to mid-2008 before the acceleration of the crisis did not reflect an economy-wide condition—there was a near total shutdown in much of the American commercial paper market in 2008, and borrowers were forced to take out bank loans (M3) instead. The commercial paper market had yet to recover during mid and late 2008 while M3plunged, thus collectively the economy's broad bank and near-bank (commercial paper etc.) money and near-money supplies declined dramatically in mid-2008 (a point in time when the Fed and others thought that the spreading 'sub-prime mortgage crisis' was largely contained).
- Governments need to be explicit in their desire to impose regulation on financial markets that recognizes the large degree of economic externalities (positive and negative) that issue from the activities of FIs. This regulation needs to insure transparency as well as an internationally agreed-upon system for bankruptcy of FIs.
- Regulation is also needed that insures transparency as well as an internationally agreed-upon system in situations when countries are unable to honor sovereign debt (as per Mexico 1994-5 and Iceland 2008 discussed earlier).Whether the IMF and others move toward a formal bankruptcy procedure for countries or towards other Sovereign Debt Restructuring Mechanisms, given recent financial globalization it is clear that nations increasingly need to be coordinated like the 'states' in the U.S. or the euro-zone for purposes of monetary coordination and central banking.
- Along the way toward globalization of financial institutions, which has lagged globalization of financial markets, encouragement and support needs to be given to the creation of more organized regional currency blocs such as the euro model in Europe, so that destabilizing financial flows between currencies are reduced, and so that the dominant US dollar core of the global system gains less "money-mercantilist benefits" (Allen, 2009, p. 137-44) at the expense of other less organized currency areas—thus reducing the risk of financial crisis and further inequalities of wealth across the global system.
- Governments should foster the development of more stable forward-looking financial markets with larger secure reserve facilities, so that financial market participants of all types can better manage their levels of future risk against destabilizing changes in interest rates, exchange rates, financial crises and recession, etc.Because of the "non-identification of troubled assets" problem faced by central banks due to securitization and globalization, lender of last resort intervention by central banks often needs to flood entire markets with liquidity.Unlike the days of J.P. Morgan, intervention targeted only toward 'high-profile' bad asset holders is not likely to be as sufficient;

thus, larger reserve facilities are necessary.An analogy here is the use of strong systemic antibiotics to fight infection in the human body vs. smaller doses of localized antibiotics.

- Working cooperatively, governments should maintain better money-liquidity throughout the global system with continued research and better monetary policy responses. The econometric research of author Allen (1989, 2009) indicates that greater money supplies have been necessary to accommodate the growth of money-absorbing financial activity as well as non-financial activity. Based upon the quantity equation (m x v) = (p x q), changes in the income velocity of money (v) need further study so that appropriate supplies of money (m) can be directed to productive uses in the rest of the economy as for non-inflationary economic growth—appropriate levels of inflation as measured by the economy-wide price index (p) and real GDP (q). In this regard, there has been a revival of interest in theories of endogenous money creation, as by the non-SBFIs discussed earlier, that can be contrasted with the more dominant theories of exogenous money creation by the central banks and SBFIs (Lavoie, 2003, and Kinsella, 2009).

- New thinking about the dynamics of the global financial system should be encouraged, including greater attention to evolutionary and complex system approaches as discussed earlier, and greater attention to psychological and social factors. In this regard, 'Human Ecology Economics (HEE)', as recently developed by author Allen (2008), as a new heterodox approach to doing economics, expands upon evolutionary and complex systems approaches and includes a formal role for psychological and social system drivers. In Allen's view, HEE is a superior framework for the political economy of financial crisis and central banking, because unlike traditional economics and most other social sciences, HEE: (1) allows a long run time perspective consistent with evolutionary approaches; (2) it encourages use of the humanities including a formal role for belief systems and 'ways of being' within the economic system; (3) it allows everything to vary within the economic system—including belief systems, ways of being, and social agreements—in complex, co-evolutionary ways; (4) it emphasizes global systems and (5) it effectively juxtaposes 'sustainability' and other interdisciplinary issues alongside traditional economic issues. Each of (1–5) is needed, in the view of the authors, to best sort out and apprehend the 'creative chaos' of financial crisis, institutional change and related instabilities in the environment for central banking over recent decades.

- Finally, regulatory systems should be expanded to include the non-SBFIs and be flexible enough to recognize the formation of new FIs. This means defining FIs by function and not by narrow corporate form or balance sheet structure. For example, in the current crises, the Federal Reserve purchased more than $1 trillion in mortgage backed bonds to add liquidity and monetary oversight to the housing market, and the Fed created a "Term Asset-Backed Securities Loan Facility" (TALF) to supply approximately $200 billion to the student, auto, credit card, and small business loan markets. Also, U.S. reclassification of investment banks such as Goldman Sachs and Morgan Stanley as bank holding companies in the current crisis brought them into the 'public utility' supervision of the Federal Reserve to a much greater degree.

Terrible economic and social costs are associated with the current crisis; however it has already provoked some healthy change.Central banks*begin to* reform themselves along the lines described above, so that they *begin to* reflect the political economy of the early 21st century more accurately than the political economy of the early 20th century.Surely change in these stately institutions will continue to lag changes in the ecologies that they are obliged to serve, but it is the authors' hope that this lag time can be reduced.As Minsky states at the end of his classic work on this topic:The analysis argues for a system of changes, not for isolated changes.There is no simple answer to the problems of our capitalism...After an initial interval, the basic disequilibrating tendencies of capitalist finance will once again push the financial structure to the brink of fragility.When that occurs, a new era of reform will be needed.There is no possibility that we can ever set things right once and for all; instability, put to rest by one set of reforms will, after time, emerge in a new guise (Minsky, 2008, p. 370).

REFERENCES

Allen, Roy E. (2009), Financial Crises and Recession in the Global Economy, Third Edition, Edward Elgar Publishing Ltd.: Cheltenham, UK and Northampton, MA, USA.

Allen, Roy E., and Donald Snyder (2009), 'New Thinking on the Financial Crisis', Critical Perspectives on International Business, Vol. 5 No. 1/2 p. 36-55.

Allen, Roy E. (ed.) (2008), Human Ecology Economics: A New Framework for Global Sustainability, Routledge: Oxon, UK and New York.

Allen, Roy E. (1989), 'Globalisation of the US Financial Markets: The New Structure for Monetary Policy', in *International Economics and Financial Markets*, 266–86, Oxford University Press: Oxford.

Barron's (4 May 1987) 'The Globalization of the Industrialized Economies', p. 45.

Board of Governors of the Federal Reserve System (2010) http://www .federalreserve.gov/aboutthefed/section13.htm

Brown, Brendan (1996), Economists and the Financial Markets, Routledge: London and New York.

Cerny, Philip G. (ed.) (1993), Finance and World Politics: Markets, Regimes and States in the Post-hegemonic Era, Edward Elgar Publishing: Aldershot, UK and Brookfield, US.

Chandler, Lester Vernon (1958), Benjamin Strong: Central Banker. Brookings Institution: Washington, D.C.

Cohen, Benjamin J. (2004) The Future of Money, Princeton University Press: Princeton and Oxford.

Dopfer, K., J. Foster and J. Potts (2004), 'Micro, Meso, Macro', *Journal of Evolutionary Economics*, 14, 263–79.

The Economist, (12 Nov 2009). "Over the Counter, Out of Sight,"

The Economist, (5 December 2009), "Banks and Information Technology," p. 83.

The European Central Bank, "Constitution of the ESCB", http://www.ecb .int/ecb/legal/pdf/en_statute_2.pdf

Financial Times (1 December 2008), "*Harbours of Resentment*", p. 11.

Foster, John (2005), 'From Simplistic to Complex Systems in Economics', *Cambridge Journal of Economics*, 29, 873–92.

Foster, J. and P. Wild (1999a), 'Detecting Self-organizational Change in Economic Processes Exhibiting Logistic Growth', *Journal of Evolutionary Economics*, 9 109–33.

Gates, Bill, with Nathan Myhrvold and Peter Rinearson (1995), The Road Ahead, Viking Press: New York.

Greenspan, Alan (1998), 'The Globalization of Finance', The Cato Journal, 17 (3), Winter.

Greenspan, Alan (2008), *The Age of Turbulence: Adventures in a New World*, Penquin Press: New York.

Helleiner, Eric (1995), 'Explaining the Globalization of Financial Markets: Bringing States Back In', *Review of International Political Economy*, 2 (2), 315–41.

IMF (2002), IMF Board Holds Informal Seminar on Sovereign Debt Restructuring, Public Information Notice 02/38, Washington: International Monetary Fund.

Kambhu, John, Scott Weidman and Neel Krishnan (2007), New Directions for Understanding Systemic Risk: A Report on a Conference Co-sponsored by the Federal Reserve Bank of New York and the National Academy of Sciences, National Academic Press: Washington, D.C..

Keynes, John Maynard (1936), *The General Theory of Employment, Interest, and Money*, Macmillan: London.

Kindleberger, Charles P. (1989), Manias, Panics, and Crashes: *A History of Financial Crises*, Basic Books: New York.

Kinsella, Stephen (2009), "Theories of International Money," Working Paper, Department of Economics, Kemmy Business School, University of Limerick, Ireland.

Leathers, C.G. and J.P. Raines (2004), 'The Schumpeterian Role of Financial Innovations in the New Economy's Business Cycle', *Cambridge Journal of Economics*, 28 (5), September, 667–81.

Lavoie, Marc (2003), "A Primer on Endogenous Credit-Money," in Modern Theories of Money: The Nature and Role of Money in Capitalist Economies, Edward Elgar Publishing Ltd.: Cheltenham, UK and Northampton, MA, USA, Chapter 21, p. 506-543.

Lewis, Nathan K. (2007), Gold: the Once and Future Money, John Wiley and Sons: New Jersey.

Lindgren, Carl-Johan, Gillian Garcia and Matthew Seal (1995), "Bank Soundness and Macroeconomic Policy", International Monetary Fund: Washington, D.C.

Mandelbrot, Benoit and Richard Hudson (2004), *The Misbehavior of Markets,* Basic Books: New York.

Marchionatti, Roberto (1999), 'On Keynes' Animal Spirits', Kyklos, 52 (3), 415–39.

Meltzer, Allan (2003), *A History of the Federal Reserve* (vol. 1) University of Chicago Press: Chicago, IL

Minsky, Hyman P. (2008), Stabilizing an Unstable Economy, McGraw Hill: New York.

Norton, Robert (1993), 'Offshore Funds Maximise Reward and Minimise Risk', The European, 3 December.

Rees-Mogg, William (1993), 'Down and Out on Trillionaire's Row', Financial Times, 11 October, p. 14.

Reinhart, Carmen M. and Kenneth S. Rogoff (2007), 'Is the 2007 US Sub-prime Financial Crisis So Different? An International Historical Pattern', *American Economic Review: Papers and Proceedings,* 98 (2), 339–44.

Reinhart, Carmen M. and Kenneth S. Rogoff (2008), 'This Time is Different: *A Panoramic View of Eight Centuries of Financial Crises'*, Working Paper.

Reinhart, Carmen M. and Kenneth S. Rogoff (2009), 'The Aftermath of Financial Crises', paper presented at the American Social Sciences Association Annual Meeting, January 2009, San Francisco.

Schumpeter, Joseph (1934), Theory of Economic Development, Harvard University Press:

Cambridge, MA.Time, (28 December 2009) "Person of the Year: Ben Bernanke" pp.76-78.

In: After the Crisis: Rethinking Finance
Editor: Thomas Lagoarde-Segot

ISBN 978-1-61668-925-4
© 2010 Nova Science Publishers, Inc.

Chapter 8

IN SEARCH OF RELEVANT REGULATORY POLICIES: A MINSKYIAN ANALYSIS OF THE CURRENT FINANCIAL CRISIS

Faruk Ülgen

ABSTRACT

In the light of 2007-2008 global financial crisis this study shows that when deep distress comes into the picture, markets are cleared by rationing and provoke consequences exceeding the intrinsic significance of the distress such that a panic behaviour sets in and freezes the markets. To deal with this issue, the Minsky's approach of the economic instability as a result of cumulative euphoric expectations is used as theoretical guideline. This phenomenon seems to cast doubt on the belief that the self-regulatory market mechanisms are able to correct errors of judgment of decentralized actors without necessitating collective regulation. In view of the current crisis, a specific Minsky's financial-instability-hypothesis based analysis would lead monetary and financial authorities into more consistent policies.

"Even as we continue working to stabilize our financial system and reinvigorate our economy, it is essential that we learn the lessons of the crisis so that we can prevent it from happen again. Because the crisis was so complex, its lessons are many, and they are not always straightforward. Surely, both the private sector and financial regulators must improve their ability to monitor and control risk-taking. The crisis revealed not only weaknesses in regulators' oversight of financial institutions, but also, more fundamentally, important gaps in the architecture of financial regulation around the world."
Ben S. Bernanke, January 3, 2010, Atlanta, Georgia

1. INTRODUCTION

The 2007-2008 global financial crisis has once again raised the issue of how interdependencies between idiosyncratic individual risks and the monetary and financial system's stability might be better managed to prevent the recurrence of such crises. Many analysts referred to the current crisis as a Minsky moment even though main monetary and financial authorities all around the world have implemented emergency policies without considering the current market-oriented monetary and financial regulatory framework weaknesses throughout an explicit analysis of the financial instability hypothesis.

The aim of this study is to identify the actual nature of the current financial crisis and to search for guidelines of a consistent intervention framework. In order to tackle this crisis a crucial issue comes into the picture: do we need of a simple up-dating of current rules or should we, on the contrary, imagine a new regulatory framework accompanying the reality of globalized private capital markets? To deal with this issue, I consider Minsky's approach of the economic instability which identifies financial crises as a result of market-oriented cumulative euphoric expectations. In this vein, one should bring to the fore the uncertain nature of the market economy and the limits of individual rationality regarding the viability concern of liberalized financial systems. Therefore, I use the Keynesian explanation of the working of the entrepreneurial economy where individual financial investors' preference is mainly for short-term investments. Founded on mass psychology, such behaviour can be called herd behaviour which reduces the real knowledge in the valuation of investments and increases the macroeconomic volatility. The striking ignorance of the interdependency among the macroeconomic effects of the (microeconomic) behaviours of economic actors comes out as the underlying factor that can allow us to understand the main systemic difficulties of our capitalism.

The last decades have witnessed structural changes of monetary and financial regulatory mechanisms towards more open and liberalized markets. The regulatory framework of the highly finance-based modern capitalism had been moved through more market-oriented rules since the 1980s. Increased competition and generalized opening of national economies allowed banks and financial intermediaries to imagine various ways of making competition in order to defend their market shares or to enter new markets. Consequently, a spectacular process of innovation took place offering new products, using new processes and new ways of marketing financial products while the monetary and financial authorities withdraw explicitly from the previous (more centralized) regulatory schemes. Therefore, more decentralized and private control practices settled instead of the public supervision rules. This radical change permitted an unprecedented expansion of the means and methods of funding economies throughout a rich set of market-oriented activities. The "quantitative efficiency" of financial relations gained strength both in terms of variety and time-saving at national and international levels. A virtual and speculative economic growth all around the world reached high levels allowing several developing countries to access to new sources of financing and to attract capital flows.

This growth had been accompanied also by an increase of the role of banks and financial holdings that enlarged the financing of Leveraged Buy Outs (LBOs), takeovers and mergers of firms, and deficit adjustment operations of governments. Under this evolution, the developed as well as the developing market economies achieved their monetization and the development of financial systems -more liquid, deeper/diversified and broader- is generalized. But the improving of the allocation (quantitative) efficiency of banking and financial systems has not been accompanied by the creation of new relevant control mechanisms (qualitative efficiency) so searching the length and breadth of the financial relations for the stability of economies became more difficult than in the past. The current market-oriented regulatory framework of the world financial system did not succeed in improving the stability of economic relations. Numerous severe crises hit developing and emerging markets and the so-called subprime crisis is shaking today the most developed economies and seems to endanger the continuity of open international relations through the increasing threat of protectionism. This distress reappraises the viability of the world growth path.

To hold the case of the Horses of the Lake Ladoga[1] up as an example, one can consider the super-fused water imprisoning the unfortunate horses as a metaphor of instabilities which can occur in an unforeseen way by a movement of mass under latent individual economic decisions and (de)regulatory policies. As Kindleberger emphasized (1989), in case of distress, markets are suddenly cleared by rationing, obtaining funds becomes difficult and this worsens information about borrowers and then implies more deterioration of monetary and financial relations. Therefore, distress provokes consequences exceeding its intrinsic significance and generates systemic vicious circle. In such a situation, a panic behaviour sets in and freezes the markets.

In view of this situation, the continuity of economic relations calls for a coordinated and well planned intervention of authorities and new regulatory schemes are to be developed and implemented beyond the ideological beliefs of liberal conception. However, it is obvious that one should state unambiguously the very nature of such a crisis before imagining relevant schemes that could be able to cope with the current financial distress. A more specific analysis, aiming to clarify the very nature of the distress, can be developed through the Minsky's financial fragility hypothesis which seems to be able to suggest some consistent intervention frameworks in view of the expansion of the speculative-finance-based markets.

In the second section, I present briefly the emergence of a new financial world backed up with the hypothesis of the efficiency of free market mechanisms and show that the evolution of the financial markets is related to a new accumulation schema through more speculative and short-term oriented market operations. The third section considers a Minskian lecture of the business cycle and deals with the characteristics of the securitization process in order to point out the origins of the current crisis. The fourth section questions the relevance of some principles of intervention in order to tackle recurrent financial instabilities in an open economic world. The last section concludes.

2. MARKET EFFICIENCY HYPOTHESIS LEADING TO A NEW FINANCIAL WORLD AND A NEW ACCUMULATION PROCESS

2.1. The Paradox of Efficiency of Free Market Mechanisms

The efficient markets paradigm dominates, since the late 70s, contemporaneous conceptions of monetary and financial systems. It holds that free market mechanisms provide economies with the best way to elaborate and implement production and consumption decisions as well as to resolve any possible malfunctioning. Such a paradigm asserts that the market prices give any time the fundamental values, so neither bubbles nor crashes can be expected (by definition). This equilibrium paradigm stipulates that the market prices provide

---

[1] of *Kaputt* of Curzio Malaparte (1943).

all required information to render separate individual behaviours globally compatible each with other (Fama, 1970). Such mechanism, in Adam Smith's vein of the invisible hand picture, is supposed to be the best way of allowing the economy to function spontaneously so as to secure equilibrium conditions and not to necessitate an external state intervention on markets. Consequently, the regulatory models are changed into more free and private evaluation (rating) schemas and allowed economic units to adopt original and globally unconstrained market strategies.

However, the original sin of the contemporaneous regulatory structure is related to the confusion between the market economy (and its stability) and the exuberant monetary and financial deregulation. The self regulatory mechanisms of markets are founded on partial and subjective microeconomic criteria of individual units and cannot cope with the issue of global viability of monetary systems. Actually, the main systemic issue to deal with in our financial world is related to the interdependencies among agents, places and economies which are not taken into account in the standard belief of the well working of markets through deregulated and decentralized mechanisms. The interpenetration and the deep links between different economies and firms make that the weight of idiosyncratic risks on the system's stability becomes decisive and the interconnections gain strength in the explanation of worldwide financial disequilibria. More explicitly, perfect market models cannot consider, by definition, problems of information asymmetries, disaster myopia, limits of the individual fear behaviours against increasing distress and, last but not least, interdependencies reinforced by herd behaviour.

In the neoclassical synthesis which assumes that the free market mechanisms are able to work in the long run without disequilibrium, a serious depression cannot occur endogenously. The instability is then supposed to come from policy errors or from institutional weaknesses. The working of the monetary and financial systems is also analysed through this assumption and is considered as a technical detail concerning the techniques of exchange in the economy. Then there is no room for the analysis of the sophisticated financial structure that a capitalist economy generates in its own evolution regarding the problem of the stability. So, in a monetary economy of which the foundations are conceptually ignored in the neoclassical theory of markets, financing arrangements (which involve lenders and borrowers through deficit-spending operations) cannot find attention.

2.2. New Finance and New Accumulation Schema in an "Old" Debt-Economy

In the context of more and more liberalized markets and institutions, the evolution of the financial system is related to a new accumulation principle founded on the profitability of a debt burden that is more and more important without any corresponding sustainable economic growth all around the world. To be more precise, in last three decades we are in a specific environment where the little growth rates and persistent unemployment had been the results of conservative economic policies. The monetary policy[2] has led to wage-deflation process, accompanied in the US by a sustained consumption thanks to low levels of interest rates and

---

[2] The price stability or inflation targeting rule is announced as the scientific and ethical rule to follow by the authorities.

to easier credit system allowing households to spend more and more without increasing regular revenues. In such a case, it was not the full employment optimism but the spending-ease optimism that permitted individuals and institutions to borrow/lend more and more. A kind of attractive bubble emerging and speculative gains increasing over time, the optimism had been very large.

The case of the US economy is a perfect example of this new principle: "growth over the past few decades has been driven largely by rising household spending on consumption and residential investment. Consumption as a percent of GDP was 63% in 1980, 67% in 1998 and 70% in 2008. Since real wages were stagnant and real family income growth was slow, rising household spending was increasingly driven by the combined effects of rising debt and the increase in household wealth created by stock market and housing booms. Household debt was 48% of GDP in 1985, about where it had been in 1965. But it grew to 66% by 1998 then accelerated to over 100% by late 2008" (Crotty, 2009: 576). To bring to the fore the new reproduction schema in this accumulation process, Fernandez, Kaboub and Todorova (2008) argue that the subprime crisis has structural origins that extend beyond the housing and financial markets and the rise of inequalities since the 1980s formed the breeding ground for the current meltdown. In fact, between 1980 and 2004, wage income hardly changed in the US while worker productivity has increased by 68% and the Gini coefficient has been rising with a widening gap between the bottom and second quintiles and the top 20% (Fernandez, Kaboub and Todorova, 2008: 8-9). In such a downward adjustment context, the only possibility to include large popular masses into the new speculative bubble had been the subprime loans policy both of by banks and of the government[3]. Thus, the rise in homeownership since 2001 was not really due to the change of traditional variables as the rise of real income, the decrease of real estate prices or the enlargement of government subsidies, but to a new accumulation schema using a new speculative tool, the house industry through new mortgage techniques. This created a fictitious increase in the demand for homes "fuelled by innovative financing schemes that misled residential real estate developers into increasing the supply of new homes and setting up the industry for one its worst declines in decades" (Fernandez, Kaboub and Todorova, 2008: 3).The space left by the end of the euphoria of new technologies backed markets in the second half of the 1990s is filled by the swelling of the mortgage bubble while such a bubble was provoked financial instabilities in the late 90s in the US, followed by Japan and, a little later in 1997, in Asia. Such a development is permitted by financial deregulatory policies letting monetary and financial institutions imagine and implement innovations to enlarge various profit opportunities without considering the underlying systemic fragilities.

Minsky (1984, 2008) asserts that stable growth is inconsistent in an economy in which debt-financed ownership of capital assets exists, and the extent to which such debt-financing can be carried is market determined. In such an economy the evolution of private debts affects the pace of investment which determines in its turn both aggregate demand and the viability of debt structures. Then financial innovations are permanent features of financial markets and they increase the types and amounts of available financing for different activities. This availability bids up the prices of assets relative to the prices of current output. As the Real

---

[3] President G. W. Bush declared in 2002 the increase of popular homeowners as a goal of the first decade of the new millennium. See "President calls for Expanding Opportunities to Home Ownership", June 17, Washington, DC. Available at: http://georgewbush-whitehouse.archives.gov/news/releases/2002/06/20020617.html.

Estate Investment Trusts that engaged in speculative finance in 1970-73, banks and other financial intermediaries used the real estate sector to generate high speculative profits in the 2000s turning mortgage markets into euphoric easy-profit devices as agents believed that the future would promise perpetual expansion.

The confident expectations of continuously rising profits increase the willingness to assume less sound liability structures and lead banks to finance acquisitions of additional capital goods and real estate assets. Then the supply conditions for financing these acquisitions reinforce also the willingness to issue liabilities to finance such acquisitions. Thus, there is a frank rise in the value of existing capital which allows to the increase of the willingness to finance new acquisitions by issuing new liabilities (increasing of the borrower's risk) and to stronger willingness of lenders to accept low-yield assets regarding the lenders' risk (Minsky, 1984: 122 and 282). The willingness to issue liabilities is constrained by the need to hedge agents against the failure. When the perception of such an occurrence is reduced, the willingness to enter into new debt relations increases. Therefore, the boom financed by the euphoria generates pervasive transformations in portfolios the liquidity level of which becomes decreasing. The securitization is the main way by which such a euphoria had been created through the support of lax regulation in the 2000s.

3. FINANCIAL INSTABILITY OF DEREGULATED CAPITALISM

It seems to be analytically suitable to comprehend the financial instability of modern market economies through the booms and busts cycle studied by Hyman Minsky in its several insightful works (1984, 1992, 2008)[4]. The first characteristic of the Minsky cycle that paves the way for a critical "moment" is the evolution of the economy through three types of investors: the hedge, the speculative and the Ponzi borrowers. The second characteristic is the evolution of the regulatory framework through the size and duties of public authorities (government, central bank and other supervision agencies) and through the loosening of credit standards. These characteristics lead to the core feature of the Minskian analysis, the endogenous financial instability hypothesis of monetary market economies. As in the new-Keynesian framework, the instability appears in the loans and equity markets in particular thus the origin lies in the way market economies operate and not in rigidities nor in exogenous shocks[5]. This instability has been experimented, among other cases around the world, in the last two US credit booms and asset bubbles that ended up in a recession: the SandL boom and bust in the late 1980s; and the tech bubble and bust in the late 1990s. Currently, we witness another Minsky credit cycle that can be related to a particular evolution of the securitization process.

---

[4] For a global presentation of the Minky's analysis, see the insightful synthesis of Papadimitriou and Wray (2001).
[5] See Nasica (2000) for an original interpretation of the new-Keynesian framework regarding Minskian financial instability hypothesis.

3. 1. The Way to Great Depression

Minsky (1984) defines a great depression -"It"- as the great collapse along with a deep and long-lasting depression of which the spectre haunts the public as well as the politicians since 1930s. In his analysis of "It", Minsky emphasizes three points:

- The fact that it would be misleading to separate the real economy from the financial system. Actually, one can observe the divorce between the expansion of the financial innovations and speculation and the development of the productive system;
- The need to integrate the effects of evolving institutional structures into economic theory. At this level, one can study the non adaptation of the regulatory system to the financial development;
- The assumption that the financial instability is an inescapable part of any decentralized capitalist economy while the financial instability needs not lead to a great depression (Minsky, 2008). Here, that is the conception of new economic policies which is needed to strengthen the financial system in accord with the needs of the productive system.

Three financial postures, identified by Minsky[6] in the evolution of monetary commitments among agents -hedge, speculative and Ponzi-, determine the stability of the economy's financial structure[7]. The hedge financing gives greater stability while an increasing weight of speculative and Ponzi schemes indicates an increasing fragility. The hedge finance is founded on the expectations of an excess of cash flows from participation in income production even though the foreseeable future cash flows exceed the total cash payments on outstanding debt. The vulnerability of speculative finance units usually comes from sudden liquidity problems when for some periods the cash payment commitments on debts exceed the expected gross capital income: "The speculation is the refinancing will be available when needed" (Minsky, 1984: 26). So, "(...) a speculative unit has near term cash deficits and cash surpluses in later terms" (id.: 27). Thus a speculative unit finances a long position in assets by short run liabilities. Consequently, higher interest rates lower the present value of cash receipts and cash flows yield a negative excess at high interest rates. In a Ponzi finance scheme the outstanding debts grow due to interest on existing debt such that the near term cash flows fall short of the near term interest payments on debt. In this case, the fulfilling of payment commitments depends on the continuity of near borrowings. The Ponzi unit faces a solvability problem[8] such that its viability in time "depends upon the expectation that some assets will be sold at a high enough price sometime in the future" (id.: 23). A Ponzi finance consists in borrowing to hold assets which yield no or little income in the expectation that at some date the market value of the assets held will yield enough to clear debt. As the present value of assets held depends on interest rates, the solvency of a Ponzi agent is related to the changes of interest rates and to the expectations of future cash flows. Therefore the core

---

[6] See for instance the Appendix A in Minsky (2008) for the presentation of these three financial structures.
[7] For more details, see Minsky, 1984: 22; 66-67; 105-106, etc.
[8] Minsky defines the solvency as follows: "In as much as a unit is solvent only as the value of its assets exceeds the value of its debts, changes in interest rates cannot affect the solvency of a unit that hedge finances" (1984: 25) while the liquidity means "that one can meet all of his or her commitments for cash outflows as they come due" (Davidson, 2008: 670).

problem is not that the working of the economy is founded on debt-financing relations; that is the very nature of a monetary and decentralized market economy. The problem is rather related to the fact that in a global financial world the debt commitments can be swelled according to speculative expectations which are fuelled by the aim of making money through available opportunities on markets without considering the development of the productive capacities of income-creating units. This can be possible thanks to expanded financial liberalization and to financial innovations. The financial liberalization usually induces "two speculative pressures: expectations-induced and competition-coerced, both of which contribute to the increased presence of short-term, high-risk speculative transactions in the economy and to increased vulnerability to financial crises" (Arestis, 2001: 172). The innovations allow markets to imagine various types of techniques and products that spur agents to take a positive stand on the future of the economy while the commitments move away from the real state of macroeconomic imbalances. When the split between the economic development and the debt commitments is consumed, the speculative and Ponzi agents seem to be unable to fulfil their debt commitments.

3. 2. Innovative Dynamics: Does the Securitization Secure the Positions?

In the development of economies since the 80s, it was a prolonged period of increase of pyramidal debt creation[9] where the borrowing has been continuously needed to meet existing loans and large financial market underwriters transformed illiquid noncommercial mortgages into liquid assets via securitization. The innovative dynamics of the financial capitalism enlarges these operations and lead agents through various techniques –as securitization- to create profitable activities in the short run. Such an evolution is a characteristic of developed financial economies where market mechanisms –thanks to loose regulation- can generate new speculative areas after fizzled out bubbles on previous profit-making activities. Expansion of lenders' markets into less creditworthy borrowers begins with financial innovations such as "interest-only" mortgages and "option adjustable rate" mortgages with low payments at the outset, but rising monthly payments later.

On these mortgage markets banks play multiple roles:

- They are initiators as paper creators structuring the credit and accepting the borrowers' promises to repay.
- They are investment banks creating securities and presenting them as sound investment vehicles –through their cooperation with credit-rating agencies-.
- Banks are also market makers (of a secondary market) as underwriters of securities issued

---

[9] In such a process, the Ponzi finance purchaser can issue successive sets of debt securities that aim to provide enough cash inflow to meet the upcoming contractual cash outflows. This increases the level of future contractual cash outflows at any time (Davidson, 2008). In the subprime mortgages, borrowers have expected the rise of the value of their assets (houses, securities, etc.) as the speculative bubble continued to rise. The repeal of the Glass-Steagal Act in 1999 allowed bank loans to be readily sold to underwriters which were often an affiliate of the parent bank within 30 days. After this period, the mortgage is put out the banks' books. The underwriters sold tranches of these mortgage loans to investors (local governments, banks, private investors, etc.) that believed that under the guarantee of underwriters the risk of capital loss was reduced.

- Thus, banking system bundles mortgages into mortgage-backed securities and sell these packaged products to investment funds which use them as collateral for highly leveraged loans as these securities are highly rated by private evaluators. These loans are used in turn to buy more mortgage bundles. By this way, such products are used to create other securitization conduits that are also connected to short-term asset-backed commercial paper.

Calomiris (2007) reports that between 2000 and 2005, securitized non-conforming mortgages had increased from 35% to 60% (and to 65% in 2007), and subprime mortgage originations rose from $160 billion in 2001 to $600 billion in 2006. In the same way, the share of prime mortgage finance decreased from 78.9% in 2002 to 50.1% at the end of 2006 letting the non-prime credit increasing sharply[10]. This interconnectedness of innovations in products and processes permitted securitized mortgages to become re-securitized as backing for collateralized debt obligations[11]. This process of securitization as other financial derivatives involves expectations about the uncertain future and its evolution depends on fragile and not well ordered microeconomic behaviors. When expectations back-fires on marked-to-market values, homeowners' default increases, homes and mortgages are not selling, investors try to sell out positions and assets are devalued.

The securitization is not a new phenomenon. As Minsky stated it (1984), the securitization began in the US mortgage market and enabled the saving and loan banks to continue to initiate mortgage even though their funding ability was sorely compromised. The ambiguous advantage of the securitization is that it reduces limits of bank initiative to create credits (there is no direct need of bank capital) for the credits do not absorb bank reserves. Then the securitization reduces the weight of the part of the financing structure that the central bank is committed to protect. But for holders, a change in interest rates (a sudden rise) or in expectations on future values of assets (fizzling out of speculative expectations) can provoke a need to sell position which may lead to a drastic fall in the price of securities. Whalen (2007) points out that the fizzling out of mortgage market in the US seems to start explicitly in August 2007 when a third of home loans failed to close as brokers could not sell them to investors because investors remarked that they could not sell existing loans in their portfolios at any price. In the same time, Whalen reports that $1.2 trillion asset-backed commercial paper market was freezing up (id.: 9).

Illing (2008) argues that new financial instruments such as securitization are clever instruments to risk sharing between different generations as securitized assets are held by pension funds instead of banks. Thus the old participate in the market risk of loans and when asset prices' fluctuations are passed through the old the fire sales forced by defaults would be limited. But the problem, however, is that the highly leveraged institutions which transform risk into securities (as Fannie Mae and Freddie Mac) "usually increase their exposure to systemic risk. They seem to hold the riskiest tranches of the loans they initiate (...). Thus in the case of serious aggregate shocks, the economy will be made even more fragile: as soon as

---

[10] According to the *Mortgage Market Statistical Annual* of 2008.

[11] For instance, at the end of 2006, 39.5% of existing collateralised debt obligations pools covered by Moody's consisted of mortgage-backed securities, of which 70% were subprime or second-lien mortgages (see Calomiris, 2007). Chomsisengphet and Pennington-Cross (2006) show also that the securitized share of subprime loans increased from 40.5% in 2000 to 58.7% in 2003. This share passed to 74.8% in 2006 (the securitization rate=securities issued divided by origination in dollars).

managers try to minimize their losses by selling bad loans, fire sales will be triggered. (…) There is thus the danger that, beyond a certain threshold, the virtuous cycle turns into a vicious one, creating the risk of a financial meltdown" (Illing, 2008: 82-83).

This financial development began in the 1980's when the LBOs movement led to growth in highly leveraged firms: "The growth in the money market mutuals in the 1980's led to a large demand for short term marketable corporate liabilities. The combined effect of these two developments was the growth in speculative financing. Leveraged buy outs often included "payment in kind" bonds, i. e. the capitalization of interest (Ponzi finance)" (Minsky, 1992: 19).

3. 3. The Ponzi Finance Scheme in Mortgage Markets

In the 2000s, two phenomena can be observed. First, the households re-leveraged excessively rising consumption through increasing debt burdens and over-borrowing. This increase was supported by rising asset prices (housing and also equity). These new Ponzi borrowers and their funders were founded their expansion on negative amortization mortgages without verification of income and assets in a reasonable way. At the beginning, they were usual speculative borrowers who expected to be able to refinance their mortgages and debts in time thanks to the expected increase of market values of their assets. Second, in the same time the loosening of credit standards among mortgage lenders (accompanied by the retreat of regulators believing in the spontaneous equilibrating mechanisms of free markets) reinforced the current credit cycle. This process spread to the corporate and financial system through the switch from equity to debt that took the form of LBOs that sustained the private equity and swelled the bulk of the equity market bubble. The previous optimism of lenders and borrowers is driven in part by the unprecedented growth in liquidity from hedge fund and private equity, feeding hot money funds. The Ponzi borrowers that would have been forced into debt default were unfortunately able to obtain refinancing packages because of the reckless credit and liquidity conditions in bubbly markets.

While in Minsky analysis it is assumed that housing is typically financed by hedge financing (1984: 32), one can observe some common points with the Ponzi financing. Although Ponzi finance is often tinged with fraud, every investment project with a long gestation period and somewhat uncertain returns has aspects of a Ponzi finance scheme. Minsky shows that many of the real estate investment trusts that came upon hard times in 1974-75 in the US were, quite unknowing to the household investors who bought their equities, involved in Ponzi schemes: "Many of these trusts were financing construction projects that had to be sold out quickly and at a favourable price if the debts to the trusts were to be paid. A tightening of mortgage credit brought on slowness of sales of finished construction, which led to a "present value reversal" for these projects" (1984: 106). The Ponzi scheme is related to this reversal of the present value of real estate assets. As Minsky remarks "Consumer and mortgage debt can become Ponzi-like only if actual wage income falls short of anticipated and other sources of disposal income" (1984: 30). As the wage income did not increase in the period (see above), a speculative boom came into the picture when substantial and growing payment commitments had been related to the rising expectations that asset values would continue to be appreciated. In such a boom, the current and near term expected cash flows from participating in the production and distribution of income are not sufficient to meet the payment commitments but the expectations on the future market values of households' assets remain high.

By the same manner that a capitalist economy only works well as an investing economy, for investment generates profits (in a Kaleckian and Keynesian vein), the financing of the households' debt positions can only be continuous if the expected value of the real estate assets is growing enough in order to permit households to reimburse their debts, i.e. when the expected value of houses is at least as high as the commitments necessitate: "In an ordinary home mortgage the primary source of the cash needed to fulfil the contract is the income of the homeowner. The secondary source or fallback source of cash is the market value of the mortgaged property" (Minsky, 1984: 19-20). In the development of the mortgage-based financial relations, the primary source of the real estate industry had been confused with the secondary source that overcame the primary source such that the expansion of the market had been founded on the speculative expectations on the future market value of properties. As the evolution of this market value is related to the swelling of the home price bubbles, banks and other financial intermediaries did not take care of the multiplication of the commitments which contributed to the swelling of the bubble. The bubble had been self-fed by the expectations.

It is obvious that there are strong links between the mortgage market and the leveraged loan markets. Margin requirement for hedge funds and for other leveraged operations becomes lower as the competition among lenders for prime brokerage services for hedge funds became fierce. The corporate borrowers' high leverage ratios decline credit standards. And the negative-amortization-based loans fuel "originate and distribute models" while the evaluation of such loans is below what could be justified by the economic fundamentals. Subsequently to the fall of home prices, the re-pricing of risk in credit markets led in the last sequence to a credit crunch in the LBOs and corporate credit markets with the rise of the risk aversion of investors and of the credit default spreads.

4. WHAT LEARNINGS FOR ECONOMIC POLICIES: EMERGENCY EXIT OR STRUCTURAL REFORMS?

In the aftermath of scandals of governance of some large firms, unstable geopolitical evolutions and the bubble on equity markets, bursting with optimism the IMF asserts in September 2003 that the financial markets showed a remarkable resilience and they are self reinforced despite a low economic growth in developed economies. This report underlines particularly that the vulnerabilities on mature markets began to be lessened:

> "The bursting of the equity bubble, geopolitical developments, and corporate governance scandals have severely tested the global financial system in recent years. In the fall of last year, these developments contributed to high levels of risk aversion, increased market volatility, widening credit spreads, and limited access to external financing for many emerging market countries. Even in the face of these strong headwinds, however, financial markets have remained remarkably resilient. Indeed, markets strengthened in the first half of 2003, notwithstanding continued lacklustre economic growth".

Since the March 2003 issue of the *GlobalFinancial Stability Report* (GFSR), further progress has been made in addressing the lingering effects of the bursting of the equity price bubble. Household and corporate balance sheets have continued to improve gradually and corporate default levels have declined. Companies in mature markets have cut costs, enhancing their ability to cope with slower growth and other potential difficulties. While unambiguous signs of stronger growth are still lacking, corporations—particularly in the United States—have made good progress in their financial consolidation efforts and are in a better financial position to increase investment spending" (IMF, 2003: 1)

However, these conclusions seem to have been revealed erroneous in the aftermath of the current financial crisis and the stability of financial markets needs to be sustained by structural reforms that call for a new public intervention and regulatory framework for the viability of the entire economic system.

4. 1. Some Paradoxes of the Lax Regulation and Self-Regulation: Bad Incentives

The deregulation of financial markets since the 1990s is related to the central hypothesis of the efficiency of free market mechanisms which asserts that capital markets price securities correctly with respect to expected risk and return and actors are able to make optimal decisions to correctly manage risks. Then it is assumed that free financial markets minimise the possibility of financial crises and the need for government bailouts[12]. This belief constitutes the base of what Crotty calls the New Financial Architecture (NFA):

"(…) structural flaws in the NFA created dangerous leverage throughout the financial system. Annual borrowing by US financial institutions as a percent of gross domestic product (GDP) jumped from 6.9% in 1997 to 12.8% a decade later. From 1975 to 2003, the US Securities and Exchange Commission (SEC) limited investment bank leverage to 12 times capital. However, in 2004, under pressure from Goldman Sachs chairman and later Treasury Secretary Henry Paulson, it raised the acceptable leverage ratio to 40 times capital and made compliance voluntary (Wall Street Watch, 2009, p. 17). This allowed large investment banks to generate asset-to-equity ratios in the mid to upper 30s just before the crisis, with at least half of their borrowing in the form of overnight repos, money that could flee at the first hint of trouble" (Crotty, 2009: 574).

Thus, instead of reconsidering the regulatory weakness of the system, the Fed implemented easy money policies facilitating leverage operations and then to avoid a deep financial crisis in the aftermath of the late 1990s booms, she continued to hold short-term interest rates at record lows through to mid-2004. In this period, some crucial weaknesses can be brought to the fore. The first one is the self-regulation principle that generates a conflict of interest. The credit-rating agencies that constitute in the new (de)regulatory framework of the 2000s the main self-control mechanism of debt markets, have two opposite roles: they

---

[12] See the speech of Paul Volcker to the Economic Club of New York, 8 April 2008.Also, New York Fed Chairman, and current Secretary of the Treasury, Timothy Geithner stated in 2006 that"In the financial system we have today, with less risk concentrated in banks, theprobability of systemic financial crises may be lower than in traditional bank-centeredfinancial systems". (Comments by New York Fed President Timothy Geithner, Wall Street Journal, 30 May2008).

evaluate the quality of banks and financial institutions' products and processes and they elaborate with these institutions new debt packages to be rated. As they are paid by the users of the securities, they are usually inclined to give good ratings for these products. This provokes confusion between two sides, the rating agencies and those they have to rate as agencies are paid by banks whose products they rate. Their profits therefore depend on whether they rate these banks nicely, thus there is an incentive to high ratings. For instance, Crotty (2009: 566) remarks that:

> "In 2005, more than 40% of Moody's revenue came from rating securitised debt such as mortgage backed securities (MBSs) and collateralised debt obligations (CDOs). If one agency gave realistic assessments of the high risk associated with these securities while others did not, that firm would see its profit plummet. Thus, it made sense for investment banks to shop their securities around, looking for the agency that would give them the highest ratings, and it made sense for agencies to provide excessively optimistic ratings."

It is also revealed that the rating agencies based their evaluations on the information given by those they should rate. This led to highly leveraged mortgage lenders and holders of mortgage-backed securities. Therefore, investors have been encouraged to invest by the high ratings given to the instruments issued while the risk embodied in various forms of securities was of growing opacity and complexity. Actually the deregulation allowed financial conglomerates to become so large and complex then neither insiders nor outsiders could accurately evaluate their risk. Unfortunately, the deregulatory scheme enhanced financial fragility and enabled micro-units to adopt strategies without worrying about the systemic instabilities. National regulators allowed banks to evaluate their own risk through Value at Risk (VAR) models[13] and ceded to banks and to ratings agencies the core of the regulatory power.

In addition, fee incomes are generated by the mortgage securitization operations to banks and brokers (the sellers) as well as to investment bankers and institutions which transforming the loans into securities and serviced them and rating-agencies that evaluate them (thus affect the market price of the final products)[14]. Moreover, as there was no compensation mechanism when the securities issued suffer losses, incentives to augment the issue of loans have been strong notwithstanding the possible unsoundness of the products sold. Obviously, such payment matrix creates counter-incentives in the market bonus system as it induces evaluators to be less objective and thus to give high ratings to non-transparent structured financial products[15].

---

[13] As Crotty emphasizes: "VAR-determined capital requirement are just one of many possible examples of totallyineffective regulatory processes within the NFA. Financial markets were not just lightlyregulated, such regulation as did exist was often 'phantom' regulation—ineffective bydesign" (2009: 572).

[14] Total fees from home sales and mortgage securitizationfrom 2003 to 2008 have been estimated byFinancial Times at $2 trillion (reported by Crotty, 2009: 565).

[15] Wall Street Journal reports that its survey among first 23 US financial actors (banks, various funds) indicates that Wall Street would pay its employees a total of $140 billion (all payments included) in 2009 after a light drop in 2008 ($117 billion)(14 October 2009)! Bonuses at Goldman are expected to average $570,000 in 2009 in the midst of the crisis. About 700 employees of Merrill Lynch received bonuses in excess of $1 million in 2008from a total bonus pool of $3.6 billion in spite of the fact that the firm lost $27 billion (losses reported by Merrill totalled $35.8 billion in 2007 and2008). Another enlightening example of counter incentives is the case of the AIG's Financial Products unit:"This division, which gambled on credit default swaps(CDSs), contributed substantially to AIG's rising profits in the boom. In 2008 the unit lost$40.5 billion. Though the US

4. 2. Suitable Policy Principles

As Minsky (1984) states as a general feature of the capitalism, the turbulence of the economy operates against prudent investment and finance. Since the 60s the general economic orientation has been conducive to short-run speculation rather than to the long-run capital development of the economy. For Minsky the problems observed in modern economies are not due to vagaries of budget deficits or to bad money supply policies but they reflect the normal way economies operate after a run of successful years. Although it seems to be unconsidered to suggest unique and standardized remedy to endogenous financial instability of the modern capitalism because policies which work in one financial regime may not be effective in another regime and the policy to implement does change according to the dominant financial structure, one can imagine some general policy principles that could be suitable in the aim of more stabilizing the working of the financial markets.

In his study of some threats of financial crisis occurred in the post-war period[16], Minsky argues that each of these threats has been aborted by a combination of support operations by the Fed and a large government sector trying to sustain the reproduction of a "paper world" (1984: 63). In these episodes of instability, the Fed bolstered the system through its protection of banks and other financial institutions and this was accompanied by a large government deficit substitutes for investment in sustaining deficit profits (id.: 84). Thus, the absence of great depression in the post-war period is due to the presence of a big government in the economy and to the willingness of the Fed to act promptly as a lender of last resort. The big government, through the combined effects of its policies and interventions as a provider of high-grade default-free liabilities to financial markets in case of reversion from private debt, can calm markets' ardour down and help to stop to plunge to a deep depression: "If an economy is given to intermittent endogenously determined incoherence then devices (regulations and interventions) that contain the incoherence or impose coherence can improve performance. Central banks are just such devices; big government whose deficits sustain aggregate profits in times of recession[17] are another such device" (Minsky, 1992: 12). Then beside the government financial presence in the economy, the central bank plays a crucial role through its two main functions: the stabilizer and the lender of last resort. From this angle, the main differences between the collapse of the 1930s and the post-World War II period (where there was no great depression in developed economies) are due to:

- The larger size of the government with much greater deficit in case of downturn;
- A large outstanding government debt setting a floor to liquidity;

---

government owns 80% of AIG's shares and invested $180billion in the corporation, AIG nevertheless paid the 377 members of the division a total of $220 million in bonuses for 2008 (…)" (Crotty, 2009: 565).

[16] The first is credit crunch of 1966 centred around a run on bank-negotiable certificates of deposit, the second observed in 1970 was a run on the commercial paper market after the failure of the Penn-Central Railroad and the third has occurred in 1974-75, centred around the speculative activities of big banks with the failure of the Franklin National Bank of New York in December 1973 through a run on its overseas branch.

[17] Minsky shows that in the period before the Great Depression, the size of the government was such that there was no way an automatic response of government spending or taxation could offset the drop of investment. This structure led the gross investment to fall from $16.2 billion to 1.4 billion and the gross retained earning from $11.7 to 3.2 billion between 1929 and 1933. On the contrary, in the recession period of 1973-75, with a big government, business gross retained profits rose from $140.2 billion in 1973 to 176.2 billion in 1975 despite the rise of unemployment rates and the decline in industrial production (1984: 45)

- The rapid expansion of central banks as lender of last resort whenever a financial crisis threatens, preventing a collapse of asset values.

But these functions may be in conflict. Bernanke points out that "Monetary policy is also a blunt tool, and interest rate increases in 2003 or 2004 sufficient to constrain the bubble could have seriously weakened the economy at just the time when recovery from the previous recession was becoming established" (2010: 21-22). And Minsky says that: "If constrained action, undertaken to stabilize income, threatens the solvency of financial institutions, the central bank will be forced to back away from the policy of constraint" (1984: 152) and "If a financial crisis occurs, the central bank must abandon any policy of constraint" (id.: 199).

The time of interventions seems to be of great importance. Comparing too late and too little interventions and too soon and effective exercise of the lender of last resort function of the central bank, Minsky remarks that in the first case, the decline in asset prices would lead to a deeper recession. Therefore, he says that the error of easing too soon only delays the problem of constraining a euphoric situation, it may be that the best choice for monetary policy really involves preventing those more severe losses in asset prices that lead to deep depression, rather than preventing any disorderly or near-crisis conditions.

In case of generalized financial meltdown, Minsky (1992: 13) argues that the specific aim of the government refinancing of banks is to prevent a broad set of institutions to need to improve positions by fire sales. He suggests that failing banks should be treated as institutions which would continue to operate after an infusion of equity through 'The Reconstruction Finance Corporation' that becomes the banks owner and replaces the management. By this way many non-performing assets could be treated as 'work outs' rather than as requiring foreclosures and liquidations: "Continuing the "failed" banks as refinanced independent institutions, though government owned, is more conducive to economic recovery that the [present] treatment, in which organizations are destroyed and the non-performing assets of failed institutions act to depress asset prices" (1992: 14).

In front of the current meltdown, the policies implemented by the main central banks (Fed, ECB, BoJ, etc.) have been in the Minskian vein; for instance the Fed reduced its discount rate and federal funds rate, eased conditions on overnight borrowing and injected cash into monetary markets. Some government supported institutions as Fannie Mae and Freddie Mac have been used to protect mortgage holders. But these interventions are rescue plans and cannot lead to structural reforms to improve the soundness of the financial system. More rigorous bank supervision and tighter regulation of financial markets should be elaborated. In this aim, the "all liberalization" of financial markets must be discarded in favour of more realistic and objective regulatory framework which should have to deal with the characteristics of a monetary/decentralized market economy.

The identification of the financial vulnerability through some observable phenomena can give public authorities a relevant direction to channel their interventions. For instance, when there is a strong growth of financial payments relative to income payments, a decrease in the relative weight of outside and guaranteed assets in the totality of financial asset values and a rapid growth of asset prices nourished by high euphoric expectations, the authorities (external supervision agencies[18] and central banks) should intervene in order to tighten regulatory conditions on speculative markets. The central bank should use its monetary powers to guide

---

[18] and not profit-seeking private institutions.

the evolution of financial markets in directions that are compatible with financial stability in the longer run rather than improvise controls that put out fires but which allow the underlying market situation to remain unchanged[19]. But it is obvious that these policies cannot be elaborated or imagined if the prudential supervision agencies do not believe that the spontaneous free market mechanisms can involve the economy in deep instability. As Bootle states, "economies can get stuck in a state of depression from which individual actors, whether people or companies, can find escape. The state is the only agent in society capable of working for the collective interest on a sufficient scale" (2009: 34). That seems to be one of the most important lessons that we should learn from the current disarray which give us a chance for rethinking with humility the role of the markets. That does not means that we have to over-centralize the working of our economies but to leave a priori reasoning about the nature of the capitalist economy. In our modern world, "For the viability of economic relations, we have to imagine a good financial society in which the tendency by business and banks to engage in speculative finance is constrained" (Minsky, 1984: 69)[20]. The simplification of financial structure is one of the ways of achieving greater stability while there is no economic model that solves the problem of economic policy for all times: "I am afraid economists can never become mere technicians applying an agreed-upon theory that is fit for all seasons within an institutional structure that does not and need not change" (1984: 114).

The harmony of self-interests seems not to be guaranteed in a multi-dimensional financial world which needs to be constrained by regulation (Leijonhufvud, 2009). We have to take into account the error that consists to make no distinction between free markets and unregulated markets (Acemoglu, 2009) and to avoid the ambiguous belief that market mechanisms are sufficient to reallocate resources towards efficient uses. So a new regulatory framework that contains rules aiming the systemic financial stability and new supervision principles to check the implementation of such rules still remain to be elaborated (Ülgen, 2009)[21]. Therefore, one can consider various propositions for a macro-prudential approach (Borio, 2009) focusing on the financial system as a whole and not on individual institutions in order to treat aggregate risk as endogenous[22] and to limit the risk of episodes of system-wide distresses and their costs for the economy.

5. CONCLUSION

For a theory to be useful guide to policy for the control of instability, it must show how instability is generated. The Minskian lecture of the working of financial markets can give us

---

[19] See Minsky, 1984: 181 and 184.

[20] Here, one can find what Henry Simons has called "the reappearance of prohibited practices in new and non prohibited forms" and what Kane (1988) named the dialectic of regulation, and Goodhart (1995) emphasized as the phenomenon of financial innovations to avoid existing regulatory constraints.

[21] For example, one can consider that the usually dominant tendency to decentralize various prudential supervision mechanisms is not an efficient way of organizing the financial control and protection functions in a complex financial environment "especially since an effective defense against an emerging financial crisis may require coordination and consistency among the various units with lender of last resort functions" (Minsky, 1984: 4).

[22] Coming from the collective effects of individual institutions whose behaviours affect prices and quantities and hence the strength of the economy itself.

a relevant analytical grid to cope with this question. In the aftermath of the 1970s crises, one can observe a radical policy shift which is theoretically and practically founded on the efficient markets theory. The liberal capitalism became therefore the philosophical reference of a new deregulated financial system. The deep cause of the current crisis is related to this set of institutional and political principles which led economies into myopic practices. Numerous instabilities since the 1980s through accelerated deregulatory reforms and financial innovations had been accompanied by governments' bailouts that permitted continuous expansion of financial markets. Financial markets grew more than the real economy, the complexity and the opacity of new products and processes had been developed and became the dominant aspect of market relations.

These changes belong to the natural behaviour of the capitalist economy which was underlined in Minsky's analysis through two phenomena. The first is the evolution of the financial structure affecting the nature of primary assets, the extent of financial layering, and the evolution of financial institutions. The second consists of the financial impacts over a short period due to the existence of a euphoric economy that decreases the domain of stability of the financial system through portfolio transformations. The growing importance of speculative market operations leads agents to have more vulnerable postures. The assets that agents hold reveal to be of longer term than their liabilities thus a rise in both long and short-term interest rates can lead to a greater fall in the market value of their assets than of their liabilities. Furthermore, the views as to acceptable liquidity structures are subjective and a shortfall of cash receipts relative to cash payment commitments can lead to quick and wide revaluations of desired and acceptable financial structures. When this kind of sensitivity spreads throughout markets, a general reluctance to finance appears and leads to a decline in the ability to sustain existing debt structure. This initiates doubts about the reproducible future agents try to hedge their positions and funders to reconsider financing plans of future investments. An explosive combination of commitments, inherited from the euphoria and of current revenues which seems to be less than expected levels, comes into the picture. When a large number of agents resort to extraordinary sources of cash, individual rationality implies the option of saying "I don't know" (Minsky, 1984: 131) and the postponing of decisions. The retreat from markets and the refusal of refinancing positions dry monetary and financial markets up. Markets clear on a downward path and attempts by agents with shrunken income to meet their commitments by selling assets adversely affect other initially quite liquid and solvent agents and may have a destabilizing impact upon the entire economy. A consistent system of institutions and interventions that can contain the threat of financial collapse becomes necessary to refinance markets and institutions -whose perilous position defines the crisis- and to assure that the aggregate of business profits does not decline. The response to such a meltdown stems from the involvement of governments' spending programs in the creation of capital assets and from prompt and targeted interventions of central banks to restore confidence in the viability of economic relations. But, if we want to reduce the extent and the expansion of such recurring crises, a change in our minds seems to be the first condition to be fulfilled in our reflection about the working of the market economy and of its consequences. So we have to ask ourselves what the suitable regulatory framework could be in order to establish a security cushion in front of sudden and rapid changes of expectations and to guarantee the viability of monetary and financial markets.

It seems also to be necessary that the leaders should put their heads together not for a fall -persisting in implementing the 'great moderation era' policies- but for new realistic and structural monetary and financial management schemes. Morgan (2009) remarks that the great moderation provided by low inflation levels in central economies led central banks to have more confidence in their deregulated managing rules of monetary and financial markets. As long as the inflationary pressures were maintained in an acceptable interval, central banks were considering the speculative debt-related economic growth as a suitable way for a sustainable growth. Consequently, the central bank interventions had been event-led without trying to identify the problem as a structural crisis. Then Minsky asserts that the new use of central bank powers as they affect uncertainty is a form of financial brinksmanship: "The central bank acts so that the range of "possible" market conditions increases (…and) instead of acting as an insurer (substituting certainty for uncertainty) central banking has taken on some aspects of a casino (substituting uncertainty for certainty" (1984: 180).

But Minsky does not believe that the system can be definitely stabilized even if central banks and governments adopt rigorous financial policies: "If capitalism reacts to past success by trying to explode, it may be the only effective way to stabilize the system, short of direct investment controls, is to allow minor financial crises to occur from time to time" (1984: 153). Actually the efforts of central banks are part of a broader challenge of strengthening the safeguards against financial instability: "The basic question is how best this should be done. The answer ultimately depends on how we think of financial instability, of its ultimate causes and implications" (Borio, 2003: 1982). As Whalen remarks, "While the reaction of mainstream economists was 'I'm shocked', Minsky would likely have just nodded, and the twinkle in his eyes would have gently said, 'I told you so'" (2007: 18).

REFERENCES

Acemoglu, D. (2009) "The crisis of 2008: structural lessons for and from economics." Policy Insight N°28, Centre for Economic Policy Research, January.

Annual Hyman P. Minsky Conference (2009) Meeting the Challenges of Financial Crisis. The Levy Economics Institute of Bard College, April 16-17, New York City.

Arestis, P. (2001) Recent banking and financial crises: Minsky versus the financial liberalizationists. In: R. Bellofiore and P. Ferri (Eds.), Financial Keynesianism and Market Instability. *The Economic Legacy of Hyman Minsky.* Vol I, Edward Elgar: Cheltenham, UK:159-178.

Bernanke, B. S. (2010) Monetary Policy and the Housing Bubble. Address of the Chairman of Board of Governors of the Federal Reserve System to the Annual Meeting of the American Economic Association, Atlanta, Georgia, January 3.

Bootle, R. (2009) "Redrawing the Boundaries. Rethinking the role of the state and markets." *Finance and Development,* March: 34-35.

Borio, C. (2009) "Implementing the macroprudential approach to financial regulation and supervision." Banque de France Financial Stability Review, 13: 31-41.

Borio, C. (2003) "Towards a Macroprudential Framework for Financial Supervision and Regulation?" CESifo Economic Studies, 49(2): 181-215.

Calomiris, C. W. (2007) "Not (Yet) a `Minsky Moment'." voxEU.org, 23 November.

Chomsisengphet, S. and Pennington-Cross, A. (2006) "The Evolution of Subprime Mortgage Market." Federal Reserve Bank of Saint Louis Review, January/February, 88(1): 31-56.

Crotty, J. (2009) "Structural causes of the global financial crisis: a critical assessment of the 'new financial architecture'." *Cambridge Journal of Economics*, 33: 563-580.

Davidson, P. (2008) "Is the current financial distress caused by the subprime mortgage crisis a Minsky moment? Or is it the result of attempting to securitize illiquid non-commercial mortgage loans?" *Journal of Post Keynesian Economics*, 30(4): 669-676.

Fama, E. F. (1970) "Efficient capital markets: a review of theory and empirical work." *The Journal of Finance*, 25(2): 383-417.

Fernandez, L., Kaboub, F. and Todorova, Z. (2008) "On Democratizing Financial Turmoil: A Minskian Analysis of the Subprime Crisis." Working Paper N°548, *The Jerome Levy Economics Institute of Bard College*.

Goodhart, C. A. E. (1995) The Central Bank and The Financial System. Macmillan: London.

Illing, G. (2008) Financial stability and monetary policy: a framework. In J.-P. Touffut (Ed.), Central Banks as Economic Institutions, Edward Elgar: Cheltenham, UK: 68-87.

International Monetary Fund (2003) Global Financial Stability Report. Market Developments and Issues. September.

Kane, E. J. (1988) "Interaction of financial and regulatory innovation." *American Economic Review*, 78(2): 328-334.

Keynes, J. M. (1936) *The General Theory of Employment, Interest and Money*. Macmillan: London.

Kindleberger, C. (1989) Manias, Panics, and Crashes. *A History of Financial Crises*. 2nd edition, Macmillan: London.

Leijonhufvud, A. (2009) "Two systemic problems." Policy Insight N°29, *Centre for Economic Policy Research*, January.

Minsky, H. P. (2008) "Securitization." Policy Note, 2008/2, *The Jerome Levy Economics Institute of Bard College*.

Minsky, H. P. (2008) Stabilizing an Unstable Economy. McGraw-Hill: New York.

Minsky, H. P. (1992) "The Capital Development of the Economy and the Structure of Financial Institutions." Working Paper N° 72, *The Jerome Levy Economics Institute of Bard College*.

Minsky, H. P. (1984) Can "It" Happen Again? Essays on Instability and Finance. M. E. Sharpe, Inc.: Armonk, N. Y.

Morgan, J. (2009) "The limits of central bank policy." *Cambridge Journal of Economics*, 33: 581-608.

Nasica, E. (2000) Finance, Investment and Economic Fluctuations. An Analysis in the Tradition of Hyman P. Minsky. Edward Elgar: Cheltenham, U. K.

Papadimitriou, D. B. and Wray, L. R. (2001) Minsky's analysis of financial capitalism. In: R. Bellofiore and P. Ferri (Eds.), Financial Keynesianism and Market Instability. The Economic Legacy of Hyman Minsky. Vol I, Edward Elgar: Cheltenham, UK: 123-146.

Simon, H. (1936) "Rules versus Authorities in Monetary Policy." *Journal of Political Economy*, 44: 1-39.

Ülgen, F. (2009) "The current financial crisis: paving the way for reconsidering the working of market economies." Forthcoming, Idea. *A Journal of humanities*, 1(2).

Whalen, C. J. (2007) "The U.S. credit crunch of 2007. A Minsky moment." Public Policy Brief N°92, The Levy Economics Institute of Bard College.

In: After the Crisis: Rethinking Finance
Editor: Thomas Lagoarde-Segot

ISBN 978-1-61668-925-4
© 2010 Nova Science Publishers, Inc.

Chapter 9

MORTGAGE MARKETS MATTER: WHY WE NEED A BETTER UNDERSTANDING OF THE MORTGAGE MARKET TO UNDERSTAND THE FINANCIAL CRISIS

Manuel B. Aalbers

ABSTRACT

Heterodox economists as well as non-economist like economic sociologists and economic geographers have argued for years that the mainstream, neoclassical view of markets is wrong. This chapter will not review these theoretical debates, but will seek an alternative understanding of one crucial market: the mortgage market. Developments in this market were at the root of the financial crisis. Three years into the crisis, our understanding of mortgage markets is still flawed and needs to be altered to enhance our understanding of the financial crisis. I will argue that there was a conscious decision to increasingly financialize home ownership, not for the sake of increasing home ownership but to fuel economic growth. As a result, not only are home ownership and finance more entangled than ever before, but the mortgage crisis and the financial crisis also feed upon another. Home ownership has increased primarily among low-income groups – the groups that most severely experience the insecurity caused by changes in the labour market and the welfare state as well as by the mortgage market crisis. The impact of the mortgage market on both sophisticated financial markets and ordinary citizens is unique. The financialization of home ownership is not just another example of financialization but a crucial one, as mortgage markets are crucial markets in the present economy, while homes are as crucial as ever for households, but have increased their importance as indicators of the economy.

1. INTRODUCTION

Heterodox economists as well as non-economist like economic sociologists and economic geographers have argued for years that the mainstream, neoclassical view of markets is wrong. This chapter will not review these theoretical debates, but will seek an alternative understanding of one crucial market: the mortgage market. Developments in this market were at the root of the financial crisis. Three years into the crisis, our understanding of mortgage markets is still flawed and needs to be altered to enhance our understanding of the financial crisis. I will argue that there was a conscious decision to increasingly financialize home ownership, not for the sake of increasing home ownership but to fuel economic growth. As a result, not only are home ownership and finance more entangled than ever before, but the mortgage crisis and the financial crisis also feed upon another. Home ownership has increased primarily among low-income groups – the groups that most severely experience the insecurity caused by changes in the labor market and the welfare state as well as by the mortgage market crisis. The impact of the mortgage market on both sophisticated financial markets and ordinary citizens is unique. The financialization of home ownership is not just another example of financialization but a crucial one, as mortgage markets are crucial markets in the present economy, while homes are as crucial as ever for households, but have increased their importance as indicators of the economy.

The dominant view on economic action and markets comes from neoclassical economics. Neoclassical economic perspectives rest on a number of premises: (1) actors have complete information; (2) information is free; (3) therefore, all actors act in the same rational way according to exogenously given preferences; (4) actors are oriented towards profit or utility maximalization; (5) state intervention negatively alters the workings of the market; and (6) market equilibrium appears by itself as a result of market forces. All of these assumptions have been challenged by a large number of critics, both from within and outside economics (e.g. Amin, 1999; Bourdieu, 2005; Boyer, 2004; Courpasson, 1995; Fligstein, 2001; Granovetter, 1985; Hirsch et al., 1990; Hogdson, 1988; Kornai, 1971; Lawson, 1997; North, 1990; Scott, 2000; Smelser and Swedberg, 2005) and it is not my intention to repeat their arguments here. Rather than proposing an alternative view, I will only briefly discuss one version of the economic sociological approach to markets, thereby heavily relying on the work of Neil Fligstein.

Like heterodox economists and economic geographers, most economic sociologists do not deny that actors are rational, but they do take a much wider definition of rationality than neoclassical economists. For example, Weber and Polanyi define rational action as "choice of means in relation to ends" and argue that rational does not refer to either ends or means, "but rather to the relating of means to ends" (Polanyi, 1992: 31). Rationality in this broader sense does not necessarily refer to maximizing profit, but can also refer to the firm's survival; in order to survive and reproduce, the owners and managers "will do anything to control others" (Fligstein, 2001: 19), whether these are other firms, customers or state institutions. Firms do no only aim to control state institutions, but also turn to state institutions to attain stability. This is not a paradox: in order to increase their own control, firms need the state to intervene and (re-) define the borders and the rules of the market: "Once institutionalized, these rules both enable and constrain subsequent behavior" (Fligstein, 2001: 19). Moreover, rational behavior is learned rather than innate: "Rationality is motivated and guided by systems of shared beliefs, customs, norms and institutions (Weber, 1968); it is context-bound and embedded in interpersonal ties because human agency is "intendedly rational, but limitedly so" (Simon, 1957: xxiv) due to uncertainty, information asymmetry and imperfect cognitive ability (Nee, 2005). Rationality is not just bound due to lack of information, but also because there is often too much information to process and to use in making decisions. Information can take many forms and not all information can be easily codified into rational decisions in a neoclassical fashion.

Markets are social constructions, but to make the institutionalization of markets successful, it requires an inherently political process (Fligstein, 2001). In the end, market organization is "a mix of the historical and the political. The chosen solutions for organizing for markets depend on who writes the rules and how these rules help a given set of actors" (Fligstein, 2001: 65). Markets depend on a 'conception of control', that is, "collective understandings about what the actions of other market actors mean" (Fligstein, 2005: 192; see also Fligstein, 2001). Both the stability and the dynamics of markets are made possible by this extensive social organization as "economic actors are totally dependent on social arrangements to make profits" (Fligstein, 2001: 23) whereby "market theories need non-market coordination to make them work" (Stuart, 2003: 68). Indeed, as Polanyi (1944) argues, regulation is not only a necessary component of (semi-) capitalist societies, but one that actually facilitates the workings of markets.

The mortgage market is an economic field structured by power relations between different actors, which are maintained through combinations of not only financial capital, but also social, cultural and symbolic capital. Within this field firms orient their actions toward one another (Bourdieu, 2005; Fligstein, 2001; White, 1981). The relations between firms can be characterized both by a struggle of competition and by coordination (Weber, 1898). Coordination enables power and information advantages in the interest struggle, in this case between lenders and consumers. In this struggle lenders do not just respond to consumer demand, but provide 'incentives and opportunities that pull and mould behaviors, locational preferences and choices of individual consumers' (Gotham, 2002: 87; see also Feagin and Parker, 1990; Gottdiener, 1994). Competition in many markets "is tempered by the recognition that if all prosper, all survive" (Fligstein, 2001: 50). Moreover, we cannot explain the rise of subprime lending or the roots of the financial crisis by purely relying on the neoclassical idea of 'rational choice' and should pay more attention to the institutional and social environment. Rationality is context-bound and guided by systems of shared beliefs, customs, networks, norms and institutional arrangements.

In both popular and academic accounts, the roots of the current global financial crises in the US housing market are presented as a problem in which homeowners took out risky loans that were pushed by greedy loan brokers and lenders who didn't care about the riskiness of these loans as they would be packaged and sold off as residential mortgage-backed securities (RMBS) anyway. This popular account of the financial crisis continues to present a network of agents that have not paid enough attention to risk: not only borrowers and lenders, but also the state, regulators, investors and rating agencies. Three roots to the financial crisis are often discussed: greed, the bursting of a real estate bubble and the fact that "everyone made mistakes". This image of the roots of the financial crisis is not wrong, but it is limited in explaining what went wrong. Greed is nothing new, real estate bubbles need to develop before they can burst and we need to understand in which context actors made mistakes. In this paper I will discuss the roots of the financial crisis within the mortgage market. I will continue to argue that, although there was no 'master plan' to commodify home ownership even further, it was a conscious decision by a range of actors – including state actors and financial market actors – to increasingly financialize home ownership, not for the sake of increasing home ownership but to fuel economic growth. As a result, not only are home ownership and finance more entangled than ever before, but the mortgage crisis and the financial crisis are also feeding upon each other. As home ownership has increased primarily among low-income groups, it is these groups that experience the most insecurity because of changes in the labor market, changes in the welfare state and the mortgage market crisis. I will argue that the impact of the mortgage market on both sophisticated financial markets and ordinary citizens is unique. The financialization of home ownership is not just another example of financialization but a crucial one, as mortgage markets are crucial markets in the present economy, while homes are as crucial as ever for households, but have increased their importance as indicators of the economy.

The pairing of the home as an individual good *and* as a societal good is important here. Individualism is deeply rooted in American society. Actors interested in expanding financial markets through the expansion of home ownership have mobilized this American trait very well. A "home" is the first thing most people mention when they think of the American Dream. The American Dream is, in a wider sense, about the prospect of prosperity, but throughout the years this prospect has increasingly been coupled to home ownership. Home ownership became one tangible result of prosperity, but – as I will explain in this chapter – through financialization home ownership also became mobilized for prosperity. The image of the home as an ATM, as a cash dispenser, is one that has become one that is connected to the financial crisis. For many people, in particular the millions faced with foreclosure, the crisis has turned their home, their American Dream, into their American Nightmare.

In this chapter, I will first discuss three contributing factors to the crisis. First, I look at how the US mortgage market has developed and how securitization and deregulation play a role in this. Second I focus on two subsets of mortgage lending that were at the basis of the current crisis, namely subprime and predatory lending. Third, I focus on the part played by bubbles and wrong incentives. After discussing these three factors, I take a step back to discuss the concept on financialization and what financialization means for mortgage markets. By doing this, I am able to place the crisis into a bigger picture: a picture in which greed, deregulation, real estate bubbles and incentives all play a role, but come about in a certain context. The concept of financialization, which is at the same time the explanandum and the explanans, provides a heuristic that helps us to make sense of the financial crisis. Finally, I ask the question if the financial crisis necessarily had to start in the mortgage market, or if it is a coincidence and could have started in other financial markets as well.

2. Securitization and Deregulation

The current financial crisis originates in the housing and mortgage markets, but it affects financial markets around the world. A few decades ago most mortgage lenders were local or regional institutions. Today, most mortgage lenders are national lenders who tap into the global credit market. This is not so much the case because lenders are global financial institutions – most lenders are national in scope – but because they compete for the same credit in a global market. Before the financial crisis of the late 1980s, savings and loans institutions (SandL's) granted loans based on the savings that got into the bank. Generally speaking, the savings and loans were made in the same geographical market. The fact that the SandL's only worked in local markets was seen as a problem: what if savings are available in one area, but loans are needed in another; and what if a local housing market goes bust? The 'solution' was to connect local markets and to spread risk. The idea was that interest rates on loans would fall because there was now a more efficient market for the demand and supply of money and credit. Moreover, national lenders could more easily take the burdens of a local housing market bust because risk would be spread.

The trend from local to national mortgage lenders was one thing, but, it was argued, mortgage markets could be even more efficient if they were connected to other financial markets and not just to savings. In the wider credit market it would be easy for mortgage lenders to get money as mortgages were considered low-risk. Mortgages would be an ideal investment for low-risk investors and cheaper credit, in return, would lower interest rates on mortgage loans. Securitization was already introduced in the 1960s by Fannie Mae and Freddie Mac, two government sponsored enterprises that were meant to spur home ownership rates for low and middle income households. Securitization enables mortgage lenders to sell their mortgage portfolio on the secondary mortgage markets to investors. Following the SandL crisis, deregulation favoured securitization, not only through Fannie Mae and Freddie Mac, but also through so-called "private labels". Gotham (2006) has studied the deregulation of the mortgage market and demonstrates how the federal government, step-by-step, has enabled securitization, e.g. by the Financial Institutions Reform, Recovery and Enforcement Act (1989) that pushed portfolio lenders to securitize their loans and shift to non-depository lending. In other words, the state was at the origins of the current crisis.

Deregulation also removed the walls between the different rooms of finance, thereby enabling existing financial firms to become active in more types of financial markets and providing opportunities for new mortgage lenders. Securitization meant that mortgage lenders could work according to a new business model whereby mortgages are taken off-balance. This frees up more equity for more loans and enabled non-banks to enter the mortgage market. Many of these new "non-bank lenders" had different regulators than traditional lenders and were also assessed by other, i.e. weaker, regulatory frameworks. In addition, it is not always clear which regulator watches what, but even if this is clear, this is no guarantee that regulators actually execute their regulatory powers, sometimes due to a lack of interest and sometimes due to a lack of manpower. In many cases, companies can actually shop around for a regulator. It is obvious that they won't opt for the hardest regulator. Mortgage portfolios could now be sold to investors anywhere in the world and because these investors thought mortgage portfolios were low-risk and there was a lot of money waiting to be invested, especially after the dot-com bubble crash (2000-2002), there was a great appetite for RMBS. In other words, the SandL crisis, the following bank merger wave (Dymski, 1999), securitization, the entry of non-bank lenders and the demand for low-risk investments together shaped the globalization and financialization of mortgage markets (Aalbers, 2008).

Lenders, rating agencies and investors not only underestimated the risks of RMBS but also overestimated the returns. Even though housing prices on average fell by 20% between summer 2006 and summer 2008, the impact on the RMBS market was much bigger. This is not just a result of inflationary prices, but also of leveraging. Major players in the RMBS market, such as investment banks, basically invested with borrowed money (ratio's of 1:20 were not uncommon, 1:14 being the average) and because of this leveraging both profits and losses would be disproportionally large. For example, if an investment bank is able to borrow money on a 6% interest rate and expects a return of 8% on low-risk, prime RMBS and 16% on high-risk subprime, it effectively makes, respectively, 2% and 10% by doing almost nothing. By investing more than they borrow, they are able to rapidly increase profit margins.

However, when returns are lower than the interest rate on which they have borrowed money, for example, respectively, 4% and 2%, the investment banks not only miss 4% or 14% calculated profit, they also have to take their losses on their equity, for instance: 14 (the average leverage factor) times, respectively, 2% (6%-4%) and 4% (6%-2%) equals equity losses of, respectively, 28% and 56%. Since the leverage factors in many cases were even much higher than 14, some financial institutions and investors that were heavily involved in RMBS, and especially subprime RMBS, effectively went bankrupt.

3. SUBPRIME AND PREDATORY LENDING

Subprime mortgage lending has been growing fast, from about $35 billion (5% of total mortgage originations) in 1994 to $600 billion (20%) in 2006 (Avery et al. 2006), 75% of which is securitized. In some states like Nevada, subprime loans accounted for more than 30% of the loans originated in 2006. In 2006, 13% of outstanding loans were subprime, but 60% of the loans in foreclosure were subprime, up from 30% in 2003 (Nassar, 2007). Neither the media nor academic economists ever pass an opportunity to point out that many borrowers took out loans they could not afford. This is correct, but in most cases this was not because borrowers were eager to take on large loans even though they had bad credit. A majority of the subprime loans went to borrowers with prime credit (Brooks and Simon, 2007; Dymski, 2007). This implies that lenders systematically overcharged borrowers. Subprime lending is often defined as lending to a low-income borrower with poor credit, but this would be a misrepresentation of the essence of subprime lending, which is lending at higher fees and interest rates whether or not the borrower actually has bad credit or a low income (Aalbers, 2009). Subprime loans were pushed on borrowers – low and moderate-income as well as middle and high-income – because they brought in more money. not just because lenders were pushed to sell them.

Selling subprime loans to prime borrowers was good business for both mortgage lenders and brokers. Lenders could charge higher interest rates on subprime loans and thus make more money. For this reason lenders gave brokers bigger sales fees for selling subprime loans. Brokers did not have negative results as a result of defaulting borrowers, as they only get paid for what they sell. And defaulting borrowers actually created a bigger market for refinancing, which implied that brokers could make more money on clients by selling them another loan.

In addition, it is often argued that subprime lending enabled many people that were formerly excluded from home ownership, i.e., low-income and ethnic minority groups, to buy a house and enjoy the benefits of home ownership. This is questionable for at least two reasons. Firstly, many of these borrowers had bought properties at the low-end of the market that needed improvement work and because of the high interest rates their monthly expenses often went up much faster than their income and became unmanageable. Home ownership for many subprime homebuyers became a burden rather. Secondly, most subprime loans were not enabling home ownership as more than half of them were refinance loans and second mortgages – in other words, loans for people who already owned a mortgaged property. Most of the refinance loans were designed in such a way that they looked cheaper than the original loan, but would, in fact, turn out more expensive for the borrowers and more profitable for the mortgage broker and the lender. Adjustable Rate Mortgages (ARMs) are a good example: one type of ARM known as a 2/28 or 3/37 will start with a low interest rate, but after 2 or 3 years the interest rate resets to a much higher rate. Borrowers are shown the initial, low interest rate while the higher interest rate is hidden in the small print of the mortgage contract, which is typically unreadable.

A subset of subprime lending is known as predatory lending. Predatory lenders charge excessive fees and interest rates and originated loans that were not beneficial for borrowers. Originally predatory lending was seen as a small part of the subprime mortgage market, but research from the past five years has demonstrated predatory lending is not an exception but rather something very common in subprime lending. Often homeowners don't have a full understanding of the mortgage lending process and fail to hire experts, not only at the time of mortgage origination, but also when the first payment problems arise (Engel and McCoy, 2002). There is mounting evidence that subprime and predatory lenders use sophisticated marketing techniques to reach people with little education or prior lending experience (Carr and Schuetz, 2001; Quercia et al, 2004; Newman, 2009). Predatory loans were sold mostly in neighborhoods with ethnic minority populations. Almost half of the loans in minority areas were predatory compared to 22% in white areas (Avery et al., 2007). African-Americans receive more than twice as many high-priced loans as Whites, even after controlling for the risk level of the borrower (Schloemer et al., 2006). It then comes as no surprise that foreclosures are concentrated in certain parts of the city. These problems are not new: for at least ten years researchers have pointed out how subprime and predatory lending result in rising default and foreclosure rates (e.g. Pennington-Cross, 2002; Squires, 2004; Wyly et al., 2006). Yet, this was not considered a major problem until house prices started declining and the value of RMBS fell.

4. BUBBLES AND WRONG INCENTIVES

The root of the mortgage crisis, according to some observers, is in the housing market: the rapid increase of house prices forced people to take out bigger loans (Shiller, 2008). The housing bubble, like all bubbles, depended on a constant inflow of liquidity to sustain the rising market as well as the illusion that all participants in the market are winners (Lordon, 2007). Once the housing bubble burst, homeowners got in trouble, not just because their homes were worth less, but also because so many of them had taken out big loans with small down-payments and high interest rates. Negative equity, default and foreclosure were some of the negative results. Indeed, there was a strong housing bubble, but this did not so much fuel the mortgage market – the mortgage market, in the first place, fuelled the housing bubble. House prices increased first and foremost because mortgages allowed borrowers to buy more expensive homes, but since almost everyone could now afford a mortgage loan – and generally speaking a much bigger loan than a decade ago – the expansion of the mortgage market resulted in higher house prices forcing people to take out ever bigger loans. In that sense, the mortgage market created it own expansion. Thus, mortgage and housing markets fuelled one another, but it is crucial to understand that the driving force here is the mortgage market. Surowiecki (2009: 38) summarizes it as follows:

"With the housing bubble (...) there was no meaningful development in the real economy that could explain why homes were suddenly so much more attractive or valuable. The only thing that had changed, really, was that banks were flinging cheap money at would-be homeowners, essentially conjuring up profits out of nowhere".

As argued in the previous sections, this was enabled through deregulation and re-regulation.

Old and new lenders alike had an interest in making loans that could be sold off and in loans that generated higher yields. This resulted in riskier loans with higher interest rates (subprime lending). Mortgage brokers were rewarded with higher fees if they would sell loans with higher interest rates (i.e., riskier loans); many of these were not loans to buy a home, but refinanced loans and second mortgages, or, in other words, loans that did not contribute to increasing home ownership rates. The higher risk of default on these loans was taken for granted, not just because they would be sold off, but also because default presented a risk to the borrower who would loose her/his home; the lender could repossess the home and sell it quite easily as house prices continued to rise.

There were enough investors who had an appetite for RMBS, first in so-called conforming loans because of their low-risk that was considered to be comparable to state obligations. But since the late 1990s, and increasingly so after the dot-com bubble crash (2000-2002), they also showed an interest in subprime loans issued as RMBS: in an evermore competitive search for yield "each stage of market development replayed a dynamic of over-speculation based on competitive pressures to adopt riskier borrowers and loan products" (Ashton, 2008). Investors, in return, "had concentrated risks by leveraging their holdings of mortgages in securitized assets, so [when the bubble burst] their losses were multiplied" (Mizen, 2008: 532). Subprime loans were considered riskier, but this was compensated by higher returns and since the rating agencies still supplied high ratings, such RMBS were seen as low-risk/high-return. Rating agencies saw the increased likeliness of default on such loans, but like the lenders they didn't see this as a major problem, more as an inconvenience. In addition, rating agencies get paid by the firms whose securities they have to rate.

It is too easy to argue that this made the rating agencies less critical of RMBS. After all, they were also dependent on rating other financial products and if they would give high ratings to all of them, they would soon not be taken seriously anymore. So what did cause rating agencies to be so late in realizing the risk of these securities? First, as I suggested above, they simply did not realize the risk as they believed in rising house prices, just like homeowners, lenders, and the media – like everyone essentially. Second, because the rating agencies had become so heavily involved with securities that their own growth now depended on rating more and more of them. Third, throughout the years the most basic RMBS were complemented by ever more complicated products that few had an understanding of, not even the rating agencies on which investors trusted. It is sometimes argued that the rating agencies cannot be blamed for this as others in the mortgage network also didn't understand the complexity and riskiness of these products, but since it is their job to understand and then rate financial products, it could be argued, in an almost tautologically fashion, that the rating agencies are responsible for rating high-risk products as low-risk.

These RMBS were now traded on global markets that are localized in places like New York and London (Pryke and Lee 1995; Sassen 2001). While in the past a mortgage bubble or a housing bubble would affect the economy through homeowners, the current bursting of these bubbles affects the economy not just through homeowners, but also through financial markets. Because lenders are now national in scope this no longer affects only some housing markets, but all housing markets throughout the US. Housing markets may still be local or regional, mortgage markets are not. Since primary mortgage markets are national, the bubble in the national mortgage market affects all local and regional housing markets, although it clearly affects housing markets with a greater bubble more than those with a smaller bubble (Aalbers, 2009a). In addition, secondary mortgage markets are global markets, which means that a crisis of mortgage securitization implies that investors around the globe, and therefore economies around the globe, are affected. The mortgage market crisis affects the US economy on both sides of the mortgage lending chain – through homeowners and through financial markets – while it affects other economies in the world mostly through financial markets, not just because investors around the globe have invested in RMBS, but also because the mortgage market has triggered a whole chain of events that have decreased liquidity and this affects even agents in financial markets that have never been involved in RMBS.

5. FINANCIALIZATION

It is no coincidence that the securitization of mortgage loans went too far and created a mortgage bubble – and thereby also a housing bubble. Securitization may have started out for the sake of increasing home ownership, but the last 15 to 20 years the growth in securitization had little to do with increasing home ownership – this was simply a by-product – and more with the dependence of the US economy on the financial sector for economic growth. Due to the slowing down of the overall growth rate and the stagnation of the real economy, capitalism has increasingly become dependent on the growth of finance to enlarge money capital (Sweezy, 1995; Foster, 2007). Therefore the capital accumulation process becomes financialized: focused on the growth of finance not to benefit the real economy but to benefit actors within financial markets such as investors. Boyer (2000) speaks of a finance-led regime of accumulation. Financialization is a pattern of accumulation in which profit-making occurs increasingly through financial channels rather than through trade and commodity production (Arrighi, 1994; Krippner, 2005). It signifies that the financial industry has been transformed "from a facilitator of other firms' economic growth into a growth industry in its own right" (Engelen, 2003). Financialization refers to the increased role of finance in the operations of capitalism and implies that "the inverted relation between the financial and the real is the key to understanding new trends in the world" (Sweezy, 1995: 8). Financialization can be characterized as the capitalist economy gone extreme: it is not a producer or consumer market, but a market designed only to make money.

Much like globalization, financialization can be seen as 'a *process* that has introduced a new form of competition within the economy and that has the capacity to become ever more pervasive' (French et al., 2007: 8, emphasis in original). Financialization is by no means limited to financial markets and entails the financialization of non-financial sectors of the real economy that become heavily involved in capital and money markets. Of course, actors (e.g. firms) in the real economy have always been dependent on credit, but with financialization they are increasingly ruled by financial actors and their interests: 'finance more and more sets the pace and the rules for the management of the cash flow of non-financial firms' (Foster, 2007: 7). The rules and logics of Wall Street are increasingly becoming the rules and logics outside Wall Street. Financialization not only refers to the growth of financial actors such as banks, lenders, private equity and hedge funds, but is reflected in the operations of non-financial firms in different parts of the economy, such as the car industry (Froud et al., 2002), the 'new economy' (Feng et al., 2001) and real estate (Aalbers, 2008; Smart and Lee, 2003). Finally, financialization not only affects businesses, but increasingly also consumers: 'It asks people from all walks of life to accept risks into their homes that were hitherto the province of professionals. Without significant capital, people are being asked to think like capitalists' (Martin, 2002: 12; cf. Mandel, 1996).

Mortgage markets were originally designed to facilitate households who wanted to buy a home, but they also fueled house prices (Aalbers, 2008). In the US, in the late 1990s, the expansion of mortgage markets entered a new stage in which mortgage markets no longer only facilitate home ownership, but are increasingly, yet not exclusively, designed to facilitate the growth of credit itself. Home ownership has always been dependent on finance, but today investment in real estate markets is more than ever before dependent on the development offinancial markets. The push for home ownership has increased the importance of home ownership at both the individual and the societal level (Aalbers, 2005). The expansion of the mortgage market is not just meant to increase home ownership, but is also intended as a means to further the neo-liberal agenda of private property, firms and growing profits. In this process, homeowners also become more dependent on financial markets. Old arrangements of social rights have been replaced and continue to be replaced by new arrangements in which social rights and guarantees are transferred from the state to financial markets. Indeed, the restructuring of welfare states has resulted in a "great risk shift" in which households are increasingly dependent on financial markets for their long-term security (Hacker, 2006).

Due to the financialization of home ownership, housing risks are increasingly financial market risks these days – and vice versa. The financialization of home ownership forces more and more households to see acquiring a house not just as a home, as a place to live, but as an investment, as something to put equity into and take equity from – the ATM or cash dispenser image of the home I mentioned before. This can be a financially gainful experience, but is not necessarily so. As home ownership has increased primarily among low-income groups, there are also more groups that have become vulnerable to the risks of home ownership. It is these groups that experience the most insecurity because of changes in the labor market, the welfare state and the mortgage market crisis. It is also these groups that are hit disproportionally hard by predatory lending.

Financialization has resulted in an increase in the number of homeowners, but also, and more importantly, in a rapid and huge increase in the value of homes. It is not recent homeowners who benefit most, but those who have been property owners for decades. The financialization of home ownership is of course the most beneficial for those who invested earlier and who were able to invest more: the "upward pressure on house prices restricts access to home ownership and adds to the wealth of the 'insiders' at the expense of the 'outsiders'" (Stephens, 2007: 218). More available and, in particular, bigger mortgage loans may, at first sight, seem to benefit people who want to buy a house, but since it has resulted in dramatic increases in house prices, home ownership has paradoxically become both more accessible and more expensive.

In addition, the US financial system made other types of credit more and more dependent on home equity. Simply put, owning a home made it easier and cheaper to get credit and, in addition, the growth of the economy in recent decades has become increasingly dependent on credit rather than on income. Home equity was and is an important part of what needs to keep the system going. Consequently, the current mortgage crisis and the related fall in house prices affect not just households that need to refinance their homes or that want to sell their homes, but the whole economy. Home equity has become so entangled with other parts of the economy, that problems in housing affect other parts of the economy. A crisis in the mortgage market is therefore a crisis in the accumulation patterns of financialization and affects the economy at large. If a rise in home equity can keep the market going, a stagnation or decrease in home equity can result in a stagnation of other sectors of the economy and can depress economic growth.

Housing is a central aspect of financialization. Through the rise of securitization and the vast expansion of secondary mortgage markets, not only in the US but also in other countries, the mortgage market becomes financialized. Increasingly, lenders become intermediaries who sell mortgages, but don't manage, service or fund them (Aalbers, 2009b; Dennis and Pinkowish, 2004). But the financialization of homeownership is not limited to the development of secondary mortgage markets; it can also be witnessed in the financialization of (potential) homeowners. The financialization of home was never designed to enable homeownership; it was first and foremost designed to fuel the economy. The expansion of the mortgage market was a necessary component in the financialization of home, but wideraccess to mortgage loans resulted in higher house prices (Aalbers, 2008). Access does not equal affordability. The result is not improved access to homeownership, but an increase in risk and insecurity. Higher mortgage loans enabled not only homeownership, but also higher house prices; subsequently, access needed to be widened further to enable continued securitization. It is a vicious circle that had reached its absolute limits in 2007-2008. By simultaneously expanding the mortgage market, by means of granting bigger loans (as a percentage of income and as a percentage of home value), and by giving access to more households (so-called 'underserved populations'), the growth machine kept on working smoothly for a while.

6. THE UNIQUE CONTRIBUTION OF THE MORTGAGE MARKET

Greed, the bursting of real estate bubbles and the credo that "everyone made mistakes" cannot explain the current financial crisis. The roots of the crisis are in the structural developments of the mortgage market. Deregulation supported both securitization and subprime lending. While the primary mortgage market after the SandL crisis of the late 1980s developed into a national market, the secondary mortgage market (i.e., the market for RMBS) developed into a global market in which mortgage funding is increasingly tied to other credit markets. It is this combination of deregulation, securitization and financialization that is at the root of the current crisis. This not only resulted in more connected mortgage markets, but also in vastly expanding mortgage markets. This fueled housing prices, but also extended mortgage funding beyond what was deemed good business in the past (and beyond what is deemed good business again today). Homeowners were lured into overpriced loans, often through expensive refinancing. The subprime and predatory boom were not meant to increase home ownership, as is often argued – instead, they were designed to maximize profits for lenders, mortgage brokers, investment banks, rating agencies and investors in RMBS, not borrowers. In short, the financialization of the mortgage market means that it is not only the global and the local that have become interdependent, but also the financial and the built environment – and indeed, the volatility of financial markets and the daily life of households (Aalbers, 2008).

Some commentators (e.g. Mizen, 2008) would argue that it is a coincidence that the financial crisis started in the mortgage market. They argue that the whole financial system is so rotten that, sooner or later, it had to fail: the mortgage market is the trigger of the downturn, but the actual causes are much deeper and have affected all financial sectors. Other commentators (e.g. Ashton, 2009) would alternatively argue that it is no surprise that the fall down of the financial sector was caused by the mortgage market. They argue that the mortgage market was far more rotten than any other financial sector and that in no other financial sector money had been provided as recklessly. In fact, the mortgage market was not unique in its financial excesses; other financial markets also showed developments that were getting out of hand. For example, at Lehman Brothers, the American investment bank that failed, it was possible to speculate on almost anything, including the weather. Investing in a house by taking out a mortgage loan, albeit a risky one, in that respect looks less risky; and also investing in RMBS, even in subprime RMBS, does not seem so excessive anymore.

Nevertheless, the mortgage market is different from other financial markets in at least two important ways. First, the market for mortgage lending and the market for RMBS, not necessarily in turnover but certainly in outstanding volume, are simply much bigger than most other financial markets. If the market for weather speculation or even that for the securitization of car loans would far apart, the impact would be far less reaching. Second, unlike many other financial markets, a downturn in the mortgage market hits not only agents active in the credit and securities markets, but also homeowners. Since a home is the most expensive thing most households will ever buy and because it is such a basic need, the impact of a mortgage crisis – in a country like the US that is heavily depended on mortgage loans to make the housing market work – could only be dramatic. In the sense that there were too many wrong incentives in the market, mortgages and RMBS were not so different from many other financial markets, but in its impact on both 'sophisticated' financial markets and ordinary citizens, the mortgage market is unique.

By simultaneously expanding the mortgage market – by means of granting bigger loans (as a percentage of income and as a percentage of home value) and by giving access to more households (so-called "underserved populations") – the growth machine (cf. Molotch, 1976) kept on working smoothly for a while. Yet, every growth machine needs to keep on growing to function smoothly and the current crisis has announced the beginning of the end of ever expanding mortgage markets. In addition, the reduced liquidity of mortgages in the secondary market will make it harder for lenders to securitize loans. And considering that two-thirds of the US mortgage market is securitized, the impact could only be massive. This is why major bank lenders are hit hard and have lost billions of dollars in the crisis, but the ones going bankrupt (e.g. New Century Financial Corporation) or closing down (e.g. American Home Mortgage) are the non-bank lenders that fully rely on the secondary mortgage to sell their portfolios. In addition, foreign investors, such as European banks and pension funds, are hit because many of them have bought MBS.

Crises have often been blamed on a lack of openness and transparency. Yet, the current credit crunch originates in a market made open, liquid, and transparent; located in a country that prides itself on its free, open markets. In addition, an analysis of financial crisis since 1945 demonstrates that financial liberalization, whether de jure or de facto, precedes the majority of crises (Kaminsky and Reinhart, 1999) – the current crisis is no exception. Liberalization-enabled securitization and financialization, by embracing risk rather than avoiding it, act against the interests of long-term investments. Though securitization was designed to limit risk by spreading it over a wider area and to increase efficiency as a result of economies of scale, the spread of risk gives the crisis wider latitude, not only affecting subprime loans, but also prime loans; not only affecting mortgage markets, but also other credit markets; and not only affecting the US, but also other places around the globe. Through financialization, the volatility of Wall Street has entered not only companies off-Wall-Street, but increasingly also individual homes – home ownership and finance are more entangled than ever before. It could be argued that the state has facilitated the privatisation of profit and the socialisation of risk.

The current credit crunch exemplifies how the fate of homeowners is increasingly tied to the fate of financial markets. In its origins, this is not because rising default rates and foreclosures trouble financial markets, but because the financialization of mortgages and homeowners has led to the extraction of capital from homeowners to financial investors. In other words, the mortgage crisis is a direct result of the financialization of both mortgage markets and homeowners. The financialization of home ownership is not just another example of financialization but a crucial one, as mortgage markets are crucial markets in the present economy, while homes are as crucial as ever for households, but have increased their importance as indicators of the economy.

REFERENCES

Aalbers, M. B. (2005) "The quantified customer", or how financial institutions value risk, in P. Boelhouwer, J. Doling and M. Elsinga (eds), *Home ownership: getting in, getting from, getting out.* Delft: Delft University Press, 33-57.

Aalbers M. B. (2008) The financialization of home and the mortgage market crisis. *Competition and Change* 12: 148-66.

Aalbers, M. B. (2009a) *Geographies of the financial crisis.* Area 41(1): 34-42.

Aalbers, M. B. (2009b) The Globalization and Europanization of Mortgage Markets. *International Journal of Urban and Regional Research* 33(2): 389-410.

Amin, A. (1999) An institutionalist perspective on regional economic development. *International Journal of Urban and Regional Research* 23(1): 365-378.

Arrighi, G. (1994) The long twentieth century: *Money, power, and the origins of our times.* London: Verso.

Ashton, P. (2008) Advantage or disadvantage? The changing institutional landscape of underserved mortgage markets. *Urban Affairs Review* 43: 352-402.

Ashton, P. (2009) An appetite for yield: the anatomy of the subprime mortgage crisis. *Environment and Planning* A 41.6, 1420–41.

Avery, R. B., Brevoort, K. P. and Canner, G. B. (2006) Higher-priced home lending and the 2005 *HMDA data*. *Federal Reserve Bulletin* 92: 123-66.

Avery, R. B., Brevoort, K. P. and Canner, G. B. (2007) The 2006 HMDA data. *Federal Reserve Bulletin* 93: 73-109.

Bromley C et al. (2008) Paying more for the American dream. *The subprime shakeout and its impact on lower-income and minority communities.* The California Reinvestment Coalition et al., San Francisco, CA.

Brooks, R. and Simon, R. (2007) Subprime debacle traps even very credit-worthy. *Wall Street Journal* 3 December: A1.

Bourdieu, P. (2005) *The social structures of the economy.* Cambridge: Polity.

Boyer, R. (2004) Une théorie du capitalisme est-elle possible? Paris: Odile Jacob.

Cagan, C. (2007) Mortgage payment reset: The issue and the impact First American. CoreLogic, Santa Ana, CA.

Carr, J. and Schuetz, J. (2001) Financial services in distressed communities: framing the issue, finding solutions. Fannie Mae Foundation, Washington DC.

Courpasson, D. (1995) Éléments pour une sociologie de la relation commerciale. Les paradoxes de la modernisation dans le banque. Sociologie du travail 37(1): 1-24.

Dennis, M. W. and Pinkowish, T. J. (2004) Residential Mortgage Lending: Principles and Practices, fifth edition. Mason, OH: Thomson South-Western.

Dymski, G. A. (1999) The bank merger wave: *The economic causes and social consequences of financial consolidation.* Sharpe, Armonk, NY.

Dymski, G. A. (2007) *From financial exploitation to global banking instability: two overlooked roots of the subprime crisis.* Working paper, University of California Center Sacramento, Sacramento.

Engel, K. and McCoy, P. (2002) A tale of three markets: *The law and economics of predatory lending.* Texas Law Review 80: 1255-381.

Engelen, E. (2003) The logic of funding European pension restructuring and the dangers of financialization. *Environment and Planning* A 35(8): 1357-72.

Feng, H., Froud, J., Haslam, C., Johal, S., Haslam, C. and Williams, K. (2001) A new business model? The capital market and the new economy, *Economy and Society,* 30(4): 467–503.

Fligstein, N. (2001) *The architecture of markets.* Princeton: Princeton University Press.

Fligstein, N. (2005) The political and economic sociology of international economic arrangements. In: N.J. Smelser and R. Swedberg (eds), *The handbook of economic sociology.* Second edition, pp. 183-204. Princeton: Princeton University Press.

Foster, J. B. (2007) *The financialization of capitalism.* Monthly Review 58(11): 1-12.

French, S., Leyshon, A. and Wainwright, T. (2007) Financializing space, working paper, School of Geography, University of Nottingham.

Froud, J., Haslam, C., Johal, S. and Williams, K. (2002) Cars after financialisation: a case study of financial under-performance, constraints and consequences, Competition and Change, 6(1): 13–41.

Gotham, K. F. (2002) Race, real estate, and uneven development. The Kansas city experience, 1900-2000. Albany: State University of New York Press.

Gotham, K. F. (2006) The secondary circuit of capital reconsidered: Globalization and the U.S. real estate sector. *American Journal of Sociology* 112: 231-75.

Gottdiener, M. (1994) *The social production of urban space.* Second edition. Austin, TX: University of Texas Press.

Granovetter, M. (1985) Economic action and social structure: The problem of embeddedness. *American Journal of Sociology* 91(3): 481-510.

Harvey, D. (1985) The urbanization of capital. Studies in the history and theory of capitalist urbanization. Blackwell, Oxford

Hirsch, P., Michaels, S. and Friedman, R. (1990) Clean models vs. dirty hands: Why economics is different from sociology. In: S. Zukin and P. DiMaggio (eds) Structures of capital: *The social organization of the economy,* pp. 39-56. Cambridge: Cambridge University Press.

Hodgson, G. M. (1988) Economics and institutions: *A manifesto for a modern institutional economics.* Cambridge: Polity.

Kaminsky, G. L. and Reinhart, C. M. (1999) The twin crises: The causes of banking and balance-of-payment problems. *American Economic Review* 89(3): 473-500.

Kornai, J. (1971/1991) Anti-equilibrium: On economic systems theory and the tasks of research. Fairfield, NJ: Augustus M. Kelley (originally published, Amsterdam/London: North-Holland).

Krippner, G. (2005) The financialization of the American economy. *Socio-Economic Review,* 3: 173-208.

Lawson, T. (1997) Economics and reality. London: Routledge.

Lobel, M. (2008) A free and fair market. Miller-McCune 1(5): 30-33.

Lordon, F. (2007) Spéculation immobilière, ralentissement économique. Quand la finance prend le monde en otage. Le Monde diplomatique Septembre.

Mandel, M. J. (1996) The High-risk society: Peril and Promise in the New Economy. New York: Random House.

Martin, R. (2002) Financialization of Daily Life. Philadelphia: Temple University Press.

Mizen, P. (2008) The credit crunch of 2007-2008: A discussion of the background, market reactions, and policy responses. *Federal Reserve Bank of St. Louis Review* 90(5): 531-67.

Molotch, H. (1976) The city as a growth machine: Towards a political economy of place. *American Journal of Sociology* 36: 309-32.

Nassar, J. (2007) Foreclosure, predatory mortgage and payday lending in America's cities. Testimony before the U.S. *House Committee on Oversight and Government Reform,* Washington DC.

NCRC (2002) Anti-predatory lending toolkit. *National Community Reinvestment Coalition,* Washington, DC.

Nee, V. (2005) The new institutionalism in economics and sociology. In N.J. Smelser and R. Swedberg (eds), *The handbook of economic sociology.* Second edition, pp. 49-74. Princeton: Princeton University Press.

Newman, K. (2009) Post Industrial Widgets: Capital Flows and the Production of the Urban. *International Journal of Urban and Regional Research* 33(2): 325-42.

North. D. C. (1990) *Institutions, institutional change, and economic performance.* Cambridge: Cambridge University Press.

Pennington-Cross, A. (2002) Subprime lending in the primary and secondary markets. Journal of Housing Research 13: 31-50.

Polanyi, K. (1944) The great transformation: *The political and economic origins of ourtime.* Boston: Beacon.

Polanyi, K. (1992) The economy as instituted process. In: M. Granovetter and R. Swedberg (eds), The sociology of economic life, pp. 29-51. Boulder, CO: Westview.

Sassen, S. (2001) *The global city: New York, London, Tokyo.* Second edition. Princeton University Press, Princeton, NJ.

Schloemer, E., Li, W., Ernst, K. and Keest, K. (2006) Losing ground: Foreclosures in the subprime market and their cost to homeowners. *Center for Responsible Lending,* Washington DC.

Scott, A. J. (2000) Economic geography: The great half-century. In: G.L. Clark. M.P. Feldman and M.S. Gertler (eds), *The Oxford handbook of economic geography,* pp. 18-44. Oxford: Oxford University Press.

Shiller, R. J. (2008) The subprime solution. Princeton University Press, Princeton.

Simon, H. A. (1957) Models of man: Social and rational. New York: John Wiley and Sons.

Smart, A. and Lee, J. (2003) Financialization and the role of real estate in Hong Kong's regime of accumulation, *Economic Geography,* 79(2): 153–171.

Smelser, N. J. and R. Swedberg (eds) (2005) *The handbook of economic sociology.* Second edition. Princeton: Princeton University Press.

Squires G. D. (ed.) (2004) Why the poor pay more. *How to stop predatory lending.* Praeger, Westport.

Stephens, M. (2007) Mortgage market deregulation and its consequences. *Housing Studies* 22(2): 201-20.

Stuart, G. (2003) Discriminating risk: *The U.S. mortgage lending industry in the twentieth century.* Ithaca. NY: Cornell University Press.

Surowiecki, J. (2009) Monsters, Inc. The New Yorker May 11: 38.

Sweezy, P. M. (1995) Economic reminiscences. Monthly Review 47(1): 1-11.

Taylor, J., Silver, J. and Berenbaum, D. (2004) The targets of predatory and discriminatory lending: Who are they and where do they live? in Squires G D ed Why the poor pay more. *How to stop predatory lending,* Praeger, Westport, 25-37.

Weber, M. (1968) Economy and society: An outline of interpretive sociology. Berkeley: University of California Press.

White, H. (1981) Where do markets come from? *American Journal of Sociology* 87: 517-547.

Wyly, E., Atia, M., Foxcroft, H., Hammel, D., and Philips-Watts, K. (2006) American home: predatory mortgage capital and neighbourhood spaces of race and class exploitation in the United States. Geografiska Annaler B 88: 105-32.

In: After the Crisis: Rethinking Finance
Editor: Thomas Lagoarde-Segot

ISBN 978-1-61668-925-4
© 2010 Nova Science Publishers, Inc.

Chapter 10

PRIVATE EQUITY AND THE CURRENT FINANCIAL CRISIS: RISK AND OPPORTUNISM

David Weitzner and James Darroch

ABSTRACT

The early years of the 21st century saw profound changes in the global financial system, particularly in North America and the UK, with the rise of the "new power brokers" of sovereign funds, hedge funds, Asian central banks and private equity (PE).(Farrell, Lund Gerlemann, and Seeburger 2007). The ease of financing not only made previously unimaginable deals possible, they made them possible in ways that did not promote the enhanced governance discussed by Jensen (1987). The lack of enhanced governance combined with the financial opportunism evident in some deals should cause genuine concerns for policy makers and business ethicists. While the general response from the PE industry has been to point to the good performance of the average deal, this chapter argues that the extreme deals are the fault line that reveal fundamental issues that need to be addressed. When late boom deals try to climb the maturity cliff, the opportunism demonstrated in several large PE deals will be shown to have increased the level of risk in the financial system.

1. INTRODUCTION

The early years of the 21st century saw profound changes to the global financial system marked by tremendous growth in financial assets. According to Farrell et al. (2008) the ratio of financial assets to GDP grew more rapidly than GDP from 2006 to 2007 as global financial assets grew to be $196 trillion dollars and over 350% of GDP. In part the growth of financial assets can be explained by a shift in corporate financing from institutions (banks) to markets which helped to allow unprecedented growth in leverage and sparked a new wave of corporate deal making producing new financial assets. (Tett, 2009) The innovations that fueled the growth of financial assets had profound effects on financial markets, particularly in the market-based financial systems of the US and UK. This growth was accompanied by the emergence of the "new power brokers" of sovereign wealth funds (SWFs), hedge funds, Asian central banks and private equity (PE).(Farrell, Lund, Gerlemann, and Seeburger, 2007; Roxburgh et al., 2009). During the golden years of borrowing the world was awash in liquidity and this liquidity promoted easy credit conditions which gave birth to what has become known as Old World PE deals(Tett and Davies, 2007; Partners Group, 2009) Moreover, there was tremendous optimism that the new capitalists would resolve some long standing conflicts between stakeholders and shareholders as pension funds - essentially the general public - became the owners of enterprises– a phenomenon foreseen first by Drucker (1949) (Davis, Lukomnik, Pitt-Watson, 2006)

This chapter focuses upon the implications of the emergence and unprecedented growth of the shadow banking system upon leveraged buyout (LBO) PE deals and the impact of these deals on the economy. We focus on the LBO sector as it is an area of considerable concern to policy makers because of the importance of the market for corporate control to governance of public firms in the market based economies of the Anglo-American world. For the more bank-based economies of Europe(Demirguc-Kunt and Levine, 1999; Beck and Levine 2002), the growing power of financial markets posed new problems. Since Adam Smith recognized the problem that arose from separating management and ownership, agency theorists have considered different ways to align the interests of owners and managers. In the modern era Berle and Means (1932) again brought attention to the long held concerns about the abilities of agents to act in the best interests of their principals. Jensen (1989) in a seminal article even argued for the "eclipse of the public corporation" in the previous era of LBOs.It is now held that PE promotes better management through better governance. Beroutsos, Freeman and Beroutsos (2007) study found that top PE firms were more committed to actively asserting the rights of ownership over management and aligning management interests via high and appropriately structured forms of compensation. A major studyfor the World Economic Forum co-edited by Anuradha Gurung, of WEF and Josh Lernerof the Harvard Business School of 21,397 private equity transactions between 1970 and 2007 came to the same conclusion.

Elsewhere we have argued that there was a general failure of governance - opaque instruments combined with lack of centralized information made it impossible for the full credit exposure of many issues and deals to be properly assessed. (Weitzner and Darroch, 2009) Smooth functioning markets depend upon information and when information is lacking or is deliberately made asymmetrical, market governance cannot function properly. Did the recent credit bubble show the "eclipse" of the highly leveraged PE portfolio company? We will argue that we need to take a finer grained approach to PEand will focus upon firms taken private with the intention of returning them to public markets via an initial public offering (IPO). In studying these firms, we need to consider both how PE firms create value and claim value. In order to do that, we first need to define what PE is and how large the LBO segment is. Then we will consider the methods by which PE firms create value and then claim value. Next we consider how changes in the global financial system may have changed both how PE firms could create and claim value before proceeding to consider some particularly salient examples. We will conclude with considerations some remaining open questions and a discussion of whether voluntary codes will be sufficient to deal with the problems identified.

2. WHAT IS PE AND HOW CAN IT CREATE VALUE?

This section explores the ways in which PE can create value both for the general economy and investors, but first we need to define what we mean by PE. Campbell and Campbell (2008) define PE in the following way:

> "Private equity is an organization type has its roots in venture capital. The most common form is now the leveraged buyout (LBO) and this is the type of investment under challenge. The private equity vehicle for leveraged buyouts is comprised of General Partners (GPs) who manage an investment fund, and Limited Partners (LPs) who provide the money for the fund
>
> The GPs use the money in the fund, together with loans from banks (the leverage), to buy companies. A typical fund is "closed-end" with a life of around ten years, extendable to 14 years. At the end of the period the fund is wound up and the LPs receive their share of the proceeds.
>
> A typical deal will be financed by 60-80% of loans from banks and 20-40% of equity from the fund. The GPs are looking for companies whose performance can be transformed. This can be achieved by increasing cash flows through better management of the business or by selling of underused assets (such as property or non-core businesses) and hence reducing debt".

Some have presented PE as a new source of good because PE firms provide stable capital and are consequently are able to take a long term view unaffected by the short-termism promoted by the quarterly reports demanded by equity markets. In addition, PE creates the possibility for industrial restructuring and rationalization in many industries and enhanced competitiveness by bringing value adding skills and and/or replacing bad management (Thornton, 2007; WEF 2008). This view of PE stresses that the firms most likely to be taken private are the ones that offer the greatest opportunity for value creation due to mismanagement. A recent research report by Partners Group (2009) sampled a 100 PE deals made between January 2005 and June 2009 to discover what was the typical (median) business case for deals in the buyout sector. Table 1 presents their finding for what is labeled "old world" deals or those taking place between 2005 and 2008.

The results suggest that the firms taken private may have been starved for investment since most of the value creation comes from revenue growth and operational improvements. Both of these depend not only upon knowledgeable management but ready access to needed cash. Interestingly despite these improvements the contraction of the multiple of Earnings Before Interest Tax and Depreciation (EBITDA) suggest that markets will actually use lower evaluation metrics for the firm than the PE firm used in making the acquisition suggesting a hot market for deals. This could also be taken as supporting the assertions that public markets are too short sighted to appreciate and consequently invest in long term value creation or that the deal market was overheated leading to higher multiples at time of acquisition.

We also need to appreciate the role of leverage- the key term in Leveraged Buy Outs - in magnifying returns and losses. The PE portfolio firm is much more highly leveraged than a typical SandP firm and recently higher than the median deal presented by Partners Group as Table 2 shows.Farrell, Lund, Gerlemann, and Seeburger (2007) also noted the increasing use of leverage and covenant light loans after 2005. By covenant light loans, we mean loans that lack the usual positive and negative covenants restricting management's actions. Issuance of covenant light loans went to S48 billion in the first quarter of 2007, twice the amount issued in 2006.

Table 1. Value Creation in "Old WorldPE"

		Old World PE Deal 2005-2008		
		Planned Equity Value Creation	% of Value Creation	Results of Value Creation
		Multiple Expansion/Contraction	(10)	
		Revenue Growth	64	
		Operational Improvements	32	
		Deleveraging	14	
Equity Cost	40%			2.7 X Cost 22% IRR
Debt	60%			
Typical Deal Size	S2Bn			
Assumed Increase in Enterprise Value	57%			

Source: Partners Group 2009.

Table 2. Leverage of LBOs vs SandP Average[1]

	SandP 500		LBOs	
	Debt	Equity	Debt	Equity
1990	35	65	79	21
1991	31	69	79	21
1992	30	70	78	22
1993	29	71	75	25
1994	28	72	74	26
1995	24	76	77	23
1996	21	79	70	30
1997	19	81	68	32
1998	16	84	64	36
1999	15	85	62	38
2000	18	82	59	41
2001	22	78	60	40
2002	26	74	60	40
2003	22	78	65	35
2004	21	79	67	33
2005	21	79	66	34
AVG	23.6	76.4	68.9	31.1
AVG 2000 - 2005	21.7	78.3	62.8	37.2

Source:Farrell, Lund, Gerlemann, and Seeburger, October 2007: Exhibit 5.5

---

[1] At times due to rounding to the nearest.2 digit number, the percentages do not add up to 100%.

Private Equity and the Current Financial Crisis: Risk and Opportunism 189

As can be seen there are cycles in credit markets and while leverage was high in the early part of the 21st century it was not as high as it had been seen in the first LBO boom of the 1990s.Nonetheless, the levels of debt are dramatically higher than for the average SandP company. The level of debt is not determined by a banker, but rather what level the capital markets will allow. It further needs to be recognized that the high levels of debt can be seen as essential for improved performance and governance by instituting specific contractual relations in place of the rather loose relationship of promised equity returns.In essence high levels of debt promoted better governance by limiting the free cash flows available to managerial discretion. (Jensen, 1989; Jensen, 2007). With high levels of debt came both the positive and negative covenants to control further managerial discretion on the use of funds. Debt investors should be cautious and active in asserting their contractual rights since their downside risk is not offset by participation in the upside of the equity holders. The above portrays a structural shift in governance mechanisms from equity markets to debt holders at a time when governance was lax in the credit markets.

However, PE firms have also been charged with being quick buck artists stripping assets and making healthy companies fragile as employment and future investments are reduced. The issue of PE was sufficiently controversial, particlarly in Europe, to lead to the WEF study mentioned earlier. In general, the report led to favourable, although possibly misleading, press reports on PE concerning employment and the financial health of PE companies (Hall, 2008).Hall (2008) prepared Table 3 on the size and geographic scope of LBOs from data in WEF 2008.

Table 3. WEF Demography of LBOs: LBOs by Type and Region

Type	2001-2007		Region	1970-2000	**2001-2007**
	% of deals by value			% of deals by value	% of deals by value
Public-to-private	28.9		USA	64.5	42.8
Divisional buyout	31.6		Canada	1.5	2.4
Private-to-private	14.7			0	0
Financial vendor	23.5		UK	15.0	15.5
Distressed/bankrupt firms	1.4		Scandinavia	2.3	4.5
			Eastern Europe	0.2	1.0
			Rest of Europe	13.2	26.1
			Africa and middle east	0.3	1.3
			Asia	1.8	4.0
			Australia	0.3	1.3
			Latin America	0.9	1.2
Total value of deals	$2,679billion			$1,242 billion	$2,679billion

Source: Hall (2008) using WEF 2008 Demography study Table 2a and 2b.

Some observations are in order.First, the value of deals done between 2000 and 2007 was more than double the deals done between 1970 and 2000 showing significant growth of the market. As Jensen (2009) asked is this another example of the "success breeds failure phenomenon?" Second, the market based financial systems of the USA, Canada and the UK dominate the world of LBOs with slightly over 80% of the LBO deals. While companies selling off a division is the largest segment of deals, 28.9% of the deals done between 2001 and 2007 saw firms disappearing from public markets. Interestingly from 2002 to 2006, the global number of firms being taken private exceeded the global number of IPOs. (Farrell, Lund, Gerlemann, and Seeburger, 2007) If we consider that divisional buyouts also materially alter the character of a publicly traded firm, then over 60% of LBOs had significance for publicly traded firms. It is also interesting that the LBO seems to have spread out from the US and grew in all other regions. Once a new business model was developed and refined in possibly the world's most significant capital markets it disseminated and grew in other markets.Table 4 below focuses upon the period 2003 to 2008 which is of greatest concern to us.

Table 4. LBO Assets Under Management By Region 2003-2008

		2003	2004	2005	2006	2007	2008
North America	LBO $ Bil	255	243	269	398	553	750
	Growth in %		-5	11	48	39	36
	As % of LBOs	64	61	56	59	61	60
			-5	-7	4	4	-2
Europe	LBO $ Bil	134	143	183	241	293	399
	Growth in %		7	28	32	22	36
	As % of LBOs	34	36	38	35	32	32
Asia	LBO $ Bil	2	7	11	11	13	27
	Growth in %		250	57	0	18	108
	LBO as a %	1	2	2	2	1	2
Rest of the World	LBO $ Bil	4	2	4	8	15	30
	Growth in %		-50	100	100	88	100
	As % of LBOs	1	0	1	1	2	2
Total LBO $ Bil			399	401	478	679	906	1,249

Source: Roxburgh et al., 2009 Table 4.1.

While the PE world studied by the WEF may have a broader geographic focus this has little to do with the matter under study here. In fact, it is quite likely that in other parts of the world where institutions play the dominant role in the pooling of capital that PE would be a welcome addition to the stock of capital and provide needed funds to cash starved firms. In addition where market governance is weak, PE will definitely improve governance. Further, just as we saw a tremendous growth in the 2001 to 2007 period, the aggregation did not call attention to the significance of the tremendous growth taking place in 2005 and showing itself in 2006. Despite the tremendous growth in the earlier part of the 21st century the LBO boom was gaining further momentum – growing virtually in sync with the growth of structured credit and the shadow banking system which took a step change at the end of 2004 and (Tett and Davies, 2007;Tett 2009; Shivdasani and Wang, 2009)

Jensen (2007) raised the key governance question in going private: Why don't publicly traded firms use the tools that PE uses that are available to them? The centrality of the question is demonstrated by data showing that Management Buy Outs (MBOs) in which the existing management stays in place outperforms Management Buy Ins (MBIs) where new management is put in place. This suggests that existing management in underperforming companies have the skill set to perform at a higher level. Consequently either motivation or some other resources are missing. The following table summarizes employment results from Amess and Wright (2007).

Table 5. Differences Among Companies in Employment Performance

	Average Annual Change In Employment %	**Average Annual Change in Wages %**
Non-buyout companies	0.26	0.93
MBOs	0.77	0.62
MBIs	-0.55	-0.04

Source: Ammess and Wright, 2007.

We should interpret this table with some caution, agreeing with Wright, Bacon and Amess (2007) that PE is a heterogeneous phenomenon so that it is important not to compare apples and oranges. That having been said, it is interesting that the MBOs' average annual change in employment which one would suspect is highly correlated with growth outpaces both non-buyout companies and MBIs. This certainly raises doubts about the ability of PE firms to improve management per se since it is clear that performance is significantly greater when management is retained. Clearly PE firms reduce agency costs by better aligning the interests of owners and management as the mindset of management is changed, not management per se. A possible limitation to this could be that the MBI target firms were was in significantly worse condition than the MBOs. Yet, it is interesting that the existing managers in MBOs failed to convince their existing boards or equity holders to support their growth plans. Or did they not make sufficient efforts preferring to claim the rewards through an LBO? If this is the case, then what are the long term implications of replacing governance via equity markets with governance of institutions (PE firms) and debt markets given the goal of harvesting returns through an IPO?

3. HOW PE FIRMS CLAIM VALUE: NEW CAPITAL STRUCTURE AND EXITS

There can be little doubt that Private Equity (PE) has been an important financial player has provoked controversy between the European Union and Anglo-American world. (McCreevy, 2009; Rasmussen, 2009). The source of the dispute is over the difference between the value created by PE and the value claimed by PE firms.Campbell and Campbell (2008) list and offer market based economic arguments to refute the following charges against PE: Asset stripping: selling off assets to reduce debt and thereby damaging the companies future; Reducing employment; Paying too little tax; Undermining Pensions; and, Poor returns to investors. In addition, The International Organization of Securities Commissions (IOSCO, 2008) also produced a report concerning issues raised by PE. While the report raised a number of issues which are of relevance to us: the effects of increasing leverage – in particular where public firms taken private retain publicly listed securities; conflicts of interest – particularly in the case of MBOs; and concentrations of risk. We will not be able to examine all of these charges above but do intend to analyze topics related to the level of value that PE firms can claim with specific reference to late cycle deals:

1. Increased Leverage;
2. Harvests (Exits); and
3. Investor returns.

3.1. Increased Leverage

As Campbell and Campbell (2008) note PE typically employs high levels of debt in the capital structure of its acquisitions. As noted earlier, in the recent wave of PE, the capital structure of most firms taken private is much heavier on debt than their publicly traded counterparts and this has raised concerns about defaults (Gilligan and Wright, 2008).Therefore before studying exits to test for increased bankruptcy rates, it makes sense to consider the issue of leverage. Moreover high levels of debt are important to improved governance via the surveillance of debt holders (Jensen, 1989; Jensen, 2007). Yet, as the current crisis has made clear, capital is the ultimate defense in bad times. Clearly increased levels of debt with hard interest payments, and, restrictions on the scope of management actions will make the portfolio company more vulnerable to changes in interest rates and refinancing risks due to the dependence upon debt markets. Increased leverage then in important both to improved governance necessary to improve performance but it comes at the risk of making the portfolio company more vulnerable to changes in debt markets.

Table 6 Private Equity and Leverage

	$ Mil	$ Mil
Target Company Purchase Price	100	50
Equity from PE Fund	20	50
Debt	80	
Sale Price	140	100
Time of Sale from Purchase	2 Years	6 Years
PE Gain	40	50
Return	3X	2X
IRR	44%	10%

Source: Arnold 2008a.

In this context, it is important to recognize the importance of leverage for the profitability of PE deals. Arnold (2008a) presents two "typical" deals in Table 6 – one representative of the bull market of prior to 2007 and the extreme in the credit crunch model that followed.

In this presentation, two key factors drive the dramatic difference in the return structure of the PE deal:

4. Amount of leverage; and
5. Time to exit.

Since PE firms are driven to make money, we should anticipate them pushing leverage to the highest possible levels and recognize the temptation for early exit. Both of these factors depend upon the financial strategies of the firms and/or market governance.In the credit crunch model, the financing and exit options may be unduly limiting to PE firms, but in a bull market there is the opportunity for excess or opportunism as we shall see. We would further expect that more experienced firms with a more comprehensive knowledge of business cycles might restrain their opportunism recognizing the riskiness of being too equity light. New firms with only knowledge of the low interest covenant light era may not recognize the riskiness of possible deal structures. We should also note the different size of the deals. The stronger the bull market, the larger the firms that come into play. The reverse is also true, as Roxburgh et al. (2009) note two thirds of the decline in deals between 2007 and 2008 was in the so-called megadeals over $3 billion.

When one sees the very high levels of expected returns as portrayed above it is obvious as to why funds flow into these investment funds and investors are prepared to pay high fees to the managers of successful funds. However, at what point does the business change from doing appropriate deals to having funds to invest and chasing deals? One constant feature of financial crises is that as funds flow into the hot new areas returns go down and risks go up. And as new funds flow into an asset class returns typically go down as risk goes up. In the trade uninvested capital is known as "Dry Powder" and it is interesting to note the growth of "Dry Powder" during the bull market presented in Table 7.

Table 7. Buyout funds and "Dry Powder"

	2004	2005	2006	2007	2008
Dry Powder	170	209	331	439	535
Invested Capital	231	269	348	467	714
Total	401	478	679	906	1249
% of Dry Powder	42	44	49	48	43

Source: Roxburgh et al 2009: Exhibit 4.3.

As the table makes clear the bull market made it relatively easy to raise funds for existing and new PE funds just as the current climate makes it very difficult to raise new funds. (Roxburgh et al Exhibit 4.2) Pressures do high levels of uninvested funds create for managers serve to increase competition for deals among both old and new funds. Farrell, Lund, Gerlemann, and Seeburger (2007) suggest that there was evidence that PE firms broadened the range of companies and sectors in which they participated. The move may also reflect increased competition which was bidding up prices of targets not only other PE firms, but also from growing infrastructure funds. This in part helps to explain the growth in leverage in 2006 and 2007 noted above given the need to maintain high levels of returns.

Earlier we commented that PE was a heterogeneous phenomenon and recognized the opportunities for significant transfers of wealth and risk in deals. In that vein we need to consider the differing financial strategies of the PE firms as analyzed in Moody's 2008 Report. The research excluded deals which suffered a downgrade 18 to 24 months following the initial rating because the firm had issued a large dividend but this event was followed by an IPO where the proceeds were used to pay down debt leading to a ratings upgrade. Fifty-Eight companies were downgraded, roughly 3 times the number of firms that was upgraded. Dividends were a significant factor in many of the downgrades, although even more important was less than expected financial performance.Private Equity sponsors took dividends in over 45% of the deals rated prior to September 2006 and of these equity virtually disappeared in 30% of the deals. In 50 of the deals, dividends wiped out 80% or more of the cash equity used to finance the deal. The report further reveals striking differences among the firms in their financial strategies with Welsh Carson, Cerberus, Providence Equity Partners, Carlyle, Madison Dearborn and TH Lee being particularly aggressive in their dividend policy. Despite the increased leverage, Moody's does note that the deals had a default rate of only 1.1% compared to the 3.4 % for high yield debt during the same period.

To conclude this section it must be asked whether an excessive belief in markets and financial engineering led players, policy makers and regulators to ignore dangerous risk concentrations developing in the markets as the bull market conditions changed important conditions in PE deals. In this context, Europeans who often have a preference for institutions over markets may have been more prescient about the risks in some financial innovations.

3.2. Value Claiming From Old Investors and New

Given the above description of the role of debt, it is interesting to think about possibilities to lower the price of debt and lessen restrictive covenants. Ivashina and Kovener (2008) found the ability of private equity firms to leverage bank relationships to be a source of funding advantage. Ongoing relationships and the possibility of earning fees from the PE firms often led banks into terms that raised the higher equity returns. However, there is an even more attractive way to lower the price and restrictions on debt: take firms private who have outstanding bonds with no change of control covenants. Billett, Jiang, and Lie (2008) found that firms whose bonds lacked such clauses were twice as likely to be a target for an LBO. Interestingly this became a concern to practitioners near the height of the boom. (Barclay's 2006). In addition, bondholders suffered an immediate loss on average of approximately 6.76%. Baran and King (2008) found that investment grade bonds holders suffered significant losses especially when the target was larger. A possible explanation for this could be that the possibility of a buyout was inconceivable and this was exactly the case with Bell Canada Enterprises (BCE) as we shall see later.

When fees are excluded, PE firms outperform the SandP index by 3%, however since their fees are typically 6% this means that they underperform the index. (Phalippou and Gottschalg, 2009; Phalippou, 2009). The paradox of investors flocking to an underperforming asset class is an interesting phenomenon for those believing that investors are rational. Farrell, Lund, Gerlemann, and Seeburger (2007) found that on a 10 year time horizon PE slightly underperformed US equities although the top quartile funds far outperformed equities. Since higher leverage generally raises risk, PE investors should expect returns higher than the market. A possible counter to this is the stability of returns available from top performing funds as the BCG by Meerkatt et al (2008) argues.In any event, it is unclear that PE creates value for investors.

Interestingly, if PE was to solve the agency problem, once PE firms become publicly traded, many of the traditional conflicts of interest that PE was supposed to resolve reemerge (Harris, 2010; Schwartz, 2009; FSA, 2006; IOSCO, 2008).One of the largest investors in PE, the California State Teachers' Retirement System (Calstrs) is critical of the move by PE firms to claim value by going public. As publicly traded firms the PE firms will face the same pressures to make short term decisions as the firms that they benefitted by taking private. (Guerrera, 2007). The world of PE raises many issues of conflicts of interest. Just as when risk is transferred it does not go away, neither do certain agency issues.

Table 8. PE Exits by Percentages

With Financial Sponsor	1970 to 1984	1985 to 1989	1990 to 1994	1995 to 1999	2000 to 2002	2003 to 2005	2006 to 2007	Average
Bankruptcy	7	6	5	8	6	3	3	6
IPO	28	25	23	11	9	11	1	14
Sold To Strategic Buyer	31	35	38	40	37	40	35	38
Sold to Financial Buyer	5	13	17	23	31	31	17	24
Sold to LBO Backed Firm	2	3	3	5	6	7	19	5
Sold to Management	1	1	1	2	2	1	1	1
Other/Unknown	26	18	12	11	10	7	24	11
Total Exits	100	100	100	100	100	100	100	100
No exit	3	5	9	27	43	74	98	54
Bankruptcy as a % of Known Exits	10	8	6	10	7	4	4	7

Source: WEF (2008)

3.3 Harvests and Exits

If leverage is essential to high returns so too are time and mode of exit. Table 8 presents exit data taken from considers only the deals done with a financial sponsor, not all deals and provides insight into this question. First, it is worth noting the level of bankruptcy is 6% and if post-2002 deals which may not have had time to enter financial distress are excluded the rate is 7%. This is twice the level of publicly traded US companies during the same period according to WEF (2008) and we expect when the clouds clear significantly higher rates for late cycle deals. Partners Group (2009) estimates returns for old world deals between negative 4 and 7% suggesting that many deals are in serious trouble even without higher cost refinancing– a topic we return to in Section 4.0.

We now turn to the mode of exit and note that the two dominant forms are selling to a strategic buyer or IPO. Analyzing exits or "harvests" raise fundamental questions concerning what the WEF or McKinsey data can tell us. The percentage of IPOs should not be seen as the desired or intended outcome but rather what IPO markets allow.From a governance perspective, there also seems something odd about returning firms to public market which had demonstrated their inability to promote good governance. While Jensen's (1989) claims concerning the eclipse make all the sense in the world from an agency point of view, the return of companies to market governance does not. As Jensen has noted, most of the techniques use by PE are available to publicly traded companies, but managers and boards do not make use of them. (Jensen, 2007) He then goes on to say that this failure to change the mindsets of managers and boards is evidence of the agency costs of publicly traded firms. If this is the case, then for PE firms to make lasting changes they must be able to have changed the mindsets of managers and boards when they re-take the firms public.

Cao and Lerner (2006) studied 525 Reversed Leveraged Buyouts (RLBOs) between 1981 and 2003 and found the following:

- In cross-sectional analyses, RLBOs appear to consistently outperform other IPOs and the market as a whole.
- In the calendar-time portfolio, the performance of RLBOs does not significantly differ from the market;
- The performance of RLBOs appears to have deteriorated in more recent years, and RLBOs that are more underpriced do more poorly.
- There is no evidence that more leveraged RLBOs or ones with more insider sales perform more poorly than their peers.

The metaphor would seem to be that these firms are taken from neglectful parents nurtured by good adoptive parents and reenter the world as productive citizens. However, there does seem to be a bit of a recidivist problem as the RLBOs seem to deteriorate over time – in essence return to their bad ways. It also seems that the amount of time that they spend with the foster parents matter since the study also found that quick flips – firms held under a year – underperformed. We would also remind the reader that the time period covered by Cao and Lerner (2006) is prior to the one of concern to us and prior to the full development of the shadow banking system. The earlier time period also precedes the rush into PE by a number of new and less experienced players who may have been under increased pressures to harvest early and or lacked the skills to change the mindsets of the acquired company. Once again looking at the average case may be misleading. The importance of holding period is made manifest and can be seen in Table 9:

Table 9 Holding Period for Exited Sponsored LBO Transactions

	Exited deals only					% of exited and non-exited deals		
	Mean	Median	N	Minimum	Maximum	% of	% of	% of
	(months)	(months)		(months)	(months)	Exits	Exits	Exits
						within	within	within
						12 months	24 months	60 months
1970-1984	87	63	114	4	323	1.7	14.2	46.7
1985-1989	80	72	453	2	246	2.1	11.8	40.1
1990-1994	60	51	830	3	204	4	14.2	53.3
1995-1999	54	50	2,550	1	145	3.2	12.9	40.9
2000-2002	43	43	1,367	1	89	2.7	9	40.4
2003-2005	25	24	998	1	54	2.9	12.8	
2006-2007	9	10	47	1	17	2.1		

Source: WEF 2008 Table 5.

In order to assess properly the time horizon of PE firms we would need to study the investment time horizon on individual deals and then see how close the harvest timing comes to that which Partners Group suggest is 5 years for the median deal. To simply consider averages means that failed investments that cannot be harvested will overstate the degree to which PE represents patient capital. While one needs to read the table with caution, it is interesting that the trend in the mean is constantly towards a shorter holding period. While not as strong, in general this can be said for the median too. Given the then bull market conditions for IPOs we should not be surprised at the harvesting activities of PE firms.

A report by Moody's Global Corporate Finance Group, "Private Equity: Tracking the Largest Sponsors" issued in January of 2008 is an intriguing analysis of the different financial strategies of PE firms and the implications for ratings. The study analyzed 220 transactions from 2002 to the end of the third quarter of 2007 that had been rated by Moody's. The methodology excluded deals that had not had sufficient time to establish a track record before the 2007 credit crisis. Their research found that "roughly 20% of the deals resulted in initial public offerings or were flipped (that is, sold to another private-equity firm or a strategic buyer) within the first three years of the initial rating." This offers some support for the critics of PE who argue that the prime motive in taking companies private is not to improve their long-term performance but to quickly claim short-term value for a few financed by the credit of many. It also suggests that he era may have differed materially from the one studied by Cao and Lerner (2006). The Private Equity Council, a lobby group for the industry, reports research that supports that quick flips at 16% are the exception, not the rule. (Gottschalg, 2007). Earlier the Council had reported findings from WEF (2008) that "quick flips represented less than 12% of all transactions. We do not dispute these studies, but rather suggest that the boom times following these studies promoted or allowed different behaviour as Moody's research suggests. We would ask policy makers to decideswhat is the right percentage of quick flips as recent times have shown dangers from the extremes of conduct, not the average.

3.4. Some Examples of Late Cycle Deals

The risk of opportunism given market conditions of high liquidity because previously unimagined deals become possible. Taking a firm private by itself cannot create more value. Rather, it allows value to be claimed by new owners. The act of taking a firm private should be seen as virtually an arbitrage opportunity – where a firm is bought in the equity markets and sold into the debt markets. The arbitrage aspect is important to recognize because it makes the transaction virtually risk-less for the arbitrageur. But risk cannot go away, it can only be transformed and the risk in these transactions is frequently on by the old debt holders as well as new ones.While these deals may be a long time in the making, the actual nature of the value claiming is relatively quick and the risk transfer is relatively robust. Classical theories have focused on the equity holders – those with the most at risk – as being in control of management decisions, but in the new world, in many ways the debt holders have taken on much of the risk and should be looked on to take on more control – especially if firms get into trouble. PE has played a valuable role in restructuring many industries, but its record in the US retailing industry is less than stellar as we can see from Table 10:

Table 10. The Sad Story of Retail and PE

Company	Buyers	Purchase Date	Bankruptcy Date
Linens Holding	Apollo Silver Point Capital Tri-Artisan Capital NRDC Equity	February 2006	May 2008
Mervyns	Cerberus Capital Sun Capital Lubert-Adler	August 2004	July 2008
Sharper Image	Sun Capital Windsong Brands	May 2007	February 2008
Goody's Family Clothing	Prentice Capital GMM Capital	October 2005	June 2008
Value City	Emerald Capital Crystal Capital	January 2008	October 2008
Home Interiors And Gifts	HM Capital	April 1999	April 2008

Source: *BusinessWeek*November 26 2008.

It is instructive to focus upon the Mervyn deal done by Cerberus, Sun Capital, and Lubert-Adler as reported by Emily Thornton (2008) to understand the risks created by asset stripping and taking cash out too early. According to Thornton:

"When those firms bought Mervyns from Target (TGT) for $1.2 billion in 2004, they promised to revive the limping West Coast retailer. Then they stripped it of real estate assets, nearly doubled its rent, and saddled it with $800 million in debt while sucking out more than $400 million in cash for themselves, according to the company. The moves left Mervyns so weak it couldn't survive".

The result of the restructuring and asset sale is "[i]ts 149 remaining stores are being liquidated. More than 18,000 people have been thrown out of work—without severance and, in many cases, weeks of vacation pay—amid the toughest job market in a generation." Naturally the deal made a profit for the PE firms (Lattman, 2008). While improved governance led to improved shareholder performance, it is clear that many stakeholders did not benefit. It is interesting that at least one study of the effectiveness of PE versus public boards found PE boards to be far more effective in driving financial performance, but far "less experienced and skilled in engaging with broader stakeholders" (Acharya, Kehoe, and Reyner, 2009). Just as we saw in the case of subprime mortgage securitization, if the originator does not have sufficient skin the game, there are potential problems. Perhaps the purchasers of debt should have been more aware of the potential risks and that is the question that policy makers need to address in establishing the free market caveat emptor approach with regulatory intervention.

There are several reasons for focusing upon the BCE deal not the least of which BCE is typical of other Private Equity (PE) deals involving national telecom companies that have had performance issues following deregulation. BCE is the largest telecommunications in Canada and operates under the Bell name. Following deregulation, BCE has come under attack for its level of performance. It also has certain classic features of the type of PE deals that should concern both policy makers and business ethicists. It is worth noting that BCE was the classic widows and orphans investment vehicle in Canada. The deal is also noteworthy because of the size of the deal. The $ (US) 51.8 billion deal was one of the largest and last of the major private equity deals of the boom. According to Michael Sabia, CEO of BCE, he had approached Goldman Sachs a few years earlier about going private, but was told that the money was not there. (McLean 2007) This confirms our point that there are risks when market conditions can significantly alter who is in play.

Below is a brief chronology of the relevant facts taken from the decision by the Quebec Supreme Court – the relevant sections are provided in Appendix 1.

1. the Board accepted that its primary obligation was to maximize shareholder value;
2. BCE was widely held;
3. "Over the years, Bell Canada made representations to the investment community regarding the importance it attached to maintaining investment grade ratings and protecting the credit quality of the company" (p.6)
4. shareholders benefitted by about 14% while debenture holders suffered approximately a 18% loss;
5. BCE and its US advisor, Goldman Sachs, depended upon a US court ruling in Revlonto support its position on shareholder maximization;

6. The court held that "The Canadian legal landscape with respect to stakeholders is unique. Creditors are only one set of stakeholders, but their interests are protected in a number of ways" (emphasis in original, p.24);

7. In Canada, the directors of a corporation have a more extensive duty. This more extensive duty embodied in the statutory duty of care encompasses, depending on the circumstances of the case, giving consideration to the interests of all stakeholders, which, in this case includes the debentureholders. They must have regard, inter alia, to the reasonable expectations of the debentureholders, and those may be more extensive than merely respecting their contractual legal rights.

8. The Court

- ALLOWS the appeal, with costs to the appellants;
- SETS ASIDE the judgment of the Superior Court dated March 7, 2008;
- DISMISSES the Motion for Final Order;
- RETURNS the file to the Superior Court for the determination of the costs in the Superior Court, in accordance with the agreement of the parties. (p.40)

We accept that certain aspects of the case are peculiarly Canadian, but that is the point, different societies have different goals or standards and the financial system evolves in this institutional context. In this context, it is important to note that the Court emphasizes that Canada is different in terms of the duties of directors and that the debenture holders are explicitly discussed both specifically but also under the general category of "stakeholders." We would further emphasize the Court's presentation of the discussion by BCE's management of its intentions – specifically to uphold the investment grade rating of the debentures – in facilitating an interesting discussion concerning the differences between the law and ethics. The decision of the Quebec Court was overturned by the Supreme Court of Canada who found that the debenture holders had failed to establish their claims. If that were the end of the story, it would be illustrative of the effect of market conditions upon who is in play, but the story continues. The deal collapsed just before Christmas 2008 (Arnold, Sender, and Guerrera, 2008) when accountants at KPMG decided that the deal would render BCE insolvent. Too much debt was being placed on the company. In this case bankers and bondholders breathed a sight of relief as the delays caused by the appeals probably saved their investments.

The BCE deal stands in stark contrast to what happened in Germany. In 2005 Blackstone, one of America's most renowned PE players became aware that the German government was interested in selling a significant stake in Deutsche Telekom and that many of Blackstone' rivals were interested. Wiesmann (2007a) provides a fascinating account of how Merkel came to see that PE could play a positive role in restructuring the German economy. During the previous election, a Social Democrat politician had labeled hedge funds as "locusts" ravaging the German industrial landscape. If PE was to play a role it would have to be because of the "long term perspective" that Merkel saw in PE.

While both Merkel and Stephen Schwartzman, CEO, of Blackstone saw the need to reform Deutsche Telekom, at issue was how large a stake Blackstone would be allowed to take and how would the culture of American PE work in the more consensus driven German governance structure where workers are represented on the supervisory board. Fundamental to Berlin's position was the need to maintain control over Deutsche Telekom – it decided to hold 25 % of the company plus one share. Thus it was able to exert control over important decisions – especially concerning labour. Eventually Blackstone took a 4.5% stake with the tacit agreement that the government would quietly support that reforms needed to unlock the true value of the asset. While the stake was lower than normal, and probably even lower than desired, it did come with a seat on the board and allowed Blackstone to move far more quickly than its rivals. As is often the case with rushed deals, problems ensued. When financial results were poorer than expected, Blackstone began to push for senior management changes. Despite the ongoing conflicts between the interests of labour and the economic interests of shareholders, the deal has held together – albeit in a somewhat disappointing fashion for Blackstone.

There are some important lessons from the German case. First, the plan to reform the company is working, albeit more slowly than the normal PE deal and the partnership between Blackstone and Berlin appears to be working. Blackstone has had to learn the lessons of working in a different institutional framework – one which has at time rejected outright its plans for reform. The true success of the deal though is uncertain. German officials have announced that there will be no more selloffs to PE (Wiesmann 2007b) and one can only wonder if the returns are worth the headaches to Blackstone. The underlying question is to what degree can the traditional practices of PE be modified to work by providing growth capital in different institutional settings – including minority positions -and it is too early to answer that question. There is also the question of what does governance mean. Does it mean solely maximizing returns to shareholders or are there issues of corporate social responsibility. The work by Acharya, Kehoe and Reyner (2009) shows this to be an important question since their study comparing Private Equity Boards with public boards in the UK found that the expected performance results from the tightened focus on performance came at a cost of worse stakeholder management and lower effectiveness in audit, compliance and risk.

WHAT IS HAPPENING NOW AND WHAT WILL HAPPEN?

Weitzner and Darroch (2008) were among the early academics to warn of dangers in PE deals, especially those done late in the cycle. There is not doubt that many PE firms identified as more conservative by Moody's have created value and by creating a vibrant market for corporate control improve governance of all firms, as Jensen pointed out. There can also be little doubt that there were excesses and depending upon the length and depth of the economic problems and its effects upon refinancing, worse troubles may lie ahead not only for the PE firms but for the all of the other stakeholders including employees, suppliers, and even customers involved. Given our focus on late cycle deals, European events merit special consideration because leverage and firm weakening was still going on in Europe while it was diminishing the US. During 2008 and most of 2009 stories concerning failures of PE portfolio companies were pretty much a constant in the *Financial Times*.Articles reporting on research by Centre for Management Buy-Out Research (CMBOR) at Nottingham University were typical:

- The number of private equity-owned companies falling into receivership rose by almost half last year to 106, its highest level since the end of the last economic slowdown in 2003, according to research to be published on Wednesday.
- More than a quarter of the 400 companies disposed of by private equity last year went into bankruptcy, according to the annual survey of buy-out exits (Arnold, 2008b)
- Nearly three-quarters of all UK private equity exits ended in administration in the three months to June, underlining the scale of challenges facing the industry as the value of new buy-out deals shrank to a 14-year low. Out of 108 buy-out exits this year, nine were secondary buy-outs, 25 were trade sales and 74 ended in receivership. (Arnold, 2009b)

We should also return to the paradox of PE of investors flocking to an asset class with below average performance. Arnold (2009) report "European buy-out funds left bruised" is revealing and reinforces the point that firms that loaded up at the top of the cycle – late boom deals – are facing significant problems, although some firms did perform well. It is also unclear that the worst is behind us as $400 billion of debt needs to be repaid over the next five years with amounts peaking in 2013 and 2014 (Saigol and Arnold, 2009). As Arnold (2009) noted, the credit crunch will hit many PE firms very hard as they work to refinance. The true depths of the LBO problem cannot be assessed until we are past the peak years of refinancing in 2013 and 2014.

If that were not bad enough, there is also an issue of funds coming close to their sell-by date which means a significant percentage of the holdings will need to be sold. This should further depress returns in the years ahead. Lex provides the information on table 11 on the expiry PE funds..At the end of 2009, there are some clear signs of recovery in the PE world. Arnold (2009b) on recent PE activity and research report by the respected investors, Partners Group (2009), "The New Buyout" compares deals done between January 2005 and June 2009 with deals done since. While the typical deal dramatically fell in size from $2bn to $300 mn between 2005 and 2008, there has been a return of the large deal with TPG and Canada Pension Plan's 5.2 billion takeover of IMS Health, Ajax Partners acquisition of Marken a pharmaceutical logistic company for $1.6 bn and the announced acquisition of Springer Science by EQT for $2.3 bn.

Table 11. Sell-by Date: Remaining Time Horizon on Current Fund

Years Remaining	% of Total Funds
1 Year	18
2 Years	15
3 Years	22
4 Years	15
5 Years	8
6 or more years	22

Source: Lex: Financial Times October 26 2009.

But the general world of PE buyouts has changed. The pricing of deals has fallen to 6x EBITDA from 9x with leverage falling from 60% debt (6.0xEBITDA)t o 35% debt (2.3xEBITDA). Surprisingly the median of expected return has risen from 22% to 28% in the New World to compensate for the higher risk. The manner of achieving the return has changed too:

> "The largest portion of equity returns in the median Old-World private equity transaction was expected to be created through revenue growth, which was projected to account for 64% of equity value creation. Operational improvements and debt reduction were expected to drive 32% and 14% of value creation, respectively. Interestingly, the median Old-World private equity transaction was underwritten with the assumption that the company would ultimately be sold at a lower valuation multiple than the private equity manager paid at entry, leading to partial offset of the other value creation initiatives.
> The median New-world private equity transaction, on the other hand, assumes that operational improvements will be the largest driver of equity returns, delivering 42% of budgeted equity value creation. Revenue growth, debt reduction, and valuation multiple expansion are expected to drive 28%, 20% and 10% of value creation, respectively". (Partners Group 2009)

PE has successfully adjusted to the new conditions of financial markets. The question that policy makers must ask is twofold:

1. Can regulation improve the functioning of markets? And,
2. Is the damage caused by bubbles excessive?

One should not be too encouraged by Partners Group study of median deals because the extremes are still out there. Recently Moody's has again warned investors that there has been a return to the loosely structured covenants that was typical of pre-crisis bonds (Hughes, 2009). It seems that the chase for yield over-rides fears of risk.

5. CONCLUSION

There can be little doubt that PE can play a valuable role in enforcing market discipline and promoting better governance of many ventures through moving firms to the appropriate capital structure. There can also be no doubt that there were excesses, as there are during any time of too easy credit. Kindleberger (2005) reveals a depressingly similar pattern to most financial crises and further suggests either an inability to learn from history or that capital market players have a disturbingly short memory. Perhaps while the current pain is fresh in our mind and we are questioning the hyper-rational models of modern finance, it would be useful for finance professionals and policy makers to read the classic work on the mania of crowds by Charles MacKay first published in 1841 to develop an enhanced appreciation of the importance of human behavior for financial markets.

The differences between Anglo/American and European approaches is deep rooted and evidenced by their differing approaches to financial systems. While the Anglo/Americans put their faith in a market-based approach, Europeans have traditionally held to a more bank-based approach. It is clear in 2007 that both systems let us down. It is clear that the US was the epicenter of the current crisis but it does not necessarily follow that the market-based system is inferior to the bank-based system since the institutional governance provided by the bank-based approach failed as badly as that provided by market-based approaches. What the current crisis has made clear and is different from previous crisis is the role of derivatives, other financial engineering products, and the shadow banking system in creating an excessive expansion of credit. If we wish to avoid or limit such problems in the future, we would be well advised not to focus on particular institutions, e.g., PE, but to focus on the root of the problem, unconstrained growth of credit. While the opaque instruments of modern finance played an important role, focusing on the instruments per se is to miss the point as the work by MacKay and Kindleberger make clear. In the current crisis, opportunism flourished in the "shadows" and public policy must create lights to dispel the shadows. The task for public policy is to not let itself be unduly influenced by those promoting conditions in which opportunism can flourish, nor by those who wish to unduly restrain the forces of innovation in financial markets. While many self-serving statements about the role of free markets lack credibility, we should not forget that many of the financial innovations have also made home ownership easier, growing firms easier, and facilitated risk management.If we want the benefits of innovation, the challenge is to come to an understanding of how in the complex, interdependent financial world of the 21st Century we need improved market governance and institutional governance to limit the damage of inevitable financial crises. The growth of the investment books of banks makes it clear that without improved market governance that institutional governance will fail. Consequently, when players argue for shadows, policy makers must turn on the lights.

REFERENCES

Acharya Viral V. Conor Kehoe Michael Reyner (2009) "Private Equity vs. PLC Boards: A Comparison of Practices and Effectiveness - Summary of Research Findings" *Journal of Applied Corporate Finance* 21:1, 46-58

Amess K. and Wright M. (2007) "The Wage And Employment Effects Of Leveraged Buyouts In The UK," *International Journal of Economics and Business*, 14: 2 (July): 179–195

Arnold, Martin. (2008a) *"Failure rate rockets for buy-out companies,"* Financial Times, April 21.

Arnold, Martin (2008b) *"Buy-outs bypass bank debt in all-share deals,"* Financial Times, November 21.

Arnold, Martin (2009a) "European buy-out funds left bruised," Financial Times April 15.

Arnold, Martin 2009b. *"Buy-outs bitten hard by credit crunch,"* Financial Times, December 10.

Arnold, Martin, Henny Sender and Francesco Guerrera (2008) "Collapse of BCE plan fuels private equity concern," Financial Times December 11.

Baran, Lindsay and Tao-Hsien Dolly King (2008) "Bondholder Wealth Effects in Going Private Transactions." http://www.fma.org/Texas/Papers/Going_Private_Bonds_Jan08_Cover.pdf

Barclay's, (2006) "Special Focus: Poison Pills In The Corporate Bond Market," 22 Marchhttp://www.stockbrokers.barclays.co.uk/content/research/reports/specialreports/doc

uments/Special%20Focus%20-%20Poison%20pills%20in%20the%
20corporate%20bond% 20market~2006-03-22%2012_42.pdf

Beck, Thorsten and Ross Levine (2002) "Industry growth" *Journal of Financial Economics*, 64:2 (May): 147-180

Berle, Adolph and Means, Gardiner(1932) The Modern Corporation and Private Property. Transaction Publishers: New York.

Beroutsos, Andreas, Andrew Freeman, Conor F Kehoer (2007) "What Public Corporations Can Learn From Private Equity Firms," McKinsey on Finance 22(Winter): 1-6.

Billett, Matthew T., Zhan Jiang, and Erik Lie (2008) "The Role of Bondholder Wealth Expropriation in LBO Transactions" March. Available at SSRN: http://ssrn.com/abstract=1107448

Bullock, Nicole (2009) "Maturity cliff still an uphill climb," Financial Times August 18, p18.

Campbell, Duncan and Andrew Campbell, (2008) "The Economic Impact of Private Equity," The Ashridge Journal Spring, 1-5. http://www.ashridge.org.uk/Website/IC.nsf/wFARATT/The%20economic%20impact%20of%20private%20equity/$File/TheEconomicImpactOfPrivateEquity.pdf

Cao, Jerry and Josh Lerner (2006), "The Performance of Reverse Leveraged Buyouts" Swedish Institute for Financial Research Conference on The Economics of the Private Equity Market. Available at SSRN: http://ssrn.com/abstract=937801

Davis, Stephen, Jon Lukomnik, David Pitt-Watson (2006) The New Capitalists: How Citizen Investors are Reshaping the Corporate Agenda. Harvard University Press: Boston.

Demirguc-Kunt, Asli and Ross Levine (1999) "Bank-Based and Market-Based Financial Systems: A Cross Country Comparison," *World Bank Working Policy Research Paper* 2143.

Drucker, Peter (1942) The Future of Industrial Man. J. Day: New York.

Farrell, Diana, Susan Lund, Eva Gerlemann and Peter Seeburger (2007) The New Power Brokers: How Oil, Asia, Hedge Funds, and Private Equity Are Shaping Global Capital Markets. McKinsey Global Institute, October. http://www.mckinsey.com/mgi/publications/The_New_Power_Brokers/index.asp

Farrell, Diana, Susan Lund, Oskar Skau, Charles Atkins, Jan Philipp Mengeringhaus, and Moira S. Pierce (2008) Mapping Global Capital Markets: Fifth Annual Report. October.

Financial Services Authority (FSA) (UK) (2006) Private equity: a discussion of risk and regulatory Engagement. November.

Gilligan, John and Mike Wright (2008) Private Equity Demystified: An explanatory guide (http://www.nottingham.ac.uk/business/cmbor/privateequity.pdf)

Gerrera, Francesco (2007) "Flotations of buy-out groups under fire," Financial Times, July 17.

Gottschalg, Oliver (2007) "Private Equity and Leveraged Buy-outs Study," (IP/A/ECON/IC/2007-25)

Hall, David (2008) "Private equity and employment – the Davos/WEF/Harvard study," Public Services International Research Unit, February 1. http://www.psiru.org/reports/2008-02-PE-WEF.doc

Harris, Lee (2010) "A Critical Theory of Private Equity," Delaware Journal of Corporate Law 35:1 (forthcoming)

Hughes, Jennifer (2009) "Moody's warns on bond covenants," Financial Times, December 11.

IOSCO, Technical Committee Of The International Organization Of Securities Commissions (2008) Private Equity: Final Report. May.

Ivashina, Victoria and Anna Kovner (2008) "The Private Equity Advantage: Leveraged Buyout Firms and Relationship Banking," http://ssrn.com/abstract=1017857

Jensen, Michael C. (1989) "The Eclipse of the Public Corporation," Harvard Business Review, 67: 61-74.

Jensen, Michael C. (1986) "The Takeover Controversy: Analysis and Evidence," Midland Corporate Finance Journal, 4:2 http://papers.ssrn.com/sol3 /papers.cfm? abstract_id=173452

Jensen, Michael C. (2007) "The Economic Case for Private Equity (and Some Concerns)," -- pdf of Keynote Slides (November 27, Harvard NOM Working Paper No. 07-02; Swedish Institute for Financial Research Conference on The Economics of the Private Equity Market. Available at SSRN: http://ssrn.com/abstract=963530

Kindleberger, Charles P. (2005) Manias, Panics, and Crashes: A History of Financial Crises. 5th Edition. Wiley: New York.

Lattman, Peter (2008) "Mervyn's Deal Yielded Profit," Wall Street Journal. November 24, B2.

Lund, Susan and Charles Roxburgh (2009) "The new financial power brokers: Crisis update," McKinsey Global Institute. September.

MacKay, Charles (2008 (1841)) Extraordinary Popular Delusions and the Madness of Crowds. Wilder Editions: Radford VA.

Meerkatt Heino, John Rose, Michael Brigl, Heinrich von Liechtenstein, M Julia Prats, and Alejandro Herrera, 2008. "The advantage of persistence: How the best private-equity firms "beat the fade"", The Boston Consulting Group, February http://www.bcg.it /attachments/pdf/007_TheAdvantageOfPersistence.pdf

McLean, Catherine (2007) "He didn't want it to be easy," Report on Business, The Globe and Mail, July 4, B1

Moody's Investor Services, "Rating Private Equity Transactions, July 2007. http://www. collectif-lbo.org/international/Moodys_on_private_equity

Partners Group (2009) The New Buyout: How the financial crisis is changing private equity. Partners Group Research Flash November http://www.partnersgroup.com/docs/library/ 20091125_Direct_Research_Flash.pdf

Phalippou, Ludovic (2009) "Beware of Venturing into Private Equity," SSRN http://papers.ssrn.com/sol3/papers.cfm?abstract_id=999910

Phalippou, Ludovic and Oliver Gottschalg (2009). "The Performance of Private Equity Funds," The Review of Financial Studies 22:4 1747-1776.

Rasmussen, Poul Nyrup (2009) "Direct EU regulation for Private Equity and Hedge funds: The real economy comes first," Commission conference on private equity and hedge funds 26 February

Roxburgh, Charles, Susan Lund, Matt Lippert, Olivia White and Yue Zhao (2009) The New Power Brokers: The new power brokers: How oil, Asia, hedge funds, and private equity are faring in the financial crisis. McKinsey Global Institute July.

Schwartz, Jeff (2009) "Reconceptualizing Investment Management Regulation," George Mason Law Review, 16:3: 521-586.

Saigol, Lina and Martin Arnold (2009) "Private Equity groups in $400bn of debt," Financial Times August 2.

Shivdasani, Anil and Yihui Wang (2009) "Did Structured Credit Fuel the LBO Boom?" Atlanta Meetings Paper. Available at SSRN: http://ssrn.com/abstract=1285058

Sunshine, Mark (2009) "Commentary- How Did Economists Blow It (Part 3) The Assumed Markets Theory," Erisk, Wednesday, September 16. http://seekingalpha.com/article/161612-how-did-economists-blow-it-part-3-the-assumed-markets

Tett, Gillian (2009) Fool's Gold: How the Bold Dream of a Small Tribe at J.P. Morgan Was Corrupted by Wall Street Greed and Unleashed a Catastrophe. Free Press: New York.

Tett, Gillian and Paul J Davies (2007) "Out of the shadows: How banking's secret system broke down," Financial Times, December 17.

Thornton, Emily (2008) "How Private Equity Strangled Mervyns" BusinessWeek November 26.

Thornton, Phil (2007) Inside the Dark Box: Shedding Light on Private Equity. The Work Foundation.

Wiesmann, Gerritt. (2007a) "How Merkel and Blackstone changed German capitalism," Financial Times, July 2.

Wiesmann, Gerrit (2007b)"Germany to halt sell-offs to private equity," Financial Times July 3.

Weitzner, David and James Darroch (2008) "The Growth of Private Equity and the Institutional-effect of Greed, Academy of Management," Anaheim, California, Tuesday, August 12.

Weitzner, David and James Darroch (2009) "Why Moral Failures Precede Financial Crises," Critical Perspectives on International Business. 5:1/2

World Economic Forum, Globalization of Alternative Investments Working Papers Volume 1: The Global Economic Impact of Private Equity Report 2008. http://www.weforum.org/pdf/cgi/pe/Full_Report.pdf

In: After the Crisis: Rethinking Finance
Editor: Thomas Lagoarde-Segot

ISBN 978-1-61668-925-4
© 2010 Nova Science Publishers, Inc.

Chapter 11

SUB-PRIME CRISIS: MARKET FAILURES OR HUMAN FOLLIES?

Arvind K. Jain

ABSTRACT

The impact of the subprime crisis has been so far reaching that the crisis deserves to be dissected from all possible angles. This chapter examines some aspects of the behavior of various players including regulators, public officials, bankers and wealthy investors in order to understand how certain decision-making processes may have led to the crisis. Most observers agree that the trigger for the crisis had its origin in a combination of three occurrences – the issuing of subprime loans, the securitization of those loans, and an almost total neglect of any regulatory effort to take seriously the potential negative impact of those two developments.These three developments were occurring in a global macroeconomic context in which one group of countries was encouraging excessive domestic consumption and the other excessive domestic investment, each to stimulate their own economies. The macroeconomic policy makers ignored both the long term implications of such strategies as well as the potential consequences resulting from a significant global imbalance. The reigning philosophy during the epoch was that markets take care of such problems. One strand of discussion since the onslaught of the crisis has been that the market model has failed. There may be a grain of truth in that argument. Very little attempt has been made to examine whether the failure was on the part of those who found it easier to engage in hubris rather than make some difficult decisions. This chapter examines the information that was available before the crisis began and analyzes whether the explanation of the crisis lies more in human behavior than in fundamental flaws of the market system itself.

1. INTRODUCTION

If one were forced to identify a single culprit for the present economic and financial crisis, it would have to be the collective amnesia towards the faults of a market system. The assessment that "with all its faults the market system is the best human societies have been able to develop to satisfy our material needs" is taken to mean that nothing needs to be done to tackle the faults that do remain.[1] Hubris, or worse self-interest, allows us to pepper over any evidence that things are nowhere near as good as we pretend, or want, them to be. Best assume that everyone is being rational – it is an assumption that has served us well over the past decades as economics has pashed aside other guides to human behavior – anthropology, psychology, sociology and indeed – ethics.

The key assumption that supports the notion of superiority of a market system – actors behave rationally – does not obtain in the contemporary global economy – if it ever did. Ignorance, selfishness, laziness, manipulation and deceitfulness combine in various proportions to create situations which can cause havoc and, in retrospect, create "what were they thinking" moments. The rationality assumption faces challenges on yet another flank – our inability to learn from past mistakes. In this, our collective behavior does not even satisfy the requirements of the simplest form of market efficiency, which claims that past information has been fully taken into account in making current decisions.

The current economic crisis is a gold mine for the skeptics of the market system and scholars of behavioral economics. In this crisis, which clearly originated in the United States, private actors made untenable assumptions and allowed their greed to ignore reality. Policy makers and regulators allowed moral hazard situations to exist, failed to assess potential systemic consequences of private actions and completely ignored lessons of the past.[2] Regulators seemed oblivious to the decisions of private actors whose consequences were distributed asymmetrically such that these actors would gain in one state of nature and the public would lose in the other. Policy makers demonstrated perhaps the worst case of short-term thinking; what will happen tomorrow is someone else's concern. Regulators thought they were omnipotent – just as everyone was saying they were – there was not a crisis whose consequences they could not manage. The mentality that prevailed was "why bother trying to prevent disasters, they cannot happen under our watch and, should minor land-slides occur, the consequences can be cleaned very easily."

This chapter attempts to document the behaviors of private actors, policy makers and regulators that defy notions of rationality. The decisions they made were irrational, not because they turned out to be bad decisions *ex-post*, but because they were bad decisions when they were made. It is the responsibility of private actors to analyze available information before making decisions. It is the responsibility of policy makers to identify events and trends with uncertain outcomes and take corrective actions when there are chances of potentially severe costs to the system – costs that outweigh any potential benefits. It is the responsibility of the regulators to ensure that the private interests of those they do regulate do not trump public interest. What is sometimes privately rational, herding for example, may not be collectively rational. Regulators have been given the authority precisely to prevent such behavior from dominating market developments. This chapter suggests that these three groups of players failed in their responsibilities to act rationally.

There are two fundamental reasons why many of the decisions made preceding the financial crisis can be considered "bad." First, decisions were made without ascertaining that the underlying assumptions were justifiable. By their very nature, most investment decisions

---

[1] This criticism is shared by academics and practitioners. See Acemoglu (2009, pp. 4-5).

[2] Johnson (2009) goes one step further and draws the parallel between the elite in the industrialized countries and that in "banana republics" colluding with the oligarchs of the society to channel the wealth of the society in a particular direction during periods before and after financial crises.

are made without full knowledge about the future; assumptions must be made about the distribution of key variables. Rational behavior would require that the assumptions about the future conform to available information. Many of the assumptions made by financial institutions and investors, however, bore no relationship to reality. Second, policy makers and regulators must weigh the benefits and costs of their policies assigning reasonable probabilities to favorable and unfavorable outcomes. It is painfully obvious that many policies and regulatory decisions (including decisions not to take an action) were made while assigning negligibly small (subjective) probabilities to unfavorable events. This behavior exhibits characteristics of "disaster myopia." Assignment of unreasonably low probabilities to unfavorable outcomes also allowed policy makers and regulators to ignore situations of moral hazard that were being created in the financial markets.

Table 1 below summarizes some activities of financial institutions, investors, policy makers and regulators that appear not to have been based on rational analysis. The table identifies the key assumptions behind those activities. The rest of the chapter develops the context in which these decisions were made and illustrates the weaknesses behind the assumptions. The first section below summarizes the key details of the events that led to the current financial crisis. The subsequent sections discuss the decisions of three groups of players in order to demonstrate why it would be difficult to describe their decision making as rational. We separate the decisions of private participants which are banks, rating agencies and investors, from those of policy makers and regulators.

2. THE SUBPRIME CRISIS

By all accounts, the origin of the present financial crisis lies in the expansion of subprime mortgages in the United States. Although subprime mortgages (and their close cousin "alt-A" mortgages) offered to borrowers with impaired credit histories and with little or no equity are not a new phenomenon, their growth in the first decade of 2000s was truly extraordinary. The originations of subprime mortgages increased from about 1.1 million in 2003 to 1.9 million in 2005 and those of Alt-A mortgages from about 0.3 million to 1.1 million during the same period. The combined shares of these two groups of mortgages increased to 32 percent of all mortgages in 2005 compared to only 10 percent in 2003 (Mayer et al, 2009, p. 28).[3] In common parlance, these were known as NINJA (No INcome, Job or Assets) loans.

At the peak of the cycle in 2006, $600 billion worth of subprime mortgages were issued compared to $180 billion in 2001.[4] The subprime mortgages accounted for about 20 percent of all mortgages in 2006 compared to only about seven percent in 2001. Many of these mortgages were issued with a loan-to-value (LTV) ratio of 100 percent and others with limited documentation. In the years before subprime lending became the norm, banks and federally-sponsored institutions like FANNIE MAE and FREDDIE MAC did not finance mortgages if the LTV exceeded 80 percent. In 2006, 11 percent of all mortgages issued had

---

[3] See Mayer et al (2009) for many other details of such mortgages. These details, like fraudulent practices used to issue the mortgages, lack of documentation and use of these mortgages, highlight the risks associated with this segment of financial markets.
[4] The data in this paragraph are quoted in Sahlman (2009, p. 9).

LTV ratio of 100 percent and limited documentation. The ratio for such mortgages in 2001 was less than one percent.

Table 1. Key activities and assumptions

Activity/decision	Key assumption/basis for the decision
Banks offering mortgages	
Subprime loans	House prices will continue rising
CDO issuers	
Securitization of mortgages and sales in three tranches of increasing risks	Data are available to carry out statistical analysis that justifies separating the risks of three tranches Risk assessment without appropriate data; Lack of any data on past nation wide mortgage market downturns ruled out estimation of risks of various tranches of CDOs
Rating agencies	
Provided risk ratings for the three tranches	Are the data available? Conflict of interest: rating securities issued by their paymasters
Investors	
Purchases of CDOs based on mortgages	Purchases based on ratings given by rating agencies
Insurance companies	
Issued credit default swaps	Requires expertise on derivatives and data on default rates
Policy makers	
Treatment of global imbalances	What are the causes of such imbalances and what could be the consequences if they are allowed to continue?
FED and regulators of financial markets	
Permit subprime loans	Process is free of fraud on the part of the lenders

Activity/decision	Key assumption/basis for the decision
Estimation of systemic risks	Understanding of where the risks of a complex web of derivatives lie; Complexity of markets by itself does not add to the risks – risks become exaggerated.
Treatment of subprime loans	Accounting for herding; each subprime loan to NINJA borrower could make sense for the lending bank as long as the bank in not overextended; what will be the consequences for the system as a whole – where 20% of mortgages were subprime –if those 20% become delinquent – not an unreasonable scenario to contemplate
Creation of moral hazard situations	Incentives for financial institutions to take excessive risks do not threaten the financial system
Disaster myopia	Consequences of (manageable) collapses of asset bubbles are less harmful than the consequences of not allowing bubbles to form

While it might make sense for borrowers to take such loans, why would lenders knowingly lend to borrowers who were likely to default? There were two reasons. First, this market segment expanded during a period of rising real estate prices. During the peak of this lending boom, when the borrower was unable to meet his/her obligations and the lender had to repossess the property, the value of the property would have increased sufficiently to return the lender's funds, even after administrative expenses had been taken into account. Second, and equally importantly, these mortgages were increasingly being securitized. The lenders pooled mortgages into mortgage-backed securities, then sold them to investors looking for short-term investments that would earn them more than risk-free rates available in the financial markets at that time.[5] The monetary policy during this epoch had been guided by the philosophy of "growth at any cost" and the interest rates had been kept low since the crash of the IT-bubble in 2001. Low interest rates had created incentives for investors to purchase what would appear to be very low-risk investments if they offered slightly higher rates of returns.

The securitization process attracted a number of non-traditional lenders to the mortgage market.[6] Banks that had not been traditionally involved in the mortgage market earlier relied upon mortgage brokers who could bring such contracts to banks. Banks would temporarily invest their funds, securitize the mortgages into instruments known as collateralized debt obligations (CDO for short) and pass on the risks to investors. To further differentiate between investors, these instruments were usually separated into three tranches based on their

---

[5] In 2006, about 60 percent of all home mortgage issued were securitized. Mortgage-backed securities accounted for about 62 percent of all securitizations in that year; Gillian Tett and Aline Van Duyn, "Under restraint," Financial Times, July 7 2009.

[6] By 2005, non-banks had captured about 27 percent of the mortgage market, having increased their share from less than ten percent in 1980s.

risks. The prime tranche of these debt instruments was supposed to be practically risk-free. The process of securitization was aided by rating agencies who accepted the challenges associated with assessing the risks of mortgage markets and who provided ratings for various tranches of the mortgage-backed-securities. Insurance companies, not to be left behind in this rapidly growing market, helped the intermediation of funds further by offering insurance against defaults of the CDOs through instruments that came to be known as credit-default-swaps. Insurance companies, whose expertise included offering insurance against all kinds of calamities and misfortunes, saw a systemic failure of the mortgage market as just one of many disasters that would have a small probability of occurrence and whose financial consequences were measurable and manageable.

There was a curious absence of regulators and policy makers in this process. The rapid pace of financial innovation in the decades before the crisis had created an environment in which financial markets, financial intermediaries and investors were seen as informed and rational players who understood the risks of the activities they performed, and who were able to assess and price the risks of instruments with which they dealt. In this environment, there were no externalities and hence no need for regulators to limit activities of private entities. Deregulation of financial markets continued along the trend that had begun since the early 1990s. The wall that had separated commercial and investment banking since the 1930s met the same fate as the one in Berlin. Banks were allowed to set their own risk standards and measure risks of their derivatives activities as they themselves saw fit. Restrictions on trading activities were dismantled and any attempts to control the behavior of unscrupulous mortgage lenders were voted down in the US Congress. Those were glorious days for proponents of free markets.

Unfortunately the events took unpredicted turn sometimes in 2006. The number of borrowers who were delinquent in their mortgage payments had been creeping up ever so slightly till 2005. In 2006 and 2007, however, this rate began to show a strong upward trend as the upward trend in real estate prices softened and a downward momentum took hold. Exhibit 1 shows the relationship between the percent of delinquent amounts for mortgages and the year of issue.[7] About 17 percent of the mortgages issued in 2007 were delinquent 12 months after issue compared to about 2 percent of the mortgages issued in 2003. Banks that had issued the mortgage-backed securities but had yet to market those securities found that the investors had begun to withdrawn from the market. The secondary market for these securities, which was far from a liquid market to begin with, imploded.[8] By 2008, the banking sector's losses were being calculated in trillions of dollars. IMF estimated that the total losses amounted to about $4.1 trillion. Governments around the world had spent about $800 billion to rescue banks. AIG alone reported a loss of $99 billion in 2008 and its rescue had cost the US government about $182 billion. In addition, there were the costs of the fiscal stimuli that were needed to prevent a global depression.

---

[7] Data from IMF, Global Financial Stability Report, October 2008.

[8] For a description of this implosion, see Gillian Tett, "Big Freeze: How it Began," Financial Times, August 4 2008. The illiquidity of these markets was partly due to the absence of any designated market makers.

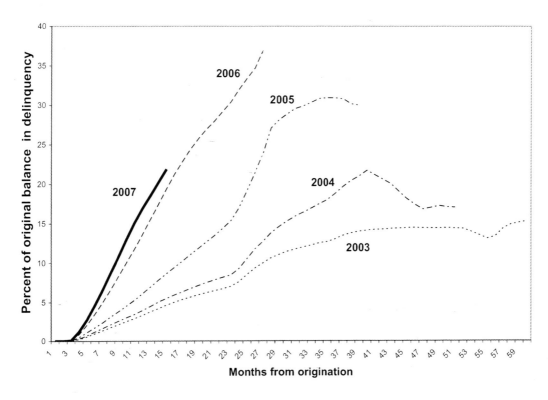

Figure 1. Delinquency Rate of Mortgages Issued from 2003 to 2007.

3. PRIVATE PLAYERS

There are two groups of private players whose behavior during the period preceding the present economic crisis could hardly be described as rational. These players include the mortgage lenders and the investors who bought the securitized mortgage obligations. A third group played an important role in the sequence of events that led to the crisis, but this group, the rating agencies, were merely doing what was good for themselves. It was really the responsibility of those who accepted the reports and the ratings of the rating agencies to ensure that the rating agencies were operating under correct incentives.

Rational behavior on the part of mortgage lenders and the investors who invested their funds in the non-prime (that is, subprime and Alt-A) mortgages would have been to assure themselves that the returns on these mortgages were justified given the risk of defaults. There were two key requirements to keep the risks of these mortgages manageable: (i) that housing prices had to keep rising, and (ii) defaults that would occur would arise from randomly distributed individual reasons not from system-wide shocks.

Given both the high loan-to-value ratios of these loans, and the fact that borrowers had very poor credit histories, it was obvious that defaulting on their mortgages would have very little adverse consequence for the borrowers. They would service the loans only as long they had some equity in the investment. Unlike prime mortgage borrowers, they had few, if any, other assets at stake in the process. Even a slight decline in real estate prices would result in the borrower being left with a negative equity, with little incentive to service the mortgage.

The default rates of these mortgages would remain low as long as the reason for non-payment resided in the borrower. However, were there to be systemic reasons affecting the ability of a large subset of borrowers to service their obligations, default rates could reach levels that would never justify the small margins that were being offered on the risky tranches of mortgage-backed securities. Lenders made a key assumption based on recent history. Since there had never been a systemic failure of the housing market since the great depression, they assumed that such a failure could not happen in the future. Hence their assumption of uncorrelated defaults appeared to be justified.

Investors who bought mortgage-backed securities relied heavily on ratings provided by agencies such as Moody's and Standard and Poor's. Banks were busy "slicing and dicing" debt obligations into different risk groups, and rating agencies were happy to rate various slices or tranches into prime and below-prime categories. The belief underlying this slicing strategy was that the data were available to separate mortgages into different categories of risks. The plain truth is that such data did not exist. Tett (2009, Chapter 4) describes how analysts in one bank refused commercial deals for which they could not estimate risks because of a lack of data on mortgage default rates. Other banks, however, proceeded with their analysis by assuming that the data from the period during which there had been no systemic failures or systemic mortgage defaults provided a good basis for estimating risks for the future. As with many previous crises, the assumption was made that small probability events just do not occur. In retrospect, the tails of probability distributions turned out to be much fatter than had been arbitrarily assumed.

Insurance companies carried over the assumption that the recent past is a good basis for predicting the future to credit-default swaps. Buyers of mortgage-backed securities who wished to eliminate perceived small risk purchased swaps that would compensate them in the unlikely event that their debtors would not fulfill their obligations. Estimations of the costs of such swaps required the same data that were required for the estimation of the risks of the various tranches of mortgage-backed securities. Insurance companies, like AIG, accepted the estimates of risks that the banks had prepared and, without much in-house expertise on derivatives, offered credit default swaps worth hundreds of billions of dollars.

The financial system was operating under the faulty impression that reallocation of risks from lenders to investors had somehow made the financial system safer. Investors believed that since mortgages had traditionally been a safe investment, they would remain so in the future regardless of the quality of the borrowers who were being allowed into the market. Even supposedly sophisticated investors, the hedge funds, were unable to escape this trap. In one of the most ironic turn of events in this saga, leading hedge fund managers failed to accept responsibility for the investments they had made – instead blaming the rating agencies for having misled the managers of the hedge funds![9]

---

[9] At a hearing of the US Congress in November 2008, Mr. Soros, one of the most prominent hedge fund managers, "pinned blame on the "financial system itself", while James Simons, president of Renaissance Technologies, criticised credit ratings agencies, which he said had facilitated the sale of "sows' ears ... as silk purses" through "fanciful" ratings of mortgage-backed securities." Stephanie Kirchgaessner and Henny Sender, "Hedge Fund Chiefs blame the System for the Financial Crisis," Financial Times, November 14, 2008.

4. POLICY MAKERS AND GLOBAL MACROECONOMIC IMBALANCES

For about a decade before the crisis, the global economy was marked by large and persistent imbalances in the financial and trade flows between countries. Some countries had persistent current account deficits, others persistent surpluses. These imbalances, however, did not fluctuate randomly between countries from year to year. Exhibit 2 shows that the pattern of imbalances was very stable. Only one change occurred in the list of the five largest deficit or surplus countries between 2003 and 2007 – Saudi Arabia replaced Switzerland in 2005 – and only minor changes in the rankings within the top five.

Readers who have not delved into external balances for a while need to be reminded of some very important equivalences between the external and the domestic sectors of an economy. A current account surplus implies that the country is absorbing (whether for consumption or for investments) less goods than it produces. It also implies that the country is saving more than it is investing within the economy. A deficit, of course, implies the opposite – that the country is saving less than it invests domestically. International exchange of goods and services becomes the mechanism through which countries bring their domestic output and demand as well as their savings and needs for investments in balance. A deficit in one country implies that the rest-of-the-world will have a surplus. The algebra of balance of payments, while being quite simple, saysnothingaboutthe causationbetweenthe variableswithinand between countries. Which country, for example, is responsible for current account imbalances between two countries – the deficit country or the surplus one? In a two-country world when one country has, say, an unsustainable deficit, the second would have, by definition, an unsustainable surplus. Since some policy measures must be taken to redress the situation, which country should take measures to reduce or eliminate the imbalances? Ideal policy measure should focus on the country that was causing the imbalance. In practice, however, it is often impossible to assign blame to one country as being the source of this type of a problem. Similarly it is often difficult to determine whether a country's current account deficit is being caused by excessive investments or by a shortage of savings.

Although both – a surplus or a deficit – may represent an unsustainable situation, a deficit presents an immediate problem for the country. While a surplus country can avoid facing the issue by accepting foreign currency reserves, a country planning to continue with deficits has to ensure that sufficient funds will be available to finance those deficits. As shown in Exhibit 3, the US economy had had a long period of large and increasing deficits in the years preceding the crisis. Were these large deficits sustainable and in the interest of the US economy or should the policy makers have taken steps to reduce them? These deficits implied that the US economy was absorbing more goods than it was producing. Whereas these deficits were being financed by most of the surplus countries increasing their dollar reserves at least since the bust of the IT bubble in 2001, questions had to be asked about the desirability of excessive consumption within the country represented by current account deficits, the long term possibilities of foreign countries continuing to increase their reserves, and the desirability of foreign countries holding large volume of US government debt obligations in their reserve accounts.

In the years preceding the financial crisis, policy makers in the United States took the convenient approach of accepting a "savings-glut hypothesis" proposed by Ben Bernanke in 2005 (Bernanke 2005).

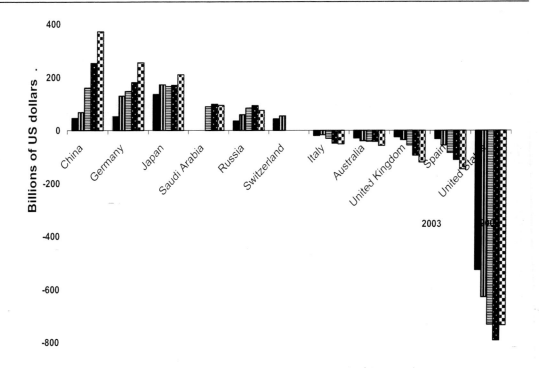

Figure 2. Five Largest Surplus and Deficit Countries, 2003-2007.

According to this hypothesis, the US economy was running current account deficits merely because a number of other countries had a "savings glut." Those countries were not able to absorb all their savings and the global economy would have been awash with excess savings if nothing had been done. The US economy, by running current account deficits, was thus absorbing the excess savings in the global economy. The causation in this analysis was from the surpluses to the deficits. Acceptance of the savings-glut hypothesis took the pressure off the US policy makers to do something about the deficits; in this version of events US policies were saving the world. The fact that most surplus countries were increasing their foreign currency reserves (mostly in US dollars) was proof positive that the surplus countries were satisfied with the then status quo.

This explanation made life easy for policy makers in the United States: "They have the surpluses. We, by accepting deficits and thus absorbing their savings, are doing the world a big favor." There was very little examination of the possibility that this was merely a convenient explanation that allowed the US to assume an attitude of benign neglect towards a key problem of the global economy and whether the long term consequences of this development would be desirable for the US economy. Policy makers failed to examine at least one alternate hypothesis that excessive domestic consumption – which in this case was happening simultaneously with reduced levels of domestic savings – was driving the inflow of global savings to the United States. If this alternate hypothesis were to be correct and the imbalances were driven by a lack of savings, then the correct policy measure would have been to take steps to restore levels of savings and curb consumption. Increased consumption was feeding back into the housing market that was leading to increased levels of domestic indebtedness simultaneously with a rise in the subprime mortgage lending and current account deficits. The US household debt as a ratio of disposable income grew as much between 2000 and 2007 as it had in the previous quarter century. The ratio of US households' debt to income ratio increased from 62 percent in 1975 to 101 percent in 2000 and to 138 in 2007.[10]

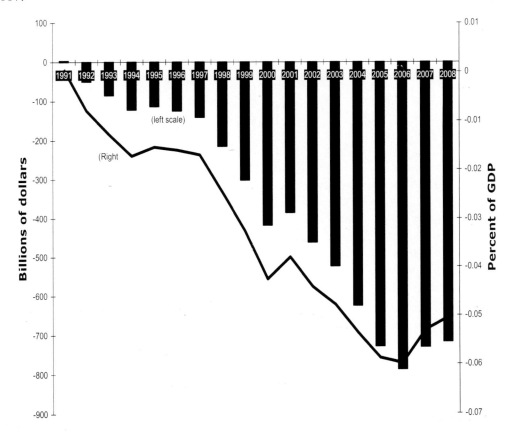

Figure 3. US Current Account Deficits, 1991-2008.

If the true reason for the US current account deficits were debt-financed consumption, then increasing levels of debt would have sooner or later become unsupportable. At some point, the debt levels would become so high that households would be unable to maintain their consumption levels, house prices would stop rising and a large number of subprime mortgages would no longer remain attractive for the borrowers. As mortgage holders default, the supply of houses would increase faster than the demand, further fueling the downward spiral of real estate prices. With subprime and Alt-A mortgages accounting for about one-third of all mortgages, lenders or investors holding subprime loans may find it difficult to remain solvent.

It was the responsibility of policy makers to examine competing hypotheses to "savings-glut hypothesis" and estimate the consequences, however small the probability, of the savings-glut hypothesis being wrong. Given the importance of the issue – which was the build up of both high consumer debt and current account deficits – it was incumbent upon policy

---

[10] Data from Exhibit 2 in Baily et al (2009).

makers to ensure that their assumptions were correct. It was not enough to merely present a plausible explanation that the equivalence between excess savings in the rest-of-the-world and the deficits in the US current account justified a policy of benign neglect.

The explanation provided by the savings glut hypothesis has been challenged on the grounds that most of the logical predictions of this hypothesis have not been borne out by the data. A global savings glut should raise global savings rate and increase investment rate in the global economy as well as in the savings-absorbing country which was the United States. Laibson and Mallerstrom (2010) fail to find support for these likely outcomes. Their analysis also fails to find the link between purported savings glut and the decline in the real interest rates in the global economy. They find that about half of the current account deficits in the United States are explained by housing price bubbles in the country rather than by excess savings in the rest of the world (p. 18).

The savings-glut hypothesis was nothing more than an algebraic convenience. It is indeed true that the surplus countries were saving more than they were investing. An algebraic equality, however, does not provide clues to the causality. Which was the driving force for the imbalanced: excess of savings or deficit of savings? Moreover, was the imbalance in savings caused by a change in the rates of savings or in the rates of investments? Even a cursory examination of the data reveals that one big change had been in the savings rates of countries like the United States.[11] The seeming lack of concern to deal with this issue was due to the same phenomenon that justified high levels of consumption and poor quality loans – that savings from disposal income were being replaced by rising asset prices and that households were not obliged to save their current income.[12]

5. REGULATORS

The purpose of regulation is, ostensibly, to protect public interest. Groups that can benefit from regulation (or its absence) will organize in an attempt to influence political decisions regarding the regulation of their industries (Stigler 1971). Since it is difficult for the public to understand and respond to every regulatory issue, it is the responsibility of regulators, as agents of the public, to take public interest into account when setting regulatory rules. Regulators must keep in mind that the public can influence the political process through other means and can reward or punish poor regulation.

In the years preceding the financial crisis, regulators became oblivious to their role as agents of the public and allowed their faith in the market system to override simple common sense. This faith in the market system had led regulators to assume that nothing needed to be done to ensure that the market system delivered on its promises. Market imperfections, especially power that incumbents have to distort the market process, were ignored. Externalities that arose from the profit motive were not neutralized. It was clear that there was a serious conflict of interest between those whom the regulators were supposed to represents

---

[11] US savings rate shows a secular decline from abut 10 percent of disposable income in 1980 to about 1 percent in 2007 (Baily et al 2009, Exhibit 5.)

[12] For a large number of households in the US, real estate is the larger part of their wealth; they view changes in real estate prices as permanent changes in their wealth; if the wealth was increasing, and would remain at high levels, there would be less need for saving the same proportions of current disposable income as in the past.

and those who were actually able to influence regulation. This conflict of interest does not appear to have entered into the calculations of the regulators.

Regulatory behavior during the years preceding the crisis provides no indication that regulators were aware of the externalities associated with subprime loans. While each loan itself may have been legal, with manageable risks, for a particular financial institution or investor, a large number of such loans created asymmetric bankruptcy risks for a lending institution. In theory, default risks of mortgages should be unsystematic, but positive bankruptcy costs create a dead weight loss for the system when an institution fails. While the financial system as a whole was lending almost one-third of its mortgages to non-prime borrowers, the possibility that a large percentage of these mortgages would default and create system-wide costs should have been assessed by the regulators and steps should have been taken to discourage such loans. There is no evidence that regulators attempted to educate investors or markets about the risks of purchasing mortgage-backed securities in the countries where subprime lending was booming, particularly in the United States and the United Kingdom.

Over the past few years, the financial services industry has found it desirable to influence the political process for reduced regulations as the financial markets have become more globalized, the pace of financial innovations has increased and advances in telecommunications technology have reduced banking and information costs. For approximately two decades prior to the financial crisis, there was a consistent dismantling of regulatory restrictions on the financial services industry within the United States. A partial list of this dismantling includes "the repeal of Depression-era regulations separating commercial and investment banking, ..., a congressional ban on the regulation of credit-default swaps, ..., an international agreement to allow banks to measure their own riskiness, and an intentional failure to update regulations so as to keep up with the tremendous pace of financial innovation."[13]

Although the reigning philosophy of the epoch – that markets take care of any problems that may arise and hence should be left free of government interference – justified the removal of regulatory restrictions, it did not hurt that the financial services industry became one of the biggest contributors to the legislators in the United States through their political action committees. Though not an irrefutable proof, improved performance of this industry during this period gives credence to the claims of the increased political power of this industry. Towards the end of this period, the average pay-per-worker in the financial services industry reached 181 percent of the pay-per-person in all domestic industries after having hovered around 100 to 110 percent before 1980. The profits of this industry reached an unprecedented 41 percent of all U.S. business profits before the financial crisis.[14]

In the years preceding the financial crisis, firms in the financial services industry had been very actively involved in lobbying legislators and policy makers to pass legislation that would allow these firms unrestricted freedom of action in the financial markets. In 2006, firms in the finance/insurance/real estate industry spent about a half-million dollars per firm, the highest average spending level of any economic sector that year, on lobbying activities – a trend that had been followed since at least 1999.[15] Within the mortgage market, these firms

---

[13] This is a partial list from Johnson (2009).

[14] See Johnson (2009) for long term trends in both these measures.

[15] Figure 1 in Igan et.al (2009) compares data for contributions by various sectors in 2006 and Figure 2 compares lobbying expenditures of this industry to the average expenditure of all industries since 1999.

managed to prevent the passing of legislation that would have protected consumers.[16] Lobbying firms, moreover, were able to focus their efforts on legislation that would direct benefits toward the lobbying firms. Research shows that "lenders that lobby more intensively (i) originate mortgages with higher loan-to-income ratios, (ii) securitize a faster growing proportion of loans originated, and (iii) have faster growing mortgage loan portfolios" (Igan et at, 2009, p. 5). These authors find that, consistent with principles of moral hazard, lobbying firms took more risk before the crisis and suffered higher losses during the crisis.

Regulators, as agents of the public, must be aware of, and counter, the influence of lobbying efforts by the financial services industry to introduce legislation that would serve the industry's interests at the cost of the public. The reality, unfortunately, does not provide evidence for such behavior. Regulators failed to account for the influence of those who were purchasing the ears of the policy makers – an activity that should be interpreted, per se, as contrary to the public interest. Policy makers must include interests of various groups when setting government policy. However the practice where policy makers ignore their roles as agents of the public and focus solelyon the interest of those who can organize and pay to be heard, leads to decisions that can have damaging consequences. In general, regulators must be aware that private agents influence policy makers mostly when the natural tendency of the policy makers would have been be make decisions that would favor public over private interests.

Regulators completely ignored the costs that financial crises inflict on the economic systems. Their most serious error seems to have occurred in the area of ignoring the lesson of the past. Many previous crises, for example the Latin American debt crisis, the savings and loan debacle, and the Long Term Capital Markets crisis, had created systemic risks out of poor decisions by individual institutions. In most of those crises, concerted efforts and influence of policy makers and regulators around the world were required in order to prevent serious damages to the international financial system. Finally, regulators seem to operate under a disaster myopic mind set – if a crisis has not happened in recent memory, it was unlikely to happen again.

Regulatory behavior in this area exhibits characteristics of disaster myopia. Disaster myopia refers to the tendency to assign lower subjective probabilities to an event than its objective probability as the event fades from our memory (Guttentag and Herring, 1984). Since system wide mortgage failures had not occurred since the great depression, a negligibly smallprobability was assigned to the chances of a large number of mortgages defaulting. There were two problems with this approach. First, even small probability events have a tendency to happen, and moreover they sometimes happen with very serious consequences. Second, the system had no experience, in the entire economic history, with such proportions of mortgages being of such a low quality. There was no history to draw upon.

---

[16] The following quote from Igan et al (2009, p.1) illustrates this quite well:
"On December 31, 2007, Wall Street Journal reported that Ameriquest Mortgage and Countrywide Financial, two of the largest mortgage lenders in the nation, spent respectively $20.5 million and $8.7 million in political donations, campaign contributions and lobbying activities from 2002 through 2006. The sought outcome, according to the article, was the defeat of the anti-predatory lending legislation. In other words, timely regulatory response that could have mitigated reckless lending practices and the consequent rise of delinquencies and foreclosures was shut down by some mortgage lenders."In 2009, Ameriquest agreed to pay $295 million to settle lass action suits arising from its involvement in unlawful mortgage-lending practices.

6. CONCLUSION

Behavioral economists have identified many individual or institutional characteristics and biases that defy the assumption of rationality. The present financial and economic crisis provides ample evidence for the absence of rationality at many levels of decision making – private and public, individual and institutional. Hubris, herding and over-confidence abounded. At the highest level of policy making, there is evidence of institutions suffering from disaster myopia and a gross inability to learn from the past.

The greed of bankers and their unethical behavior alone do not explain this crisis. Sahlman (2009) has pointed out that "even greedy executives would not have wanted to see their companies disappear or their net worths vaporize." As Acemoglu (2009, p. 5) aptly points out, "... greed is neither good nor bad in the abstract...But when unchecked by the appropriate institutions and regulations, it will degenerate into rent-seeking, corruption and crime."

Policy makers and regulators can be accused of hubris. To do nothing seemed the more politically expedient move than "taking the punchbowl away just as the party gets going." There was also the attitude that "it is better to clean up the consequences of a bubble busting than to prevent it from forming in the first place." There is widespread recognition that regulatory authorities failed in their assigned tasks. Three large countries at the center of this crisis - the United States, the United Kingdom and the European Union – have all proposed quite dramatic changes in the way financial markets should be regulated. While much of the discussion focuses on the issue of moral hazard and the resulting "too big to fail" mentality[17], steps are being proposed to ensure that consumer protection is strengthened, at least in the United States.[18]

The crisis was not just a string of unexpected bad events. Financial institutions and investors had placed themselves in positions where their ability to manage adverse shocks was seriously impaired. Regulators of financial institutions had created situations of moral hazard, effectively allowing a mentality of "too big to fail" to dominate the decisions of financial institutions. These regulators became oblivious to the lessons of previous crises in which they had seen that financial derivatives create a tangled web of obligations in which it becomes very difficult to separate exposures; as such the poor decision-making of individual institutions becomes exaggerated at the level of the financial system.

The failure of individuals is not a failure necessarily of the market system. Rather it is failure of those who manage economies to recognize that a market system needs regulations. In the absence of full information, a good guide for an individual decision maker may be to herd behind others; such a behavior, however, is not rational for the system as a whole. Regulators may create good conditions for economic growth in the short run by reassuring financial institutions that the government will stand behind them. Such assurances, however, create moral hazard situations that do not help financial markets in the long run.

---

[17] See the opinion of one influential ex-central banker in Gerald Corrigan, "The FED's role in Financial Regulation," Financial Times, December 10, 2009.

[18] A summary of proposed regulatory changes can be seen at http://www.ft.com/cms/s/0/313aeca4-7864-11de-bb06-00144feabdc0.html.

REFERENCES

Acemoglu, Daron, 2009, "The Crisis of 2008: Structural Lessons for and from Economics, Working paper, Boston: Massachusetts Institute of Technology.

Baily, Martin N., Susan Lund, and Charles Atkins, 2009, Will US Consumer Debt Reduction Cripple the Economy? McKinsey Global Institute.

Bernanke, Ben S., 2005, "The Global Saving Glut and the U.S. Current Account Deficit," speechgiven on March 10, at the Sandridge Lecture, Virginia: Virginia Association of Economists, Richmond.

Igan, Deniz, Prachi Mishra, Thierry Tressel, 2009, "A Fistful of Dollars: Lobbying and the Financial Crisis," Working paper, WP/09/287, Washington D.C.: International Monetary Fund.

Guttentag, Jack, and Richard Herring, 1984, "Credit Rationing and Financial Disorder," *The Journal of Finance,* 39 (5), 1159-82.

Johnson, Simon, 2009, "The Quite Coup," The Atlantic, May.

Laibson, David, and Johanna Mallerstrom, 2010, "Capital Flows, Consumption Booms and Asset Bubbles: A Behavioral Alternative to the Savings Glut Hypothesis," Working paper no. 15759, Cambridge: National Bureau of Economic Research.

Mayer, Christopher, Karen Pence, and Shane M. Sherlund, 2009, "The Rise in Mortgage Defaults," *Journal of Economic Perspectives,* 23 (1), 27-50.

Sahlman, William A., 2009, "Management and the Financial Crisis: (We have met the Enemy and He is us …), Working Paper 10-033, Harvard Business School.

Stigler, George J., 1971, "The Theory of Economic Regulation," *Bell Journal of Economics and Management Science,* vol. 2, no.1, 3-21.

Tett, Gillian, 2009, Fool's Gold: How Unrestrained Greed Corrupted a Dream, Shattered Global Markets and Unleashed a Catastrophe, Little Brown

Chapter 12

PORTFOLIOS, INFORMATION AND GEOMETRY: *SIMPLEX ORBIS NON SUFFICIT*

Eric Briys, Brice Magdalou, Richard Nock

ABSTRACT

Mark Twain once said "Put all your eggs in the one basket and – Watch that basket." Financial theory teaches the exact opposite: Investors should buy and hold the market portfolio. If they do so, they enjoy diversification benefits and carry less risk. The verdict of history is not very kind to financial theory. As the recent crisis has once again shown, diversification does not hold to its promises when most needed. What is then the value of a theory that is 95% of the time right but fails to recognize the utmost importance of the remaining 5%? The objective of our paper is to thoroughly revisit the "working horse" of finance, namely the mean-variance approach, and to show that it is just a particular case of a more general approach very well-known in information theory but rather ignored in financial economics.Our first objective is to show that, if we still assume that investor's preferences are of VNM type, associated risk measures can be derived accordingly. These measures involve Bregman divergences. Our second objective is to show how to build portfolios based on trade-offs between expectation and risk defined as divergences. To do so, we use an illustrative example where investors exhibit Constant Absolute Risk Aversion (CARA) and asset returns obey the exponential family of distributions. We contrast our results with the standard results obtained in a standard Markowitz setting with CARA investors and multivariate Gaussian distributions. This simple example illustrates all the benefits that can be drawn from the use of Bregman divergences in financial economics.

1. INTRODUCTION

According to Stephen A. Ross (1978), "modern financial theory derives its analytical power from a few strong assumptions it imposes on models it develops." The modeling of portfolio choices is one such area where significant efforts have been deployed to produce tractable results. It was indeed long understood that asset risk and return were the key ingredients to build risky portfolios. What was missing though was a way to model these portfolio choices in a tractable way. Markowitz and Tobin were the first to frame the tradeoff between risk and return in a solid analytic setting. This setting is grounded on the assumption that investors seek to maximize the expected utility of their final wealth, and that they act as if additional amounts of money have diminishing marginal utility. In other words, they prefer more to less and they are risk averse. To make the optimal portfolio determination analytically tractable, Markowitz and Tobin moreover assume that investors care for the mean and variance of their final wealth only.

For arbitrary distributions of asset returns, the mean-variance framework can be motivated by assuming that investors exhibit quadratic utility. Indeed, when expected rates of return and variances are finite, quadratic utility is sufficient for asset choice to be completely described in terms of a preference relation defined over the mean and variance of expected returns. Unfortunately, there is no such thing as a free lunch and quadratic utility yields the undesirable consequence that risky assets are inferior goods.

For arbitrary preferences, the mean-variance model can be justified by assuming that asset returns are multivariate normally distributed. Normality is usually motivated by a loose application of the central limit theorem: Final wealth is the sum of many separate assets, hence its distributions will tend towards normality. The argument is rather weak as individual returns are neither independently nor identically distributed. Under normality, the higher order moments can be expressed as functions of the first two moments only. Normal distributions have the nice property that they are stable under the addition. However there is again no such thing as a free lunch. The normal distribution is incompatible with limited liability (which precludes negative wealth levels) and economic theory (which attributes no meaning to negative consumption). Indeed, the normal distribution is unbounded from below.

In all other cases, be they distribution driven and/or preference driven, mean-variance acts as an approximation. This is best seen through a Taylor expansion of the expected utility function. A Taylor series expansion is a way of approximating that function to any degree of desired accuracy depending on the number of terms of the series and the choice of the arbitrary point at which the expansion is taken. The expansion is hundred percent accurate in the two cases postulated by Markowitz and Tobin. No higher-order terms are needed beyond the second term. It is worthwhile noting that in the particular case of both an exponential utility function (constant absolute risk aversion) and a Gaussian multivariate distribution, the optimization can be directly framed in a mean-variance setting. Indeed, the general expected utility maximization is fully equivalent to that of the certainty equivalent expressed in terms of the mean of the portfolio return, of the variance of portfolio return and of the coefficient of absolute risk aversion.

All this suggests that the assumption choice is binary, either a distributional assumption and/or a preference assumption. As a matter of fact, the Taylor series expansion suggests that the true choice is between tractability and information. In a Markowitz-Tobin setting, one sacrifices valuable information about preferences and probability distributions in the hope that this loss of information won't be too damaging to optimal portfolio choices and to the robustness of diversification. But the tradeoff between tractability and information does need to be that harsh. Indeed, the tradeoff can be fine-tuned. The best way to show it is to revisit the seminal contributions by Arrow and Pratt. Arrow and Pratt derive the notions of risk premium and certainty equivalent. They show that the risk premium is intimately linked to the (size of the) risk and to an index of risk aversion. The certainty equivalent can then be expressed in terms of the expected return, the variance and the coefficient of absolute risk aversion. This expression is exact if we have normality, quadratic preference or a combination of an exponential utility and normality. Otherwise this is indeed an

$$C(\omega) \simeq E(\omega) - \frac{1}{2} a\big(E(\omega)\big) V(\omega)$$

approximation (1.1)   i.e. an expression in which the term on the left-hand side denotes the certainty equivalent of wealth and the two terms on the right-hand side the expected value of wealth and the risk premium à la Arrow-Pratt respectively. But, this is precisely where the tradeoff can be recast and fine-tuned using new tools drawn from information theory. To the best of our knowledge, very few papers have interpreted portfolio choices in an information geometric setting. This is rather odd as the information lost in the mean-variance approximation can be recovered by using proper information concepts. It is for instance well-known that investors like positive skewness. By definition, this preference for skewness is lost in a mean-variance setting. By the same token, it is now common to emphasize the notion of proper risk aversion, a notion that rests on the successive derivatives of the utility function. In a nutshell, the devil may lie in the details but in a mean-variance framework these details are assumed away: Their impact on portfolio choices are considered negligible. Information theory offers ways to bypass this "fingers crossed" approach. One popular concept of information theory is the so-called Bregman divergence. In layman's words, the Bregman divergence is equivalent to the tail of a Taylor series expansion for a convex function. It is a function that measures discrepancies between two points. Mean-variance portfolio choices are predicated on preference and distribution discrepancies. Although, there have been efforts towards incorporating some of these discrepancies (for example skewness) in the computation of optimal portfolio choices, no paper, to the best of our knowledge, has yet developed an all-encompassing approach whereby the full set of discrepancies are captured in one go. This is what a Bregman divergence performs.

Beyond the tail of the approximation argument, there are two other motives that make Bregman divergences so appealing. First, as shown in Banerjee (2005), there is a direct relationship between the Jensen inequality and Bregman divergences. This is obviously most relevant in a setting where investors are risk-averse: Risk aversion is indeed an economic way of expressing the Jensen inequality. As a result, the Jensen equality yields the equation whose unknown is the risk premium that the investor is willing to pay to avoid taking a gamble. Hence, from a preference perspective, Bregman divergences have much to deliver. Second, exponential families of probability distributions and Bregman divergences have a very intimate relationship. Indeed, there exists a unique Bregman divergence corresponding to every regular exponential family. Again, this is most relevant as it helps relax the Gaussian only assumption.

The objective of this paper is to reframe portfolio choices in an information theoretic framework that relaxes the traditional limitations of the mean-variance approach. More specifically, the aim is to show the usefulness of a tool ignored so far by financial economics, namely the Bregman divergences. We hope this paper through the simple examples it provides will contribute to make Bregman divergences more popular in financial economics.

The paper is structured as follows. Section 2 is devoted to a reminder of traditional results pertaining to risk aversion, risk premia and certainty equivalent. Section 3 introduces the concept of Bregman divergences and shows how mean variance portfolio choices can be recast in a mean-divergence setting. The exact expressions of the portfolio risk premium and of the certainty equivalent are written using the Bregman divergence framework. Section 4 illustrates the usefulness and the power of the mean-Bregman divergence approach through the specific case of exponential utility functions and exponential family of probability distributions. The purpose of section 4 is to give a flavor of what the efficient and optimal portfolios should be if one departs from the usual Markowitz approximation. Indeed, it is well known that under CARA preferences and a multivariate Gaussian distribution of returns the exact optimal portfolio of risky assets can be found by maximizing the certainty equivalent of final wealth as defined by expression (1.1). If the distribution of returns is not normal, this result is just an approximation and the resulting portfolio is inaccurate. Thanks to the use of Bregman divergences we compute the true optimal portfolio and we give the formula for the efficient frontier. Although we stick to the standard Homo Economicus expected utility framework for the sake of pedagogy, it should not be concluded that Bregman divergences apply only to this case. Bregman divergences are one of the ingredients used in machine learning and as such their domain is much wider. Hence they hold valuable promises for our understanding of optimal portfolio choices. These promises are part of the agenda of the authors future research.

2. INVESTMENT DECISIONS: THE TRADITIONAL FRAMEWORK

2.1. Notation

We first present the framework this paper is focused on. We consider an investor faced to a portfolio allocation. among m risky assets. We assume that the support of the investor's wealth denoted by ω, is bounded and defined by $\mathcal{D} := \left[\overline{\omega}, \underline{\omega}\right] \subset \mathbb{R}$. His *initial wealth* is denoted by $\omega^0 \in \mathcal{D}$. We let $\alpha_j \in [0,1]$ indicate the proportion of the initial wealth invested in the risky asset j $(j = 1,2,\cdots,m)$, such that $\alpha_j \omega^0$ represents the amount of money invested in j. We denote by $\alpha := (\alpha_1, \alpha_2, \cdots, \alpha_m)$ the list of the proportions, the investor has to determinate in the portfolio allocation. The set of the admissible α is $\mathcal{V} := \left\{\alpha : \sum_{j=1}^{m} \alpha_j = 1\right\}$. At the end of the investment period, the uncertain monetary return per unit of the asset j is indicated by r_j. Hence, the investor's *final wealth* $\omega^F \in \mathcal{D}$ can be expressed as:

$$\omega^F = \sum_{j=1}^{m} \alpha_j r_j \omega^0 .$$

(2.1)

One remarks that the quantity $\omega_j := r_j \omega^0$ represents the random amount of money obtained by the investor, in the case where he decides to completely invest the initial wealth

ω^0 in asset j. Consequently, the portfolio allocation consists in affecting weights between the random variables ω_j. We let $\boldsymbol{\omega} := (\omega_1, \omega_2, \cdots, \omega_m)$ be the list of the random variables, and we will call the composite list $(\boldsymbol{\alpha}; \boldsymbol{\omega})$, the investor's *portfolio*. The set of the admissible portfolios is simply defined by:

$$\mathcal{P} := \{(\boldsymbol{\alpha}; \boldsymbol{\omega}) : \boldsymbol{\alpha} \in \mathcal{V}, \boldsymbol{\omega} \in \mathcal{D}^m\}. \tag{2.2}$$

By using a vectorial notation, relation (2.1) can be rewritten as $\omega^F = \boldsymbol{\alpha} \, \boldsymbol{\omega}^\mathsf{T}$ where subscript T indicates the transpose. Letting $\mu_j := \mathrm{E}(\omega_j)$ be the expected return of the risky asset j, the list of the expected returns is defined by $\boldsymbol{\mu} := (\mu_1, \mu_2, \cdots, \mu_m)$. The covariance between assets i and j is indicated by $\sigma_{ij} := \mathrm{E}\big[(\omega_i - \mu_i)(\omega_j - \mu_j)\big]$. The covariance matrix, denoted by Σ, is obtained from:

$$\Sigma := \begin{bmatrix} \sigma_{11} & \cdots & \sigma_{1m} \\ \vdots & \ddots & \vdots \\ \sigma_{m1} & \cdots & \sigma_{mm} \end{bmatrix}. \tag{2.3}$$

Finally, the list of the variance of each asset j, the diagonal of the matrix Σ, is represented by $\boldsymbol{\sigma} := (\sigma_1^2, \sigma_2^2, \cdots, \sigma_m^2)$, where $\sigma_j^2 := \sigma_{jj} = V(\omega_j)$. The objective of the investor is to build an optimal portfolio – that is to choose the optimal allocation $\boldsymbol{\alpha}$ – according to his risk preferences, based on the expected return and on the risk of the portfolio. The traditional theory of investment behavior hypothesizes that the investor prefers more to less, and that he is risk averse.

2.2. Preferences and Expected Utility

Suppose that the wealth $\omega \in \mathcal{D}$ is uncertain. It may correspond to the final wealth ω^F, presented in the previous section. We assume that the investor's preferences are represented by a *binary relation* $\succcurlyeq$ on $\mathcal{D}$, such that $\omega \succcurlyeq \omega'$ is interpreted as meaning wealth ω' is not preferred to ω by the investor. The asymmetric and symmetric components are $\succ$ and $\sim$, respectively. Then, we suppose that there exists a continuous utility function $U: \mathcal{D} \to \mathbb{R}$, defined up to an increasing affine transformation, which fully characterizes the investor's preferences under the *expected utility framework*. Precisely, we assume that, for $\omega, \omega' \in \mathcal{D}$, we have:

$$\omega \succcurlyeq \omega' \iff EU(\omega) \geq EU(\omega'). \tag{2.4}$$

This approach can be justified, applying some well-known properties on the relation $\succcurlyeq$. We consider throughout that the utility function is monotonically non-decreasing: any additional amount of money always creates an additional satisfaction.

The essential features of the investor's preferences are captured by the risk premium and the certainty equivalent. We define the *risk premium of the uncertain wealth* ω, denoted by $\pi(\omega)$, as the maximum amount of money the investor is willing to pay, in order to accept the expected value of the risky wealth, whereas accepting the risk. Precisely, for all $\omega \in \mathcal{D}$, we have:

$$\big(E(\omega) - \pi(\omega)\big) \sim \omega. \tag{2.5}$$

Since the amount $\big(E(\omega) - \pi(\omega)\big)$ is certain, we deduce:

$$U\big(E(\omega) - \pi(\omega)\big) = EU(\omega). \tag{2.6}$$

Equivalently, the expected utility of the risky wealth is equal to the utility of its expected return, minus the risk premium. The *certainty equivalent*, which is the sure amount received by the individual - if he decides to pay the risk premium, in order to obtain the expected value of ω - is represented by $C(\omega) := E(\omega) - \pi(\omega)$. Consequently, it follows that $U\big(C(\omega)\big) = EU(\omega)$. If we assume that U is invertible, another formulation of the certainty equivalent is $C(\omega) = U^{-1}[EU(\omega)]$, recalling equation (2.6).

If the investor's preferences are consistent with the expected utility model, and if he is risk averse, then the investor has to allocate his portfolio by maximizing the certainty equivalent of the final wealth. Since $C(\omega) = E(\omega) - \pi(\omega)$, his optimization strategy can be decomposed in two steps: first, minimizing the risk premium $\pi(\omega)$ for a given expected return, then maximizing the expected return.

2.3. Risk Aversion and Measure of Risk

The investor is strictly risk averse if he strictly prefers the expected return whereas accepting the risk. So $E(\omega) \succ \omega$, or equivalently $U\big(E(\omega)\big) > EU(\omega)$. Following the well-known Jensen's inequality, one deduces that the investor is strictly risk averse if and only if the utility function U is concave. It follows that the risk premium is positive, $\pi(\omega) > 0$, and that $C(\omega) < E(\omega)$. Nevertheless, we have no indication about the investor's risk aversion degree, nor about the risk level of the uncertain wealth ω.

Pratt (1964) has shown that the second derivative of the utility function $U''(\omega)$ - assuming that U is twice continuously differentiable - is not an appropriate candidate to evaluate the investor's risk aversion degree. The main justification is that U is defined up to an increasing affine transformation. He has proposed a measure of local risk aversion, using a Taylor series expansion at the neighborhood of $E(\omega)$, of both hands of equation (2.6). For the right hand, one obtains:

$$EU(\omega) = U(E(\omega)) + \frac{1}{2} V(\omega) U''(E(\omega)) + O(V(\omega)), \qquad (2.7)$$

where the rest $O(V(\omega))$ depends on the central moments of ω and the successive derivatives of U, of order higher than two. For the left hand of (2.6), one obtains:

$$U(E(\omega) - \pi(\omega)) = U(E(\omega)) - \pi(\omega) U'(E(\omega)) + O(\pi(\omega)). \qquad (2.8)$$

If one neglects the residual terms O in (2.7) and (2.8), one immediately deduces the following expression for the risk premium:

$$\pi(\omega) \simeq \frac{1}{2} a(E(\omega)) V(\omega), \qquad (2.9)$$

where $a(t) := -U''(t)/U'(t)$ corresponds to the Arrow-Pratt coefficient of absolute risk aversion, evaluated at a certain wealth $t \in \mathcal{D}$. Equivalently, since $C(\omega) = E(\omega) - \pi(\omega)$, one deduces an approximation of the certainty equivalent:

$$C(\omega) \simeq E(\omega) - \frac{1}{2} a(E(\omega)) V(\omega). \qquad (2.10)$$

This result provides a theoretical background for the usual mean-variance approach of portfolio allocation. The certainty equivalent is separated, in a linear fashion, between the expected return of the portfolio and its variance, weighted by the investor's risk aversion: The higher the risk aversion, the higher the negative impact on the certainty equivalent of the variance. Nevertheless the approximations proposed in (2.9) and (2.10), are based on rather counter-intuitive restrictions imposed on the utility function U, and/or on the probability distribution of the wealth ω. For example, if the coefficient of absolute risk aversion is constant over $\mathcal{D}$ and if the uncertain wealth is normally distributed, then the approximations in (2.9) and (2.10) become exact. The normality assumption is, however, an empirically inconsistent assumption. Such approximations are also exact if the utility function is quadratic, because the derivatives of U, of order higher than two, are equals to zero. Unfortunately a quadratic utility function exhibits an increasing absolute risk aversion, an assumption traditionally viewed with suspicion since it entails that risky assets are inferior goods.

3. From Mean-Variance Efficiency to Mean-Divergence Efficiency

3.1. Bregman Divergence

In the approximation of the certainty equivalent in (2.10), all the central moments of the distribution of ω, but the first and the second (mean and variance), are neglected. So the risk is captured by the variance only, and the investor's preferences over other central moments are sacrificed. The standard theory has embraced a simple tradeoff: the tractability and the interpretation of the results at the cost of a potentially harmful loss of information. This loss of information pertains simultaneously to the probability distributions and the investor's preferences. Hence a fundamental question arises: Does the concern for tractability truly justify to act blindly? Obviously not. We propose in this paper to present the *only possible strategy* to preserve an exact definition of the certainty equivalent, without assumption on the utility function - apart from concavity - and without restriction imposed on the probability distribution of the uncertain wealth. This tool is standard in information geometry but almost unknown in economics - and totally ignored in financial economics -: It is named Bregman divergences. Under this new framework, no approximation is required to capture the risk and there is no reason why one should restrict oneself to the usual variance approximation. There is indeed life beyond order 2.

In a first step, we define the notion of Bregman divergence. Consider two certain amounts of money $\omega, \omega' \in \mathcal{D}$, and a continuous function $\varphi : \mathcal{D} \to \mathbb{R}$. A *Bregman divergence with generator φ*, is an asymmetric function $D_\varphi : \mathcal{D} \times \mathcal{D} \to \mathbb{R}$, defined by:

$$D_\varphi(\omega \parallel \omega') := \varphi(\omega) - \varphi(\omega') - (\omega - \omega')\varphi'(\omega'), \tag{3.1}$$

where φ' denotes the first derivative of φ. The interaction between the expected utility model and the notion of Bregman divergence is not immediately intuitive. The best way to gain intuition is to go back to a tool that is familiar to financial economists, namely Taylor expansions. First one remarks that, for two certain amounts $\omega, \omega' \in \mathcal{D}$, a Taylor series expansion of the utility function $U(\omega)$ at the neighborhood of ω', gives:

$$U(\omega) = U(\omega') + (\omega - \omega')U'(\omega') + O(\omega - \omega'). \tag{3.2}$$

From (3.1), we deduce that the tail of the expansion $O(\omega - \omega')$ is the following Bregman divergence:

$$O(\omega - \omega') = D_U(\omega \parallel \omega'). \tag{3.3}$$

It is traditionally assumed that the first derivative of U represents the marginal utility of wealth, and that higher-order derivatives capture the investor's risk preferences. Consequently, an exact Taylor series expansion of the utility function, isolating the first derivative of U and taking into account all higher dimensions of the risk and the risk aversion, is possible only if we appeal to a Bregman divergence. As we show in the remaining sections of this paper, this way of rewriting things is not just a cosmetic one. It opens up the whole panoply of information theory. Accordingly, in the following subsection, we introduce another concept, the so-called Bregman information, closely associated to the notion of Bregman divergence. Then we link these notions to the expected utility model.

3.2. Bregman Information

Now suppose that the wealth is a uncertain, as for example the final wealth ω^F of the investor. We introduce the notion of *Bregman information*, as proposed by Banerjee *et al.* (2005) in information geometry, and defined by:

$$I_\varphi(\omega) := E\big[D_\varphi\big(\omega \,\|\, E(\omega)\big)\big]. \tag{3.4}$$

We will establish that the certainty equivalent $C(\omega)$ can be exactly decomposed between the expectation $E(\omega)$ and a Bregman Information, with a generator derived from the utility function U. First, Banerjee *et al.* (2005) observe that the Bregman information exactly quantifies the difference between the two sides of the Jensen's inequality. Precisely, we have:

Claim 3.1 Consider a uncertain wealth ω with values in $\mathcal{D}$ and a utility function $U : \mathcal{D} \to \mathbb{R}$.. The expected utility of ω can be expressed as:

$$EU(\omega) = U\big(E(\omega)\big) + I_U(\omega). \tag{3.5}$$

Proof: The result follows immediately from the definition of the Bregman information:

$$I_U(\omega) = E\big[D_U\big(\omega \,\|\, E(\omega)\big)\big] = E\big[U(\omega) - U\big(E(\omega)\big) - \big(\omega - E(\omega)\big)U'\big(E(\omega)\big)\big] \tag{3.6}$$

or equivalently:

$$I_U(\omega) = EU(\omega) - U\big(E(\omega)\big) - U'\big(E(\omega)\big)E\big[\omega - E(\omega)\big]. \tag{3.7}$$

The equality holds, noting that the last term of (3.6) is equal to zero.

If the investor is risk averse, then $U\big(E(\omega)\big) > EU(\omega)$. The result establishes that the loss between the utility of the expected $U\big(E(\omega)\big)$ and the expected utility $EU(\omega)$, is exactly measurable by the Bregman information $I_U(\omega)$. From relations (2.7) and (3.5), one observes:

$$I_U(\omega) = \tfrac{1}{2} V(\omega) U''\big(E(\omega)\big) + O\big(V(\omega)\big). \tag{3.8}$$

Thus the Bregman information $I_U(\omega)$ captures the variance of the probability distribution and its marginal contribution on the expected utility, equal to $U''(E(\omega))/2$.

This contribution depends on the investor's risk preferences: if he is risk averse $(U'' < 0)$, then the contribution is negative. But $I_U(\omega)$ also incorporates the *entire* tail of the Taylor series expansion. Precisely, letting $M_i(\omega) := E[\omega - E(\omega)]^i$ be the i-th central moment of ω, and U^i be the i-th derivative of U, one observes that:

$$I_U(\omega) = \frac{U^2(E(\omega))}{2!} M_2(\omega) + \frac{U^3(E(\omega))}{3!} M_3(\omega) + \frac{U^4(E(\omega))}{4!} M_4(\omega) + \cdots (3.9)$$

Consequently, if the utility function is continuously differentiable, the Bregman information $I_U(\omega)$ appears as a linear combination of all the central moments ω, weighted by the corresponding marginal contribution. These contributions depend on the successive derivatives of the utility function, which characterize the investor's risk preferences. We propose a similar result for the certainty equivalent.

Claim 3.2 Consider a uncertain wealth ω with values in $\mathcal{D}$ and an invertible utility function $U : \mathcal{D} \to \mathbb{R}$. The risk premium is equal to $\pi(\omega) = I_{U^{-1}}(U(\omega))$, and the certainty equivalent $C(\omega)$ is such that:

$$C(\omega) = E(\omega) - I_{U^{-1}}(U(\omega)). \tag{3.9}$$

Proof: From Claim 3.1, we know that $I_U(\omega) = EU(\omega) - U(E(\omega))$, hence:

$$I_{U^{-1}}(U(\omega)) = EU^{-1}(U(\omega)) - U^{-1}[EU(\omega)] = E(\omega) - C(\omega). \tag{3.10}$$

That corresponds to the definition of the risk premium, $\pi(\omega) = E(\omega) - C(\omega)$. $\blacksquare$

In the traditional Arrow-Pratt setting, the risk premium is approximated on the basis on the variance and the absolute risk aversion coefficient, such that $\pi(\omega) \simeq [a(E(\omega))V(\omega)]/2$. The risk premium identified in Claim 3.2 incorporates all the central moments of ω. Using the notation $\rho_i(t) := -U^i(t)/U'(t)$ for all $t \in \mathcal{D}$ (noting that $\rho_2 = a$), it follows:

$$I_{U^{-1}}(U(\omega)) = \frac{\rho_2(E(\omega))}{2!} M_2(\omega) + \frac{\rho_3(E(\omega))}{3!} M_3(\omega) + \frac{\rho_4(E(\omega))}{4!} M_4(\omega) + \cdots (3.11)$$

In most theoretical and empirical studies, the certainty equivalent $C(\omega)$ is approximated from the two first central moments of the risky wealth ω, namely the mean and the variance. Variance is seen as a measure of risk. But, we have shown in Claim 3.2 that an exact definition of the certainty equivalent is possible, using the notion of Bregman information. Following this new approach, we propose to substitute a *mean-divergence* criterion of portfolio allocation, to the traditional *mean-variance* strategy.

Some clarifications are nevertheless required. The main advantage of the usual mean-variance strategy is twofold. First a distinction between risk aversion (captured by the absolute risk aversion coefficient) and the measure of risk (approximated by the variance) is easily identifiable. Second, this theory is tractable and allows portfolio allocations, using a well-known two steps procedure: first, minimizing the variance for a given expected return, then maximizing the expected return for a given level of variance. But the cost is far from being insignificant. Valuable features of the probability distributions are neglected, and the investor is assumed to act as if he were unaware of them or as if he considered them harmless. The mean-divergence criterion we present in this paper is a promising one, since no approximation is required even though a distinction between risk aversion and the measure of risk is not immediate. The risk premium $I_{U^{-1}}\big(U(\omega)\big)$ incorporates both dimensions simultaneously. But, as already pointed out, this immediacy does not come for free. Second, the tractability of this new risk premium, in order to obtain portfolio allocations, is not guaranteed. But who said tractability is the one and only way to go? The main objective of the present paper is not to provide all the solutions that Bregman divergences and Bregman information allow: Given the novelty of the Bregman notions in financial economics, it is to pave the right way for future researches. One can reasonably hope that rapid advances will be made in the elaboration of this new setting.

4. PORTFOLIO SELECTION UNDER CONSTANT ABSOLUTE RISK AVERSION (CARA)

4.1. The Framework

In Section 3, we have pointed out the usefulness of the Bregman divergences in the definition of the risk premium and the certainty equivalent, in an expected utility framework. We show in this section that the notion of Bregman divergence makes tremendous sense if, for instance, we focus on the probability distributions, instead of the utility function. It is well-known that the mean-variance approach can be justified if asset returns are multivariate normally distributed: the higher order moments can be expressed as functions of the first two moments only. But the normality assumption is too demanding in practice. For the sake of Bregman pedagogy, we will use an example where the distributions belong to a more general class. It appears that the Bregman divergences are closely associated to a large class of probability distributions - which admits as a special case the Gaussian distribution - called the exponential families of distributions.

The objective of this section is to show Bregman tools in action. For the sake of clarity - recalling that we focus on the probability distributions aspect of things, instead of utility functions - we restrict attention to the case where there is no wealth effect on the risk premium. This assumption implies that the investor's preferences exhibit *constant absolute risk aversion.* Precisely, for a random wealth ω with values in $\mathcal{D}$ and a constant $c \in \mathcal{D}$, we have:

$$\pi(\omega + c) = \pi(\omega).$$

(4.1)

The following result, already known in the literature, establishes that the utility function is necessarily exponential.

Claim 4.1 Consider a uncertain wealth ω with values in $\mathcal{D}$ and a utility function $U : \mathcal{D} \rightarrow \mathbb{R}$. The risk premium is such that $\pi(\omega + c) = \pi(\omega)$ for all $c \in \mathcal{D}$, if and only if the utility function, defined up to an increasing affine transformation, is of the form:

(4.2) $U(\omega) = -\exp(-a\omega), \forall a \in \mathbb{R}$

Moreover the investor is risk averse $(U'' < 0)$ if and only if $a > 0$.

Proof : By definition $C(\omega + c) = E(\omega + c) - \pi(\omega + c)$. Letting $\pi(\omega + c) = \pi(\omega)$, it follows that $C(\omega + c) = E(\omega) - \pi(\omega) + c$, or equivalently $C(\omega + c) = C(\omega) + c$. Hence the certainty equivalent $C(\omega) = U^{-1}[EU(\omega)]$ is translatable. The implication on the utility function is known in the literature, see for example Nock et al. (2009), Theorem 2, point (E), page 8. _

In the Arrow-Pratt's risk premium approximation (equation 2.9), a constant absolute risk aversion is equivalent to $a(\omega) = - U''(\omega)/U'(\omega) = a$ for all certain wealth $\omega \in \mathcal{D}$.

It is convenient, in the following, to present the expected utility model in a multidimensional setting: the expected utility of the *unidimensional* final wealth becomes the expected utility of the *multidimensional* portfolio. Let us recall that the final wealth ω^F is such that $\omega^F = \sum_{j=1}^{m} \alpha_j \omega_j = \alpha\omega^T$, where $\omega_j = r_j \omega^0$ represents the investor's final wealth in the case where his portfolio is totally invested in the risky asset j $(j = 1, 2, \cdots, m)$. Also α_j is the proportion of asset j in the portfolio, and $(\alpha; \omega)$ is called the portfolio. If we assume constant absolute risk aversion, then the utility function can be rewritten as:

$$U(\omega^F) = U(\alpha\omega^T) = -\exp(-a\alpha\omega^T), \forall a > 0.$$

(4.3)

The certainty equivalent of the final wealth is $C(\omega^F) = E(\omega^F) - \pi(\omega^F)$. In the multidimensional setting the expected return becomes $E(\omega^F) = E(\alpha\omega^T) = \sum_{j=1}^{m} \alpha_j E(\omega_j) = \alpha\mu^T$, which implies:

$$C(\alpha\omega^T) = \alpha\mu^T - \pi(\alpha\omega^T).$$

(4.4)

As exposed in Section 2, the certainty equivalent can be approximated by a linear combination of the expected return and the variance of the final wealth. After simplification, the variance is equal to:

$$V(\alpha\omega^{\mathrm{T}}) = E\left[\left(\textstyle\sum_{j=1}^{m} \alpha_j\omega_j - \sum_{j=1}^{m} \alpha_j E(\omega_j)\right)^2\right] = \alpha\Sigma\alpha^{\mathrm{T}}. \tag{4.5}$$

Hence the Arrow-Pratt's approximation of the certainty equivalent gives:

$$C(\alpha\omega^{\mathrm{T}}) \simeq \alpha\mu^{\mathrm{T}} - \frac{a}{2}\,\alpha\Sigma\alpha^{\mathrm{T}}. \tag{4.6}$$

Under constant absolute risk aversion, it is well-known that such an approximation is exact if and only if the vector of the random variables ω_j, for all $j = 1, 2, \cdots, m$, is multivariate normally distributed. So we have to assume that the investor chooses a portfolio belonging to the set:

$$\mathcal{P}(\Sigma) := \left\{ (\alpha; \omega) \in \mathcal{P} : p(\omega; \mu, \Sigma) = \frac{1}{(2\pi)^{m/2}\sqrt{\det\Sigma}}\,\exp\left(-\frac{(\omega-\mu)\Sigma^{-1}(\omega-\mu)}{2}\right)\right\}, \tag{4.7}$$

where p indicates the probability density function of ω. Nevertheless, this assumption is highly questionable from an empirical standpoint. Hence, we propose to extend the set of portfolios under consideration.

Before introducing our main results, we have to present the notion of Bregman divergence in a multidimensional setting. Consider two lists of certain amounts of money, $\omega, \omega' \in \mathcal{D}^m$, and a continuous function $\varphi : \mathcal{D}^m \to \mathbb{R}$. A (*multivariate*) *Bregman divergence with generator* φ, is an asymmetric function $D_\varphi : \mathcal{D}^m \times \mathcal{D}^m \to \mathbb{R}$, defined by:

$$D_\varphi(\omega \| \omega') := \varphi(\omega) - \varphi(\omega') - (\omega - \omega')\nabla_\varphi(\omega'), \tag{4.7}$$

where the *gradient* ∇_φ denotes the list of the first derivatives of φ, such that:

$$\nabla_\varphi(\omega) := \left(\frac{\partial\varphi(\omega)}{\partial\omega_1}, \frac{\partial\varphi(\omega)}{\partial\omega_2}, \cdots, \frac{\partial\varphi(\omega)}{\partial\omega_m}\right). \tag{4.8}$$

4.2. CARA and Exponential Family of Distributions

As already mentioned in the previous section, we restrict attention to portfolios characterized by a multivariate parametric distribution function, belonging to the *exponential family of distributions* (Banerjee et al., 2005; Nielsen and Nock, 2009a,c). Precisely, we focus on the following set of portfolios:

$$\mathcal{P}_\psi(\theta) := \left\{(\alpha; \omega) \in \mathcal{P} : p_\psi(\omega) = \exp\left(\omega\,\theta^{\mathrm{T}} - \psi(\theta)\right)b(\omega)\right\}. \tag{4.9}$$

$\boldsymbol{\theta} := (\theta_1, \theta_2, \cdots, \theta_m)$ defines the *natural parameters* of the family, depending on the multivariate random variable $\boldsymbol{\omega}$ with values in $\mathcal{D}^m$. The *cumulant function* ψ is strictly convex, and its range depends on $\mathcal{D}^m$. This function, also called the log-partition function, is obtained from:

$$\psi(\boldsymbol{\theta}) = \log \int_{\mathcal{D}^m} \exp(\boldsymbol{\omega}\,\boldsymbol{\theta}^{\mathsf{T}}) b(\boldsymbol{\omega}) d(\boldsymbol{\omega}) . \tag{4.10}$$

Note that ψ also defines the usual moments of $\boldsymbol{\omega}$:

$$\mu = \nabla_\psi(\boldsymbol{\theta}) , \tag{4.11a}$$

$$\sigma = \nabla^2_\psi(\boldsymbol{\theta}) . \tag{4.11b}$$

where $\sigma = \nabla^2_\psi(\boldsymbol{\theta})$ is the *Hessian* of the function ψ. Bernoulli, normal, Poisson, Laplacian, negative binomial, Raylegh, Wishart, Dirichlet and Gamma are just few examples of exponential families (see Nielsen and Nock, 2009c). In the particular case of an univariate gaussian distribution, the natural parameter θ is defined by $\theta := \mu/\sigma^2$, where μ denotes the mean and σ^2 the variance of the distribution. We assume in this paper that the exponential family is sufficiently large to encompass the distributions, commonly encountered in the real financial world.

Our first result establishes that, under constant absolute risk aversion, and considering a multivariate risk belonging to the exponential family of distributions, the certainty equivalent and the risk premium can be expressed without approximation. Note that, in order to alleviate the technicalities of the paper, the proofs of the results are omitted. They are available from the authors upon request.

Proposition 4.2 For all portfolios $(\boldsymbol{\alpha}; \boldsymbol{\omega}) \in \mathcal{P}_\psi(\boldsymbol{\theta})$, *under constant absolute risk aversion, denoted by* a, *the certainty equivalent of the final wealth is equal to:*

$$C(\boldsymbol{\alpha}\boldsymbol{\omega}^{\mathsf{T}}) = [\psi(\boldsymbol{\theta}) - \psi(\boldsymbol{\theta} - a\boldsymbol{\alpha})]/a , \; \forall\, a \neq 0 . \tag{4.12}$$

The risk premium is then deduced from the relation: $\pi(\boldsymbol{\alpha}\boldsymbol{\omega}^{\mathsf{T}}) = \boldsymbol{\alpha}\mu^{\mathsf{T}} - C(\boldsymbol{\alpha}\boldsymbol{\omega}^{\mathsf{T}})$.

Thus the certainty equivalent only depends on the cumulant function ψ which characterizes the multivariate probability distribution. It is worthwhile to remark that the risk premium can be simplified, as demonstrated by the following result.

Proposition 4.3 For all portfolios $(\boldsymbol{\alpha}; \boldsymbol{\omega}) \in \mathcal{P}_\psi(\boldsymbol{\theta})$, *under constant absolute risk aversion, the risk premium simplifies as follows:*

$$\pi(\boldsymbol{\alpha}\boldsymbol{\omega}^{\mathsf{T}}) = D_\psi(\boldsymbol{\theta} - a\boldsymbol{\alpha} \,\|\, \boldsymbol{\theta})/a , \; \forall\, a \neq 0 . \tag{4.13}$$

The risk premium is exactly equal to a Bregman divergence, with the cumulant function ψ as generator. Unlike the results presented in Section 3, we are now able to distinguish the risk aversion, captured by the parameter a, and the measure of risk, calculated by D_ψ. However, as intuitively expected, the two dimensions cannot be linearly separated. The risk aversion has a *distortion effect* on the natural parameters of the distribution. Recalling that α_j is the proportion of asset j in the portfolio, the distortion is stronger for assets highly weighted in the portfolio.

This approach generalizes a well-known result in financial economics. As mentioned earlier, the mean-variance approach is exact if the distribution is multivariate normally distributed and if the absolute risk aversion is constant. Recalling that the set of portfolios with a multivariate normally distribution is denoted by $\mathcal{P}(\Sigma)$, and such that $\mathcal{P}(\Sigma) \subset \mathcal{P}_\psi(\boldsymbol{\theta})$, on obtains the usual following result.

Proposition 4.4 For all portfolios $(\boldsymbol{\alpha}; \boldsymbol{\omega}) \in \mathcal{P}(\Sigma)$, under constant absolute risk aversion, the risk premium simplifies as follows:

$$\pi(\boldsymbol{\alpha}\boldsymbol{\omega}^\mathsf{T}) = \tfrac{a}{2} V(\boldsymbol{\alpha}\boldsymbol{\omega}^\mathsf{T}). \tag{4.14}$$

4.3. Finding the Optimal Portfolio

Under the assumption that the multivariate probability distribution of the portfolio belongs to the exponential family, one observes that the risk premium can be exactly expressed by a Bregman divergence. Whereas it is generally assumed by the usual theory that the complexity of portfolio selection need to focus on a restrictive model, for example the mean-variance approach, we establish now the tractability of our approach. Recalling that $\mathcal{V} := \left\{\alpha : \sum_{j=1}^m \alpha_j = 1\right\}$, the portfolio selection amounts to solve the following problem:

$$\text{find } \boldsymbol{\alpha}^* = \arg\max\nolimits_{\alpha \in \mathcal{V}} \ C(\boldsymbol{\alpha}\boldsymbol{\omega}^\mathsf{T}) = \arg\max\nolimits_{\alpha \in \mathcal{V}} \ \boldsymbol{\alpha}\boldsymbol{\mu}^\mathsf{T} - \pi(\boldsymbol{\alpha}\boldsymbol{\omega}^\mathsf{T}). \tag{4.15}$$

In other words, the investor has to determinate the proportions of the initial wealth invested in each risky asset, in order to maximize the expected utility of the final wealth, or equivalently in our setting to maximize its certainty equivalent, $C(\boldsymbol{\alpha}\boldsymbol{\omega}^\mathsf{T})$. The following result identifies the optimal portfolio selection in our framework.

Proposition 4.5 For all portfolios $(\boldsymbol{\alpha}; \boldsymbol{\omega}) \in \mathcal{P}_\psi(\boldsymbol{\theta})$, under constant absolute risk aversion, the solution to (4.15) is:

$$\boldsymbol{\alpha}^* = \tfrac{1}{a}\left(\boldsymbol{\theta} - \nabla_\psi^{-1}(-\lambda\mathbf{1})\right), \tag{4.16}$$

for some $\lambda \in \mathbb{R}_+$, where $\mathbf{1} := (1,1,\cdots,1)$ denotes the unit vector in $\mathbb{R}^m$.

We know that the multivariate Gaussian distribution is one particular case of the exponential family. Thus this result allows to derive the solution for the Markowitz' framework, as demonstrated below.

Proposition 4.6 For all portfolios $(\alpha; \omega) \in \mathcal{P}(\Sigma)$, under constant absolute risk aversion, the solution to (4.15) is:

$$\alpha^* = \frac{\Sigma^{-1}\mathbf{1}^T}{\mathbf{1}\Sigma^{-1}\mathbf{1}^T} + \frac{1}{a\mathbf{1}\Sigma^{-1}\mathbf{1}^T}(\mathbf{1}\Sigma^{-1}\mathbf{1}^T\Sigma^{-1}\mu^T - \mathbf{1}\Sigma^{-1}\mu^T\Sigma^{-1}\mathbf{1}^T), \qquad (4.17)$$

for which:

$$C(\alpha^*\omega^T) = \frac{1}{2a}(\mu\Sigma^{-1}\mu^T - (a - \mu\Sigma^{-1}\mathbf{1}^T)^2) \qquad (4.18)$$

It is not hard to check that Proposition 4.6 indeed corresponds to Theorem 1.4 in Steinbach (2001). The generalization we propose is most useful in cases where the domain of the expectation and/or natural parameters of the exponential family is not $\mathbb{R}^m$. This is for example the case for Poisson, binomial, multinomial and Bernoulli distributions (among other exponential families). In such cases, reducing the general solution obtained in Proposition 4.5 to the traditional Markowitz mean-variance solution (Proposition 4.6) may trigger significant losses. To see this, it is worthwhile remarking that a simple Taylor expansion yields that α^* may also be given by $\alpha^* = (1/a)(H^{-1}\mu^T + \tilde{\lambda}H^{-1})$, for some particular value of the Hessian of ψ taken in its domain, denoted by H. If we denote for short $C_{H^{-1}} := C(\alpha^*\omega^T)$, the value of the certainty equivalent as given by this new expression, then little algebra brings

$$C_{\Sigma^{-1}} = C_{H^{-1}} + C_{\Sigma^{-1}-H^{-1}} + (a/2) - (1/a)\mu\Sigma^{-1}\mathbf{1}^T\mu H^{-1}\mathbf{1}^T.$$

Hence a bad choice for the approximation of the Hessian by a constant value Σ over the domain (*i.e.* Markowitz's mean-variance solution) yields significant differences in the certainty equivalent, that may blow up with the risk aversion --- not to mention the additional error incurred by the approximation of the Hessian, $C_{\Sigma^{-1}-H^{-1}}$.

4.4. Portfolio Choice and the Efficient Frontier

The optimal solution for the portfolio selection is possible through a one stage optimization process. But it may be useful to consider a two-stage decomposition, in order to characterize the *efficient frontier* for the portfolios. We are going to see that the efficient frontier match important concepts of information geometry.

The first possibility, in order to obtain the efficient frontier, is to maximize the expected return of the portfolio, under a maximal risk premium constraint. We are left with the following problem:

$$\text{find } \alpha^* = \arg\max_{\alpha \in V} \alpha \mu^T \text{ s.t. } \pi(\alpha \omega^T) \leq \kappa. \tag{4.19}$$

where $\kappa > 0$ is fixed. This amounts to a constrained maximization of the certainty equivalent $C(\alpha \omega^T)$. To be more explicit, (4.19) is equivalent to solving the following convex problem, with $\delta := \kappa/a > 0$:

$$\text{find } \alpha^* = \arg\max_{\alpha \in V} \alpha \mu^T \text{ s.t. } D_\psi(\theta - a\alpha \| \theta) \leq \delta. \tag{4.20}$$

or equivalently, fixing for short $V_{a,\theta} := \{x \in \mathbb{R}^m : (1/a)(\theta - x) \in V\}$, and remarking that this set is convex,

$$\text{find } \theta^* = \arg\max_{\theta' \in V_{a,\theta}} \frac{1}{a}(\theta - \theta')\mu^T \text{ s.t. } D_\psi(\theta' \| \theta) \leq \delta, \tag{4.21}$$

which simplifies to the final problem on which we focus:

$$\text{find } \theta^* = \arg\max_{\theta' \in V_{a,\theta}} \theta' \mu^T \text{ s.t. } D_\psi(\theta' \| \theta) \leq \delta. \tag{4.22}$$

Note that the constraint in (4.22) is convex in its left argument (see Nock and Nielsen, 2009b, Lemma 4). The solution of this problem characterizes the efficient frontier of the portfolios, if we assume constant absolute risk aversion and a multivariate distribution of the risk, belonging to the exponential family.

Proposition 4.7 For all portfolios $(\alpha; \omega) \in \mathcal{P}_\psi(\theta)$, under constant absolute risk aversion, the solution to (4.21) which characterizes the efficient frontier of the portfolios is:

$$\theta^* = \nabla_\psi^{-1}\left((1 - \lambda)\nabla_\psi(\theta) + \lambda \beta \mathbf{1}^T\right), \tag{4.23}$$

for some $\lambda, \beta \in \mathbb{R}$, that depend on κ and a.

The solution provided by Proposition 4.7 is well-known in information geometry. Letting $\mathbf{1}_{\beta,\psi} := \nabla_\psi^{-1}(\beta \mathbf{1}^T)$, the expression (4.23) is a *generalized mean*, also called *Bregman average* (see Nielsen et al., 2007; Nielsen and Nock, 2009a):

$$\theta^* = \nabla_\psi^{-1}\left((1 - \lambda)\nabla_\psi(\theta) + \lambda \nabla_\psi(\mathbf{1}_{\beta,\psi})\right). \tag{4.24}$$

That is, θ^* is of the form $f^{-1}\left((1 - \lambda)f(u) + \lambda f(v)\right)$, and thus θ^* is located on a curve crossing points θ and $\mathbf{1}_{\beta,\psi}$ in the natural parameters' space. Furthermore, as we make κ vary, θ^* moves along this curve, thereby defining the efficient frontier for portfolios.

It can be further remarked that this curve bears very interesting properties. For example, it is a line if and only if the exponential family is a multivariate Gaussian (Nielsen et al.,

242   Eric Briys, Brice Magdalou and Richard Nock

2007; Nielsen and Nock, 2009a). Furthermore, it has geometric properties similar to those of geodesics in Riemannian manifolds, provided an information measure --- which is not a metric --- is used in lieu of metrics (Nielsen et al., 2007; Nielsen and Nock, 2009a). Powerful geometric algorithms allow to compute or estimate $\boldsymbol{\theta}^*$ (Nielsen and Nock, 2009a).

Another possibility to obtain the efficient frontier is to minimize the risk premium, under a minimal expected return constraint. The problem becomes:

$$\text{find } \boldsymbol{\alpha}^* = \arg\min_{\alpha \in \mathcal{V}} \pi(\boldsymbol{\alpha}\boldsymbol{\omega}^\mathrm{T}) \text{ s.t. } \boldsymbol{\alpha}\boldsymbol{\mu}^\mathrm{T} \geq \kappa, \tag{4.25}$$

which reduces to a convex optimization problem, which parallels (4.22). It follows:

$$\text{find } \boldsymbol{\theta}^* = \arg\max_{\boldsymbol{\theta}' \in \mathcal{V}_{\alpha,\theta}} D_\psi(\boldsymbol{\theta}' \| \boldsymbol{\theta}) \text{ s.t. } \boldsymbol{\theta}'\boldsymbol{\mu}^\mathrm{T} \leq \boldsymbol{\theta}\boldsymbol{\mu}^\mathrm{T} - \delta, \tag{4.26}$$

with $\delta := \alpha\kappa$. The solution to (4.26) is given in the following proposition, whose proof parallels that of Proposition 4.7.

Proposition 4.8 For all portfolios $(\boldsymbol{\alpha}; \boldsymbol{\omega}) \in \mathcal{P}_\psi(\boldsymbol{\theta})$, *under constant absolute risk aversion, the solution to (4.26) has the same expression as (4.23).*

5. CONCLUSION

Traditional portfolio theory à la Markowitz is a cornerstone of financial economics. It is the basis on which standard asset pricing models such as the CAPM are built. Diversification and mutual fund theorems are usually drawn from this framework where investors are driven by mean-variance preferences. The limitations of the mean-variance framework have long been recognized and numerous attempts have been made to relax the restrictive assumptions that the standard Markowitz approach entails. More refined expected utility models, non-expected utility models have been introduced on the preference front. Higher moments (than the variance) like skewness, Pareto-Lévy distributions have been considered on the distributional front. At the risk of oversimplifying these various attempts, although interesting, do not convey the global picture of the problem at hand. They each focus on one aspect of the portfolio problem. Our ambition in this paper has been to recast the portfolio problem in a new territory, namely that of information geometry. After all, the costs of the Markowitz approach can be understood as information losses, be they preference information or distributional information. In this paper, instead of trying to isolate bits of information lost (such as, say, skewness), we take a global stance by introducing powerful information geometry concepts, namely Bregman divergences and Bregman information. In a nutshell, Bregman divergences capture all the dimensions that the mean-variance approach hides "under the rug" in the name of analytical tractability.

To make our point more vivid, we have deliberately focused in this paper on the special illustrative case of CARA preferences and the exponential family of distributions. In a Markowitz setting, CARA preferences combined with a multivariate Gaussian distribution of asset returns yield exact mean-variance portfolios. As soon as the Gaussian assumption is lifted, these results are just approximations, the issue being that not much is said about the portfolio costs of such approximations. But, there is no reason why one should stick to this "fingers crossed" attitude. Indeed, we show that under the broad exponential family of distributions we can compute the exact optimal portfolio choices and the exact efficiency frontier. These computations are made possible because we use the proper information theoretic tools, namely the Bregman divergences. Among other things, we show that Markowitz optimal portfolios may be rather incorrect and we explain why: We give the true portfolio weights (expression 4.16) and compare them to the approximate portfolio weights (expression 4.17).

These results carry fruitful promises and we hope to have convinced the reader that financial economics can get a new lease of life by working with proper information geometry tools such as Bregman divergences. Let us suggest one area where much can be expected. It is a well known result that when markets are complete there is unique risk-neutral probability measure that yields the unique price of any derivative asset. It is also well-known that when markets are incomplete there is an infinite number of such martingale probabilities and hence an infinite number of derivative asset prices. Many papers have been written to find "ad-hoc" ways (much in Markowitz spirit) to pick and choose a "right" martingale probability measure rather than another one. But, after all what matters, loosely speaking, is a notion of distance between these various probability measures. Here again, Bregman divergences can be of great help in properly modeling the problem. In forthcoming papers, we intend to show the broad applicability of information geometry concepts to financial economics problems.

REFERENCES

Arrow, Kenneth J. (1971). "Essays on the Theory of Risk-Bearing", Markham, Chicago

Banerjee, A., Merugu, S., Dhillon, I. and Ghosh, J. (2005). Clustering with bregman divergences. *Journal of Machine Learning Research,* 6, 1705-1749.

Chavas, J.P. (2004). Risk analysis in theory and practice. Academic Press Advanced Finance, *Elsevier Science and Technology Books.*

Briys, E., Magdalou, B. and Nock, R. (2010). Exact measure of risk under expected utility, *CEREGMIA working paper* 2010-01.

Markowitz, H. (1952). Portfolio selection. *Journal of Finance,* 6, 77-91.

Menezes, C., Geiss, G. and Tessler, J. (1980). Increasing downside risk. *American Economic Review,* 70, 921-932.

Nielsen, F., Boissonnat, J.D. and Nock, R. (2007). On Bregman Voronoi diagrams. In Proc. of the 19th ACM-SIAM *Symposium on Discrete Algorithm,* 746-755, SIAM-ACM Press.

Nielsen, F. and Nock, R. (2009a). Sided and symmetrized Bregman centroids. *IEEE Trans. on Information Theory,* 55, 2882-2904.

Nock, R., Magdalou, B., Sanz, N., Briys, E., Célimène, F. and Nielsen, F. (2009). Information geometries for microeconomic theories, *Computing Research Repository* (coRR), abs/0901.2586.

Nock, R. and Nielsen, F. (2009b). Bregman divergences and surrogates for learning. IEEE Trans. on Pattern Analysis and Machine Intelligence, 31(11), 2048-2059.

Nock, R. and Nielsen, F. (2009c). Intrinsic geometries learning. In F. Nielsen (ed.), Emerging Trends in Visual Computing, 175-215, Springer-Verlag.

Pratt, John (1964). Risk aversion in the small and in the large, Econometrica, 32

Ross, Stephen A. (1978). Mutual fund separation in financial theory – The Separating Distributions. *Journal of Economic Theory*, Vol 17, n°2, 254-86

Steinbach, M.C. (2001). Markowitz revisited: Mean-variance models in financial portfolio analysis. SIAM Review, 43, 31-85.

Tobin, James (1958), Liquidity preference as behavior toward risk. *Review of Economic Studies*, 25, 65-85.

INDEX

9

'long boom' 1980–2006, 133

A

absorption, 3, 41
academics, vii, 2, 201, 210
access, xiii, 13, 37, 40, 48, 57, 66, 70, 71, 72, 85, 88, 137, 150, 159, 178, 179, 180, 187
accountability, 12
accounting, 4, 5, 14, 59, 74, 75, 76, 141, 219
accreditation, xiii
acquisitions, 154, 192
activism, 85, 86, 87, 89
adjustment, 134, 150, 153
Africa, 25, 189
age, 20, 21, 29, 105, 135
agencies, 5, 6, 12, 13, 59, 62, 154, 161, 163, 176, 212, 215, 216
aggregate demand, 153
aggregation, 5, 27, 190
Allen, R.E., 135, 137, 145
alternative energy, x
alters, 137, 170
Amable et Palombarini, 23
American Recovery and Reinvestment Act, 93, 99
amnesia, 209
amortization, 60, 158, 159
anatomy, 181
applications, 29, 44, 51
appointments, xii, 6
appraisals, 33, 49, 60
arbitrage, 30, 133, 198
Asia, xii, xiv, 153, 189, 190, 205, 206
Asian crisis, 121
aspiration, 37
assessment, xiii, 48, 55, 167, 209, 212
assessment procedures, xiii

assets, 5, 39, 42, 43, 44, 49, 50, 58, 59, 60, 66, 67, 77, 78, 90, 91, 127, 130, 131, 132, 133, 134, 135, 137, 144, 153, 154, 155, 156, 157, 158, 159, 163, 165, 176, 185, 187, 189, 191, 199, 216
assumptions, vii, 3, 59, 84, 170, 210, 211, 212, 220
Attorney General, 55, 72, 79
authorities, 7, 25, 89, 149, 150, 151, 152, 154, 163, 223
authority, 104, 128, 210
authors, 42, 55, 101, 144, 145, 146, 222

B

background, x, 23, 26, 128, 183
bail, 91, 98, 107, 135
balance of payments, 36, 131, 141, 217
balance sheet, 40, 41, 43, 50, 52, 54, 57, 75, 77, 130, 145, 160
bank debt, 10, 88, 204
bank failure, 90
Bank for International Settlements, 135
Bank of England, 83, 131, 138
bankers, 12, 54, 96, 142, 200, 209, 223
banking, x, xii, xiv, 4, 10, 12, 13, 36, 39, 40, 41, 42, 44, 49, 58, 59, 75, 81, 82, 86, 87, 88, 90, 93, 98, 102, 125, 126, 128, 129, 130, 131, 132, 133, 134, 138, 139, 141, 142, 143, 145, 150, 157, 166, 182, 183, 186, 191, 196, 204, 207, 214, 221
banking sector, 36, 39, 41, 42, 44, 82, 87, 88, 90, 134, 214
bankruptcy, 5, 40, 48, 65, 74, 76, 82, 134, 144, 192, 195, 202, 221
behavior, xii, xiii, 105, 106, 136, 140, 170, 209, 210, 211, 214, 215, 221, 222, 223
behaviors, 114, 115, 122, 157, 171, 210
Belgium, 86
belief systems, 145
    role in economics, 145
beliefs, 141, 151, 170, 171
beneficial effect, 37
benign, 35, 218, 220

Bhagwati, 104, 122
bias, 107, 113, 117, 118
biotechnology, xiii
Birnbaum et Leca, 18
bondholders, 194, 200
bonds, 3, 42, 55, 130, 133, 137, 145, 158, 194, 203
borrowers, 53, 55, 59, 62, 74, 144, 151, 152, 154,
 156, 158, 159, 171, 174, 175, 176, 180, 211, 213,
 214, 215, 216, 219, 221
borrowing, 39, 155, 156, 158, 160, 163, 186
Boyer, 23
Brazil, 95, 108, 109, 135
breeding, 153
Britain, 84, 89, 97, 133
broad money, 130, 143, 144
budget deficit, 162
building societies, 11, 40
business cycle, 151, 193
business ethics, xiv
business management, 13
business model, 5, 50, 52, 73, 75, 173, 182, 190
buyer, 51, 55, 76, 130, 196, 197

C

Canada, xi, xii, xiv, 14, 108, 109, 137, 189, 194, 199,
 200, 202
capital accumulation, 177
capital controls, 132
capital flight, xii, 142
capital flows, 7, 8, 86, 87, 150
capital gains, 39, 41
capital goods, 135, 154
capital markets, 150, 160, 167, 189, 190
capitalism, 13, 14, 83, 105, 135, 136, 146, 150, 162,
 165, 166, 177, 182, 207
categorization, 101, 107, 109, 122
causality, 30, 136, 220
causation, 13, 217, 218
Cayman Islands, 131
Cerny, P., 136
certificates of deposit, 162
challenges, 25, 30, 94, 107, 202, 210, 214
channels, 85, 105, 177
character, 4, 56, 92, 190
checks and balances, 5
China, x, 10, 81, 86, 93, 94, 98, 100
CHIPS, 130
circulation, 2, 9
CitiCorp, 134
City, ix, xii, 55, 72, 85, 166, 198
civil action, 48, 49, 50, 77
clarity, 77
class period, 74, 75

classes, 73, 94
classification, 27, 62
Clearing House Interbank Payments System. *see*
 CHIPS
clients, 5, 49, 54, 56, 57, 58, 60, 77, 78, 132, 133,
 174
cognitive ability, 170
cognitive capacities, 26
Cold War, xii, 81, 91
collaboration, 8, 12, 104, 105
collateral, 39, 40, 41, 42, 43, 56, 60, 62, 66, 157
collateral damage, 56
collateralized debt obligations, 130
combined effect, 153, 158, 162
commerce, 92, 107, 127, 129
commercial bank, 54, 131, 132
commodity, xii, 177
commodity futures, xii
common law, 70, 71
communication, 73, 84, 105, 129, 130
community, ix, 21, 22, 24, 25, 27, 28, 31, 141, 199
comparative advantage, 43
compensation, 57, 67, 89, 91, 161, 186
competition, 1, 5, 63, 133, 150, 156, 159, 171, 177,
 193
competitive advantage, xiv, 140
competitiveness, 42, 43, 44, 187
competitors, 72, 108
complaints, 49, 56, 62, 66
complex adaptive systems, Error! Not a valid
 bookmark in entry on page 136
complexity, xiii, 2, 3, 5, 6, 12, 23, 29, 30, 49, 52, 53,
 55, 78, 86, 87, 161, 165, 176
compliance, 160, 201
components, 6, 8, 13
composition, 38, 41, 83, 127
concentration, 10, 11, 41, 143
conception, 151, 155, 171
conceptualization, 2
conference, 140, 206
confidence, 20, 90, 94, 165, 166, 223
conflict, 83, 87, 129, 160, 163, 220
conflict of interest, 160, 220
Congress, 7, 15, 55, 71, 132, 138, 214, 216-
connectivity, 2, 10
consensus, 37, 121, 200
consolidation, 6, 90, 160, 182
conspiracy, 66, 68, 69
construction, 18, 19, 22, 27, 28, 38, 39, 41, 109, 158
consumer demand, 171
consumer protection, 223
consumers, 27, 28, 65, 171, 178, 222

Index

247

consumption, 19, 29, 151, 152, 153, 158, 209, 217, 218, 219, 220

contamination, 27

continuity, 105, 151, 155

control, 4, 8, 13, 14, 19, 23, 54, 59, 63, 70, 85, 88, 89, 91, 92, 107, 112, 113, 114, 116, 127, 129, 131, 132, 138, 139, 140, 142, 143, 149, 150, 164, 170, 171, 186, 189, 194, 198, 201, 214

controversies, 47

convention, 18, 24, 26, 141

coordination, xiii, xiv, 24, 101, 115, 121, 137, 139, 144, 164, 171

corporate finance, 32

corporate governance, 159

corporations, 12, 25, 84, 85, 128, 133, 139, 160

correlation, 111, 114, 116

corruption, x, xii, 223

cost, 9, 43, 51, 59, 74, 78, 84, 184, 196, 201, 213, 214, 222

costs, 38, 42, 44, 51, 52, 74, 76, 82, 105, 121, 140, 160, 164, 191, 196, 200, 210, 211, 214, 216, 221, 222

credibility, 25, 113, 122, 204

credit availability, 138

credit market, 82, 139, 159, 172, 173, 179, 181, 189

credit rating, 5, 6, 7, 13, 216

credit squeeze, 44

creditors, 44, 88, 90, 129, 133

criticism, 24, 40, 210

critics, 126, 170, 197

culture, xii, 22, 30, 31, 200

currency, 3, 8, 39, 44, 82, 88, 90, 103, 104, 126, 129, 130, 131, 132, 138, 139, 143, 144, 217, 218

current account, 91, 217, 218, 219, 220

current account deficit, 91, 217, 218, 219, 220

current account surplus, 217

customers, 24, 43, 52, 88, 89, 108, 170, 201

cycles, 43, 189

D

debts, 44, 90, 153, 155, 158, 159

decision making, 211, 223

decision-making process, 85, 209

decisions, xii, 17, 18, 25, 26, 29, 30, 36, 44, 48, 83, 85, 109, 151, 160, 165, 170, 195, 198, 201, 209, 210, 211, 220, 222, 223

defendants, 49, 70, 71, 72, 73, 75, 76, 77

defense, 56, 58, 69, 72, 73, 76, 164, 192

deficit, 42, 150, 152, 162, 217, 220

definition, 4, 15, 26, 84, 126, 127, 128, 134, 139, 151, 152, 170, 217

Denmark, 85, 90

Department of Justice, 65, 69, 74

dependent variable, 107, 109, 113, 115, 117, 118 -

deposits, 10, 11, 36, 39, 44, 75, 88, 89

depression, 122, 152, 155, 162, 163, 164, 214, 216, 222

deregulation, 3, 6, 84, 133, 152, 160, 161, 172, 173, 176, 179, 184, 199

derivatives, 1, 2, 3, 4, 5, 6, 8, 9, 13, 14, 15, 41, 86, 125, 130, 131, 157, 204, 212, 213, 214, 216, 223

destruction, 40, 136, 137, 143

developing countries, xii, 43, 108, 109, 150

differentiation, 21

diffusion, 121

direct investment, 166

directors, 43, 59, 73, 74, 75, 76, 200

disappointment, 43

disaster, 103, 152, 211, 222, 223

discipline, vii, 18, 27

disclosure, 12, 56, 76, 77

discourse, vii, xi, 35

disposable income, 219, 220

distress, 144, 149, 151, 152

distribution, 66, 117, 158, 211

distribution of income, 159

diversification, vii, 41, 43

diversity, 25, 29, 44, 66

domestic demand, 84

domestic economy, 83, 94

domestic investment, 209

domestic markets, 85

drawing, 12, 24, 107, 109

dream, 21, 22, 182

dumping, 102, 109, 124

duties, 56, 109, 154, 200

dynamics, xiii, 21, 145, 156, 171

E

early warning, 66, 91, 137

earnings, 43, 50, 57, 59, 67, 75, 85

East Asia, xiv, 134

Eastern Europe, 189

ecology, 125, 126, 129, 134, 138, 139, 140

economic activity, 37, 92, 93, 94, 135

economic behaviour, 9

economic boom, 37, 38, 42

economic crisis, vii, xi, xii, 2, 90, 101, 102, 103, 104, 105, 106, 114, 115, 121, 133, 210, 215, 223

economic development, xii, xiv, 25, 156, 181

economic downturn, 52, 107, 112, 115, 116, 118

economic fundamentals, 159

economic growth, 37, 38, 138, 141, 145, 150, 159, 166, 169, 170, 171, 177, 179, 223

economic institutions, 102

economic performance, 143, 183

economic policy, 1, 88, 92, 111, 164
economic problem, 138, 201
economic sociology, 182, 183, 184
economic systems, 183, 222
economic theory, 13, 22, 155
economics, vii, xiii, xiv, 13, 20, 28, 29, 33, 37, 136, 138, 139, 140, 143, 145, 166, 170, 182, 183, 210
economies of scale, 51, 181
educational system, 13
emerging markets, 151
emigration, 35, 36, 37
emotion, 28
employees, 24, 65, 68, 161, 201
employment, 2, 39, 40, 44, 60, 88, 133, 189, 191, 192, 205
EMU, 36, 40, 44
encouragement, 144
energy, x, 38, 86, 93, 94, 140
energy efficiency, 93
enforcement, 74, 102, 109, 111, 122
engineering, xiii, 1, 2, 3, 5, 6, 13, 140, 194, 204
England, 95, 131
entrepreneurs, 140, 143
entrepreneurship, xii
environment, xiv, 3, 6, 8, 9, 30, 36, 44, 63, 87, 88, 92, 94, 100, 104, 106, 145, 152, 164, 180, 214
environmental policy, 93
equation of exchange (quantity equation), 145
equilibrium, 101, 136, 151, 170, 183
equity, 40, 44, 53, 57, 60, 62, 63, 76, 81, 82, 85, 86, 132, 154, 158, 159, 160, 163, 173, 174, 175, 178, 179, 185, 186, 187, 189, 191, 193, 194, 197, 198, 199, 202, 203, 204, 205, 206, 207, 211, 215
equity market, 154, 158, 159, 187, 189, 191, 198
ethics, xiv, 30, 200, 210
ethnic minority, 174, 175
EU, 38, 41, 86, 94, 96, 97, 106, 107, 108, 109, 113, 118, 206
euphoria, 153, 154, 165
Euro, ix, xiii, 45, 46
Eurocurrency, 131
Europe, 22, 36, 84, 99, 105, 130, 139, 143, 144, 186, 189, 190, 201
European Central Bank, 138, 146
European Commission, ix, xii, 107
European Community, x, 139
European Monetary Union, 36
European Union, 37, 95, 106, 111, 191, 223
Eurozone, 144
evolution, xii, xiii, 2, 4, 6, 7, 48, 82, 83, 137, 139, 142, 150, 151, 152, 153, 154, 155, 156, 157, 159, 164, 165
exchange controls, 103, 131

exchange rate, xii, 36, 40, 88, 90, 103, 128, 140, 144
exercise, 25, 29, 30, 73, 163
expertise, 44, 54, 72, 107, 212, 214, 216
experts, 121, 140, 175
exploitation, 1, 182, 184
export subsidies, 102, 107
export-led growth, 37, 44
exposure, 36, 41, 59, 69, 89, 157, 186
external constraints, 20
external environment, 37
external financing, 159
externalities, 92, 144, 214, 221
Eymard-Duvernay, 23

F

failure, 48, 67, 76, 85, 88, 105, 133, 154, 162, 186, 189, 196, 209, 214, 216, 221, 223
family, 20, 28, 50, 62, 153
family income, 153
Favereau, 23
FDI, 36, 37, 38, 43
federal funds, 163
Federal Reserve Bank, 130, 135, 136, 140, 143
Federal Reserve Board, 14, 58, 135
financial capital, 7, 24, 156, 167, 171
financial crisis, 2, 8, 35, 36, 42, 44, 48, 81, 82, 83, 84, 85, 91, 92, 93, 103, 125, 132, 134, 137, 140, 144, 145, 149, 150, 160, 162, 163, 164, 167, 169, 170, 171, 172, 179, 180, 181, 206, 209, 210, 211, 217, 220, 221
financial development, 155, 158
financial distress, 109, 151, 167, 195
financial fragility, 132, 151, 161
financial instability, 136, 150, 154, 155, 162, 166
financial institutions, xiv, 7, 8, 36, 39, 43, 48, 49, 50, 52, 53, 55, 59, 76, 77, 83, 129, 133, 137, 139, 144, 149, 153, 160, 161, 162, 163, 165, 172, 174, 181, 211, 213, 223
financial intermediaries, x, 51, 126, 127, 130, 132, 150, 154, 159, 214
financial liberalisation, 38
financial performance, 194, 199
financial regulation, 84, 85, 149, 166
financial sector, 6, 36, 87, 102, 137, 177, 180
Financial Services Authority, 11, 45, 205
financial stability, 89, 164
financial system, xiv, 7, 12, 43, 120, 126, 127, 128, 129, 132, 136, 138, 139, 140, 141, 143, 145, 149, 150, 151, 152, 155, 158, 159, 160, 163, 164, 165, 179, 180, 185, 186, 189, 200, 203, 213, 216, 221, 222, 223
financial vulnerability, 163

Index

financing, xiii, 22, 23, 25, 40, 42, 44, 51, 52, 75, 93, 142, 150, 152, 153, 154, 155, 157, 158, 159, 165, 185, 193
fiscal policy, 41
fluctuations, 88, 140, 157
focusing, 53, 92, 121, 140, 164, 199, 204
foreclosure, 52, 53, 65, 74, 77, 78, 172, 174, 175
foreign banks, 59, 132
foreign direct investment, 36
foreign exchange, 130
foreign firms, 87
foreign investment, 133
Foster, J., 137, 146
foundations, vii, 18, 37, 152
France, ix, xiii, xiv, 22, 32, 33, 43, 85, 86, 92, 99, 108, 109, 166, 204, 205
fraud, 49, 50, 52, 54, 55, 57, 65, 66, 68, 69, 70, 71, 72, 73, 158, 212
freedom, 6, 20, 22, 221
fuel, 141, 142, 159, 169, 170, 171, 175, 179
funding, 13, 40, 43, 51, 52, 75, 83, 92, 93, 94, 150, 157, 179, 182, 194
funds, 3, 10, 40, 43, 55, 56, 57, 58, 69, 70, 71, 75, 82, 83, 85, 86, 93, 94, 127, 128, 131, 132, 151, 157, 158, 159, 161, 178, 180, 185, 186, 189, 190, 193, 194, 200, 202, 204, 206, 213, 215, 216, 217

G

Galileo, 18
GATT, xii, 123
GDP, 38, 39, 41, 42, 43, 87, 112, 113, 114, 115, 116, 117, 118, 119, 120, 132, 133, 134, 136, 137, 138, 145, 153, 160, 185
world, 132
General Agreement on Tariffs and Trade, 106
General Motors, 79
generation, 37, 77, 90, 136, 199
Georgia, 74, 149, 166
Germany, xiii, 42, 43, 85, 86, 99, 108, 109, 118, 200, 207
GIRO, 130
global economy, 36, 82, 84, 127, 128, 131, 133, 134, 138, 210, 217, 218, 220
global markets, 143, 176
global trade, 102, 103, 104, 128
globalization, x, 84, 92, 101, 102, 104, 106, 121, 125, 126, 129, 133, 135, 136, 143, 144, 173, 177
Globalization, v, x, xi, 14, 46, 99, 101, 131, 135, 146, 147, 181, 182, 207
GNP, 37, 38
goods and services, 22, 26, 36, 217

governance, xi, 1, 11, 25, 82, 83, 85, 87, 92, 93, 102, 104, 159, 185, 186, 189, 190, 191, 192, 193, 196, 199, 200, 201, 203, 204
government policy, 35, 39, 42, 222
government revenues, 41
government securities, 137
government spending, 40, 162
Great Britain, 22, 29, 103, 105
Great Depression, 101, 102, 103, 104, 106, 121, 155, 162
gross domestic product, 130, 160
gross investment, 162
groups, 22, 55, 85, 109, 112, 169, 170, 172, 174, 178, 205, 206, 210, 211, 215, 216, 222
growth rate, 35, 36, 37, 38, 39, 41, 44, 101, 143, 144, 152, 177
guardian, 95, 96, 99, 100
guidance, 58, 59, 62, 63
guidelines, 56, 58, 63, 67, 143, 150

H

hands, 127, 129, 183
hard currency, 103
harvesting, 191, 197
health, xiii, 37, 86, 93, 127, 189
health care, xiii, 93
hedging, 9, 41, 58, 59, 66, 67, 73
Helleiner, E., 136
heteroskedasticity, 114
holding company, 48, 53, 54, 57, 58, 65, 66, 68, 69, 70, 72
holism, 18
home ownership, 169, 170, 171, 172, 173, 174, 176, 177, 178, 180, 181, 204
home value, 62, 179, 180
homeowners, 50, 60, 72, 153, 157, 171, 175, 176, 178, 179, 180, 181, 184
Hong Kong, 10, 98, 131, 184
House, 11, 39, 52, 80, 112, 130, 175, 183, 212
households, 42, 153, 158, 159, 169, 170, 172, 173, 178, 179, 180, 181, 219, 220
housing, ix, 2, 13, 38, 39, 41, 49, 50, 52, 56, 75, 76, 77, 145, 153, 158, 171, 172, 173, 175, 176, 177, 178, 179, 180, 215, 216, 218, 220
human agency, 170
human behavior, 203, 209, 210
human capital, 43
hybrid, 2, 7, 10, 14, 82, 83, 87, 88, 92, 93, 94, 95
hypothesis, 17, 18, 20, 22, 102, 106, 115, 149, 150, 151, 154, 160, 217, 218, 219, 220

I

Iceland, 81, 82, 87, 88, 89, 90, 91, 92, 95, 96, 97, 98, 99, 133, 144
identification, 29, 59, 133, 144, 163
ideology, 7, 8, 12, 20, 23, 121
idiosyncratic, 149, 152
illiquid asset, 5
illusion, 20, 31, 175
image, xiii, 130, 171, 172, 178
imagination, 3, 19, 20
imbalances, xii, 156, 212, 217, 218
IMF, 5, 8, 10, 12, 37, 90, 91, 96, 97, 109, 112, 133, 134, 135, 138, 142, 144, 147, 159, 160, 214
immigration, 37, 38, 39
impacts, 6, 87, 115, 165
implementation, 102, 164
import restrictions, 102
import substitution, 36
incentives, 7, 13, 37, 39, 43, 93, 161, 171, 172, 180, 213, 215
income, 8, 40, 41, 50, 59, 60, 62, 74, 75, 76, 138, 142, 145, 153, 155, 158, 159, 163, 165, 169, 170, 172, 173, 174, 178, 179, 180, 182, 219, 220, 222
income tax, 40, 41
increased competition, 59, 193
incumbents, 220
independence, 109
independent variable, 109
India, xii, 115, 116, 118, 119, 120
indication, 38, 221
indicators, 169, 170, 172, 181
individual action, 21, 22, 29
individualism, 20, 21, 29
industrial relations, 24
industrial restructuring, 187
industrialized countries, 210
industry, xii, 6, 38, 39, 48, 62, 63, 85, 86, 93, 109, 128, 129, 137, 153, 159, 177, 178, 184, 185, 197, 198, 202, 221, 222
inflation, 37, 39, 145, 152, 166
inflation target, 152
information processing, 133
information technology, 14, 126, 129
infrastructure, 93, 94, 134, 136, 193
innovation, 1, 13, 30, 50, 93, 94, 150, 167, 204, 214, 221
insecurity, 94, 169, 170, 172, 178, 179
instability, x, 10, 44, 129, 135, 140, 146, 149, 150, 152, 154, 155, 162, 164, 166, 182
institutional change, 145, 183
institutional economics, 183
institutional infrastructure, xiv

instruments, 1, 3, 4, 7, 8, 9, 13, 41, 50, 56, 77, 101, 111, 125, 126, 128, 129, 131, 140, 143, 157, 161, 186, 204, 213, 214
insurance, x, 9, 13, 51, 76, 128, 130, 132, 214, 221
interaction, 20, 22, 23, 29, 30, 84, 90, 105
interactions, 9, 21, 28, 29, 30, 82, 87, 95, 102, 137
interbank market, 39, 44
interdependence, 120, 121
interest groups, 39, 116, 121
interest rates, 3, 35, 38, 44, 59, 60, 89, 132, 137, 139, 140, 144, 152, 155, 157, 173, 174, 175, 176, 192, 213, 220
intermediaries, 28, 127, 128, 140, 179
international banking facilities (IBFs). *see* offshore banking facilities
international investment, 140
international law, 141
International Monetary Fund, 5, 37, 90, 97, 102, 134, 147, 167, 224
international political economy (IPE), 140
international relations, 81, 87, 121, 140, 151
international trade, x, 102, 103, 104, 105, 108
internationalization, 84
internet, 129, 130
interrelationships, 2, 6
interval, 146, 166
intervention, 37, 66, 91, 138, 139, 144, 150, 151, 160, 199
investment bank, x, 5, 6, 51, 54, 58, 68, 69, 70, 72, 132, 145, 156, 160, 161, 173, 180, 214, 221
investment rate, 220
invisible hand, 23, 152
IPO, 186, 191, 194, 195, 196
Ireland, v, x, xii, 35, 36, 37, 38, 39, 42, 43, 44, 45, 46, 147
IRR, 188, 192
IS-LM, 135
isolationism, 101, 103
issues, xii, xiv, 19, 24, 66, 73, 102, 106, 109, 113, 120, 127, 135, 145, 185, 186, 192, 195, 199, 201
Italy, ix, xiii, 109

J

Japan, xii, xiv, 51, 80, 108, 109, 143, 153
Jensen, 19, 23
judges, 74, 78
judgment, 47, 76, 149, 200

K

Kambhu, J., 140
Kazakhstan, 109
Keynes, 140, 141, 147, 167

Index

Keynes, J.M., 140, 141
Keynesian, 13, 17, 135, 150, 154, 159, 167
Kindleberger, C., 135, 140
Knight, 26
Kochen, A., 132
Korea, xii, 135
Krueger, A., 134

L

labor, 134, 170, 172, 178
labour, 1, 8, 26, 38, 43, 169, 201
labour market, 169
land, 13, 50, 77, 210
landscape, 82, 83, 84, 86, 87, 91, 92, 93, 94, 102, 181, 200
language, 45
Latin America, 133, 134, 189, 222
law enforcement, 49
laws, 22, 26, 42, 49, 50, 73, 76, 77, 109
lawyers, 49, 77, 78
layering, 6, 165
LDCs, 142
Leathers, C., 136
legislation, 12, 54, 89, 90, 221, 222
lender of last resort, 126, 128, 138, 144, 162, 163, 164
lending, xii, 3, 39, 40, 41, 42, 43, 49, 51, 59, 60, 62, 63, 72, 77, 135, 171, 172, 173, 174, 175, 176, 177, 178, 179, 180, 182, 183, 184, 211, 213, 218, 221, 222
lending process, 175
lens, 47, 82
liberalisation, 26, 36, 37
liberalization, xiv, 107, 136, 156, 163, 181
liberation, 20, 21
likelihood, 71, 102, 113, 115, 117, 119, 120, 134
Lindgren, C-J., 134
line, xiii, 51, 55, 57, 70, 107, 122, 130, 185
linkage, 107
links, x, xiv, 6, 9, 25, 27, 28, 152, 159
liquid assets, 156
liquidity, 2, 10, 11, 40, 43, 54, 67, 82, 85, 90, 91, 92, 94, 135, 143, 144, 145, 154, 155, 158, 162, 165, 175, 177, 180, 186, 198
litigation, 47, 49, 52, 53, 54, 55, 57, 69, 76, 78
lobbying, 12, 221, 222
lobbyists, 6, 8
local authorities, 89
local government, 72, 156
Lombard Street Research, 143

M

machine learning, xiii
macroeconomic policy, 143, 209
macroeconomics, xiii
majority, 4, 10, 26, 36, 82, 109, 132, 142, 174, 181
Malaysia, 98
management, xii, xiv, 12, 13, 17, 18, 19, 22, 23, 25, 28, 30, 48, 56, 57, 58, 59, 62, 63, 69, 85, 88, 127, 133, 143, 163, 166, 178, 186, 187, 191, 192, 198, 200, 201
manipulation, 13, 70, 210
manufacturing, 129
market discipline, 12, 13, 203
market economy, 23, 141, 150, 152, 156, 163, 165
market segment, 213
market share, 72, 150
marketability, 8
marketing, xi, 17, 19, 27, 28, 29, 57, 58, 70, 74, 137, 150, 175
Marx, 1, 2, 8, 9, 15, 17, 25, 135, 136
Marx, K., 135, 136
materialism, 136
matrix, 113, 161
maturation, 88
MBI, 191
measure of value, 8
measurement, 114, 141, 143
measures, 4, 18, 39, 42, 85, 93, 102, 107, 108, 109, 110, 111, 113, 114, 115, 116, 117, 118, 121, 217, 221
Meckling, 23
media, 30, 37, 39, 40, 95, 174, 176
median, 187, 197, 203
mediation, 109
Mediterranean, ix, xi, xiii, 22, 29, 32
medium of exchange, 128
membership, 37, 40, 44, 90, 102, 106, 109, 114, 115, 118
memory, 203, 222
merchandise, 134
mergers, 10, 150
metaphor, 21, 151, 196
methodological individualism, 18, 23, 29
methodology, 62, 137, 197
Mexico, xii, 84, 97, 133, 135, 141, 142, 144
minority, 175, 182, 201
Minsky, H., 140
model, 13, 19, 22, 23, 24, 28, 30, 40, 57, 103, 112, 113, 114, 116, 117, 118, 121, 136, 141, 144, 164, 192, 193, 209
model specification, 103
modeling, 58, 59, 66, 140

models, vii, 5, 7, 13, 22, 24, 28, 59, 60, 107, 114, 117, 118, 136, 140, 152, 159, 161, 183, 203
modern capitalism, 150, 162
modernisation, 182
modernity, 20, 21
momentum, 190, 214
monetary market, 154, 163
monetary policy, x, 14, 126, 139, 145, 152, 163, 167, 213
monetary union, 44
money, 8, 15, 22, 43, 48, 57, 67, 125, 126, 127, 128, 129, 130, 131, 132, 133, 134, 135, 136, 137, 138, 142, 143, 144, 145, 156, 158, 160, 162, 173, 174, 176, 177, 180, 187, 193, 199
money markets, 177
money supply, 131, 135, 137, 138, 143, 162
   (m1), 144
   (m3), 130, 143, 144
   (m4), 144
Mongolia, x
moral hazard, 42, 210, 211, 213, 222, 223
mortgage-backed securities, 3, 49, 54, 56, 57, 58, 63, 69, 157, 161, 171, 213, 214, 216, 221
Moscow, 15, 90
motion, 66, 68, 69, 71, 74, 75
motivation, 66, 85, 191
movement, 6, 10, 21, 151, 158
muscles, 53, 77
myopia, 152, 211, 213, 222, 223

N

NAFTA, 109, 111
narcissism, 22
narratives, 20
nation, 11, 36, 72, 91, 125, 212, 222
national income, 36, 39
national interests, 143
National Science Foundation, xiv
national security, 140
NATO, 91
natural resources, 36
negative equity, 216
neglect, 27, 43, 209, 218, 220
neoliberalism, 1, 12, 82, 83, 84, 87, 92, 94, 95
Netherlands, 82, 89, 91, 109
network, ix, x, xiii, 1, 25, 28, 89, 90, 94, 101, 102, 104, 105, 106, 118, 128, 171, 176
New York Stock Exchange, 6, 58
New Zealand, xii
NGOs, x
non-institutionalized, 107
normal distribution, 117
North America, 97, 99, 185, 190

Norton, R., 132
Norway, 90

O

objectives, vii, 19, 24
objectivity, 18
obligation, 43, 50, 199
observations, 121, 189
obstacles, 30, 74
OECD, 35, 37, 38, 41
offshore financial markets, 131, 135
oil, 135, 206
Onfray, 19
opacity, 161, 165
open economy, 36, 44
open market operations, 138
open markets, 181
openness, 20, 181
opportunism, 185, 193, 198, 204
opportunities, 49, 52, 81, 91, 93, 130, 131, 153, 156, 171, 173, 194
optimism, 140, 153, 158, 159, 186
order, 5, 11, 19, 24, 26, 27, 28, 29, 30, 43, 75, 78, 82, 84, 85, 87, 90, 103, 104, 105, 106, 108, 109, 113, 129, 131, 134, 135, 143, 150, 151, 159, 163, 164, 165, 170, 186, 189, 197, 209, 211, 222
orientation, 102, 162
oversight, 6, 59, 72, 127, 128, 145, 149
ownership, 2, 5, 7, 24, 26, 53, 74, 84, 85, 92, 132, 133, 153, 169, 170, 171, 172, 174, 177, 178, 181, 186
ownership structure, 85

P

packaging, 3, 13, 51, 71
paper money, 130
paradigm, vii, 22, 23, 25, 151
parallel, 111, 210
Pareto, 101
penalties, 55, 73
pension plans, 56
performance, 18, 24, 26, 33, 35, 36, 55, 59, 66, 67, 68, 129, 142, 162, 182, 185, 187, 189, 191, 192, 196, 197, 199, 201, 202, 221
pharmaceuticals, 38
plausibility, 109, 116
Poland, xii, 109
policy choice, 102, 110, 111
policy instruments, 104
policy makers, 121, 185, 186, 194, 197, 199, 203, 204, 210, 211, 214, 217, 218, 219, 221, 222
policy making, 223

policy responses, vii, 36, 183
political economy (PE), 140
political power, 91, 221
politics, xii, 9, 20, 87, 95, 104, 106, 140
pools, 51, 52, 53, 58, 67, 74, 75, 157
poor, x, 37, 66, 86, 174, 184, 215, 220, 222, 223
poor performance, 66
population, 37, 54, 62, 112, 137
portfolio, 51, 54, 62, 66, 69, 74, 165, 173, 186, 187, 192, 196, 201
portfolios, 48, 50, 133, 154, 157, 173, 180, 222
poverty, xii, 22
power, 6, 9, 10, 11, 12, 20, 22, 23, 25, 27, 51, 52, 81, 87, 91, 104, 108, 132, 135, 138, 140, 143, 161, 171, 181, 185, 186, 206, 220
power relations, 171
prediction, 112, 113
preference, 40, 134, 150, 194
preferential treatment, 111
prejudice, 74
present value, 26, 50, 155, 158
president, 68, 70, 72, 216
President Clinton, 6
pressure, 13, 54, 60, 77, 126, 140, 160, 178, 218
prevention, 13
price index, 145
price stability, 152
prices, 18, 26, 39, 40, 44, 48, 50, 54, 60, 77, 104, 135, 151, 153, 157, 158, 159, 163, 164, 173, 175, 176, 178, 179, 193, 212, 213, 214, 215, 216, 219, 220
private banks, 91, 130, 132
private firms, 82, 83, 85, 91, 92, 95
private investment, 43
private sector, ix, 13, 149
privatization, ix, 84, 137
probability, 26, 106, 113, 115, 116, 117, 118, 122, 160, 214, 216, 219, 222
probability distribution, 216
producers, 30
production, 25, 53, 59, 84, 134, 135, 136, 151, 155, 158, 162, 177, 183
productivity, 2, 38, 134, 136, 153
profit, 9, 32, 50, 73, 127, 153, 154, 156, 161, 163, 170, 173, 177, 181, 199, 220
profit margin, 173
profitability, 42, 133, 152, 192
profits, 8, 11, 72, 91, 130, 154, 159, 161, 162, 165, 171, 173, 176, 178, 180, 221
program, ix, xiv, 72, 73, 90, 91, 133
project, x, xi, xii, 20, 30, 101, 158
proliferation, 47, 136
.properties, 28, 62, 74, 78, 159, 174

property taxes, 76
prosperity, 172
protectionism, 36, 101, 102, 103, 104, 109, 121, 137, 151
psychology, 150, 210
public finance, 37
public interest, 210, 220, 222
public markets, 186, 187, 190
public opinion, vii, 18, 121
public policy, 204
public sector, xii, 6, 84
public welfare, 84
purchasing power, 134

Q

quasi-money, 131
questioning, vii, 18, 19, 23, 203

R

race, 112, 184
Raines, J., 136
range, 3, 12, 13, 20, 49, 54, 82, 83, 84, 89, 93, 94, 102, 106, 128, 143, 166, 171, 193
rate of return, 3
rating agencies, 5, 7, 156, 160, 161, 171, 173, 176, 180, 211, 212, 214, 215, 216
ratings, 5, 55, 95, 161, 176, 194, 197, 199, 212, 214, 215, 216
rationality, 18, 33, 150, 165, 170, 210, 223
Raveaud, 23
reactions, 21, 183
reading, 14, 17, 19
real estate, 13, 50, 54, 62, 76, 77, 133, 140, 153, 154, 158, 159, 171, 172, 178, 179, 182, 184, 199, 213, 214, 216, 219, 220, 221
real income, 153
real time, 66
real wage, 153
reality, 1, 9, 12, 13, 21, 24, 26, 30, 93, 128, 141, 150, 183, 210, 211, 222
reason, 20, 24, 38, 43, 54, 55, 58, 67, 90, 114, 174, 216, 219
recession, 82, 144, 154, 162, 163
reciprocal relationships, 9
recognition, xii, 12, 30, 171, 223
recovery, 35, 49, 53, 83, 92, 93, 94, 98, 163, 202
Rees-Mogg, W., 132
reflection, 23, 25, 93, 165
reforms, 11, 12, 146, 165, 201
region, ix, 27, 94

regulation, x, 1, 3, 6, 7, 8, 11, 12, 13, 25, 30, 81, 86, 92, 93, 97, 127, 128, 139, 140, 144, 149, 154, 156, 161, 163, 164, 171, 176, 203, 206, 220, 221
regulations, 6, 11, 29, 50, 62, 77, 86, 93, 102, 131, 139, 141, 162, 221, 223
regulators, 6, 41, 58, 59, 60, 62, 72, 149, 158, 161, 171, 173, 194, 209, 210, 211, 212, 214, 220, 221, 222, 223
regulatory controls, 86
regulatory framework, 150, 151, 154, 160, 163, 164, 165, 173
relationship, 1, 19, 23, 25, 28, 29, 42, 57, 65, 71, 137, 189, 211, 214
relevance, 24, 151, 192
reliability, 109
relief, xii, 200
renewable energy, x, 93, 94
repetitions, 66
replacement, 84
reproduction, 153, 162
reputation, 25, 48, 57, 58, 65
research funding, 13
reserve requirements, 131
reserves, 74, 75, 76, 91, 130, 132, 139, 140, 142, 157, 217, 218
resources, 17, 19, 25, 42, 69, 71, 164, 191
respect, 8, 9, 13, 23, 47, 48, 56, 65, 67, 70, 73, 76, 121, 138, 160, 180, 200
response time, 141
restitution, 52, 76
restructuring, 134, 178, 182, 198, 199, 200
retail, 75, 88, 89, 90, 91, 108, 129, 130
retail deposit, 90, 91
returns, 63, 83, 94, 158, 173, 176, 187, 189, 191, 192, 193, 194, 195, 201, 202, 203, 213, 215
revenue, 38, 40, 41, 92, 161, 187, 203
Review of International Political Economy, 135, 147
rights, iv, 8, 25, 52, 53, 69, 74, 77, 178, 186, 189, 200
risk aversion, 94, 159
risk management, xi, 26, 58, 59, 62, 66, 72, 204
risk society, 183
risk-taking, 149
Rivaud-Danset, 26
Russia, 81, 82, 90, 91, 98, 115, 118, 119, 120, 121

S

sales, 13, 49, 55, 60, 70, 72, 73, 75, 157, 158, 161, 163, 174, 196, 202, 212
satisfaction, 128
Saudi Arabia, 217
savings, 50, 85, 88, 89, 98, 127, 131, 132, 172, 173, 217, 218, 219, 220, 222

savings rate, 220
scale economies, 143
Scandinavia, 189
schema, 151, 153
Schumpeter, J., 136
scores, 26, 60, 113
search, 24, 74, 150, 176
searching, 21, 150
Second World, 35
Secretary of the Treasury, 160
securities, 5, 6, 18, 26, 43, 47, 48, 49, 51, 53, 54, 55, 56, 57, 58, 63, 65, 66, 67, 72, 73, 75, 76, 78, 127, 128, 130, 133, 137, 156, 157, 160, 161, 176, 180, 192, 212, 213, 214, 216
Securities Exchange Act, 69, 72, 73
securitization, 137
security, 5, 49, 51, 52, 53, 55, 57, 63, 76, 106, 128, 165, 178
self-interest, 19, 164, 210
self-regulation, 160
separation, 6, 137
settlements, 48, 71
severity, 121, 136
SGP, 42
shape, 8, 30, 35, 37, 94, 95
shaping, 11, 13, 18, 135
shareholder value, 23, 24, 51, 199
shareholders, 25, 43, 49, 51, 55, 73, 75, 82, 86, 92, 186, 199, 201
shares, 9, 39, 40, 73, 75, 162, 211
sharing, 74, 157
shock, 41, 96, 140
shores, 29
short run, 155, 156, 223
shortage, 217
short-term interest rate, 160, 165
short-termism, 187
signals, 48, 137
signs, 66, 160, 202
Singapore, 86, 98
skills, 30, 187, 196
small businesses, 43
smoking, 70, 73
social capital, 2, 5, 7, 9
social change, 27
social consequences, 182
social construct, 25, 171
social costs, 128, 146
social environment, 171
social housing, ix
social life, 9
social network, 28
social order, 29

social psychology, 27
social relations, 25, 29
social responsibility, ix, x, 23, 24, 201
social sciences, 145
social structure, 182, 183
social welfare, 24
socialization, 90
solvency, 40, 155, 163
South Africa, 109
South Korea, 81, 83, 93, 100, 109
Southeast Asia, 98
space, 1, 2, 7, 8, 9, 10, 11, 12, 13, 14, 88, 134, 153, 182, 183
Spain, 11, 86, 108, 109
stability, xiv, 77, 90, 129, 142, 143, 150, 152, 155, 160, 164, 165, 167, 170, 171, 195
Stability and Growth Pact, 42
stabilization, 84
stakeholders, 19, 24, 186, 199, 200, 201
standard error, 115, 120
standardization, 109
standards, 7, 25, 38, 58, 60, 62, 63, 73, 74, 75, 81, 154, 158, 159, 200, 214
state control, 90, 127, 139
state intervention, 84, 152, 170
state oversight, 127
state-owned enterprises, 84
statistics, 112, 113, 141
statute, 70, 146
statutes, 65, 71
stimulus, 10, 81, 83, 92, 93, 94, 95, 98
stock, 6, 18, 38, 41, 48, 51, 67, 72, 73, 75, 76, 87, 123, 130, 132, 137, 140, 153, 190
stock exchange, 6, 41
stock markets, 6
stock price, 18, 48, 75, 76
store of value, 128, 129
strategic management, xi, xiv
strategic planning, 44
strategies, vii, 17, 36, 59, 94, 105, 152, 161, 193, 194, 197, 209
strategy, xiv, 6, 23, 76, 82, 83, 85, 89, 90, 91, 216
strength, 12, 56, 150, 152, 164
stress, 7, 38, 41, 62
structural changes, 136, 150
structural reforms, 160, 163
structuring, 57, 77, 156
subprime loans, 55, 60, 63, 153, 157, 174, 176, 181, 209, 212, 213, 219, 221
superiority, 116, 210
supervision, 138, 145, 150, 154, 163, 164, 166
supply, 36, 38, 39, 142, 143, 145, 153, 154, 173, 219
supporting institutions, 128

Supreme Court, 70, 77, 199, 200
surplus, 3, 8, 9, 22, 26, 91, 127, 217, 218, 220
surveillance, 6, 7, 66, 192
survey, 18, 63, 161, 202
survival, 8, 170
suspicious activity reports, 49
sustainability, 93, 145
sustainable development, 30, 45
sustainable economic growth, 152
sustainable growth, 166
Sweden, 90, 108
swelling, 153, 159
switching, 20, 25
Switzerland, 131, 217
synthesis, 135, 152, 154
systemic change, 82
systemic risk, 41, 133, 140, 157, 213, 222

T

Taiwan, 109
Tanzania, xii
targets, 48, 184, 193
tariff, 103
tax base, 41
tax cuts, 41, 93
taxation, 4, 7, 35, 37, 40, 44, 162
teaching, xii, xiv
technical change, 50
technological developments, 1
technological progress, 51
telecommunications, 51, 199, 221
tension, 20, 21, 83
tensions, 81, 84, 87, 90, 91, 92
testing, 41, 62, 106
Thatcher, M., 131, 133
thinking, vii, 14, 40, 55, 136, 145, 210
threat, 85, 122, 151, 165
threshold, 41, 158
timing, 137, 197
trade, xii, xiv, 5, 22, 25, 26, 37, 92, 93, 101, 102, 103, 104, 105, 106, 107, 108, 109, 111, 112, 113, 115, 116, 118, 121, 122, 128, 129, 141, 143, 177, 193, 202, 217
trade agreement, xii, 102, 103, 104, 107, 111, 113, 115, 118
trade liberalization, 106, 111
trade policy, 37, 102, 103, 104, 105, 112, 113, 118, 121, 122
trade-off, 143
trading, xii, 26, 49, 72, 73, 88, 102, 103, 104, 105, 106, 107, 108, 214
trading bloc, 105
trading partner, 107, 108

256 Index

trading partners, 107, 108
tradition, 20, 21, 139
traditional practices, 201
tranches, 53, 77, 88, 94, 156, 157, 212, 213, 216
transaction costs, 105
transactions, 9, 12, 13, 23, 41, 59, 60, 62, 77, 84, 125, 126, 127, 128, 129, 130, 131, 133, 137, 156, 186, 197, 198
transfer payments, 42
transformation, 35, 37, 41, 183
transformations, 154, 165
transition, ix, x, 6, 20, 21, 82, 88, 94
transmission, 86, 137
transparency, 12, 102, 105, 106, 140, 144, 181
trends, 60, 63, 84, 177, 210, 221
trust, 9, 51, 53, 77, 128
Turkey, 109

U

U.S. Treasury, x, 132
UK, x, 6, 11, 39, 51, 82, 83, 85, 88, 89, 90, 91, 92, 93, 94, 95, 97, 98, 99, 107, 109, 131, 136, 137, 144, 146, 147, 166, 167, 185, 189, 201, 202, 204, 205
uncertain outcomes, 210
uncertainty, 26, 30, 32, 94, 101, 102, 104, 105, 121, 141, 166, 170
unemployment, 35, 37, 38, 42, 88, 101, 152, 162
unemployment rate, 38, 101, 162
unit of account, 128
United Kingdom, 10, 81, 108, 221, 223
United Nations, 106
United States, xii, 10, 25, 100, 103, 104, 118, 125, 127, 138, 143, 160, 184, 210, 211, 217, 218, 220, 221, 223
urbanization, 183
US Treasury
    Exchange Stabilization Fund, 135
USSR, 15

V

valuation, vii, 7, 41, 43, 54, 58, 60, 62, 150, 203

variables, xiii, 36, 107, 111, 112, 113, 115, 116, 117, 118, 119, 120, 136, 140, 153, 211, 217
variance, 113
vegetables, 109
vehicles, 47, 48, 77, 81, 86, 87, 133, 156
vein, 150, 152, 159, 163, 194
velocity, 7, 13, 137, 138, 145
velocity of circulation, 7
venture capital, 44, 187
volatility, 59, 129, 141, 150, 159, 180, 181
voters, 98, 116
vulnerability, 36, 44, 155

W

weakness, 12, 41, 160
wealth, 1, 17, 25, 26, 37, 38, 40, 43, 126, 127, 133, 134, 135, 136, 141, 144, 153, 178, 186, 194, 210, 220
wealth creation
    by central banks, 136
weather patterns, 140
web, xiv, 15, 213, 223
welfare, 18, 19, 22, 23, 29, 37, 84, 93, 104, 132, 169, 170, 172, 178
welfare state, 84, 169, 170, 172, 178
welfare system, 132
West Indies, x
Western Europe, 39, 97, 99
White House, 12
wholesale, 75, 129, 130
workers, 24, 41, 94, 108, 200
World Bank, 45, 112, 123, 205
World Trade Organization, 105, 111
World War I, 104, 105, 106, 162
writing, ix, xii, 2, 9, 77, 91
WTO, xii, 96, 101, 103, 104, 105, 109, 111, 118, 119, 120, 124

Z

zero growth, 144